Disputed Memory

Media and Cultural Memory/
Medien und kulturelle
Erinnerung

Edited by
Astrid Erll · Ansgar Nünning

Editorial Board
Aleida Assmann · Mieke Bal · Vita Fortunati · Richard Grusin · Udo Hebel
Andrew Hoskins · Wulf Kansteiner · Alison Landsberg · Claus Leggewie
Jeffrey Olick · Susannah Radstone · Ann Rigney · Michael Rothberg
Werner Sollors · Frederik Tygstrup · Harald Welzer

Volume 24

Disputed Memory

Emotions and Memory Politics
in Central, Eastern and South-Eastern Europe

Edited by
Tea Sindbæk Andersen and Barbara Törnquist-Plewa

DE GRUYTER

ISBN 978-3-11-061101-4
e-ISBN (PDF) 978-3-11-045353-9
e-ISBN (EPUB) 978-3-11-045334-8
ISSN 1613-8961

Library of Congress Cataloging-in-Publication Data
A CIP catalog record for this book has been applied for at the Library of Congress.

Bibliographic information published by the Deutsche Nationalbibliothek
The Deutsche Nationalbibliothek lists this publication in the Deutsche Nationalbibliografie;
detailed bibliographic data are available on the Internet at http://dnb.dnb.de.

© 2018 Walter de Gruyter GmbH, Berlin/Boston
This volume is text- and page-identical with the hardback published in 2016.
Cover illustration: Memorial to the Victims of Communism in Prague © Tomas Sniegon
Printing and binding: CPI books GmbH, Leck

♾ Printed on acid-free paper
Printed in Germany

www.degruyter.com

Table of Contents

Tea Sindbæk Andersen and Barbara Törnquist-Plewa
Introduction: Disputed Memories in Central, Eastern and South-Eastern Europe — 1

Part 1: Transnational Memory Politics

Cecilie Felicia Stokholm Banke
Global Memory and *Dialogic Forgetting*: The Armenian Case — 21

Tuomas Forsberg
Overcoming Memory Conflicts: Russia, Finland and the Second World War — 37

Davide Denti
Sorry for Srebrenica? Public Apologies and Genocide in the Western Balkans — 65

Part 2: Sites of Memory Transmission

Sophie Oliver
The Spatial Choreography of Emotion at Berlin's Memorials: Experience, Ambivalence and the Ethics of Secondary Witnessing — 95

Birga U. Meyer
The Universal Victim – Representing Jews and Roma in a European Holocaust Museum — 123

Andrej Kotljarchuk
The Memory of the Roma Holocaust in Ukraine: Mass Graves, Memory Work and the Politics of Commemoration — 149

Part 3: Local and Marginal Memory

Anna Wylegała
Forced Migration and Identity in the Memories of Post-War Expellees from Poland and Ukraine —— 177

Inge Melchior
Forming a Common European Memory of WWII from a Peripheral Perspective: Anthropological Insight into the Struggle for Recognition of Estonians' WWII Memories in Europe —— 203

Yuliya Yurchuk
Red Carnations on Victory Day and Military Marches on UPA Day? Remembered History of WWII in Ukraine —— 227

Part 4: Memorial Media Spaces

Mārtiņš Kaprāns
Framing the Ukrainian Insurgent Army and the Latvian Legion: Transnational History-Writing on Wikipedia —— 249

Volodymyr Kulyk
Negotiating Memory in Online Social Networks: Ukrainian and Ukrainian-Russian Discussions of Soviet Rule and Anti-Soviet Resistance —— 273

Tea Sindbæk Andersen
Football and Memories of Croatian Fascism on Facebook —— 297

Elvin Gjevori
Collective Memory and Institutional Reform in Albania —— 319

Igor Pietraszewski and Barbara Törnquist-Plewa
Clashes between National and Post-national European Views on Commemorating the Past: The Case of the Centennial Hall in Wrocław —— 351

Notes on contributors —— 373

Index of names —— 377

Subject index —— 379

Tea Sindbæk Andersen and Barbara Törnquist-Plewa
Introduction: Disputed Memories in Central, Eastern and South-Eastern Europe

In April 2007 the world media reported widely on violent riots that had broken out in Tallinn when thousands of people took to the streets in a clash over the decision to move the so-called Bronze soldier from its central location in the Estonian capital. For the Russian population of Estonia, the statue was a symbol of the heroic Soviet soldiers who died in Estonia fighting against Nazi Germany. However, for the majority of ethnic Estonians these Soviet soldiers were new occupiers representing the same Soviet power that had first crushed their independence in 1940 and again in 1945. The controversy over this war memorial as well the high emotions evoked by its removal illustrate well the complexity and specificity of memories in the part of Europe which until the end of the Cold War was generally called "Eastern Europe" and today is labelled, in more nuanced ways, Central, Eastern and South-Eastern Europe.

The particularity of the experiences of this part of Europe is yet not generally recognized and understood, neither among EU-elites, who in the name of integration want to unify European memory, nor by the broad Western European public, whose understanding of Europe's different war and Cold War experiences are very limited. The German historian Karl Schlögel, one of the few Western historians realizing the dilemma caused by this-asymmetry of memories in Europe, has described the complexity and specificity of Eastern European experiences in the following way:

> Eastern and central Europe was the principal theatre of the epoch of world wars and revolutions, of the new thirty years war and of the violence linked to it, a degree of violence which was in many respects unprecedented. This region of the continent found itself between the main fronts of the European civil war, between nationalism and communism, between German National Socialism and Soviet communism. It was the principal theatre of the genocide of the European Jews, of systematic social and ethnic cleansing policies; the terrain of deployment of the greatest military machines, and of burnt earth; of forced population movements, of flight; and of a liberation that was to a great extent the replacement of one foreign occupation by another. There is no point on the map of this region, no family, no biography that is not marked by this double experience. This is the central zone of the "century of extremes."[1]

---

[1] Karl Schlögel. "Places and Strata of Memory. Approaches to Eastern Europe." *Eurozine*, 19 December 2008. http://www.eurozine.com/articles/2008-12-19-schlogel-en.html (5 January 2015).

This "double experience" of two totalitarian regimes – National Socialism and Communism, plays a paradoxical role in the region. On the one hand, it constitutes a common feature that sets the whole region apart from the West of Europe and creates a bond in the form of a shared "tragic fate". On the other hand, however, the shared past events are interpreted differently by the different nations in the region, frequently in antagonistic ways. The case of the Baltic States (see Melchior as well Kaprans in this volume) is very illuminating in this respect. Due to large scale Soviet deportations of Latvians and Estonians to the Gulag, these people suffered as much, or even more, from the Soviet regime than from the Nazis. Therefore they tend to see both regimes as equally criminal, which is totally unacceptable to Russia, which responds by accusing the Balts of revisionism and by using this accusation in a political game with the West, where these issues are highly sensitive. Memories of the "Bloodlands", as Timothy Snyder called this region,[2] are also morally troubling. Categories such as victims, perpetrators, collaborators and bystanders, often used in the Western discourse about World War II, are very difficult to apply in discussing the memories of those from Central, Eastern and South-Eastern Europe. Both individuals and national and ethnic groups in this region often shifted their roles with the many, often violent, turns in the history of the "century of extremes". The same people who were victims at one stage could become perpetrators at another, and vice versa. The same military formation could be seen as heroes and liberators by one group and as criminals or traitors by another (this is for example the case with the Ukrainian Insurgent Army, UPA, – see Yurchuk). Until today expressions of moral judgment regarding these kinds of events, such as for example the mass murder of Poles in Volhynia by the UPA in 1943, continue to evoke high emotions and heated debates.

Having to live with such a troubling past, transmitted not only through various media but also via family stories, leads to people becoming personally engaged in the memories, thus contributing to emotional intensity. As a consequence, the past is not "a foreign country", memory of it is always there at hand to be used, to be referred to, leading sometimes to an excess of memory, that is, to situations where we can speak of too much memory, when a community is obsessed by the past.[3] These obsessions can complicate the situation when new political and ethnic conflicts emerge in a region. They can give continuous nourishment to memories of victimization, of enmity or of the past glory that has

---

[2] Timothy Snyder. *Bloodlands: Europe Between Hitler and Stalin.* New York: Basic Books, 2012.
[3] Jeffrey Blustein. *The Moral Demands of Memory.* Cambridge: Cambridge University Press, 2008, 15–19.

to be restored. The power of memory to exacerbate conflicts could be clearly observed during the Balkan wars in 1990s or the conflict between Russia and Ukraine that started 2014.

In order to better understand the developments in contemporary Central, Eastern and South-Eastern Europe, we need to understand the content as well as the complexity of the memories in these societies. Research is needed into questions such as how regional memories are used (or manipulated) today, who the users are and what motivates them. An important contribution to the field was made by the research project *Memory at War*,[4] which was conducted by Cambridge University and resulted in several publications.[5] Two of the researchers involved in this project, Blacker and Etkind, stated that "The fraught memory landscapes of Eastern Europe cry for more engagement with the critical perspectives of Western memory scholars".[6] Unfortunately, most publications dealing with these topics focus only on one or two countries in the region and there are still too few books that include a broader panorama of the region's memory disputes.

The present book aims to respond to the appeal by Blacker and Etkind for greater engagement by Western memory scholars "in the memory landscapes of Eastern Europe". We want to give the readers a broad insight into memory disputes in several Eastern European countries as well as disputes on memories that transcend the borders of these countries. Having a regional focus, our book at the same time has as its ambition to contribute to the overall scholarship in memory studies by presenting cases that approach memory in innovative ways. We take seriously the remark by Blacker and Etkind that this region is "a fascinating laboratory in which to study memory in action".[7] Thus a second goal of our volume is to use the thirteen carefully selected cases from Central, Eastern and South-Eastern Europe to demonstrate and investigate the interconnectedness between disputed memory, mediation of emotions and politics. The

---

[4] For extensive information about the project see http://www.memoryatwar.org/projects.
[5] *Remembering Katyn*. Ed. Alexander Etkind et al. Cambridge: Polity, 2012; *Memory and Theory in Eastern Europe*. Ed. Alexander Etkind and Uilleam Blacker. New York: Palgrave Macmillan, 2013; Alexander Etkind. *Warped Mourning: Stories of the Undead in the Land of the Unburied*. Stanford: Stanford University Press, 2013; *Memory, Conflict and New Media: Web Wars in Post-Socialist States*. Ed. Ellen Rutten and Julie Fedor. London: Routledge, 2013. However, one has to mention yet another important recent publication dealing with the subject: *History, Memory and Politics in Central and Eastern Europe Memory Game*. Ed. Georges Mink and Laure Neumayer. New York: Palgrave, 2013.
[6] Blacker and Etkind. "Introduction." *Memory and Theory in Eastern Europe*. Ed. Alexander Etkind and Uilleam Blacker. New York: Palgrave Macmillan, 2013, 10.
[7] Ibid.

chapters study representations of difficult and disputed pasts in various media, including monuments, museum exhibitions, individual and political discourse and new electronic media. At the same time the book tries to avoid the "representation bias" of memory studies, understood as the tendency to focus on the representation of a specific past within a particular media setting, without taking into account either the reception of the mediated memory or the context and conditions of its production and transmission.[8] Thus several authors of the chapters are keen to analyze memory mediation as a process, paying attention to issues of reception, that is, to reactions to the mediated memories. They also analyze carefully the social context in which the specific memories are mediated (see for example the contributions by Kotljarchuk, Yurchuk, Kaprans, Sindbæk Andersen and Pietraszewski and Törnquist-Plewa).

In their studies the authors emphasize the role of emotions in the formation and transmission of memory, an aspect that has long been downplayed in memory studies and has just recently come to the fore.[9] The case studies presented show the dynamics of affect in the interaction between individual and cultural memory (see for example Wyłęgała in this book), deal with trauma as mediatized event (see Denti) and they show how culturally mediated, deeply rooted images of the past structure our feelings when we are faced with the need to reinterpret the past (see for example the chapter by Pietraszewski and Törnquist-Plewa).

Yet another innovative aspect of the present volume is the attempt to take the study of memory beyond methodological nationalism. While recognizing the continuous importance of national memories, we want rather to emphasize region, locality and place and show their interplay with national memory. Thus we contribute to the opening of studies of memory in Eastern Europe towards a transnational perspective, described as follows by Ann Rigney and Chiara de Cesari: "'Transnationalism' recognizes the significance of national frameworks, alongside the potential of cultural production, both to reinforce and to transcend them."[10] In line with this perspective the studies in our volume investigate memory disputes on different social levels, ranging from very localized and spatially determined negotiations of memory to interpretations and uses of memory in national and international politics. Thus these studies emphasize the importance of space (including digital space) and location, which in each case define premises

---

8 Wulf Kansteiner. "Finding Meaning in Memory: A Methodological Critique of Collective memory Studies." *History and Theory* 41.2 (2002): 179–180.
9 Aleida Assmann. "Impact and Resonance – Towards a Theory of Emotions in Cultural Memory." *Södertörn Lectures*, 6 (2011): 16.
10 Ann Rigney and Chiara De Cesari. "Introduction." *Transnational Memory. Circulation, Articulation, Scales*. Ed. Ann Rigney and Chiara De Cesari. Berlin: De Gruyter, 2014, 4.

and resources and set out the type of battlefield or arena for memory negotiation.

It is also important to emphasize that, in response to the recent development in cultural memory studies, the present volume is very much a product of multidisciplinary and interdisciplinary scholarship. It not only contains contributions by historians and researchers of cultural studies but also by ethnologists, sociologists and political scientists. The latter point in their texts to the role of memories mediated in political discourse. Two of the texts (Denti and Forsberg) touch upon the question of "apology" as a memory practice, a subject very much discussed in recent studies on memory and transitional justice.

In the case studies presented in this volume the authors analyze the tense relations and mutual influences of memory, emotions and politics in contexts characterized by recent political upheaval, new nation-building and state-building projects as well as the impact of European integration processes. During the last decades, massive changes and political ruptures have brought memory disputes to the fore, resulting in a "memory boom" in Central, Eastern and South-Eastern Europe. In many places the fall of one monolithic socialist value system with a strict official interpretation of the past has opened the possibilities for new approaches to memory and history. As a consequence, an urgent need emerged to take up formerly taboo subjects. Many archives that had previously been inaccessible could be opened and this created new opportunities for rewriting history. At the same time the information uncovered has not seldom been put to ethical and/or political uses, thus leading to new confrontations. Throughout the region, difficult and disputed memories of catastrophic events in Europe's twentieth century have been approached from new angles, and new questions are being posed. Fierce debates about the past take place such as that in Poland when a book was published about Polish complicity in the Holocaust in the town of Jedwabne,[11] the treatment of the German civilian population in the Czechoslovakia after WWII;[12] the dispute over the memorial to Bandera in Lviv in

---

[11] Barbara Törnquist-Plewa. "The Jedwabne Killing – a Challenge for Polish Collective Memory. An Analysis of the Polish Debate on Jan Gross' book Neighbours." *The Echoes of the Holocaust.* Ed. Klas-Göran Karlsson. Lund: Nordic University Press, 2003, 141–176.

[12] Tomas Sniegon. "Between Old Animosity and New Mourning, Meanings of Czech Post-Communist Memorials of Mass Killings of the Sudeten Germans." *Which Memory, Whose Future? Remembering Ethnic Cleansings and Lost Cultural Diversity in Central, Eastern and South-eastern European Cities.* Ed. Barbara Törnquist-Plewa. London: Berghahn, 2016.

Ukraine;[13] the criticism of the "House of Terror" in Budapest,[14] the reassessment of WWII massacres in post-Yugoslav Serbia and Croatia,[15] to name just a few.

Often, the fall of the old memory regime leads to a reversal of memory, meaning that what was formerly regarded as positive is now judged negatively and the opposite; a process that Katherine Verdery has described as "reordering of meaningful worlds".[16] Our volume tries to capture this process in the region in a number of different contexts. In some cases this reordering opens possibilities for reconciliation and sometimes allows for changed attitudes towards former enemies (for example relations between Poles and Germans, see the chapter by Pietraszewski and Törnquist-Plewa). However, a reversal can sometimes result in the reawakening of positive attitudes toward extremely right-wing nationalist movements from the past (see for example the chapters by Melchior and Yurchuk). While it is easy to condemn such tendencies, it is important to understand what makes people, who may otherwise show pro-democratic and pro-European attitudes, produce memory representations glorifying non-democratic organizations and authoritarian figures. The chapter by Yurchuk in this volume gives some insight into this complex phenomenon by pointing to the urgent need of new nations to reclaim their past.[17] After the long period of the communist oppression, people search for stories about the resistance to communism in the past and about the national fighters whose existence could legitimate the current national state. However, the paradox and the dilemma for the new nations is that the anti-communist fighters as well as the heroes of national struggle in the past often stand for values that are incompatible with the modern democracies. What past can be reclaimed in that case? This is a challenge that several nations in the region have to face. Our volume signals the need to go behind the Western stereotype that interprets Eastern Europe as mired in primor-

---

[13] Eleonora Narvselius. "The 'Bandera Debate': The Contentious Legacy of World War II and Liberalization of Collective Memory in Western Ukraine." *Canadian Slavonic Papers* 54.3–4 (2012): 469–490.

[14] Kristian Gerner. "Hungary, Romania, the Holocaust and Historical Culture." *The Holocaust – Post-War Battlefields. Genocide as Historical Culture.* Ed. Klas-Göran Karlsson and Ulf Zander. Malmö-Lund: Sekel, 2006, 225–259.

[15] Tea Sindbæk. *Usable History? Representations of Yugoslavia's difficult past 1945–2002.* Aarhus: Aarhus University Press, 2012.

[16] Katherine Verdery. *The Political Lives of Dead Bodies.* New York: Columbia University Press, 1999, 50.

[17] For more elaborated discussion of this subject see also Yuliya Yurchuk. *Reordering of Meaningful Worlds.* Stockholm: Stockholm Studies in History 103, 2014.

dial nationalism and approaching this region using new perspectives, for example those applied in postcolonial theory.[18]

Inside countries of Central, Eastern and South-Eastern Europe, new political regimes have raised demands for reassessing recent history, confronting both the communist version of history and the history of communism itself. The ways of confronting or coping with the crimes and oppression of the communist period vary greatly across the region, spanning from judicial prosecution, and lustration to lenience and almost indifference.[19] While such differences may be explained in part by states' and politicians' different needs and motivations in the present, they are also caused by the difficulty in defining and delimiting the attitudes towards the communist past. After all, the experiences of communism vary greatly between the periods of harsh Stalinist suppression in the 1940s and 1950s and the widespread reform communism of the 1980s, and between countries, from Albania's prolonged experience of heavily oppressive Stalinism to Yugoslavia's open borders and the consumer socialism of the 1970s.

The changing memory regimes of Central, Eastern and South-Eastern Europe are also influenced by external pressure. Since the end of the Cold War, the European Union has positioned itself as an active player in European memory politics, foregrounding the Holocaust as an essential part of Europe's shared cultural memory.[20] It has been argued that the inclusion of the Holocaust as an important element of national history was one of the entrance tickets to the European Union in the 2000s.[21] Indeed, from the 1990s, the Holocaust seemed to emerge as a globally shared memory, both functioning as a standard reference of historical suffering and often challenging national and local perspectives on twentieth

---

[18] In the book *Multidirectional Memory. Remembering the Holocaust in the Age of Decolonization*. Stanford: Stanford University Press, 1999, Michael Rothberg broke new ground in combing postcolonial discourse and memory studies. This is still in need of being explored, especially in the investigation of memory in Eastern Europe, as pointed out in Blacker and Etkind. "Introduction," 15.

[19] Timothy Garton Ash. "Trials, purges and history lessons: treating a difficult past in Post-communist Europe." *Memory and Power in Post-War Europe*. Ed. Jan-Werner Müller. Cambridge: Cambridge University Press, 2002, 265–282.

[20] Aline Sierp. *History, Memory, and Transeuropean Identity: Unifying Divisions*. London: Routledge, 2014; Anne Wæhrens. *Erindringspolitik til forhandling: EU og erindringen om Holocaust, 1989–2009*. Doctoral thesis, University of Copenhagen, 2013.

[21] Tony Judt. *Postwar. A history of Europe since 1945*. London: William Heinemann, 2005, 803–804.

century history.[22] Thus, the understanding of the recent past was exposed to local and national as well as international pressure, which created confrontations and demanded negotiations about various versions of local, national, European and even global memory. Indeed, as Cecilie Banke points out in her chapter on Turkey and the Armenian genocide, global Holocaust memory may set difficult – and potentially obstructive – standards for memory negotiations, thus obfuscating attempts towards reconciliation processes. And as the informants quoted in Inge Melchior's chapter seem to suggest, the West-European foregrounding of the Holocaust as a memory standard may be perceived as more of a denial of local memory than as an invitation to a shared European memory community. Indeed, as Melchior's chapter demonstrates in the case of memory communities in Estonia, for many nations and peoples in Eastern Europe who went through the tragic double experience of the Nazi reign and Soviet-style communism, both of these regimes are of equal importance to remember. Therefore, in contrast to the West, Eastern European societies do not tend to see the Holocaust as exceptional and instead wish to universalize the memory of other genocides and violations of human rights, especially the memory of the Gulag and other communist crimes. In their view, Europe as a whole has much to learn from this legacy, which also has a potential to contribute to the formation of human rights, just as the Holocaust memories did. The representatives of Eastern European EU members have made efforts to call upon the EU to condemn and educate their members about communist crimes in a way similar to what has been done regarding Nazism.[23] One of the driving forces behind this demand is the will to have their experiences of the communist dictatorship recognized as an important part of the common European memory. Memory and identity are interconnected, as identity is to a large extent sustained by memory, by what a community remembers and what it forgets.[24] By turning the memory of the Gulag and other communist crimes into a common European, not only East European, memory, Eastern Europeans hope to broaden the scope of social understanding for their view of the past and to incorporate it into the European community of memory, thus strengthening their bonds with other EU members. The Western EU members for their part treat with a large dose of suspicion the Eastern European initiatives in the field of memory politics such as for example

---

[22] On the notion of Holocaust as a cosmopolitan memory, see Daniel Levy and Nathan Sznaider. "Memory unbound: the Holocaust and the formation of cosmopolitan memory." *European Journal of Social Theory* 5.1 (2002): 87–106.
[23] It was clearly expressed in the so called Prague Declaration, for its content see http://www.praguedeclaration.org/.
[24] Barbara Misztal. *Theories of Social Remembering*. London: Open University Press, 2003.

the establishment in 2008 of the European Day of Remembrance of the Victims of Stalinism and Nazism, perceiving these commemorative events as an attempt to relativize and diminish the importance of the Holocaust memory, with a hidden agenda of avoiding responsibility. The mistrust has some ground in the fact that several countries of Eastern Europe still have difficulty acknowledging their inhabitants' complicity in the Holocaust. This clash over memory constitutes a substantial obstacle in the construction of a common European memory.

A core question addressed in this book is how disputed and difficult memories in Central, Southern and Eastern Europe are represented, and how such representations are received and retransmitted. Indeed, it is exactly this "mediation", the presentation and transmission through various types of texts and artefacts – or "media", in the widest sense of the word – that enable memory to become known by large groups of people. As Astrid Erll and Ann Rigney point out, "memory can only become collective as part of a continuous process whereby memories are shared with the help of symbolic artefacts that mediate between individuals [...] and create community across space and time".[25] The chapters of this book examine a wide variety of types of memory transmission, including classic memory sites or in Alexander Etkind's term "hardware memories" such as monuments, memorials and museums, as well "software memories" in the form of texts in newspapers and new digital media, but also memories mediated in political rhetoric and discourse (see Forsberg's and Denti's chapters in this volume) and oral communication (see the chapter by Wylęgała). Moreover, the thematic focus on disputed or difficult memories demands an emphasis on debates and reactions, enabling the authors to look not only at memory representations but also at negotiations (for examples, see the chapters by Kulyk as well as Pietraszewski and Törnquist-Plewa). In this way, by looking at different types of communication and the interaction between them, the chapters highlight the significance of the media through which memory is transmitted.

The role of mediation is crucial not only in enabling the distribution and sharing of memory but also in investing emotional value in memory representations. We know that memory issues can be highly emotional. As Alison Landsberg has argued, memory of events that are quite remote in time and place can be made accessible and emotionally relevant to us. The ways in which historical narratives are mediated, often through modern mass culture, can create

---

25 Astrid Erll and Ann Rigney. "Introduction: Cultural Memory and its Dynamics." *Mediation, Remediation and the Dynamic of Cultural Memory.* Ed. Astrid Erll and Ann Rigney. Berlin: De Gruyter, 2009, 1.

what is in fact a personal experience, turning it into a deeply felt memory.[26] Also in new, more interactive types of media, memory representations have substantial emotional impact. Adi Kuntsman has pointed out how circulation of memory of war and violence on the Internet can intensify or transform feelings and affective states. Indeed, Kuntsman argues, these memory mediations often make an actual physical impression through what she calls the "cybertouch".[27]

When trying to understand these processes, we need to study the "emotionality of texts", as Sarah Ahmed has phrased it.[28] Text is to be understood here rather broadly to include a wide array of meaning-transmitting products such as films, photos, works of art, commemoration ceremonies as well as history books and media discourse. Identification and involvement are created through emotional appeal, Ahmed argues, by inviting the receiver to share in the emotion.[29] This is where mediations and text also obtain physiological functions, adding extra layers of emotion and affect to the representations of memory. We need to take seriously the fact that acts of remembering and of experiencing representations of memory are done by physically embodied individuals, and memory is perceived, processed and transmitted through bodies, brains, senses and capacities for communication. Emotions cannot be separated from bodily senses, and thus the reading or viewing of certain types of memory representations may cause affective and bodily reactions. This encourages us to consider what representations of memory and participation in memory transmissions may do to human beings as bodies and brains. Patricia Clough has described the challenge of analyzing representations of extreme violence and suffering: as pity, disgust and horror rise in the reader, she says, "affect is at work" and could be used to mobilize for both compassion and aggression.[30] Memory transmissions can have similar effects, creating identification and involvement and touching us across time and space. A key question is which types of mediation may have such effects and how? While certain memory representations and sites

---

[26] Alison Landsberg. *Prosthetic memory. The transformation of American remembrance in the age of global mass culture.* New York: Columbia University Press, 2004, 3, 8–9.
[27] Adi Kuntsman. "Online memories, digital conflicts and the cybertouch of war." *Digital Icons: Studies in Russian, Eurasian and Central European New Media* 4 (2010): 9; Adi Kuntsman. "Introduction: Affective Fabrics of Digital Cultures." *Digital Cultures and the Politics of Emotion.* Ed. Athina Karatzogianni and Adi Kuntsman. Basingstoke: Palgrave Macmillan, 2012, 1.
[28] Sara Ahmed. *The Cultural Politics of Emotions.* Edinburgh: Edinburg University Press, 2004, 12.
[29] Ibid, 1.
[30] Patricia Ticineto Clough. "War By Other Means: What Difference Do(es) the Graphic(s) Make?" *Digital Cultures and the Politics of Emotion.* Ed. Athina Karatzogianni and Adi Kuntsman. Basingstoke: Palgrave Macmillan, 2012, 27.

of memory cause strong affective reactions, as Sophie Oliver's chapter demonstrates, others only provoke a vague response, as is implied in the chapter by Birga Meyer or expressed in the relative lack of engagement of Yuliya Yurchuk's informants (see Oliver, Meyer and Yurchuk in this volume).

The importance of space and location for practices of memory is a fundamental concern within memory studies. Specific places or sites of memory function as prisms through which we can observe the complex dynamics of memories meeting and interacting. Sites of memory memory can be concrete physical entities, such as monuments, memorials, and cemeteries set aside to embody both private and collective remembering and mourning.[31] They are places where individuals are confronted with remnants and expressions of our shared history, catalyzing individual responses and commemorations, but they can also take on more political functions as places to ceremoniously celebrate collective identity and shared glorious history.[32] Sites of memory may also be wider spaces or cityscapes, characterized by the multi-layering of fragments from the past in an urban palimpsest and in topographies of memory.[33] Yet, sites of memory need not be physical or localized at all; the term may also refer to an image, a text, a narrative or an event. The point is that such "sites", whether material or discursive, become the focus of collective remembrance and of historical meaning. They tend to attract intense attention from those involved in remembering and are constantly being invested with new meaning.[34]

Investigating the entanglement of memory with emotion, mediation and place, this book seeks to demonstrate in particular the social power and political impact of painful and troubled memory. It aims to emphasize that memory of difficult and painful pasts is often heavily invested with politics and emotion, and therefore disputes about memory are rarely easily reconcilable. The chapters in this book show how and why memory may be different and how transmission of memory may act upon individuals, interest groups and political units. Indeed, memory of Europe's troubled past may crucially influence relations between individuals, memory communities and states. By presenting this series of chapters on disputed memories of troubling pasts across Europe, we seek to emphasize

---

[31] Jay Winter. *Sites of memory, sites of mourning: The Great War in European cultural history.* Cambridge: Cambridge University Press, 1995.
[32] James E. Young. *The Texture of Memory. Holocaust Memorials and Meaning.* New Haven: Yale University Press, 1993; Pierre Nora. *Realms of memory: rethinking the French past.* New York: Columbia University Press, 3 vols., 1996–1998.
[33] Young. *The Texture of Memory.*
[34] Ann Rigney. "Plenitude, scarcity and the circulation of cultural memory." *Journal of European Studies* 35.1 (2005): 18.

the complexity of the layers of memory of the troubled twentieth century in Central, Eastern and South-Eastern Europe. Across Europe, different memory narratives dominate and different aspects of the past are foregrounded, depending on historical experience, memory traditions, political needs and the means of memory transmission. There is an urgent need to understand the complexities of Europe's twentieth century and the memory of it, and to include all of Europe's regions in this process. We are far from suggesting any kind of relativism with regard to interpretations of the difficult pasts, for we strongly believe that there is a need to understand as thoroughly as possible the troubling events our societies struggle to remember. But we argue that there is a need to recognize a plurality of memory perspectives.

The chapters in this book investigate memory disputes played out around very different types of memory sites, from the very concrete such as monuments and memorials, to heroes or victims, to memory sites in the form of difficult and disputed events such as the Ottoman genocide against Armenians or the Srebrenica massacre, and on to sites of memory in media and cyberspace. Moreover, the chapters investigate memory disputes at very different spatial and social levels. While some chapters look at conflicting and complex interpretations of one singular site of memory, others study the negotiation of memories within particular, more or less established groups, and others again investigate memory as a factor in the establishment of national politics and as a cause for dispute on the international arena and across national borders.

The chapters are organized according to the different social spaces investigated. The first part of the book looks at memory disputes and negotiations over troubling pasts that have had an effect on, or may affect international and regional politics. It focuses on the negotiation of memory in political discourse on public and official levels. We decided to begin the book with Cecilie Felicia Stockholm Banke's chapter on the Armenian genocide since, as Blacker and Etkind has pointed out,[35] this genocide has become a historical prototype for many Eastern European developments, a paradigmatic case of mass violence of "the century of extremes". Banke's chapter presents the genocide as part of international memory and points to the strong emotions caused by the international political actualization of a human catastrophe that took place 100 years ago. Banke investigates how the memory of the Armenian genocide is negotiated in foreign politics and how strategies of remembering, not remembering and dialogically forgetting are at play. The chapter that follows, written by Tuomas Forsberg, deals with the role of World War II memory in the relationship between

---

35 Blacker and Etkind. "Introduction," 8.

Russia and Finland. Forsberg shows how a difficult and divided memory may constitute a challenge to foreign policy but may also be addressed politically and diplomatically, amongst others through the use of apologies. While Forsberg touches upon the subject of apology, the next author, Davide Denti, looks more closely at the role of apologies as a tool of reconciliation and at its functions in the domestic, international and regional politics of Serbia and Bosnia. Denti's chapter examines how a memory as recent and as emotionally troubling as the massacre in Srebrenica in 1995 may be addressed politically.

The book's second part is concerned with sites of memory not as monuments reifying established narratives, but as locations that activate processes of transmission of memory and emotion. The chapters investigate the interaction between the memory site and the audience or receivers of memory transmission and look at ways in which these memory transmissions may challenge recipients and oppose other memory narratives. Sophie Oliver's chapter on Berlin's memorials studies how emotions may be transmitted through the spatial organization of sites of painful memory. Oliver analyzes the choreography of the memorial sites and the responses of visitors. In her chapter on the representation of Holocaust victimhood, Birga Meyer analyzes photographic stereotypes of Jewish Holocaust victims. Meyer's chapter points to the power of visual representation as troubling images, but also to the ways in which national and European memories collide. Andrej Kotljarchuk's chapter on the commemoration of the Roma Holocaust in Ukraine investigates how sites of memory represent public memory or the lack thereof. Looking also at the decision-making behind the erection of monuments, Kotljarchuk shows some of the dynamics and negotiation within commemorative politics.

The third part of the book focuses on local memory as memory that adheres to a periphery or border region and is somehow marginalized or at odds with larger, institutionalized memory narratives. The chapters in this part are concerned with the memories of groups, or memory communities, and with orally transmitted memories. The investigations are based on interviews with members of a marginalized memory community or with intended recipients of transmission of the marginalized local memory. Anna Wylęgała's chapter on the memory of forced migrations in Poland and Ukraine studies individuals' narratives about their deportation and the interrelations between memory and identity in the small communities of expellees. Wylęgała points to shared characteristics of these memory communities and their relations to the surrounding society. In her chapter on the memory of World War II in Estonia, Inge Melchior investigates how memory actors and small memory communities react to experiences of being marginalized by national and European memory politics. Melchior's chapter demonstrates how feelings of non-recognition may lead to defensive strategies and polarization of memory communities. Yuliya Yurchuk's chapter investigates the development of the memory of Ukraine's nationalist insurgent army during World War II and how this relatively newly expressed memory interacts with established Soviet era memory narratives. Yurchuk looks at ways in which the new memory is activated and received and suggests that the two memories, though potentially diverging, can coexist without significant difficulty.

The last and largest part of the book examines transmissions of memory in media spaces. Though memory is always mediated, these chapters show the ways the media as such play a crucial role, setting a more open and fluctuating stage for memory transmission. Unlike oral memory transmission, which demands personal presence and a degree of intimacy, and sites of memory that suggest a more carefully calculated and stable memory narrative, media such as newspapers, internet sites and social networking sites engender both fast and far-reaching memory transmission, creating new and diverse memory communities. Moreover, digital social media allow for new forms of engagement and participation in memory negotiation. This part of the book contains five chapters. Giving it more space in the book, we want to emphasize the importance of the digital sphere for negotiations of memories in Central, Eastern and South-Eastern Europe. In some contexts in the region, this is one of the few spaces where alternative memories can be voiced. However, this openness does not mean that the Internet is only used by democratic forces. Frequently it is also a forum for political propaganda, sometimes disguised as independent, and using digital tools in ways that are perceived as adhering to rules of independence and objectivity. The Internet is also far from being a "de-nationalised space".[36] Martins Kaprans' chapter on memory wars on Wikipedia, which opens the last section of our book, deals with the above-mentioned challenges of memory work in digital spaces. This chapter is followed by Volodymyr Kulyk's chapter on the memory of Soviet rule and resistance. It studies memory negotiations, or the lack thereof, on online networks, arguing that web debates, often highly affective, in many cases contribute to establishing borders between irreconcilable viewpoints. Yet in certain cases, the online networks can create alternative rooms for real dialogue, creating particular Internet memory communities around specific questions. Tea Sindbæk Andersen's chapter on football and memories of Croatian fascism on Facebook investigates how the meaning of a historical symbol, in this case a chant used by Croatia's Second World War quis-

---

[36] Ellen Rutten and Vera Zvereva. "Introduction." *Memory, Conflict and New Media: Web Wars in Post-Socialist States*. Eds. Ellen Rutten, Julie Fedor and Vera Zvereva, London: Routledge, 2013, 1–17.

ling regime, is negotiated on social media, and how different memory agents, including a large audience of individual Facebook users, contribute to this negotiation. Facebook and other digital media are thus shown to facilitate quick and unlimited transmission of memory narratives, potentially enabling fast and wide mobilization of a digital memory community. Yet, there are very different ways of participating, and the nature of the media itself makes the memory narratives transmitted somehow fragmentary. Elvin Gjevori's chapter on memory and institutionalization in Albania explores how a troubling past can also serve as a resource for political reform and institution building. Gjevori shows how newspaper comments draw on the memory of a very repressive communist regime and of state crises in the transition period in order to promote current reform initiatives. And finally, Igor Pietraszewski and Barbara Törnquist-Plewa's chapter on the debate about the Centennial Hall in Wrocław shows how newspapers and online discussions forums may be the site of struggle between national and post-national Europeanized perspectives on memory. Pietraszewski and Törnquist-Plewa point to the complex and difficult relations between national and European memory narratives and to the problem of respecting the memories of the Other when it is at odds with our own memory. Indeed, the printed and often also digitalized media created a discursive public space in which highly emotional transmissions of memory and views of memory could take place.

References

Ahmed, Sara. *The Cultural Politics of Emotions*. Edinburg: Edinburg University Press, 2004.
Ash, Timothy Garton. "Trials, purges and history lessons: treating a difficult past in Post-communist Europe." *Memory and Power in Post-War Europe*. Ed. Jan-Werner Müller. Cambridge: Cambridge University Press, 2002. 265–282.
Assmann, Aleida. "Impact and Resonance – Towards A Theory of Emotions in Cultural Memory." *Södertörn Lectures* 6 (2011).
Blustein, Jeffrey. *The Moral Demands of Memory*. Cambridge: Cambridge University Press, 2008.
Cesari, Chiara De and Ann Rigney. "Introduction." *Transnational Memory. Circulation, Articulation, Scales*. Eds. Chiara De Cesari and Ann Rigney. Berlin: De Gruyter, 2014. 1–26.
Clough, Patricia Ticineto. "War By Other Means: What Difference Do(es) the Graphic(s) Make?" *Digital Cultures and the Politics of Emotion*. Eds. Athina Karatzogianni and Adi Kuntsman. Basingstoke: Palgrave Macmillan, 2012. 21–32.
Erll, Astrid and Ann Rigney. "Introduction: Cultural Memory and its Dynamics." *Mediation, Remediation and the Dynamic of Cultural Memory*. Eds. Astrid Erll and Ann Rigney. Berlin: De Gruyter, 2009.
Etkind, Alexander et al. Eds. *Remembering Katyn*. Cambridge: Polity, 2012.

Etkind, Alexander and Uilleam Blacker. Eds. *Memory and Theory in Eastern Europe*. New York: Palgrave Macmillan, 2013.
Etkind, Alexander. *Warped Mourning: Stories of the Undead in the Land of the Unburied*. Stanford: Stanford University Press, 2013.
Gerner, Kristian. "Hungary, Romania, the Holocaust and Historical Culture." *The Holocaust – Post-War Battlefields. Genocide as Historical Culture*. Ed. Klas-Göran Karlsson and Ulf Zander. Malmö-Lund: Sekel, 2006.
Judt, Tony. *Postwar. A history of Europe since 1945*. London: William Heinemann, 2005.
Kansteiner, Wulf. "Finding Meaning in Memory: A Methodological Critique of Collective memory Studies." *History and Theory* 41. 2 (2002): 179–197.
Kuntsman, Adi. "Introduction: Affective Fabrics of Digital Cultures." *Digital Cultures and the Politics of Emotion*. Ed. Athina Karatzogianni and Adi Kuntsman. Basingstoke: Palgrave Macmillan, 2012. 1–18.
Kuntsman, Adi. "Online memories, digital conflicts and the cybertouch of war." *Digital Icons: Studies in Russian, Eurasian and Central European New Media* 4 (2010): 1–12.
Landsberg, Alison. *Prosthetic memory. The transformation of American remembrance in the age of global mass culture*. New York: Columbia University Press, 2004.
Levy, Daniel and Nathan Sznaider. "Memory unbound: the Holocaust and the formation of cosmopolitan memory." *European Journal of Social Theory* 5.1 (2002): 87–106.
Mink, Georges and Laure Neumayer. Eds. *History, Memory and Politics in Central and Eastern Europe Memory Game*. New York: Palgrave, 2013.
Misztal, Barbara. *Theories of Social Remembering*. London: Open University Press, 2003.
Narvselius, Eleonora. "The 'Bandera Debate': The Contentious Legacy of World War II and Liberalization of Collective Memory in Western Ukraine." *Canadian Slavonic Papers* 54.3–4 (2012): 469–490.
Nora, Pierre. *Realms of memory: rethinking the French past*. New York: Columbia University Press, 3 vols., 1996–1998.
Schlögel, Karl. "Places and Strata of Memory. Approaches to Eastern Europe." *Eurozine*, 19 December 2008. http://www.eurozine.com/articles/2008-12-19-schlogel-en.html (5 January 2015).
Sniegon, Tomas. "Between Old Animosity and New Mourning, Meanings of Czech Post-Communist Memorials of Mass Killings of the Sudeten Germans." *Which Memory, Whose Future? Remembering Ethnic Cleansings and Lost Cultural Diversity in Central, Eastern and South-eastern European Cities*. Ed. Barbara Törnquist-Plewa. London: Berghahn: forthcoming.
Snyder, Timothy. *Bloodlands: Europe Between Hitler and Stalin*. New York: Basic Books, 2012.
Rigney, Ann. "Plenitude, scarcity and the circulation of cultural memory." *Journal of European Studies* 35.1 (2005): 11–28.
Rothberg, Michael. *Multidirectional Memory. Remembering the Holocaust in the Age of Decolonization*. Stanford: Stanford University Press, 1999.
Rutten, Ellen, Julie Fedor and Vera Zvereva. Eds. *Memory, Conflict and New Media: Web Wars in Post-Socialist States*. London: Routledge, 2013.
Rutten, Ellen and Vera Zvereva. "Introduction." *Memory, Conflict and New Media: Web Wars in Post-Socialist States*. Eds. Ellen Rutten, Julie Fedor and Vera Zvereva, London: Routledge, 2013. 1–18.

Sierp, Aline. *History, Memory, and Transeuropean Identity: Unifying Divisions.* London: Routledge, 2014.

Sindbæk, Tea. *Usable History? Representations of Yugoslavia's difficult past 1945–2002.* Aarhus: Aarhus University Press, 2012.

Törnquist-Plewa, Barbara. "The Jedwabne Killing – a Challenge for Polish Collective Memory. An Analysis of the Polish Debate on Jan Gross' book Neighbours." *The Echoes of the Holocaust.* Ed. Klas-Göran Karlsson. Lund: Nordic University Press, 2003. 141–177.

Verdery, Katherine. *The Political Lives of Dead Bodies.* New York: Columbia University Press, 1999.

Wæhrens, Anne. *Erindringspolitik til forhandling: EU og erindringen om Holocaust, 1989–2009.* Doctoral thesis, University of Copenhagen, 2013.

Winter, Jay. *Sites of memory, sites of mourning: The Great War in European cultural history.* Cambridge: Cambridge University Press, 1995.

Young, James E. *The Texture of Memory. Holocaust Memorials and Meaning.* New Haven: Yale University Press, 1993.

Yurchuk, Yuliya. *Reordering of Meaningful Worlds. Memory of the Organization of Ukrainian Nationalists and the Ukrainian Insurgent Army in Post-Soviet Ukraine.* Stockholm: Stockholm Studies in History 103, 2014.

Part 1: **Transnational Memory Politics**

Cecilie Felicia Stokholm Banke
Global Memory and *Dialogic Forgetting*: The Armenian Case

In January 2012, just before the annual Holocaust Remembrance Day, the French Senate passed a bill that would criminalize the denial of officially recognized genocides, including the Armenian genocide initiated in 1915. The bill was, not surprisingly, met by a firm protest from the Turkish government, which denounced the French act and demanded that, instead of interfering with Turkish history, France should admit its own past atrocities in Algeria. Even among writers and historians, and within the international community of genocide scholars, several found it wrong to introduce a law that would officially make denying the Armenian genocide a crime. The Turkish-Armenian journalist and newspaper editor, Hrant Dink, who was well known for his firm criticism of the Turkish government, was already critical when the French law first came before the parliament in 2006.[1] The British historian, Timothy Garton Ash, wrote during the debate: "The question is: should it be a crime under the law of France, or other countries, to dispute whether those terrible events constituted a genocide, a term used in international law? While not minimizing the suffering of the Armenians, the celebrated Ottoman specialist Bernard Lewis has in the past disputed that precise point. And is the French parliament equipped and entitled to set itself up as a tribunal on world history, handing down verdicts on the past conduct of other nations? The answers are: no and no."[2]

The decision on behalf of the French Senate makes it relevant to ask why something that happened over 90 years ago continues to evoke strong feelings and can even provoke a diplomatic crisis like the one between France and Turkey. When the bill was passed, Prime Minister Erdogan stated that it was "evident discrimination, racism and massacre of free speech" and reiterated Turkey's intention to institute penalties against France.[3] And diplomatic relations were af-

---

[1] *The Economist*, 31 December 2011. http://www.economist.com/node/21542225 (26 November 2012).
[2] Timothy Garton Ash. "In France, genocide has become a political brickbat." *The Guardian*, 18 January 2012. http://www.guardian.co.uk/commentisfree/2012/jan/18/france-genocide-political-brickbat (26 November 2012).
[3] "French Bill on Genocide Is Denounced by Turkey." *New York Times*, 24 January 2012. http://www.nytimes.com/2012/01/25/world/europe/turkey-lashes-out-at-france-over-genocide-bill.html (26 November 2012).

fected, even though the French foreign minister, Alain Juppé, who had openly opposed the bill, did reach out to the Turks.

To answer the question about the capacity of past events to affect us so powerfully in the present, we must not only consider the domestic politics involved, and here I refer to the voting power of approximately 500.000 French citizens of Armenian descent, but we must also understand how, in general, the politics of memory have developed in Europe over the past two decades, giving crimes of the past an increased impact on foreign relations and international politics.

The recognition of the massacre of the Armenians committed by the Young Turks and their helpers during the First World War has been an issue ever since the war ended. "The Armenian Genocide of 1915 remains one of the most painful episodes of mass killing in the history of the modern genocide," writes Norman Naimark in his preface to the co-edited volume *A Question of Genocide*.[4] Why this is the case can be explained, in part, by the controversy between the Turks and the Armenians over what actually happened – whether genocide occurred and to what extent the Ottoman state was deliberately attempting to destroy the Armenians – and whether the Turkish state should be held accountable.

The literature is in this respect considerable. From being ignored by scholars for almost fifty years, the Armenian massacres have since the mid 1960s increasingly become a focus of attention on behalf of historians, sociologists and lawyers, not least because of the emerging field of genocide studies.[5] Thus, part of the scholarly interest in the Armenian massacres can be explained by the general interest that emerged during the 1960s and 1970s in the history of the Holo-

---

[4] Ronald Grigor Suny, Fatma Müge Göcek and Norman M. Naimark. *A Question of Genocide. Armenians and Turks at the End of the Ottoman Empire*. Oxford: Oxford University Press, 2011, xiii–xix.

[5] See among others Donald Bloxham. *The Great Game of Genocide: Imperialism, Nationalism, and the Destruction of the Ottoman Armenians*. Oxford & New York: Oxford University Press, 2005; Taner Akcam. *A Shameful Act: The Armenian Genocide and the Question of Turkish Responsibility*. London: Constable & Robinson, 2007; David Gaunt. *Massacres, Resistance and Protectors: Muslim-Christian Relations in Eastern Anatolia during World War I*. Piscataway, N. J.: Gorgias Press, 2006; Richard G. Hovannisian. *The Armenian Holocaust: A Bibliography Relating to the Deportations, Massacres, and Dispersion of the Armenian People, 1915–1923*. Cambridge, Mass.: National Association for Armenian Studies and Research, 1978; Richard G. Hovannisian, Ed. *The Armenian Genocide in Perspective*. New Brunswick, N. J., and Oxford: Transaction Books, 1986; Robert Melson. *Revolution and Genocide: On the Origins of the Armenian Genocide and the Holocaust*. Chicago: University of Chicago Press, 1992. Within the field of comparative genocide studies, Leo Kuper's work is considered particularly important, see *Genocide: Its Political Use in the 20th Century*. New Haven: Yale University Press, 1981, and *The Prevention of Genocide*, New Haven: Yale University Press, 1985.

caust and other genocides. But the controversy around the recognition of the massacres as genocide and the geopolitical dimension of the issue has also lead to increased international interest. According to Klas-Göran Karlsson and Kristian Gerner, the Armenian massacres returned as an issue that could attract world attention in 1965, when thousands of Armenians demonstrated in the streets of Yerevan, the capital of the then Soviet republic Armenia, on 24 April during the fiftieth anniversary of the deportations of 1915.[6] The protests were part of the national upheavals that occurred in the Soviet-Caucasus, but in Armenia the demonstration was also a protest against the silencing of the Armenian tragedy of 1915. In that sense, the striving for national independence in the Armenian case was from the beginning strongly connected with the striving for justice and for an official recognition of the massacres. The protest was met by the Soviet government by the installation in 1967 of a monument, *Tsitsernakaberd*, to commemorate the victims. Since then, the Armenian question has been a disputed issue that also includes an important historical lesson, not only for the countries implicated, but for the international community in general.

The massacre of the Armenians during the First World War took place in full view of the international community, and the principle of nonintervention in the affairs of sovereign states won over calls for humanitarian intervention. The massacres occurred while the allies of the Ottoman Empire, Germany and Austria-Hungary, as well as the Russian Empire, and even the neutral United States of America, passively stood by. This lack of international intervention to stop the deportation and the mass killings of Armenians marks an episode in the history of modern genocide that is littered with sorrow and strong emotions.

This failure to intervene and stop the deportations could thus be mistaken for a legitimizing signal. Fewer than three decades later another authoritarian regime committed a similar, though in scale and scope more massive, crime – the deliberate mass killing of Jews during the Second World War, while other states stood passively by. Thus the experience from the First World War taught states that a crime similar to the massacre committed against the Armenians, the Assyrians, and the Greeks could, in fact, be considered an accepted, and very effective, strategy for handling religious minorities or other social groups. The lack of any sense of obligation of international parties to condemn such deeds was especially evident when the Republic of Turkey in 1923 was recognized by the major powers in the Treaty of Lausanne, which failed even to mention the Armenians or enforce minority protection on the Kemalist state. Thus, the deportations could in fact be considered "a potential solution to population

---

6 Kristian Gerner and Klas-Göran Karlsson. *Folkmordens Historia*. Stockholm: Atlantis, 2005.

problems", as Ronald Suny writes: "With the Soviet Republic as the only existing Armenian political presence, there was little incentive for Western governments to deal with this matter. In the new republic of Turkey there was a cold silence about the events of the late Ottoman period beyond the heroic nationalist narrative of Kemalist resistance to foreign aggression."[7]

In this respect, both the lack of official recognition on behalf of the Turkish state of this particular crime, and the failure on behalf of the international community to prevent this crime from happening, have made this genocide into a particularly painful episode in modern history. Neither has the perpetrator state acknowledged its guilt, nor has the international community admitted its responsibility.

Memory – terms and definitions

If we compare how the Armenian genocide and the Holocaust have been dealt with in their aftermaths, we may understand some of the difficulties embedded in the quest for an official recognition of the Armenian genocide. Most European countries have an official policy for how to commemorate the Holocaust and also for how to teach the history of the Holocaust to future generations. Since the beginning of the 1990s, several resolutions, declarations, and official statements that express these intentions have been put forward by individual states and international bodies, such as the European Parliament, the European Council, OSCE and the UN. And most European countries have an annual Holocaust remembrance day. Some countries, such as France, Belgium, and even Denmark, have acknowledged their share of responsibility for the crimes committed by Nazi-Germany during the Second World War.

When comparing this development with how other cases of genocide have been dealt with in the aftermath, we find similarities. First of all, the role of the victim communities in developing a culture of remembrance is crucial. In this respect, the global Armenian community plays an important role in continuing to push for an official acknowledgement of the Armenian tragedy as genocide. Also, several countries including Russia, France and Germany have recognized the event as a genocide and more than 135 memorials, spread across 25 countries, commemorate the Armenian Genocide. However, neither the Armeni-

---

[7] Ronald Grigor Suny. "Writing Genocide. The Fate of the Ottoman Armenians." *A Question of Genocide*. Eds. Ronald Grigor Suny, Fatma Müge Göçek and Norman Naimark. Oxford: Oxford University Press, 2011, 21.

an genocide, nor the Rwanda genocide, nor the genocide in Bosnia have a position in global memory that approaches that of the Holocaust. Why this is the case may be an interesting question, but it is not my intention to discuss it here.

Instead, I will argue that the way the Holocaust has been confronted, dealt with, and included in national remembrance activities since the late 1950s has contributed to the development of a general pattern for how memory of mass atrocities is dealt with, or rather ought to be dealt with. To a certain extent, we may say that the commemoration of the Holocaust has established a model for how other genocides and historical crimes ought to be dealt with in the present. In this sense, the politics of memory after the Holocaust has helped to set a standard for how states should behave in relation to atrocities committed in the past.

Some scholars, such as Paul Connerton, would claim that "the frequent discussion of and the apparently high value ascribed to memory in recent years is vitally connected to the accumulated repercussion of the holocaustal events of the last century."[8] Omar Bartov states that the Holocaust has generated new and particularly intense forms of memory.[9] However, as Jeffrey K. Olick, Vered Vinitsky-Seroussi and Daniel Levy argue, it is rather what Holocaust memory symbolizes that has placed this specific memory in the center of current political culture. As they say, "the image of the Holocaust victim has not simply become first among victims generally, but has supposedly placed the image of the victim at the core of contemporary culture as a whole".[10] In that sense, "the post-Holocaust landscape is one littered with victims, including not only the victims of the Holocaust but those whose victimhood is often defined by the master image of the broken Auschwitz inmate, and unfortunately often compared to or measured against him or her."[11]

In other words, what originally emerged as a quest on the part of groups and people representing the victims of the Holocaust has developed into an icon of a global memory imperative, in which victims from past atrocities claim the right to be acknowledged in the same way as victims of the Holocaust.

This *cosmopolitanization* of memory, as Daniel Levy and Nathan Sznaider define it, has led to a shift "away from the territorialized nation-state and the

---

8 Paul Connerton. *How Modernity Forgets*. Cambridge: Cambridge University Press 2009, here cited from Jeffrey K. Olick, Vered Vinitsky-Seroussi and Daniel Levy, *The Collective Memory Reader*. Oxford: Oxford University Press, 2011, 29.
9 Omer Bartov, *The Murder in Our Midst: The Holocaust, Industrial Killing, and Representation*. New York: Oxford University Press 1996.
10 Olick, Vintsky-Seroussi and Levi, *The Collective Memory Reader*, 30.
11 Ibid.

ethnically bounded framework that are commonly associated with the notion of collective memory" toward a global memory culture defined by human rights values.[12] In this global memory culture, violence, injustice, and suffering have to be addressed and, to some extent, also atoned for. While states have historically dealt with war and conflict in their aftermath by forgetting them, a paradigmatic shift occurred, as Aleida Assmann argues, with the return of Holocaust memory after a period of latency.[13]

Four models of remembering

Assmann has introduced four models for how current societies deal with, or try to overcome a traumatic history of violence.[14] These four models are (1) dialogic forgetting, (2) remembering in order to prevent forgetting, (3) remembering in order to forget, and (4) dialogic remembering.

Dialogic forgetting is, as Assmann points out, another expression for 'silence', and is based on the belief that "controlling and containing the explosive force of memory" will not only bring an end to war and conflict, but is also a necessary predicate for a society to start a new era. The model can be recognized in several historic cases, such as the Peloponnesian War in ancient Greece, and, later, after the Thirty-Years-War, when the peace treaty of Münster-Osnabrück included the formula *perpetua oblivio et amnestia*. But as Assmann also points out, "even after 1945 the model of dialogic forgetting was still widely used as a political resource."[15] This was the case in Western Europe, and particular in Germany, where silence seemed to have been an accepted strategy for how to leave the war behind and move on, not only economically, but also politically. Also in Spain, the strategy of forgetting could be applied to describe the way the memory of the Spanish civil war was contained during the whole Franco-period. Only in 2007, when a law of memory was passed by the Spanish parliament, was this strategy

---

12 Daniel Levy and Natan Sznaider. *Human Rights and Memory*. University Park: Pennsylvania State University Press, 2010. Here cited from Olick, Vintsky-Seroussi and Levi, *The Collective Memory Reader*, 31.
13 Aleida Assmann, "From Collective Violence to a Common Future: Four Models for Dealing with a Traumatic Past" in Gertraud Borea Auer and Wodak, Ruth. Eds. *Justice and Memory. Confronting traumatic pasts. An international comparison*. Vienna: Passagen Verlag, 2009.
14 Assmann, "From Collective Violence to a Common Future: Four Models for Dealing with a Traumatic Past", 32.
15 Ibid, 33

of forgetting abandoned and replaced by an explicit condemnation of the Fascist dictatorship and an acknowledgement of the suffering of the victims.[16]

The second model, *remembering in order to prevent forgetting*, is based on the paradigmatic case of Holocaust memory. The shift from forgetting to remembering is most obviously observed in the way the Holocaust was first neglected, then addressed, and finally acknowledged. Or as Raul Hilberg stated in 1988: "In the beginning there was no Holocaust. When it took place in the middle of the twentieth century, its nature was not fully grasped," meaning there was no acknowledgement of the murder of European Jewry.[17] This shift from forgetting to remembering happened in several stages, as described by, among others, Tony Judt in *Postwar*.[18] Looking at the way Europe, and more specifically West Europe came to terms with the Holocaust, we may divide the decades following the end of the war into three very generally defined phases.[19] The first phase was during the immediate post-war years, beginning with the liberation of the camps and ending with the Nuremberg trial, and was characterized by black-and-white photos being distributed by the Allies in the West-European press. The gravity of this crime, having taken place in the heart of the European continent, became known through these pictures, taken by soldiers and camp survivors. The horrors were confronted, but no questions were asked. The lesson of this phase was that Nazism was defeated, and the guilty were convicted at Nuremberg.

The second phase starting in the late 1940s, but being most intense during the 1960s, saw artists using the Holocaust to express something profound about Western civilization, capitalism, consumerism, and what was seen as a general decline of Western values. For the new generation maturing during the decades following the war, the crimes of National Socialism came to represent the utmost expression of a degenerate society, where alienation and disengagement had replaced all human dignity. As such, the Holocaust, as would soon be the term de-

---

[16] For the debate about historical memory in Spain, see Carlos Jerez-Ferran and Samuel Amago. Eds. *Unearthing Franco's Legacy. Mass Graves and the Recovery of Historical Memory in Spain*. Notre Dame: University of Notre Dame Press, 2010. See also Paul Preston. *The Spanish Holocaust. Inquisition and Extermination in Twentieth Century Spain*. New York: W. W. Norton & Company, 2012.

[17] Raul Hilberg. "Development in the Historiography of the Holocaust." *Comprehending the Holocaust. Historical and Literary Research*. Eds. Asher Cohen, Yoav Gelber and Charlotte Wardi. Frankfurt am Main: Peter Lang GmbH, 1988, 21.

[18] Tony Judt, *Postwar. A history of Europe since 1945*. New York: Penguin Press, 2005.

[19] For an extended presentation of this phase-model, see Cecilie Felicia Stokholm Banke, "Remembering Europe's Heart of Darkness. Legacies of the Holocaust in Postwar European Societies." *A European Memory? Contested Histories and Politics of Remembrance*. Eds. Malgorzata Pakier and Bo Stråth. New York: Berghahn Books, 2010.

scribing the murder against first of all European Jews, became a symbol of degeneration and moral decline, as would also be the way artists started to include references to the Holocaust in their works.[20] This artistic expression of the Holocaust embodies a great deal of political criticism on behalf of leftwing youth in the US and Europe. Some say that this kind of art could be seen as an intellectual abstraction, a way to deal with the Holocaust without really confronting it. During this phase, however, the post-war generation started asking questions, using the Holocaust as a reference for how far capitalism could go. This period also saw the publication of the first scholarly works about the Holocaust, which developed a more nuanced picture of the Holocaust and how it happened.

During this second phase, the ideological battle about how to understand the crimes of National Socialism began. Similar to the anti-fascist discourse of the 1930s, the left wing conflated the Holocaust and Nazi war crimes with colonialism and imperialism. To some extent, this way of interpreting the Holocaust relativized the crimes committed during the Second World War by comparing them to crimes committed by the European colonial powers. An example of this kind of relativism can, according to French philosopher Alain Finkielkraut, be observed in the Barbie case in France in the mid-1980s. The Nazi war criminal Klaus Barbie, also known as 'the butcher of Lyon', was captured in 1983 and brought to trial in Lyon four years later in 1987. During the trial, the lawyer for the defense, Jacques Vergés, shifted the focus from the crimes of the Nazis and those their collaborators committed in France during the Vichy Regime, to the crimes committed by France as a colonial power in Algeria and other former colonies. Thus, while following the proceedings, Finkielkraut noted that the *relativism* of this trial showed how France, again, managed to avoid confronting the active role of the Vichy Regime in the persecution and deportation of French Jews.[21] However, what Finkielkraut did not include in his criticism was the increased tendency also among scholars of modern genocides to address the crimes of National Socialism within a larger frame of genocide studies, and thus studies of political mass violence in general.[22]

Finkielkraut can be seen as representing a movement which advocates justice on behalf of the victims and the principles of international humanitarian

---

20 See Banke, "Remembering Europe's Heart of Darkness." See also Max Liljefors. *Bilder av Förintelsen. Mening. Minne. Kompromettering.* Lund: Palmkrons Förlag, 2002.
21 Alain Finkielkraut. *Remembering in Vain. The Klaus Barbie Trial and Crimes Against Humanity.* New York: Columbia University Press, 1992 (1989). See also Henry Rousso. *The Vichy Syndrome: History and Memory in France Since 1944.* Cambridge: Cambridge University Press, 1991.
22 For this development among researchers, see Dan Stone's introduction to *The Historiography of Genocide*. Houndsmill: Palgrave Macmillan, 2010.

law. This justice-oriented movement started to grow stronger in the years following the fall of the Berlin wall and received a tremendous boost with the wars of succession in the former Yugoslavia during the 1990s. The movement, which has its roots in the late nineteenth century human rights movement, was institutionalized after the Second World War by the Nuremberg Trials, the International Declaration on Human Rights of 1948, and the UN genocide convention of the same year. In addition to this, the 1980s also saw the emergence of Holocaust deniers, who questioned the Holocaust and the factual basis of the new research. Initially, a movement directed primarily by neo-Nazis, Holocaust deniers have now cloaked their bigotry, raising questions about the Holocaust in a way that may look like scientific critique. British historian David Irving is an example of this phenomenon.

The third phase saw the appearance of memorials, such as that in Berlin by Peter Eisenman, but also those in France and Belgium and Norway. Here the role of each individual country is acknowledged, and several European heads of state publicly admitted their countries' responsibility, or, as Alfred Pijpers puts it, they all acknowledge their 'holocaust guilt'.[23]

Based on the above, we may conclude that Western European countries dealt with the Holocaust in different phases. The first was the immediate confrontation with Nazi war crimes through the distribution of black and white photographs from the camps. The second was characterized by economic recovery and silence. The silence, however, was only on the surface, because, even though there was no official acknowledgement of the genocide of European Jews, artists and writers had already started, in the immediate post-war years, to address the Holocaust through works communicating and interpreting their personal experience from the camps. Then followed the trials of the late 1950s and early 1960s, which initiated a new phase – the third – the age of testimony, during which some of the first scholarly works appeared documenting the crimes of the Nazi-Regime. The final and current phase can be characterized as the "age of memory", because it is in this phase that several European states have instituted an official Holocaust Remembrance Day, admitted their share of responsibility, and developed specific programs for keeping alive the memory of the Holocaust.

In explaining this phase, Assmann uses the example of Germany. When Germany, during the 1960s, moved from, in Assmann's words, "an immediate period of *dialogic forgetting* into the phase of *remember in order to never forget*," it became a member of the transnational Holocaust community of memory, in which

---

23 Alfred Pijpers, "Now We Should All Acknowledge Our Holocaust Guilt." *Europe's World*, Autumn, 2006, 124–127.

the overall goal is to *remember in order never to forget*. And soon, other European states followed, along with the UN.²⁴ In this sense, today exists a transnational community of memory that, as Levy and Sznaider describe, has acquired the character of a civil religion.

Turkey and the dialogic "forgetting"

If we now turn to the Armenian genocide and consider how Holocaust memory has developed and affected the Armenian case, we can say that this *cosmopolitanization* of memory partly explains the ongoing controversies about applying the term, genocide, to the Armenian massacre. I say partly, because debates about terms and words can also be a strategy for exactly this, *dialogic forgetting*. Discussing which term may be the right one – massacre, tragedy, atrocities, genocide – can be a pragmatic solution for containing the explosive forces of memory. In the words of Machiavelli, as referred to by Assmann, "it is easy to conquer a people, but next to impossible to conquer their memories. Unless they are scattered and dispersed, the citizens of a conquered city will never forget their former freedom and their old memories. They will introduce them on every occasion that presents itself."²⁵ In a Machiavellian sense, as long as this *dialogic forgetting* is occurring in present Turkey, the Armenian community will never forget their old memories. They will continue to use every occasion to introduce the collective memory of the brutal deportations that destroyed the Ottoman Armenian community during the First World War. Or as Nefissa Naguib writes about the Armenian memories of relief in Jerusalem, core components of the collective memory of the Armenians are genocide, deportation and rescue and relief. These are the memories that bind the Armenians together.²⁶

Before moving on, I need to stress that the term memory – its uses and meaning – is not uncontested among scholars. Memory is about how history is perceived in the present. Memory, therefore, lives through generations, either

---

24 Assmann, "From Collective Violence to a Common Future: Four Models for Dealing with a Traumatic Past", 35.
25 Assmann, "From Collective Violence to a Common Future: Four Models for Dealing with a Traumatic Past", 45. Assmann refers to Niccoló Machiavelli. *Der Fürst*, Stuttgart: Kröner, 1955, 19.
26 Nefissa Naguib, "A Nation of Widows: Armenian Memories of Relief in Jerusalem." *Interpreting Welfare and Relief in the Middle East*. Eds. Nefissa Naguib and Inger Marie Okkenhaug. Leiden: Brill, 2007, 35–56.

in the mind of the individual or as the collective memory of a specific group.[27] While the concept of "collective memory" has been criticized for being a metaphor associated with the organic notion of a community, memory as an analytical concept can, in fact, refer both to individual memories or a *community of memory*.[28] Thus, the field has moved away from the essentialized vision of collective memory as a substitute for national communities, towards a set of analytical tools – remembrance, commemoration, discourse about the past, politics of memory, and practices of remembrance – that can be applied to the study of how societies come to terms with their past.[29]

In genocide studies, coming to terms with past atrocities has often meant developing a legal process following the atrocities, combined on occasion with local, cultural-specific reconciliation mechanisms.[30] In Rwanda, for example, a local reconciliation process was introduced with the *Gacacas* and, as in Germany after its experience with the Holocaust, it is against the law to question the 1994-genocide. In several cases, the process of coming to terms often also involves the development and institutionalization of an official narrative in museums, schools, and on days of national remembrance. As such, both institutionalized memory and individual memories of victims play important roles in how a society overcomes a traumatic and violent past.[31]

However, this process of overcoming past atrocities can often lead to new controversies about which atrocities should be recognized, especially in countries where a significant segment of the population identified with, or participated in, the crimes of previous regimes. In some cases, past atrocities are not addressed because they carry with them the potential seeds of renewed internal

---

27 Maurice Halbwalchs. *On Collective Memory*. University of Chicago Press, 1992; Paul Connerton. *How Societies Remember*. Cambridge: Cambridge University Press, 1989.
28 Aleida Assmann. "Four Formats of Memory – From Individual to collective Forms of Constructing the Past." *Cultural Memory and Historical Consciousness in the German-Speaking World since 1500*. Eds. Christian Emden and David Midgley. Bern: Peter Lang, 2004; Reinhart Koselleck. "Gebrochene Erinnerung. Deutsche und polische Vergangenheiten." *Jahrbuch der Deutschen Akademie für Sprache und Dichtung*, 20. Göttingen, 2000.
29 Bo Stråth. "Preface." *Collective Traumas. Memories of War and Conflict in 20th Century Europe*. Eds. Conny Mithander, John Sundholm and Maria Holmgren Troy. Brussels: Peter Lang, 2007, 11–12.
30 Lawrence Douglas. *The Memory of Judgment: Making Law and History in the Trials of the Holocaust*. New Haven: Yale University Press, 2005; Helen Fein. *Accounting for Genocide: Victims and Survivors of the Holocaust*. New York: The Free Press, 1979.
31 Nancy Adler, Selma Leydesdorff, Mary Cahmberlain and Leyla Neyzi. Eds. *Memories of Mass Repression. Narrating Life Stories in the Aftermath of Atrocity*. New Brunswick: Transaction Publishers, 2009.

conflict, and therefore remain 'blind spots' in the historical landscape, as in the case with Jan T. Gross' controversial book, *Neighbors. The Destrcution of the Jewish Community in Jedwabne.*[32] In this book, Gross describes how 1,600 Jews were slaughtered during the Second World War, not by the Nazis but by their Polish neighbors. The publication of the book was followed by a heated debate in Poland about relations to the country's Jewish population, and provoked at the same time a painful process of reinterpreting Polish history. In other cases, memories of one past atrocity overshadow others and create a competition for what should be remembered, as in Hungary where the crimes of communism are being commemorated and included as an important element in the post-communist Hungarian national identity, while the crimes of National Socialism receive increasingly less attention.[33]

Applying knowledge from the developments described above to the Armenian case, how can memory theory help us to understand the current controversies that exist around the Armenian genocide? The Armenian genocide is commemorated each year on 24 April, in Armenia and in several other countries around the world. The global Armenian diaspora community commemorates the tragedy that befell their families and relatives. In this sense, there exists a culture of commemoration for the Armenian genocide that keeps the memory of the massacre alive. The Armenian genocide is, in Armenia and among Armenians around the world, *remembered in order not to forget*. This was also President Obama's message in his address on the occasion of the Armenian Remembrance Day in 2011, when he spoke of the victims and how we must never forget the Armenian tragedy – the "Meds Yeghern."[34]

However, while the Holocaust has established a model for *how to remember in order not to forget*, the model has also led to a new imperative. A third model of remembering has been introduced – *remembering in order to forget*. This model was introduced as a therapeutic tool to cleanse, to purge, to heal, and to reconcile. Within international relations, commemoration can be used by countries to demonstrate that they have adopted other strategies, and that ag-

---

[32] Jan Tomasz Gross. *Neighbors: The Destruction of the Jewish Community in Jedwabne, Poland.* Princeton, NJ: Princeton University Press, 2001.
[33] See among others Julia Creet. "The House of Terror and the Holocaust Memorial Centre: Resentment and Melancholia in Post-89 Hungary." *European Cultural Memory Post-89*. Eds. Conny Mithander, John Sundholm and Adrian Velicu. Rodopi: Amsterdam/New York, NY, 2013, 326.
[34] Statement by the President on Armenian Remembrance Day, 23 April 2011, http://www.whitehouse.gov/the-press-office/2011/04/23/statement-president-armenian-remembrance-day (26 November 2012)

gression is no longer an option. In her work about apologies in international politics, Jennifer Lind describes how countries that remember and atone for past violence are signaling that they are unlikely to adopt aggressive strategies.[35] In this sense, "the way a country remembers or forgets past violence leads others to have positive or negative feelings about that country. Apologies, reparations, and so on are signs of respect: They reflect a belief that a country that is a recipient of an apology is too important to treat poorly. By contrast, a country's denials, glorification, or whitewashing of past atrocities signal contempt for a people, for their country's status, and for the future of the bilateral relationship."[36]

When turning the focus to the case of Armenia and Turkey, we may say that Turkey has made some steps towards signaling a different attitude in its relation to Armenia. But public memory after the Armenian genocide remains in the phase of *dialogic forgetting*. Some recent attempts in Turkey may signal a move towards *remembering in order to prevent forgetting*. However, it is more likely that at present, the developments in Turkey and the historical accord that was established between Armenia and Turkey in 2010 are a sign of *remembering in order to forget*. The accord is in this case used as a way to reconcile a delicate relationship between two states – a relationship that also affects how other states relate to both Armenia and Turkey. As long as this controversy between Turkey and Armenia exists, other states will have to carefully consider how to officially address the massacres against the Armenians during the First World War. In this sense, what seems to be an intimate conflict between two states about how to interpret their common past, appears to have international dimensions and affects not only the geopolitics in the Caucasus region, but also Turkey's relation to both the EU and the US.

One may ask whether, in order to move this stymied process forward, it may be advisable to separate the Armenian genocide as a historical crime from the global memory paradigm, and, with this, to also separate the quest for acknowledgement from the global memory movement which is associated with the Holocaust. As Seyhan Bayraktar has argued in her study of memory, after the Armenian genocide there is still a long way to go for a paradigmatic shift in Turkey.[37] The question is whether a necessary predicate for this shift is that the Armenian genocide no longer be understood within the framework of comparative genocides (including the Holocaust) but is moved to a broader contextual frame

---

[35] Jennifer Lind. *Sorry States. Apologies in International Politics*. Ithaca and London: Cornell University Press, 2008.
[36] Ibid, 13.
[37] Seyhan Bayraktar. *Politik und Erinnerung: der Diskurs über den Armeniermord in der Türkei zwischen Nationalismus und Europäisierung*. Bielefeld: Transcript Verlag, 2010.

that allows for a more profound understanding of the political mass violence that occurred in the Ottoman Empire during the First World War. The point I want to make here is that it may be that the term genocide and the continuous quest for having the massacres against the Armenians in 1915 recognized as such prevents Turkey and Armenia from making progress in their common understanding of this shared past.

References

Adler, Nanci, Selma Leydesdorff, Mary Cahmberlain and Leyla Neyzi. Eds. *Memories of Mass Repression. Narrating Life Stories in the Aftermath of Atrocity.* New Brunswick: Transaction Publishers, 2009.

Assmann, Aleida. "From Collective Violence to a Common Future: Four Models for Dealing with a Traumatic Past." *Justice and Memory. Confronting traumatic pasts. An international comparison.* Eds. Gertraud Auer Borea and Ruth Wodak. Vienna: Passagen Verlag, 2009. 31–48.

Assmann, Aleida. "Transformations between History and Memory." *Collective Memory and Collective Identity.* Ed. Arien Mack. *Social Research* 75.1 (2008): 49–72.

Assmann, Aleida. "Four Formats of Memory – From Individual to collective Forms of Constructing the Past." *Cultural Memory and Historical Consciouness in the German-Speaking World since 1500.* Eds. Christian Emden and David Midgley. Bern: Peter Lang. 2004, 19–38.

Banke, Cecilie Felicia Stokholm. "Remembering Europe's Heart of Darkness. Legacies of the Holocaust in Postwar European Societies." *A European Memory? Contested Histories and Politics of Remembrance.* Eds. Malgorzata Pakier and Bo Stråth. New York: Berghahn Books 2010. 163–174.

Bayraktar, Seyhan. *Politik und Erinnerung: der Diskurs über den Armeniermord in der Türkei zwischen Nationalsozialismus und Europäisierung.* Bielefeld: Transcript Verlag, 2010.

Bryld, Claus and Anette Warring. *Besættelsestiden som kollektiv erindring. Historie- og traditionsforvaltning af brig og besættelse 1945–1997.* Roskilde: Roskilde Universitetsforlag, 1998.

Connerton, Paul. *How Modernity Forgets.* Cambridge: Cambridge University Press, 2010.

Connerton, Paul. *How Societies Remember.* Cambridge: Cambridge University Press, 1989.

Dietsch, Johan. *Making sense of suffering. Holocaust and Holodomor in Ukrainian Culture.* Lund: Lund University Press, 2006.

Douglas, Lawrence. *The Memory of Judgment: Making Law and History in the Trials of the Holocaust.* New Haven: Yale University Press, 2005.

Fein, Helen. *Accounting for Genocide: Victims and Survivors of the Holocaust.* New York: The Free Press, 1979.

Finkelkraut, Alain. *Remembering in Vain. The Klaus Barbie Trial and Crimes Against Humanity.* New York: Columbia University Press, 1992 (1989).

Fogu, Claudio, Richard Ned Lebow and Wulf Kansteiner. Eds. *The Politics of Memory in Postwar Europe.* Durham, NC: Duke University Press, 2006.

Gerner, Kristian and Klas-Göran Karlson. *Folkmordens Historia.* Stockholm: Atlantis, 2005.

Gross, Jan Tomasz. *Neighbors: The Destruction of the Jewish Community in Jedwabne, Poland*. Princeton, NJ: Princeton University Press, 2001.
Halbwachs, Maurice. *On Collective Memory*. Chicago: University of Chicago Press, 1992.
Herf, Geoffrey. *Divided Memory. The Nazi past in the Two Germanys*. New Haven: Harvard University Press, 1997.
Hilberg, Raul. "Development in the Historiography of the Holocaust". *Comprehending the Holocaust. Historical and Literary Research*. Eds. Asher Cohen, Joav Gelber and Charlotte Wardi, Peter Lang: Frankfurt am Main, 1988.
Judt, Tony. *Post-War. A History of Europe since 1945*. London: Penguin Press, 2005.
Karlsson, Klas-Göran and Ulf Zander. Eds. *Echoes of the Holocaust. Historical Cultures in Contemporary Europe*. Lund: Nordic Academic Press, 2003.
Karlsson, Klas-Göran and Ulf Zander. Eds. *Holocaust Heritage. Inquiries into European Historical Cultures*, Malmö: Sekel Bokförlag, 2004.
Karlsson, Klas-Göran and Ulf Zander. Eds. *The Holocaust – Post-war Battlefields. Genocide as Historical Culture*. Malmö: Sekel Bokförlag, 2006.
Koselleck, Reinhart. *The Practice of Conceptual History: Timing History, Spacing Concepts (Cultural Memory in the Present)*. Palo Alto: Stanford University Press, 2002.
Koselleck, Reinhart. "Gebrochene Erinnerung. Deutsche und polische Vergangenheiten." *Jahrbuch der Deutschen Akademie für Sprache und Dichtung, 20*. Göttingen, 2000.
Kroh, Jens. *Transnationale Erinnerungen. Der Holocaust im Fokus geschichtspolitischer Initiativen*. Frankfurt: Campus, 2008.
Kushner, Tony. *The Holocaust and the Liberal Imagination. A Social and Cultural History*. Cambridge, Mass.: Blackwell Publishers, 1996.
Lagrou, Peter. *The Legacy of Nazi Occupation. Patriotic Memory and National Recovery in Western Europe 1945–1965*. Cambridge: Cambridge University Press, 2000.
Levy, Daniel and Natan Sznaider. *The Holocaust and Memory in the Global Age*. Philadelphia: Temple University Press, 2006.
Levy, Daniel and Natan Sznaider. "Sovereignty transformed: a sociology of human rights." *British Journal of Sociology* 57.4 (2006): 657–76.
Lind, Jennifer. *Sorry States. Apologies in International Politics*. Ithaca and London: Cornell University Press, 2008.
Machiavelli, Niccolò. *Der Fürst*, Stuttgart: Kröner, 1955.
Novick, Peter. *The Holocaust and Collective Memory*. London: Bloomsbury Publishing Plc, 2001.
Pearce, Andy. *The Development of Holocaust Consciousness in Contemporary Britain, 1979–2000*. PhD-dissertation. London: Royal Holloway College, 2010.
Pijpers, Alfred. "Now We Should All Acknowledge Our Holocaust Guilt." *Europe's World*, Autumn:, 2006, 124–127.
Rousso, Henry. *The Vichy Syndrome: History and Memory in France Since 1944*. Cambridge: Cambridge University Press, 1991.
Sniegon, Tomas. *Den Försvunna Historien. Förintelsen i tjeckisk och slovakisk historiekultur*. Lund: Lunds Universitet, Historiska Institutionen, 2008.
Suny, Ronald Grigor, Fatma Müge Göçek and Norman M. Naimark, *A Question of Genocide. Armenians and Turks at the End of the Ottoman Empire*. Oxford: Oxford University Press, 2011.

Suny, Ronald Grigor. "Writing Genocide. The Fate of the Ottoman Armenians." *A Question of Genocide. Armenians and Turks at the End of the Ottoman Empire*. Eds. Grigor Ronald Suny, Fatma Müge Göcek and Norman M. Naimark, Oxford: Oxford University Press, 2011. 15–41.

Stråth, Bo. "Preface". *Collective Traumas. Memories of War and Conflict in 20th Century Europe*. Eds. Conny Mithander, John Sundholm and Maria Holmgren Troy. Brussels: Peter Lang, 2007, 11–12.

Warring, Anette, "Demokratische Erinnerungspolitik zwischen stabilen Werten und Reflexivität." *Erinnerungskulturen im Dialog. Europäische Perspektiven auf die NS-Vergangeheit*. Eds. Claudia Lenz, Jens Schmidt and Oliver von Wrochem. Hamburg/Münster: UNRAST, 2002.

Welzer, Harald. *Der Krieg der Erinnerung. Holocaust, Kollaboration und Widerstand im europäischen Gedächtnis*. Frankfurt/M.: S. Fischer, 2007.

Wolf, Joan B. *Harnessing the Holocaust. The Politics of Memory in France*. Palo Alto, CA: Stanford University Press, 2004.

Tuomas Forsberg
Overcoming Memory Conflicts: Russia, Finland and the Second World War

The relevance of collective memory for contemporary world politics is usually understood as lying in the way the past affects our present identities and views of the other. Conflicts over memory may cause violent responses, or at least create tensions and significantly hamper mutual cooperation in cases where common interests otherwise exist. If this is so, there is a strong practical interest in overcoming such problems and developing knowledge about how memory conflicts can be reconciled.

Thus far, we have only tentative knowledge of how to overcome the limits and deal effectively with the conditions in which memory conflicts arise in world politics. Studies on transitional justice have mainly focused on the internal aspect of memory conflicts despite the fact that most civil wars have an international or transnational dimension.[1] With regard to the significance of forgiveness in international relations, there are both advocates and skeptics, but a huge gap remains between the normative and empirical research. Many empirical studies on apologies and memory conflicts are descriptive and often merely repeat the initial assumption, namely that forgiveness could play an important role in international conflict resolution. Skeptics, in turn, are not interested in studying in detail their assumptions about the inefficacy of forgiveness in international relations. Only recently, have we seen steps towards more concrete explanatory research that links theoretical and empirical elements to the aim of increasing our understanding of when and how apologies and forgiveness function positively. Probably the most significant recent study is by Jennifer Lind, who argues that apologies are not necessary for political reconciliation between states,

---

[1] David Mendeloff. "Truth-Seeking, Truth-Telling and Postconflict Peacebuilding: Curb the Enthusiasm?" *International Studies Review* 6 (2004): 355–380; Tristan Anne Borer. "Truth Telling as a Peace-Building Activity: A Theoretical Overview." *Telling the Truths: Truth Telling and Peace Building in Post-Conflict Societies*. Ed. Tristan Anne Borer. Notre Dame: University of Notre Dame Press, 2006, 1–57; Eric Brahm. "Uncovering the Truth: Examining Truth Commissions Success and Impact." *International Studies Perspectives* 8 (2007): 16–35; Michal Ben-Josef Hirsch, Megan MacKenzie and Mohamed Sesay. "Measuring the Impacts of Truth and Reconciliation Commissions: Placing the Global 'Success' of TRC's in Local Perspective." *Cooperation and Conflict* 46 (2012): 386–403.

and moreover, that attempts to extract apologies often lead to counterproductive results in the form of a conservative backlash effect.[2]

In this article, I will argue that practices related to forgiveness help reduce conflicts and foster cooperation between states and nations, even when apologies and forgiveness are only partial. I will first outline a theory of how memory conflicts and historical problems affect relations between states and then discuss the concept of forgiveness and its potential usefulness in influencing these mechanisms. I will distinguish between maximal and minimal models of forgiveness and argue that in practice, a mixed model, imperfect apology may lead to forgiveness and reconciliation. To provide an empirical basis, the article looks at the role of the memory of World War II in relations between Russia and Finland. In addition to functioning as an illustrative example of the mechanisms of overcoming international memory conflicts, the Finnish case is interesting from the perspective of mapping the collective memories of World War II because it is located between the eastern and western memory cultures in Europe.[3]

Strategies for Reconciling Memory Conflicts

There are a number of conceptual issues that need clarification when discussing the reconciliation of problems arising from the past. Although discussion of memory conflicts and the construction of views about historical problems are often strongly subjective, the factual nature of past wrongdoings cannot be entirely disregarded. Transgressions that have a certain objective magnitude in terms of harm inflicted and legal and moral norms broken are more likely to give rise to memory conflicts significant enough to affect overall political as well as economic and cultural relations. Wars of aggression, massacres and other war crimes, grave human rights violations, deportation, and stolen territory or property are often the sources of memory conflicts.[4] Yet, the wrongdoings themselves are not necessarily at the heart of memory conflicts but rather a factual disagreement about what actually happened or the interpretation of who

---

[2] Jennifer Lind. *Sorry States: Apologies in International Politics.* Ithaca: Cornell, 2008.
[3] See Patrick Finney. *Remembering the Road to World War Two: International History, National Identity, Collective Memory.* New York: Routledge, 2010 and Aleida Assmann. "Europe's Divided Memory." *Memory and Theory in Eastern Europe.* Eds. Uilleam Blacker, Alexander Etkind, and Julie Fedor. Basingstoke: Palgrave, 2013, 25–41.
[4] For discussion of different kinds of evil, see Claudia Card. *The Atrocity Paradigm: A Theory of Evil.* Oxford: Oxford University, 2002.

was responsible for what. Although what happened yesterday is already history, it is politically meaningful to see memory conflicts as related to events of a previous era defined by a change of leadership, generation or the broader international context. Sometimes memory conflicts can stem from a relatively distant past, but typically the more recent the past wrongdoing is, the more strongly the actors can identify themselves with the victims.[5]

We may also ask which actors are those who should overcome a memory conflict. While the concept of collective memory can be operationalised in various ways, the relevant aspect here is how the decision-makers and other key representatives of the state deal with the past and to what extent they are affected by the national memory culture and public concerns related to the past in conducting foreign policy.[6] Individual and social memories naturally intersect in the minds of decision-makers. They both actively shape as well as respond to the public representations of the past and the memory culture of the wider society.

Furthermore, the way in which memory conflicts affect current relations between the parties involved should also be unpacked. One way is to regard the problems of the past as psychological traumas that are emotional "wounds" (indeed, traumas are literally "wounds") that prevent normal behavior in the traumatised subject. Though a strict medical analysis is not the point here, it might be recalled that post-traumatic stress disorder is classified as an emotional illness that results in various reactions such as feelings of rejection, guilt and anger. A common feature of traumas is the avoidance effect. Normal everyday interaction with someone who brings certain memories to life can be so stressful for the traumatised subject that it is avoided.[7]

Secondly, historical problems can burden relations between states because one of the states demands some kind of justice for the perceived historical wrongs. Because of the existence of such historical problems, the state leaders or members of a nation whose rights have been violated can think that the state or nation that has committed wrongdoing has merited punishment or, at

---

[5] On victimhood, see Tami Amanda Jakoby. "A Theory of Victimhood: Politics, Conflict and the Construction of Victim-based Identity." *Millennium: Journal of International Studies* 43.2 (2015): 511–530.

[6] On collective memory and politics, see James Wertsch. *Voices of Collective Remembering.* Cambridge: Cambridge University Press, 2002; Richard Ned Lebow. "The Future of Memory." *Annals of the American Academy of Political and Social Science* 617.1 (2008): 25–41 and Eric Langenbacher. "Collective Memory as a Factor in Political Culture and International Relations." *Power and the Past: Collective Memory and International Relations.* Eds. Eric Langenbacher, and Yossi Shain. Washington D.C.: Georgetown University Press 2010, 13–50.

[7] See e.g. Judith Lewis Herman. *Trauma and Recovery: The Aftermath of Violence from Domestic Abuse to Political Terror.* New York: Basic Books, 1997.

least, is not worthy of any closer form of cooperation. There is a strong retributive instinct after wrongdoings.[8] Yet, the moral issue is not linked merely to punishment. Dealing with the past is important because, as James Booth notes, "the remembrance of past wrongs is one of the faces of justice itself".[9]

Thirdly, problems of history can restrict cooperation and increase conflicts because the way the state interprets history and, in particular, deals with its past wrongdoings is often seen as a sign of its trustworthiness and intentions.[10] The way history is treated is hence a clue for one state or group about whether or not the other has a continuing propensity to deceive or use violence in mutual relations as, for example, the degree of respect for human rights or other principles of democracy. Finally, historical problems can affect present relations adversely when they provide negative material for identity building and thus important elements in making enemy images. "National myth-making" based on history can thus have a significant impact on international relations.[11]

Furthermore, there is no consensus or clear-cut way to measure the quality of reconciliation. It is often difficult to distinguish between causal and constitutive aspects of it.[12] Yet, a rough scale can be constructed, where a minimum definition of reconciliation requires that not only have open hostilities between the parties ceased but also that there is a radically diminished likelihood for violent conflict marked by the absence of enemy rhetoric and preparation for war.[13] Even such a condition of a stable peace is often not enough, however, because reconciliation can also be needed in cases where no threat of violent conflict exists but historical problems still burden the relationship. Reconciliation at this stage would thus also mean that historical problems do not play any significant role in normal everyday interaction between the parties. The scale here is not strictly

---

8 Jeffrie Murphy. *Getting Even: Forgiveness and its Limits*. Oxford: Oxford, 2003.
9 William James Booth. "The Unforgotten: Memories of Justice." *American Political Science Review* 95.4 (2001): 777–791, here 777.
10 Jennifer Lind. *Sorry States. Apologies in International Politics*. Ithaca: Cornell, 2008.
11 Yinan He. *The Search for Reconciliation: Sino-Japanese and German-Polish Relations since World War II*. Cambridge: Cambridge University Press, 2009.
12 Siri Gloppen. "Roads to Reconciliation: A Conceptual Framework." *Roads to Reconciliation*. Eds. Elin Skaar, Siri Gloppen, and Astri Suhrke. Lanham, MA: Lexington, 2005, 17–50; Trudy Govier. *Taking Wrongs Seriously: Acknowledgment, Reconciliation, and the Politics of Sustainable Peace*. Amherst, NY: Humanity Books, 2006 and Valerie Rosoux. "Reconciliation as a Peace-Building Process: Scope and Limits." *The Sage Handbook of Conflict Resolution*. Eds. Jacob Bercovitch, Victor Kremenyuk, and Ira William Zartman. London: Sage, 2009, 543–560.
13 For examples and discussion, see Lind, *Sorry States: Apologies in International Politics*; He, *The Search for Reconciliation* and Tang, "Reconciliation and the Remaking of Anarchy." *World Politics* 63.4 (2011): 711–749.

linear, since states that have overcome the burden of the past in their relations may still prepare for a possible violent conflict with each other, but do so for reasons other than historical.

At the other end of the continuum, full reconciliation can be defined as some sort of greater harmony between the parties. Although national unity often is a stated goal after civil conflict, a common identity can be seen as a utopian and superfluous goal in relations between states and nations. Yet, integration between France and Germany, for example, may be regarded as a case where historical problems were turned into shared experiences that strengthen the relationship and created a shared identity. Thus while the concept of reconciliation should be stretched slightly further than to the simple disappearance of a threat of renewed violence and war, the expectation of "harmony" is perhaps too demanding in most contexts.

What strategies are available for states to use to overcome memory conflicts and achieve reconciliation of one or another degree? Although we cannot change the past, we can change the ways in which we remember it publicly and give significance to past events.[14] Doing nothing in terms of official history politics is, of course, also a strategic choice, and it might sometimes be a working solution. The parties can encapsulate or compartmentalise historical memories so that they do not play a role in their routine interactions. In transitional justice literature, the alternatives are usually vengeance and forgiveness, or judicial trials versus amnesty to the perpetrators.[15] In this sense, it is important to distinguish between forgiving and forgetting, since the former depends on the prior acknowledgement of the truth about the wrongdoings, whereas the latter is simply a strategy to let the past rest.

If the key problem is the subjective trauma caused by the past, then the traumatised nation simply needs time to heal. If some sort of analogy of individual therapy applies to collectives, they also need to mourn, reflect on their emotions and adjust to the new circumstances. If allowing time for healing is the best way to overcome historical problems between two states, the preferred strategy is not to intervene in the domestic memory processes. Vamik Volkan, who speaks of the "chosen traumas" of nations, argues that "forgiveness is possible only when the group that suffered has done a significant amount of mourning". In his view,

---

14 See e.g. Raphael Samuel. *Theatres of Memory.* London: Verso, 1994.
15 Martha Minow. *Between Vengeance and Forgiveness: Facing History after Genocide and Mass Violence.* Boston, MA: Beacon Press, 1998. Tuomas Forsberg. "The Philosophy and Practice of Dealing with the Past: Some Conceptual and Normative Issues." *Burying the Past. Making Peace and Doing Justice after Civil Conflict.* Ed. Nigel Biggar. Washington D.C.: Georgetown University Press, 2001, 57–72.

"the focus should be on helping with the work of mourning and not on the single (seemingly magical) act of asking forgiveness."[16] From this perspective, it can also be important that the traumatised subject can tell his or her story about the wrongdoings and be heard by the wider public.

If the key problem with the historical injustice is a moral one, then some sort of moral restoration of order is needed.[17] Then the typical strategies available are retribution or abstaining from retribution through forgiveness. There is a strong tradition of regarding reconciliation as something that can be achieved only if the moral order has been restored through retribution.[18] Yet, this tradition has been challenged by those who advocate restorative justice instead of retributive justice and see forgiveness as a means to restore the moral order without punishment.[19] Important in both cases, however, is that the truth about the past wrongdoings is spelled out and remembered, though in the case of punishment it is secondary whether the perpetrator actually accepts the truth. For the process of forgiveness as justice, a shared perception about the truth and acknowledgement of the past wrongdoings by the perpetrator are essential.

If the key problem related to past wrongdoings is related to building trust, the parties involved need to find ways to signal unambiguously the values and intentions on which such trust can be built. Lind argues that contrition and remembrance are costly signals because they make domestic mobilisation for possible future wars and political conflicts more difficult. It is not only important what the state leaders say to their counterparts and to the victims but also how they convey the message to their domestic audience.[20] Abstaining from the glorification of past violence and accepting criticism of past deeds can demonstrate peaceful intentions and increase domestic pluralism. Taking into account the views of the other country can further clear up doubts about intentions when historical interpretations constitute difficult issues in bilateral relations.

If a historical wrongdoing constitutes a national myth that supports the identities of large groups and is conducive to producing a negative image of the other, the burden of rectifying the situation often shifts to the party who

---

[16] Vamik Volkan. *Bloodlines: From Ethnic Pride to Ethnic Terrorism.* Boulder, CO: Westview, 1997, 226.

[17] Margaret Urban Walker. *Moral Repair: Reconstructing Moral Relations after Wrongdoing.* New York: Cambridge University Press, 2006.

[18] Jeffrie Murphy. *Getting Even: Forgiveness and Its Limits.* Oxford: Oxford University Press, 2003.

[19] See e.g. Dennis Sullivan, and Larry Tifft. *Handbook of Restorative Justice: A Global Perspective.* Abingdon: Routledge, 2006.

[20] Lind. *Sorry States: Apologies in International Politics,* 11.

wants to keep alive these memories of past wrongdoings, since the wrongdoer can choose to alleviate or strengthen such images. Nevertheless, apologies by the wrongdoer and other steps towards reconciliation in historical disputes can be regarded as signs of respect that can improve the overall image of the country.[21] The problem, however, is that historical memories are seldom the only source of conflicting identities. If the negative views of the other prevail, it might be hard to overcome historical problems by focusing solely on the strategies of dealing with the past. What is needed is a more profound transformation of identities. On the other hand, full convergence of the historical narratives and national identities based on them do not need to exist for stable peace and normalised relations between former enemies to emerge.

In sum, diverse mechanisms exist for solving memory conflicts depending on the way they influence the level of cooperation or the likelihood of conflict. Emotions and rationality play different roles in the solution of these problems. Healing from trauma through mourning and getting even in moral terms are strongly emotional processes.[22] Judging the other state's interpretations of historical wrongdoings and their efforts to show contrition is a more cognitive process through which intentions and capabilities to mobilise resources are revealed. Identity formation, in turn, affects the relationship in a more habitual way in terms of background thinking. The practice of forgiveness and its effectiveness as a tool of conflict resolution depend on which of these mechanisms is seen as a central aspect in the process of reconciliation. Apologies and forgiveness primarily address the problem of moral restoration but they can also transform cognitive assessments and identities.

---

21 He. *The Search for Reconciliation.*
22 Michael Ure. "Post-Traumatic Societies: On Reconciliation, Justice and the Emotions." *European Journal of Social Theory* 11.3 (2008): 283–297; Jeffrey Blustein. "Forgiveness, Commemoration and Restorative Justice: The Role of Moral Emotions." *Metaphilosophy* 41.4 (2010): 582–617; Emma Hutchison. "Trauma and the Politics of Emotions: Constituting Identity, Security and Community after the Bali Bombing." *International Relations* 24.1 (2010): 65–86 and Emma Hutchison, and Roland Bleiker. "Emotional Reconciliation: Reconstituting Identity and Community after Trauma." *European Journal of Social Theory* 11.3 (2010): 385–403.

Theories of Forgiveness

The concept of forgiveness is complex and multifaceted.[23] The purpose here is not to dwell in detail on the discussion of this concept, but rather to distinguish between maximalist and minimalist understandings of forgiveness as two almost opposing ways to conceive of its role in conflict resolution. From the maximalist point of view, apologies may be subject to a number of necessary conditions. These conditions are, for example, that the perpetrators acknowledge the injustice of the offense as a fact, deplore and regrets it, and confess their own guilt and involvement in the injustice and commits themselves at least implicitly to change their behaviour and not to repeat the same offence. An apology should also include a sincere desire to do something to compensate for violations, and to help the victims. These terms of an apology can be further elaborated and additional conditions listed. For example, Nick Smith considered "a categorical apology" a benchmark of an apology's highest manifestation. It would include, most importantly, corroborated factual record, acceptance of blame, possession of appropriate standing, identification of each harm, shared commitment to moral principles underlying each harm, recognition of the victim as a moral interlocutor, and regret.[24]

If the relevant conditions of the apology are not met, it is incomplete or partial. Merely feeling sorry and expressing remorse or regret is not an apology. An explanation for why something is not done as it should have been done is not an "apology" but an "excuse". In politics, ambiguous half-apologies are very typical. Politicians may apologise to the voters, for example, rather than to the victims. There is no clear boundary for when an incomplete apology will no longer be an apology. Interpretation is often a question of cultural and other contextual factors. Therefore, it is more meaningful to understand the effects of various complete and incomplete requests for forgiveness than to try to agree on an exact definition of apology. As Lind has noted, acceptance of an apology cannot be regarded as an indicator for how perfect an apology has been, because then we could not examine the impact of the completeness of various apologies on the settlement of disputes.[25] Sometimes incomplete apologies can be accepted while at other times they can seem like an insult and arouse resentment.

---

23 Joanna North. "Wrongdoing and Forgiveness." *Philosophy*, 62.242 (1987): 499–508; Peter Digeser. *Political Forgiveness*. Ithaca: Cornell University Press, 2001 and Nick Smith. *I Was Wrong: The Meanings of Apologies*. Cambridge: Cambridge University Press, 2008.
24 Smith. *I Was Wrong*, 140–142. See also Ernesto Verdeja. "Official Apologies in the Aftermath of Political Violence." *Metaphilosophy* 41.4 (2010): 563–581.
25 Lind, *Sorry States: Apologies in International Politics*.

For some theorists of forgiveness, the completeness of an apology is not essential because forgiveness is primarily based on empathy.[26] The minimalist view puts emphasis on the victims and their ability to understand the wrongdoer rather than on the wrongdoer and the nature of apology. Through understanding the other party and its actions from its perspective, we no longer see it as evil. Forgiveness also requires that we examine our own acts from the point of view of the other. When it is understood that we are also guilty of wrongdoing, it is easier to forgive the other. Donald Shriver has called such a policy of forgiveness the "ethics of enemies".[27]

The paradigmatic model of forgiveness is based on the normative assumption that the wrongdoer has the duty to apologise. Although granting forgiveness can be regarded more as a virtue than a duty, the model expects that the one who has suffered and whose rights have been violated, in turn, should forgive, if the conditions of apology are fulfilled. A full apology best signals the party's real desire to move closer to and overcome the old conflicts. In other words, the more complete the apology is, the better the chance for the policy of forgiveness to succeed, and past problems between states or nations to be overcome. By contrast, "the combination of apology with justification, excuse, or even explanation weakens, or perhaps, destroys the apology".[28]

The paradigmatic model of forgiveness also assumes that acknowledging the facts of the historical wrongdoing constitute the starting phase in the process of reconciliation. Elizar Barkan notes that demands for apologies and refusals of them are first steps, "a diplomatic dance that may last for a while" that paves the way for overcoming historical injustice, but an apology is not the satisfactory end result.[29] Similarly, William Long and Peter Brecke argue that the first step in the process of reconciliation is the acknowledgement of the facts.[30] Joanna

---

[26] Michael McCullogh, Everett Worthington, and Kenneth Rachal. "Interpersonal Forgiving in Close Relationships." *Journal of Personality and Social Psychology* 73.2 (1997): 321–336. Everett Worthington. "The Pyramid Model of Forgiveness: Some Interdisciplinary Speculations about Unforgiveness and Promoting Forgiveness." *Dimensions of Forgiveness: Psychological Research and Theological Forgiveness.* Ed. Everett Worthington. Philadelphia. PA: Templeton Foundation Press, 1998, 107–138.

[27] Donald W. Shriver, Jr. *An Ethic for Enemies: Forgiveness in Politics.* New York: Oxford University Press, 1995.

[28] Jane Yamazaki. *Japanese Apologies for World War II: A Rhetorical Study.* Abingdon: Routledge, 2006, 135.

[29] Elazar Barkan. *The Guilt of Nations: Restitution and Negotiating Historical Injustices.* Baltimore: The Johns Hopkins University Press, 2001, xxix.

[30] William Long and Peter Brecke. *War and Reconciliation: Reason and Emotion in Conflict Resolution.* Cambridge: The MIT Press, 2003.

Quinn contends that societies and individuals must first engage in a process of acknowledgement before any of the other steps, i.e. forgiveness and development of trust and social cohesion leading to reconciliation, can begin to take place.[31]

Yet, this sequence is not necessarily the only possibility. Equally well, it can be assumed that reconciliation can start without any shared view of the historical facts or any apologies. Rohne proposes a fourfold model of relational restoration, which starts from material reparations, leading to discussion of the past, to mutual empathy and forgiveness.[32] In other words, in this model historical problems can be overcome only when a certain level of reconciliation has already been achieved, but dealing with them is still important in deepening the process. In some cases, it is possible to think that partial apologies or acknowledgement of the facts of the historical problem can be accepted as sufficient gestures in sustaining the process of reconciliation. As Marta Valinas and Jana Arsovska remark in the context of Kosovo, even a simple public acknowledgement of the crimes by the perpetrators can be a significant factor in encouraging cooperation and enhancing dialogue.[33]

As often is the case, simplistic models are deficient in one way or another. While apologies tend to increase the sense of justice and make forgiveness more likely,[34] the paradigmatic model of forgiveness does not take into account the fact that demanding an apology may lead to counterproductive reactions in the domestic debate of the country that has committed wrongdoings and thereby increase the burden of the past.[35] By contrast, the problem with the minimalist view is that it is not always the case that the victim and the wrongdoer are equal-

---

[31] Joanna Quinn. *The Politics of Acknowledgement: Truth Commissions in Uganda and Haiti.* Vancouver: UBCPress, 2010.

[32] Holger-C Rohne, Jana Arkovska, and Ivo Aertsen. "Challenging Restorative Justice – State Based Conflict, Mass Victimisation and the Changing Nature of Warfare." *Restoring Justice after Large-scale Violent Conflicts. Kosovo, DR Congo and the Israeli-Palestinian Case.* Eds. Ivo Aertsen, Jana Arsovska, Holger-C. Rohne, Marta Valiñas, and Kris Vanspauwen. Cullompton: Willan Publishing, 2008, 3–45.

[33] Marta Valiñas, and Jana Arsovska. "A Restorative Approach for Dealing with the Aftermath of the Kosovo Conflict – Opportunities and Limits." *Restoring Justice after Large-scale Violent Conflicts. Kosovo, DR Congo and the Israeli-Palestinian Case.* Eds. Ivo Aertsen, Jana Arsovska, Holger-C. Rohne, Marta Valiñas, and Kris Vanspauwen. Cullompton: Willan Publishing, 2008, 206.

[34] Michael Wenzel and Tyler Okimoto. "How Acts of Forgiveness Restore a Sense of Justice: Addressing Status/Power and Value Concerns Raised by Transgressions." *European Journal of Social Psychology* 40 (2010): 401–417.

[35] Lind. *Sorry States: Apologies in International Politics.*

ly blameworthy. Sometimes it is very clear who the wrongdoer and who the victim is and relativising this difference through empathy and self-reflection would not help to restore moral order, provide evidence about intentions or create and strengthen common norms and identities. We thus need to relax the concept of forgiveness and even accept imperfect forms of forgiveness as potential means of overcoming conflicts.

There is little systematic research into the effectiveness of apologies, in particular when it comes to international relations. It is clear that there are huge cultural and other contextual differences in the forms and functions of apologies that do not allow for strict generalisations.[36] The realist theory still dominates the basic understanding of apologies and forgiveness in international relations. Even those who think that forgiveness has a major role to play in resolving domestic conflicts and civil wars are skeptical as to whether it would work in relations between states. On the other hand, many studies show that people have a capacity to forgive after violent conflicts and repeated violations of human rights.[37]

The Winter War and Russo-Finnish Relations

Russo-Finnish relations are often seen as being stable and friendly. The current confrontation between the EU and Russia due to the Ukrainian crisis naturally affects this image but the effects of the conflict have not yet destroyed this positive picture entirely. Unlike other EU-members bordering Russia, Finland has not joined NATO. Although various problems on the agenda already existed between the two states before the Ukrainian crisis, they mainly involved practical issues or were derivatives of broader dynamics in the relations between Russia and the EU.[38] Occasionally, the bilateral relations have been strained, and there have

---

36 J. Brewer. *Peace Processes: A Sociological Approach*. Cambridge: Polity, 2010.
37 Fabiola Azar, Etienne Mullet, and Genevieve Vinsonneau. "The Propensity to Forgive: Findings from Lebanon." *Journal of Peace Research* 36.2 (1999): 169–181; Félix Neto, Maria Da Conceiçao Pinto, and Etienne Mullet. "Intergroup Forgiveness: East Timorese and Angolan Perspectives." *Journal of Peace Research* 44 (2006): 711–728. Sabina Cehajic, Rupert Brown, and Emanuele Castano. "Forgive and Forget? Antecedents and Consequences of Intergroup Forgiveness in Bosnia and Herzegovina." *Political Psychology* 29.3 (2008): 351–363.
38 Pekka Sutela. "Finnish-Russian Relations 1991–2001: Better than Ever?" *BOFIT Online* 11. Helsinki: Bank of Finland, Institute of Economies in Transition, 2001. Tobias Etzold, and Hiski Haukkala. "Denmark, Finland and Sweden." *The National Perspectives on Russia: European Foreign Policy in the Making?* Eds. Maxine David, Jackie Gower, and Hiski Haukkala. London and New York: Routledge, 2013, 132–148.

been incidents concerning, for example, child custody issues of children with a Russian background in Finland that have negatively affected the public perception of the state of the relationship. Overall, however, these tensions have been less severe when compared to Russia's relations with the Baltic States and Poland. Many observers may thereby conclude that the relations between Russia and Finland are good because there is no burden of history. Yet, such interpretations downplay the potential of history to cause problems in terms of memory conflicts. The Finns conceive that Finland has had a long history of wars with Russia since they understand the era of Swedish rule as being part of the history of the nation. In particular, the Winter War in 1939 has been deeply ingrained in the national memory as a Soviet aggression towards an innocent victim.

The Winter War started when the Soviet Union invaded Finland at the end of November 1939 and it ended in March 1940 when peace between the parties was concluded in Moscow. Unlike the Baltic States, Finland was saved from Soviet annexation but as a result of the peace treaty Finland lost the Karelian Isthmus and other eastern areas inhabited almost entirely by ethnic Finns, including Finland's second biggest city, Vyborg. More than 400,000 people lost their homes and were resettled in the remaining Finnish territory. In June 1941, Finland joined the German attack against the Soviet Union, regained the lost territories and occupied Eastern Karelia but lost them again in the peace treaties of 1944 and 1947. A hundred thousand Finns died in the war; however, Finland was not occupied by the Soviet forces and it retained its independence, though a Soviet-led Allied Control Commission stayed in the country until 1947 and a naval base near Helsinki was leased to Russia. Finland also concluded a Friendship, Cooperation and Mutual Assistance (FCMA) treaty with the Soviet Union in 1948.[39]

The Soviet view of these events was that the Winter War was launched by the Finnish armed forces that opened fire across the border near the village of Mainila. The Finnish state before the war, despite Social Democrats being in the government, was seen by the Soviets as fascist and repressive of workers. Moreover, the Soviet side read the war history backwards: the fact that Finland was culpable of joining the German invasion of the Soviet Union in June 1941 was used to justify the Soviet invasion of 1939 and the territorial annexations. In addition, they regarded the war as strategically necessary because the Finnish border before the war ran only 30 kilometers from the centre of St. Petersburg.

---

39 See e.g. David Kirby. *A Concise History of Finland*. Cambridge: Cambridge University Press, 2006, 197–244.

The Finns, on the other hand, saw the Winter War as a one-sided aggression by the Soviets and a violation of the Covenant of the League of Nations and bilateral treaties of non-aggression. The cause of the war was attributed to Communist expansionism, to Stalin's wickedness and to the secret protocol of the Molotov-Ribbentrop treaty between the Soviet Union and Germany that allocated Finland to the Soviet sphere of interest. The Finnish view was that Finland had not posed any threat to the Soviet Union, but had conducted a policy of strict neutrality. The war and its outcome were therefore seen as deeply unjust. The Soviet side had calculated that they would get support from the Finnish working class, since there had been a bloody civil war that the Reds lost in 1918, but the Soviet attack actually united the nation. The war of 1941–1944 was seen as a consequence of the Winter War and was thus named "the Continuation War".

After World War II, Finland conducted a policy of friendship in its relations with the Soviet Union and was careful not to give grounds for Soviet criticism of it. Thus Finland did not try to seek any apologies from the Soviet side, but rather sought to cleanse its own history and politics of anti-Soviet elements. The position of Finland was defensive, as shown by the fact that 13 Finnish politicians, among them war-time President Risto Ryti but not Marshall Mannerheim, were convicted as war criminals in a domestic trial. Finland tried to stick to the interpretation that when joining Germany in the so-called Continuation War, it was conducting a separate war and was only a co-warrior and not an ally to Germany since there was no formal treaty (before summer of 1944), though German forces occupied northern parts of Finland and the war plans were in fact coordinated. This thesis of a separate war was largely invalidated first by foreign and then by Finnish historians already in the 1960s, but the interpretation that Finland was the innocent victim of the Soviet Union in the Winter War and did not have any other meaningful choice but to align with Germany in 1941 remained the standard view throughout the Cold War period. The Finnish leftist interpretation of Finland's participation in the war was of course closer to the Soviet views. Certain aspects of the war such as the Finns' crossing the old Finnish border and occupying the Soviet Eastern Karelia were widely criticised, but when an attempt was made in the 1970s to introduce the Soviet version of the Winter War in school teaching as the correct interpretation of it, it was quickly denounced.[40]

---

[40] See Ville Kivimäki. "Introduction: Three Wars and Their Epitaphs: The Finnish History and Scholarship of World War II." *Finland in World War II: History, Memory, Interpretations.* Eds. Tiina Kinnunen and Ville Kivimäki. Leiden: Brill, 2011, 1–48 and Juhana Aunesluoma. "Two Shadows over Finland: Hitler, Stalin and the Finns Facing the Second World War as History

Although Finland's official foreign policy towards the Soviet Union was friendly, the relationship remained politically precarious. Finland tried to conduct a policy of neutrality despite the FCMA treaty with the Soviet Union and was not sure whether it was able to preserve its relative freedom and perhaps even its formal independence in the future. The friendship policy was supported by the masses but at the same time it was regarded as a liturgy that did not reflect true sentiments. Nevertheless, it can be argued that the old enemy image was kept at bay and the whole nation and not only those who were politically on the left took some genuine steps towards reconciliation.[41] However, the beginnings of the friendship policy were dictated primarily by power relations and the steps towards reconciliation were taken without a mutual policy of dealing with the past. Rather, new images of the other were built as a response to present realities. But the history issue related to the Soviet invasion in 1939 had not disappeared. As Max Jakobson, the prominent Finnish diplomat and pundit wrote in 1987, the Winter War was still a neurotic question that burdened the relationship.[42]

In the mid-1980s, when the Soviet Union started a course of reform under Gorbachev's leadership, it was very much welcomed in Finland. At the beginning, the Soviet interpretations of the World War II remained largely intact, but the representatives of the Soviet Union, including its press, no longer accused the Finns of initiating the Winter War as had been done in the 1970s. The Soviet Union did not take any responsibility for initiating the war, but it was rather seen as a regrettable incident or a minor border conflict between the countries. In the late 1980s some leading Soviet war historians such as Dmitri Volkogonov had already adopted the view that the Winter War was Stalin's fault, but the issue was still sensitive in the eyes of the majority of the old Soviet establishment.[43] When Gorbachev's visit to Finland in October 1989 was planned, the reformers in the Kremlin wanted to give a positive signal with regard to history politics. They suggested two options: to recognise Finland's neutrality and to acknowledge the responsibility of the Soviet Union in launching the Winter War. The Kremlin opted for recognising Finland's neutrality, which Gorbachev then did in his speech at Finlandia Hall. An acknowledgement that the Soviet

---

1944–2010." *Hitler' Scandinavian Legacy.* Eds. Jill Stephenson and John Gilmour. London: Bloomsbury, 2013, 199–217.
41 Tuomas Forsberg. "Finnish-Russian Security Relations: Is Russia Still Seen as a Threat." *The Two-Level Game: Russia's Relations with Great Britain, Finland and the EU.* Ed. Hanna Smith. Helsinki: Aleksanteri Institute, Kikimora Publications, 2006, 141–154.
42 Max Jakobson. *Vallanvaihto.* [Succession]. Helsinki: Otava, 1992, 318.
43 Jakobson. *Vallanvaihto*, 322–324.

Union had started the Winter War was in Gorbachev's draft speech, but in the final version Gorbachev just referred to the responsible lessons that both countries had drawn from the tragedy of 1939–1944.[44]

Finland's political leadership would have preferred Gorbachev to acknowledge that the Soviet Union was responsible for the outbreak of the Winter War. Recognising Finland's neutrality was important because the status of neutrality was fiercely contested during the Cold War period, but President Koivisto wanted to avoid the impression that Finland's neutrality would depend primarily on the explicit recognition of the Soviet leader. A statement regretting the war would thus have had clear symbolic value. The Finns were nevertheless pleased that the 60th anniversary of the Winter War could be commemorated in November 1989 without fear of an anti-Soviet label, though the state leadership still kept a low profile in the issue.[45]

Nevertheless, soon after Gorbachev's visit to Finland, acts demonstrating Moscow's willingness to deal with politics of history followed. The secret protocol of the Molotov–Ribbentrop treaty was condemned in December 1989 by the Soviet Congress.[46] In Finland, the political constraints that had restrained interpretations of history were broken, followed by a "neo-patriotic turn" in collective representations of the past.[47] The Finnish leaders that had been convicted as war criminals were rehabilitated and regarded as patriotic heroes. Discussion started in the media about the loss of Karelia, but attempts to bring about the return of the lost territories did not gain support of the leading politicians, who argued that they had been lost in the peace treaties and these could not be renegotiated. The war crimes of Soviet partisans against the Finnish civilians in Lapland were taken up as a forgotten issue in light of new research.[48] At the same time, historians also revealed more details about the closeness of the Finnish-German cooperation before and during the "Continuation War" 1941–1944 and the bad treatment of the Soviet prisoners of war in Finland and of the Russian population in

---

44 Jaakko Blomberg. *Vakauden kaipuu. Kylmän sodan loppu ja Suomi* [Yearning after Stability. The End of the Cold War and Finland]. Helsinki: WSOY, 2011, 136.
45 Jakobson. *Vallanvaihto*, 318.
46 Heiki Lindpere. *Molotov-Ribbentrop Pact: Challenging Soviet History.* Tallinn: The Foreign Policy Institute, 2009, 87.
47 Tiina Kinnunen and Markku Jokisipilä. "Shifting Images of 'Our Wars': Finnish Memory Culture of World War II". *Finland in World War II.* Eds. Tiina Kinnunen and Ville Kivimäki. Leiden: Brill, 2011, 435–482.
48 Veikko Erkkilä. *Vaiettu sota. Neuvostoliiton Partisaanien iskut suomalaisiin kyliin* [The Silenced War. The Attacks of the Soviet Partisans to the Finnish Villages]. Helsinki: Arator, 1998.

the occupied Eastern Karelia.⁴⁹ Although the tune was self-critical in much of such professional history writing, it was also brought up, for example, that the German military assistance had been crucial in stopping the Soviet offensive and thus preventing the Red Army from marching to Helsinki in the late summer 1944.⁵⁰

For the Finnish politicians in the early 1990s, the key objective was to avoid Russia's political intervention in the national history debates and assure the Russians that open discussion in Finland should not be seen as a provocation against Russia. Instead of trying to demand official apologies from Russia, not to mention attempting to gain compensation or regaining the lost territories, a cooperative and pragmatic attitude was adopted towards healing the remaining wounds of history. Finland's official policy consisted of facilitating border crossings and creating possibilities to visit old home sites or war theatres in the former Finnish territory, as well as to renovate cemeteries and other cultural monuments together with the Russians. Without making an issue of it, the government also encouraged joint Finnish-Russian research projects on World War II.⁵¹

Overall, Russia's history policy towards Finland during President Boris Yeltsin's era was reconciliatory. Yeltsin's visit to Finland in the summer of 1992 demonstrated this policy most visibly. As part of the official program he laid a wreath at the Hietaniemi cemetery to the grave of war heroes. In his non-public dinner speech, he spontaneously claimed that he was sorry for the Winter War. Russia and Finland also concluded a treaty on graveyards and war monuments. During their two hour journey to Turku, Finnish President Koivisto had a chance to explain the war history from the Finnish perspective face to face to Yeltsin. His motivation was not to put pressure on the Russian leadership but to increase mutual understanding. For Koivisto, it was significant that Yeltsin listened to him and he felt that most of the pressure of these historical problems had been removed when Yeltsin understood why the historical issues such as the loss of Karelia were still discussed and remembered in Finland. "So please, take this issue calmly and in a spirit of friendship", Koivisto advised Yeltsin.⁵² In May 1994, dur-

---

49 The seminal work was that of Mauno Jokipii. *Jatkosodan synty: tutkimuksia Saksan ja Suomen sotilaallisesta yhteistyöstä 1940–41*. [The Origins of the Continuation War: Research on the German-Finnish Military Cooperation 1940–41] Helsinki: Otava, 1987.
50 See Kivimäki. "Introduction" and Aunesluoma "Two Shadows over Finland".
51 Blomberg. *Vakauden kaipuu*, 567.
52 Mauno Koivisto. *Witness to History: The Memoirs of Mauno Koivisto, President of Finland 1982–1994*. London: Hurst & Company, 1997, 250. See also Arto Mansala. "Kaotiska år i Moskva – en tid av ömsesidig anpassning i finsk-ryska relationer 1992–1996." *Säkerhetspolitik och*

ing President Ahtisaari's visit to Russia, Yeltsin publicly admitted that the Winter War was part of an offensive policy of Stalin's totalitarian regime. Also, the Russian ambassador to Finland, Yuri Derjabin, was apologetic in his many speeches and interviews. He contended that the Winter War was a Soviet invasion, and that it was shameful that the former Finnish city of Vyborg was in ruins.[53]

The few visible breaches related to politics of history during the Yeltsin era tell quite a lot about the dynamics of memory conflicts in the Russo-Finnish relations. When visiting the Karelian Republic in Russia in July 1997, Ahtisaari told the local TV reporter who asked about the discussion in Finland of the loss of Karelia that Russians had to understand those Finns who still felt that injustice had occurred during the war. When Ahtisaari then visited Moscow in November 1997, Yeltsin unexpectedly demanded in a press conference that the Finns stop discussing Karelia, but Ahtisaari replied by saying that he is the last man to forbid any discussion on Karelia in Finland. In the official dinner speech during the visit, Ahtisaari gave credit to Yeltsin for his reconciliatory gestures during his 1992 visit to Finland and assured him that the Finns understood them as such and valued his approach.[54]

President Vladimir Putin continued the reconciliatory gestures related to politics of history during his visit to Finland in September 2001. Not only did he place a wreath at the cross of the war heroes, as Yeltsin had done, but he also visited the grave of Mannerheim. This is not as perplexing as it might seem. Though Mannerheim symbolised the Finnish struggle against the Soviet Union, he was also regarded as a Russian war hero since he had been a former General in the Russian army who during the Russian civil war fought against the Bolsheviks. Moreover, Putin wanted to signal the closeness of the relations by doing the same thing as the King of Sweden had done when visiting Finland.[55] Although Putin drove the Russian politics of history in many regards towards a more conservative direction, no serious attempt followed to change the interpretation that the Soviet Union started the Winter War. In 2004, when meeting President Tarja Halonen in Moscow, Putin repeated that the Winter War was a mistake of Stalin, but reflecting the same worry as Yeltsin had had about the

---

historia. Essäer om stormaktspolitiken och Norden under sjuttio år. Eds. Mats Bergquist and Alf W. Johansson. Stockholm: Hjalmarson & Högberg, 2007, 245–262.
53 Tuomas Forsberg. "Karelia." *Contested Territory. Border Disputes at the Edge of the Former Soviet Empire*. Ed. Tuomas Forsberg. Aldershot: Edward Elgar, 1995, 202–223.
54 Alpo Rusi. *Mariankadun puolelta* [From the Mariankatu Side]. Helsinki: Otava, 2000, 258.
55 "Putin to lay wreath at Mannerheim grave during visit to Finland." *Helsingin Sanomat International Edition*, 30 August 2001. http://www2.hs.fi/english/archive/news.asp?id=20010830IE5 (15 April 2015).

potential territorial demands, he added strongly that a discussion about Karelia in Finland is detrimental and borders cannot be changed because there are too many similar border problems elsewhere.[56]

In its relations with Russia, Finland focused on concrete and pragmatic problems to do with trade, border crossings and the environment, and on developing the overall relations between the EU and Russia.[57] Memory conflicts did not play any significant role in these questions. When Prime Minister Paavo Lipponen participated in the unveiling of the first Winter War memorial in the Karelian Isthmus in 2000, he declared that "peace and reconciliation had won in the Finnish-Russian relations".[58] A good indicator of the formal reconciliation was that the Finnish leaders, unlike many other Eastern European leaders, did not see any political problem in participating at the commemorative events of the victory of World War II in Moscow and their presence there did not evoke much public debate at home. President Ahtisaari participated in the fiftieth anniversary of the Victory day in 1995 and President Halonen in the respective sixtieth anniversary in 2005 (President Niinistö decided not to travel to Moscow for the 70th in 2015 as most Western leaders had declined the invitation). Discussion about the loss of Karelia continued in civil society, and tabloids occasionally made headlines of the issue, but this discussion remained limited and politically ineffective. Border changes were not on the agenda of any government or any significant political party or decision-maker. While many of the Karelian evacuees, their descendants, and many other Finns hoped that the restoration of Karelia could have been possible, pushing the idea forward was "limited to the activities of small, albeit vociferous groups" and it did not receive support from more than one third of the citizens in public opinion polls.[59] The Karelian question is a good example how smoothly, relatively speaking, difficult questions in Russo-Finnish relations were handled.

The political problems related to the history of World War II had thus become marginal issues in Finnish-Russian relations already during the 1990s. History was sometimes debated in the media, but on the political level, it was more often the Russian representatives who wanted to check that Finnish views of the past did not lead to territorial claims or other anti-Russian attitudes rather than

---

[56] "Путин встревожен и расстроен." *Russki Reporter* (31 January 2011). http://rusrep.ru/article/2011/01/31/putin_fin/ (15 March 2012).

[57] Pekka Sutela. *Finnish-Russian Relations 1991–2001*.

[58] "Lipponen: Sovinto voittanut Suomen ja Venäjän suhteissa." *Helsingin Sanomat*, 28 June 2000.

[59] Outi Fingeroos. "'Karelia Issue': The Politics and Memory of Karelia in Finland." *Finland in World War II*. Eds. Tiina Kinnunen and Ville Kivimäki. Leiden: Brill, 2011, 483–517.

the Finnish politicians asking for more evidence of Russia's changed attitude towards the common past. One rare example exists of political interventions related to the history of World War II by the Finnish political leaders after the end of the Cold War. It was President Halonen's speech in Paris in March 2005, when she explained Finnish war history by repeating the thesis of a separate war in contrast to Finland's being an ally of Germany. This evoked some discussion both domestically as well as in Russia, but did not constitute a diplomatic incident.[60]

Because of the generally positive image that the Russian government and society had of Finland, there was no need to highlight potentially inflammatory history issues in the Russian media. For example, the meetings in Finland of former Finnish SS-soldiers who had fought in the Eastern front in 1941–1942 never gained the sort of massive negative attention as did corresponding meetings in the Baltic States. The attempts to reinterpret the history of the Winter War in Russia in accordance with the Soviet view that Finland had started it were few and they did not get much publicity.[61] Russian history textbooks in the 2000s contended that the Soviet Union had started the Winter War.[62] Putin's speech to Russian military historians in March 2013 received some public attention abroad, because he stated that he saw the key reason for the Winter War being the closeness of the Finnish border to Leningrad and the need to correct that "mistake". However, this passage of the speech was removed from the official version that was published on the Kremlin's webpage.[63] For Russia, the Winter War remained a small conflict in the Great Patriotic War and hence it was easier to admit the culpability of the Soviet Union and its leaders, in particular in starting that war, since it did not change the overall interpretation of the Soviet heroism during World War II.

Although the history issues have not been high on the political agenda in Finnish foreign policy towards Russia, it can be stated that the memory conflicts

---

60 Kinnunen and Jokisipilä. "Shifting Images of 'Our Wars'."
61 Vladimir, Baryshnikov. *От прохладного мира к зимней войне: восточная политика Финляндии в 1930-е годы.* [From the Cold World to the Winter War: Finland's Eastern Policy in the 1930s]. St. Petersburg: St. Petersburg University Press, 1997.
62 Kari Kaunismaa. *Punatähdestä kaksoiskotkaan: Neuvostoliiton romahtamisen vaikutus venäläisen keskikoulun historian oppikirjoihin* [From the Red Star to the Double Eagle. The Impact of the Collapse of the Soviet Union on the Russian Middle School Textbooks]. Turku: Uniprint, 2009.
63 Vladimir Putin. "Meeting with Founding Congress of the Russian Military Historical Society Participants." 14 March 2013, http://en.kremlin.ru/events/president/news/17677 (20 April 2015).

have not been totally overcome in the minds of Finns. In the view of Professor of Russian Studies Timo Vihavainen, the historical heritage still has a strong influence on Finnish attitudes towards Russia today.[64] He contends that people show a remarkable readiness to accept unpleasant information about developments in Russia and are not willing to engage with the Russian society properly. However, as the media researcher Pentti Raittila has pointed out, most Finns think that there is a negative bias towards Russia amongst the population in Finland, though they themselves deny that they would have any negative conceptions of Russia. Indeed, in most public opinion surveys conducted on the image of Russia in Finland, it has been hard to detect any strong negative bias. While a hostile attitude towards Russians is still strong in some segments of the Finnish people, Raittila concludes, a normalising approach emphasising neutrality and rationality is being reinforced elsewhere in the society.[65]

The Finnish foreign policy leadership did not think that Finland as a nation suffered from any particular historical trauma because of World War II. Finnish political leaders sometimes contrasted this to the Baltic States, where they saw the past as being the root cause of the problems in the relations of those states with Russia.[66] This is not to deny that probably many Finns, and especially those of the older generations, have been traumatised by the war and consequences of it such as having lost their relatives or homes. According to a recent study on the historical consciousness in Finland, three quarters of Finns disagreed with the claim that Finns are people without any major collective traumas.[67] But the traumas were felt more by the older generation rather than being a trans-generational phenomenon. The Finnish-Russian reconciliation could thus be explained as a process of healing through the passage of time. When the Russian leaders disassociated Russia from the aggressive policies of Stalin and allowed the Finns to have their truth of the war, it reduced the extent to which the bitter memories of the Soviet era were kept alive. The increased possibilities to alleviate mourning through open debate, normalising the existence of the associations of "evacuated" Karelians and the possibility of arranging nostalgic visits to the lost territories after the end of the Cold War can be seen as therapeutic for, rather than

---

[64] Timo Vihavainen. "Does History Play a Role in Finnish-Russian Relations?" *The Two-Level Game: Russia's Relations with Great Britain, Finland and the European Union*. Ed. Hanna Smith. Aleksanteri Papers 2, Helsinki: Aleksanteri Institute, University of Helsinki, 2006.
[65] Pentti Raittila. *Russia in Finnish Media and Everyday Discourse*. Paper presented at the Nordmedia Conference, Reykjavik, 13–15 August 2011.
[66] Mika Aaltola. "Agile Small State Agency: Heuristic Plays and Flexible National Identity Markers in Finnish Foreign Policy." *Nationalities Papers* 39 (2011): 257–276.
[67] Pilvi Torsti. *Suomalaiset ja historia* [The Finns and History]. Helsinki: Gaudeamus, 2012.

counterproductive to, historical reconciliation. For some, however, the absence of historical issues on the political agenda does not indicate that the trauma has been overcome. Rather there are those who have argued in the domestic debate that Finland and its foreign policy leaders suffer from a trauma that prevents it from raising the morally justified issues of territorial restoration in its relations with Russia.[68]

The moral dimension was hence present in the Finnish debate, but the need to seek for moral repair was significantly balanced by the perception that Finland also had invaded the Soviet Union and violated international norms. Moreover, Finns perceived World War II more as a success than a defeat.[69] Though Finns considered themselves more victims than perpetrators, the historical memory was not black and white. Finland's moral sense of getting even was largely fulfilled when it was no longer accused of initiating the war, and the territorial loss was mentally compensated by the ability to retain independence and avoid communist rule. This is why Yeltsin and Putin's acknowledgements of the Soviet culpability in the Winter War were seen as enough to close the books on the higher political level.

To some extent the Russian way of dealing with the past was also read as a signal of its intentions. The apologetic gestures of Yeltsin were interpreted in Finland as evidence of Russia's new values and strengthened the confidence that Russia did not threaten Finland's independence or political freedom. Similarly, Putin's policy of continuing Yeltsin's rapprochement in politics of history was also regarded as reassuring. Yet, political acts relating to history were not the most important signals in judging whether a recurrence of a military conflict with Russia would be likely. Russia's general direction towards democratisation and cooperation with the West, as well as the military force structure and the transparency of the Russian leaders to provide information on the Russian armed forces placed in the regions near Finland were more important factors in the threat calculation, particularly in the 1990s.[70]

The memories of World War II continue to be core material for Finnish identity, but the picture of the national history has become more multifaceted. When asked, the Finns today give more credit for their feelings of identity to educational achievements than to the war experience.[71] Yet, the patriotic view still holds that the war was the true test of Finland's statehood and the sacrifices that

---

68 Martti Siirala and Sirpa Kulonen. *Syvissä raiteissa: kansallisen itsetunnon matka*. [In Deep Tracks: The Journey of National Self-Confidence]. Helsinki: WSOY, 1991.
69 Torsti. *Suomalaiset ja historia*.
70 Blomberg. *Vakauden kaipuu*, 568.
71 Torsti. *Suomalaiset ja historia*.

were made on the front are something for which every Finn should be thankful even today. There is no independence day celebration that does not honour the war veterans as "cult figures" and remind Finns of the struggle in the war against the Soviet Union, which is seen as fundamental for the independence and well-being of the nation and which includes aspects of "sacredness".[72] Through this historical construction of the nation, it can be claimed that Russia automatically represents the "other" to Finland.[73] Yet, it seems that this otherness, even in neo-patriotic history, is void of strong enemy images.[74] At least to some degree, this lack of strong enemy images helped Finns to perceive Russia's half-apologetic moves relating to the history of World War II as sufficient to overcome memory conflicts rather than as a pretext for sparking new disputes in the name of openness. Similarly, Russia can be seen as some kind of cultural and political "other" for Finland even without the experience of World War II since the roots of this identity distinction run much deeper in culture, history and political belief systems. For national identity construction, Russia has been central as the other but it has not led to strong enemy images. Paradoxically, Finland may have joined the European Union in 1995 for reasons of identity defined in opposition to Russia, but the membership in the EU has also made this dimension of identity construction less palpable.[75]

Although Russia turned more authoritarian in the Putin era, and the Russo-Georgian war as well as the annexation of Crimea and the conflict in the Eastern Ukraine has reminded Finns of Russia's readiness to use military means against its neighbours, memory conflicts between Finland and Russia have not significantly intesified. Professor Vihavainen, for example, contended that discussions in a Russo-Finnish history seminar related to the 75th anniversary of the Winter War in spring 2015 were strictly professional, based on facts and reflecting high

---

[72] Heino Nyyssönen. "Remembering the Winter War in Finland." *Spivpratsia SRSR i Nimetstsini u mihvoennii period ta pid tsas drugoi cvitovoi vijni: pritsini i naclidki* [Collaboration between the Soviet Union and Germany in the interwar period and during WWII: Causes and Consequences]. Eds. S.M. Kvi, et al. Kyiv: NaUKMA, Agrar Media Group, 2012, 163–179.

[73] Sami Moisio. Eds. R. Krishtalovska and O. Pazyuk. See the list of references. "Finland, Geopolitical Image of Threat and the Post-Cold War Confusion." *Geopolitics* 3 (1998): 104–124 and Vilho Harle, and Sami Moisio. *Missä on Suomi? Kansallisen identiteettipolitiikan historia ja geopolitiikka* [Where is Finland? The History and Geopolitics of National Identity Politics]. Tampere: Vastapaino, 2000.

[74] Kinnunen and Jokisipilä. "Shifting Images of 'Our Wars'", 463.

[75] On Finnish identity construction, see Risto Alapuro. "What is Western and What is Eastern in Finland?" *Thesis Eleven* 77 (2004): 85–101. Christopher Browning. *Constructivism, Narrative and Foreign Policy Analysis: A Case Study of Finland*. Oxford: Peter Lang, 2008.

levels of mutual understanding despite the current international conflict and political tensions between Russia and the Western countries. It was as if the past wars between the Soviet Union and Finland had been honest fights that the nations had to accept as tragic episodes of their common history.[76]

Conclusions

Major historical wrongdoings can be significant factors in creating and sustaining conflicts and impeding cooperation in relations between states. Though concerns related to material interests may often suppress disputes stemming from felt historical injustice and national interpretations of historical wrongdoings, it is important to understand how memory conflicts can be overcome in their own right. The Finnish-Russian case described in this article suggests that it is not possible to reduce the nature of memory conflicts to material dimensions of strategic advantage, territorial claims or economic compensation. What was at stake were interpretations of history and acknowledgements of responsibility.

Russia and Finland succeeded in the early 1990s in normalising their relations. The historical problems were marginalised by keeping them separate from the official political agenda. For the Finnish foreign policy elite a sufficient gesture of Russia occured when Yeltsin visited Finland and acknowledged Soviet culpability in the Winter War. This process of overcoming memory conflicts in Russia's relations with Finland suggests that a full apology according to the paradigmatic model of forgiveness was not needed. The Finnish government never expected a full apology from Russia and they understood that such demands could have been counterproductive. The Finnish leaders knew that the main concern for the Russians was not that a full apology would create domestic backlash effects, because in the case of Russia this concern was secondary due to the Kremlin's ability to control mass media and political opinion formation. Instead the Finnish government realised that such demands would have violated Russia's status concerns too openly. Still, for the Finnish government and the larger foreign policy elite a clear acknowledgement that the Russian leaders regarded the Soviet Union as the initiator of the Winter War was something that they expected. A partial apology in the form of acknowledging the fact of the wrongdoing and some authentic gestures to show remorse were thus important

---

76 Timo Vihavainen. "Talvisotaseminaari Moskovassa." [A Seminar on the Winter War in Moscow.] Blog "Vihavainen" http://timo-vihavainen.blogspot.fi/2015/03/talvisotaseminaari-moskovassa.html (10 March 2015).

for the process of reconciliation, since on the basis of such symbolic acts the politicians were able to argue that the history disputes had been solved, though the key interpretations were still nationally framed. The Finnish state leadership did not, however, see the need to be active agents in the politics of history. The questions over historical facts could be left to the historians and the debates surrounding their interpretation could be seen as part of an open society.

References

Aaltola, Mika. "Agile Small State Agency: Heuristic Plays and Flexible National Identity Markers in Finnish Foreign Policy". *Nationalities Papers* 39 (2011): 257–276.
Alapuro, Risto. "What is Western and What is Eastern in Finland?" *Thesis Eleven* 77 (2004): 85–101.
Assmann, Aleida. "Europe's Divided Memory." *Memory and Theory in Eastern Europe*. Eds. Uileam Blacker, Alexander Etkind, and Julie Fedor. Basingstoke: Palgrave, 2013. 25–41.
Aunesluoma, Juhana. "Two Shadows over Finland: Hitler, Stalin and the Finns Facing the Second World War as History 1944–2010." *Hitler's Scandinavian Legacy*. Eds. Jill Stephenson, and John Gilmour. London: Bloomsbury, 2013. 199–217.
Azar, Fabiola, Mullet, Etienne, and Vinsonneau, Genevieve. "The Propensity to Forgive: Findings from Lebanon." *Journal of Peace Research* 36.2 (1999): 169–181.
Barkan, Elazar. *The Guilt of Nations: Restitution and Negotiating Historical Injustices*. Baltimore: The Johns Hopkins University Press, 2001.
Baryshnikov, Vladimir. *От прохладного мира к зимней войне: восточная политика Финляндии в 1930-е годы*. [From the Cold World to the Winter War: Finland's Eastern Policy in the 1930s]. St. Petersburg: St. Petersburg University Press, 1997.
Blomberg, Jaakko. *Vakauden kaipuu. Kylmän sodan loppu ja Suomi* [Yearning after Stability. The End of the Cold War and Finland], Helsinki: WSOY, 2011.
Blustein, Jeffrey. "Forgiveness, Commemoration and Restorative Justice: The Role of Moral Emotions." *Metaphilosophy* 41.4 (2010): 582–617.
Borer, Tristane Anne. "Truth Telling as a Peace-Building Activity: A Theoretical Overview." *Telling the Truths: Truths Telling and Peace Building in Post- Conflict Societies*. Ed. Tristan Anne Borer. Notre Dame: University of Note Dame Press, 2006. 1–57.
Brahm, Eric. "Uncovering the Truth: Examining Truth Commissions Success and Impact." *International Studies Perspectives* 8 (2007): 16–35.
Brewer, John D, *Peace Processes: A Sociological Approach*. Cambridge: Polity, 2010.
Browning, Christopher S. *Constructivism, Narrative and Foreign Policy Analysis. A Case Study of Finland*. Oxford: Peter Lang, 2008.
Booth, W. James. "The Unforgotten: Memories of Justice." *American Political Science Review* 95.4 (2001): 777–791.
Card, Claudia. *The Atrocity Paradigm: A Theory of Evil*. Oxford: Oxford University, 2002.
Cehajic, Sabina, Rupert Brown and Emanuele Castano. "Forgive and Forget? Antecedents and Consequences of Intergroup Forgiveness in Bosnia and Herzegovina." *Political Psychology* 29.3 (2008): 351–363.
Digeser, Peter. *Political Forgiveness*. Ithaca: Cornell University Press, 2001.

Erkkilä, Veikko. *Vaiettu sota. Neuvostoliiton Partisaanien iskut suomalaisiin kyliin* [The Silenced War. The Attacks of the Soviet Partisans to the Finnish Villages]. Helsinki: Arator, 1998.
Etzold, Tobias, and Haukkala, Hiski. "Denmark, Finland and Sweden." *The National Perspectives on Russia: European Foreign Policy in the Making?* Eds. Maxine David, Jackie Gower and Hiski Haukkala. London and New York: Routledge, 2013. 132–148.
Fingeroos, Outi. "'Karelia Issue': The Politics and Memory of Karelia in Finland". *Finland in World War II*. Eds. Tiina Kinnunen and Ville Kivimäki. Leiden: Brill, 2011. 483–517.
Finney, Patrick. *Remembering the Road to World War Two: International History, National Identity, Collective Memory.* New York: Routledge, 2010.
Forsberg, Tuomas. "Finnish-Russian Security Relations: Is Russia Still Seen as a Threat." *The Two-Level Game: Russia's Relations with Great Britain, Finland and the EU.* Ed. Hanna Smith. Helsinki: Aleksanteri Institute, Kikimora Publications, 2006. 141–154.
Forsberg, Tuomas. "Karelia." *Contested Territory: Border Disputes at the Edge of the Former Soviet Empire.* Ed. Tuomas Forsberg. Aldershot: Edward Elgar, 1995. 202–223.
Forsberg, Tuomas. "The Philosophy and Practice of Dealing with the Past: Some Conceptual and Normative Issues." *Burying the Past: Making Peace and Doing Justice after Civil Conflict.* Ed. Nigel Biggar. Washington D.C.: Georgetown University Press, 2001. 57–72.
Gloppen, Siri. "Roads to Reconciliation: A Conceptual Framework." *Roads to Reconciliation.* Eds. Elin Skaar, Siri Gloppen, and Astri Suhrke. Lanham, MA: Lexington, 2005. 17–50.
Govier, Trudy. *Taking Wrongs Seriously: Acknowledgment, Reconciliation, and the Politics of Sustainable Peace.* Amherst, NY: Humanity Books, 2006.
Harle, Vilho, and Moisio, Sami. *Missä on Suomi? Kansallisen identiteettipolitiikan historia ja geopolitiikka* [Where is Finland? The History and Geopolitics of National Identity Politics]. Tampere: Vastapaino, 2000.
He, Yinan. *The Search for Reconciliation: Sino-Japanese and German-Polish Relations since World War II.* Cambridge: Cambridge University Press, 2009.
Herman, Judith L. *Trauma and Recovery: The Aftermath of Violence from Domestic Abuse to Political Terror.* New York: Basic Books, 1997.
Hirsch, Michal Ben-Josef, Megan MacKenzie and Mohamed Sesay. "Measuring the Impacts of Truth and Reconciliation Commissions: Placing the Global "Success" of TRC's in Local Perspective." *Cooperation and Conflict* 46.3 (2012): 386–403.
Hutchison, Emma. "Trauma and the Politics of Emotions: Constituting Identity, Security and Community after the Bali Bombing." *International Relations* 24.1 (2010): 65–86.
Hutchison, Emma, and Roland Bleiker. "Emotional Reconciliation: Reconstituting Identity and Community after Trauma." *European Journal of Social Theory* 11.3 (2010): 385–403.
Jakobson, Max. *Vallanvaihto.* [Succession]. Helsinki: Otava, 1992.
Jakoby, Tami Amanda. "A Theory of Victimhood: Politics, Conflict and the Construction of Victim-based Identity." *Millennium: Journal of International Studies* 43.2 (2015): 511–530.
Jokipii, Mauno. *Jatkosodan synty: tutkimuksia Saksan ja Suomen sotilaallisesta yhteistyöstä 1940–41.* [The Origins of the Continuation War: Research on the German-Finnish Military Cooperation 1940–41]. Helsinki: Otava, 1987
Kaunismaa, Kari. *Punatähdestä kaksoiskotkaan: Neuvostoliiton romahtamisen vaikutus venäläisen keskikoulun historian oppikirjoihin* [From the Red Star to the Double Eagle.

The Impact of the Collapse of the Soviet Union on the Russian Middle School Textbooks]. Turku: Uniprint, 2009.

Kinnunen, Tiina and Markku Jokisipilä. "Shifting Images of 'Our Wars': Finnish Memory Culture of World War II". *Finland in World War II: History, Memory, Interpretations*. Eds. Tiina Kinnunen and Ville Kivimäki. Leiden: Brill, 2011. 435–482.

Kirby, David. *A Concise History of Finland*. Cambridge: Cambridge University Press, 2006.

Kivimäki, Ville. "Introduction: Three Wars and Their Epitaphs: The Finnish History and Scholarship of World War II". *Finland in World War II: History, Memory, Interpretations*. Eds. Tiina Kinnunen and Ville Kivimäki. Leiden: Brill, 2011. 1–48.

Koivisto, Mauno. *Witness to History: The Memoirs of Mauno Koivisto, President of Finland 1982–1994*. London: Hurst & Company, 1997.

Langenbacher, Eric. "Collective Memory as a Factor in Political Culture and International Relations." *Power and the Past: Collective Memory and International Relations*. Eds. Eric Langenbacher and Yossi Shain. Washington D.C.: Georgetown University Press 2010. 13–50.

Lebow, Richard Ned. "The Future of Memory." *Annals of the American Academy of Political and Social Science* 617.1 (2008): 25–41.

Lind, Jennifer. *Sorry States: Apologies in International Politics*. Ithaca: Cornell, 2008.

Lindpere, Heiki. *Molotov-Ribbentrop Pact: Challenging Soviet History*. Tallinn: The Foreign Policy Institute, 2009.

Long, William J., and Brecke, Peter. *War and Reconciliation: Reason and Emotion in Conflict Resolution*. Cambridge: The MIT Press, 2003.

Mansala, Arto. "Kaotiska år i Moskva – en tid av ömsesidig anpassning i finsk-ryska relationer 1992–1996." *Säkerhetspolitik och historia. Essäer om stormaktspolitiken och Norden under sjuttio år*. Eds. Mats Bergquist and Alf W. Johansson. Stockholm: Hjalmarson & Högberg, 2007. 245–262.

McCullogh, Michael E., Everett L. Worthington and Kenneth C. Rachal. "Interpersonal Forgiving in Close Relationships." *Journal of Personality and Social Psychology* 73.2 (1997): 321–336.

Mendeloff, David. "Truth-Seeking, Truth-Telling and Postconflict Peacebuilding: Curb the Enthusiasm?" *International Studies Review* 6 (2004): 355–380.

Minow, Martha. *Between Vengeance and Forgiveness: Facing History after Genocide and Mass Violence*. Boston, MA: Beacon Press, 1998.

Moisio, Sami. "Finland, Geopolitical Image of Threat and the Post-Cold War Confusion." *Geopolitics* 3 (1998): 104–124.

Murphy, Jeffrie G. *Getting Even: Forgiveness and Its Limits*. Oxford: Oxford University Press, 2003.

Neto, Félix, Maria da Conceição Pinto and Etienne Mullet. "Intergroup Forgiveness: East Timorese and Angolan Perspectives." *Journal of Peace Research* 44 (2006): 711–728.

North, Joanna. "Wrongdoing and Forgiveness". *Philosophy* 62.242 (1987): 499–508.

Nyyssönen, Heino. "Remembering the Winter War in Finland". *Spivpratsia SRSR i Nimetstsini u mihvoennii period ta pid tsas drugoi cvitovoi vijni: pritsini i nacliki* [Collaboration between the Soviet Union and Germany in the interwar period and during WWII: Causes and Consequences]. Eds. R.Krishtalovska and O. Pazyuk. Kyiv: NaUKMA, Agrar Media Group, 2012. 163–179.

Putin, Vladimir. "Meeting with Founding Congress of the Russian Military Historical Society Participants." 14 March 2013. http://en.kremlin.ru/events/president/news/17677 (20 April 2015).

Quinn, Joanna R. *The Politics of Acknowledgement: Truth Commissions in Uganda and Haiti.* Vancouver: UBCPress, 2010.

Raittila, Pentti. *Russia in Finnish Media and Everyday Discourse.* Paper presented at the Nordmedia Conference, Reykjavik, 13–15 August, 2011.

Rosoux, Valerie. "Reconciliation as a Peace-Building Process: Scope and Limits."*The Sage Handbook of Conflict Resolution.* Eds. Jacob Bercovitch, Victor Kremenyuk and I. William Zartman. London: Sage, 2009. 543–560.

Rohne, Holger-C, Jana Arkovska and Ivo Aertsen. "Challenging Restorative Justice – State Based Conflict, Mass Victimisation and the Changing Nature of Warfare." *Restoring Justice after Large-scale Violent Conflicts. Kosovo, DR Congo and the Israeli-Palestinian Case.* Eds. Ivo Aertsen, Jana Arsovska, Holger-C. Rohne, Marta Valiñas, and Kris Vanspauwen. Cullompton: Willan Publishing, 2008. 3–45.

Rusi, Alpo. *Mariankadun puolelta* [From the Mariankatu Side]. Helsinki: Otava 2000.

Samuel, Raphael. *Theatres of Memory.* London: Verso, 1994.

Shriver, Donald W., Jr. *An Ethic for Enemies: Forgiveness in Politics.* New York: Oxford University Press, 1995.

Siirala, Martti and Sirpa Kulonen. *Syvissä raiteissa: kansallisen itsetunnon matka.* [In Deep Tracks: The Journey of National Self-Confidence]. Helsinki: WSOY, 1991.

Smith, Nick. *I Was Wrong: The Meanings of Apologies.* Cambridge: Cambridge University Press, 2008.

Sullivan, Dennis, and Larry Tifft. *Handbook of Restorative Justice: A Global Perspective.* Abingdon: Routledge, 2006.

Sutela, Pekka. "Finnish-Russian Relations 1991–2001: Better than Ever?" *BOFIT Online* no.11. Helsinki: Bank of Finland, Institute of Economies in Transition, 2001.

Tang, Shiping. "Reconciliation and the Remaking of Anarchy." *World Politics* 63.4 (2011): 711–749.

Torsti, Pilvi. *Suomalaiset ja historia* [The Finns and History]. Helsinki: Gaudeamus, 2012.

Ure, Michael. "Post-Traumatic Societies: On Reconciliation, Justice and the Emotions." *European Journal of Social Theory* 11.3 (2008): 283–297.

Valiñas, Marta, and Jana Arsovska. "A Restorative Approach for Dealing with the Aftermath of the Kosovo Conflict – Opportunities and Limits." *Restoring Justice after Large-scale Violent Conflicts. Kosovo, DR Congo and the Israeli- Palestinian Case.* Eds. Ivo Aertsen, Jana Arsovska, Holger-C. Rohne, Marta Valiñas, and Kris Vanspauwen. Cullompton: Willan Publishing, 2008.

Verdeja, Ernesto. "Official Apologies in the Aftermath of Political Violence." *Metaphilosophy* 41.4 (2010): 563–581.

Vihavainen, Timo. "Does History Play a Role in Finnish-Russian Relations?" *The Two-Level Game: Russia's Relations with Great Britain, Finland and the European Union.* Ed. Hanna Smith. Aleksanteri Papers 2, Helsinki: Aleksanteri Institute, University of Helsinki, 2006.

Timo Vihavainen. "Talvisotaseminaari Moskovassa." [A Seminar on the Winter War in Moscow.] Blog "Vihavainen". 10 March 2015. http://timo-vihavainen.blogspot.fi/2015/03/talvisotaseminaari-moskovassa.html (12 March 2015).

Volkan, Vamik. *Bloodlines: From Ethnic Pride to Ethnic Terrorism.* Boulder, CO: Westview, 1997.

Walker, Margaret Urban. *Moral Repair: Reconstructing Moral Relations after Wrongdoing.* New York: Cambridge University Press, 2006.

Wenzel, Michael, and Tyler G. Okimoto. "How Acts of Forgiveness Restore a Sense of Justice: Addressing Status/Power and Value Concerns Raised by Transgressions." *European Journal of Social Psychology* 40 (2010): 401–417.

Wertsch, James V. *Voices of Collective Remembering.* Cambridge: Cambridge University Press, 2002.

Worthington, Everett. "The Pyramid Model of Forgiveness: Some Interdisciplinary Speculations about Unforgiveness and Promoting Forgiveness." *Dimensions of Forgiveness: Psychological Research and Theological Forgiveness.* Ed. Everett Worthington. Philadelphia, PA: Templeton Foundation Press, 1998. 107–138.

Yamazaki, Jane. *Japanese Apologies for World War II: A Rhetorical Study.* Abingdon: Routledge, 2006.

"Путин встревожен и расстроен." *Russki Reporter.* 31 January 2011. http://rusrep.ru/article/2011/01/31/putin_fin/ (15 March 2012).

Davide Denti
Sorry for Srebrenica? Public Apologies and Genocide in the Western Balkans

The killing of more than 8,000 Bosniak (Bosnian Muslim) men and boys in Srebrenica in July 1995,[1] perpetrated by the Army of the self-proclaimed Republika Srpska (VRS) under the command of Ratko Mladić, represents until now the only internationally and judicially acknowledged act of genocide in Europe since the end of the Second World War.[2]

The process of seeking recognition and justice for the genocide proved to be long and perilous. The war in Bosnia and Herzegovina (BiH)[3] ended without a clear military victory by one side, a situation aptly described by Mary Kaldor's model of *new wars*.[4] The 1995 Dayton Peace Agreements entrenched a consociational agreement between Republika Srpska and the Federation of Bosnia and Herzegovina (FBiH), which would be capped by a thin layer of common institutions, reconstituting the state of Bosnia and Herzegovina. On the international level, Bosnia later filed a case of genocide against Serbia and Montenegro at the International Court of Justice (ICJ),[5] while individual trials for war crimes

---

[1] The preliminary List of Missing Persons from Srebrenica includes 8,373 names. Potočari Memorial Center website, http://www.potocarimc.ba/_ba/liste/nestali_z.php#z1 (21 February 2015).
[2] In 2004, in the *Prosecutor v. Krstić* case, the Appeals Chamber of the International Criminal Tribunal for the former Yugoslavia (ICTY) found unanimously that the massacre in Srebrenica constituted genocide as defined as a crime under international law. Radovan Karadžić and Ratko Mladić are still indicted on charges of genocide and other war crimes for the war events in Prijedor, Kljuc, Foča, Zvornik and other Bosnian municipalities. ICTY. *Prosecutor v. Radislav Krstić – Sentencing Judgement.* 19 April 2004. http://www.icty.org/x/cases/krstic/acjug/en/krs-aj040419e.pdf (21 February 2015).
[3] Hereafter Bosnia.
[4] The war in Bosnia is a paradigmatic example of "new war", a category blurring the border between civil and international-conventional wars. Mary Kaldor. *New and Old Wars: Organized Violence in a Global Era.* Oxford: Polity Press, 1999.
[5] In the 2007 *Bosnian Genocide* case, the ICJ reached the conclusion that genocide had taken place, while clearing Serbia and Montenegro of direct responsibility. It found that Belgrade was in violation of international law and the 1948 Genocide Convention by having failed to prevent the 1995 Srebrenica genocide, and by having failed to prosecute those responsible or transfer them to the ICTY. ICJ. "Application of the Convention on the Prevention and Punishment of the Crime of Genocide (Bosnia and Herzegovina v. Serbia and Montenegro)." *Press Release* 8, 2007. http://www.icj-cij.org/presscom/index.php?pr=1897 &pt=1&p1=6&p2=1 (21 February 2015).

and crimes against humanity for wartime events were dealt with by the International Criminal Tribunal for the former Yugoslavia (ICTY) and by domestic Bosnian courts, entrusted with retributive justice issues.[6]

The recent conflict left a vast legacy of dynamic memories in the region, eventually waiting to be exploited for popular mobilisation by political entrepreneurs through historicising strategies. The presence of memories of conflict raises the cost of apologising for domestic actors who may fear the risk of political backlash. At the same time, since the year 2000, the countries of the region have shared the same long-term goal of EU accession, thus creating a context in which apologies may prove beneficial. They may depoliticise foreign policy issues, allow positive responses to foreign solicitation, and reduce the conflict potential of reactive memories by creating a new discourse and a new consensus about history.

The presence of these two factors pushed the domestic actors to a strategy of apologies marked by incompleteness and ambiguity, aimed at reaping the benefits of reconciliation while keeping the potential costs of a domestic political backlash at bay. In the case of Srebrenica, this is apparent in the forms and the words of the apologies offered by the actors in the conflict. These include the 2004 declaration of the Government of Republika Srpska on Srebrenica, the 2010 resolution of the Serbian Parliamentary Assembly on Srebrenica, and the 2013 apology of the Serbian president Tomislav Nikolić.

The next section of this chapter focuses on public apologies as a tool of restorative justice. Theories of justice and responsibility may help highlight the role of apologies in fostering reconciliation, and also their possible limitations. I then introduce a rational choice model of public apologies, based on the costs and benefits of reparatory decisions, in order to explain the presence of ambiguities when both the high costs and high benefits of apologising are present. I take into account the presence of two main features in the Western Balkan region concerning apologies and reconciliation: the legacies of conflict in collective memories, and the common foreign policy goal of EU accession. These two factors together make actors more likely to resort to apologies, but also to adopt strategies of am-

---

[6] Five indictees of the ICTY (Krstić, Beara, Popović, Nikolić, Tolimir), all former VRS officers, have been found guilty of genocide (among other charges) and received either 35 years or life sentences. Slobodan Milošević, accused of genocide or complicity in it, died before the verdict. Radovan Karadžić and Ratko Mladić are currently facing trial for genocide and complicity in genocide in several municipalities within Bosnia and Herzegovina, including Srebrenica. Domestic Bosnian courts have sentenced 12 indictees for charges of genocide concerning Srebrenica, as have German courts in three cases. Further prosecutions are ongoing in Bosnia, Austria and Serbia.

biguity to reduce the political risks associated. Apologies are considered as both a signal of and a catalyst for the reconciliation process. The third section traces the process of apologising for the Srebrenica genocide in the framework of the cycle of public apologies carried out among Western Balkan countries in the last decade, highlighting their features and motivations and testing the theoretical model applied. The conclusions sum up the main arguments of the chapter about the particular features of the Western Balkans, which increase both the costs and benefits of apologising, and produce the observed pattern of ambiguous apologies.

Apologies, restorative justice, and Europeanisation: a theoretical framework

Apologies as a tool of restorative justice

When dealing with past injustices, tools are available from both retributive and restorative justice. As opposed to retributive justice, aimed at establishing individual responsibilities and punishments for criminal acts, restorative (or reparative) justice focuses on the needs of the victims, as right-holders, and of the offenders, as duty-bearers, in order to achieve the satisfaction of the former, and the reintegration of the latter. Victims are considered entitled to redress and to address the causes and consequences of violations in both material and symbolic ways,[7] while offenders are encouraged to take responsibility for their actions, by offering reparation, apologising, and committing to the avoidance of future offences.

First, material reparations include concrete, appropriate and proportionate forms of compensation, resulting in a final settlement through a specific agreement between victims and perpetrators. The main risk in material reparations is failing to address the emotional damage done to the victims by the wrongdoings, thus simply "buying them off".[8] Second, symbolic reparations are policies attempting to restore to victims their sense of dignity and human worth. A particular kind of symbolic reparation is apologies, intended as a speech act performed by an appropriate person with appropriate words on an appropriate

---

[7] Shannon Jones. "Apology Diplomacy: Justice for All?" *Clingendael Discussion Papers in Diplomacy* 122 (2011): 3. http://www.clingendael.nl/publications/2011/20110900_cdsp_ discussionpapersindiplomacy_122_jones.pdf (21 February 2015).
[8] Jones. "Apology Diplomacy: Justice for All?", 4.

occasion.⁹ The reasons for which victims demand apologies include the need for a public admission of the transgression, a guarantee on future conduct, and compensation to ease the victims' reintegration in the society.¹⁰ Correspondingly, the offender's benefits include a restorative effect, as apologies may lead to forgiveness.¹¹

Apologies are, linguistically, "performative utterances", as "stating the words 'I apologise' in itself accomplishes the apology".¹² The value of an apology is therefore less in its sincerity, and more in its effectiveness in creating emotional satisfaction and closure. In fact, apologies do not only involve words, but also a series of ritualistic features including the location, speaker, audience and coverage.¹³ They can thus be usefully understood as rituals with strong performative power: as symbolic gestures, their meaning resides in the official realm rather than in "truth" or "sincerity". As argued by Horelt, "social performances are 'intrinsically effective'", as the ritual "speaks for itself".¹⁴ The lack of a requirement of sincerity is particularly important when dealing with public apologies, as it is very difficult to establish the requirements for sincerity. In fact, public apologies are mediated both institutionally, being uttered by public officials speaking on behalf of a group rather than for themselves, and mediatically, being conveyed to their addressees through means of mass communication rather than personally.

Scholars have analyzed the best and worst practices of apologies. Among the former, Matt James underlines that an *authentic apology* should be recorded in writing, clearly naming the wrongs, accepting responsibility, stating regret, promising non-repetition, not demanding forgiveness, not being hypocritical or arbitrary, and morally engaging the responsible ones through publicity, cere-

---

9 The original definition of an apology as a speech act is by J. Austin. *How to Do Things with Words*. Oxford: Clarendon Press, 1962. Quoted in Joanna Thompson. "Apology, Justice, and Respect: A Critical Defense of Political Apology". *The Age of Apology: Facing Up to the Past*. Eds. Mark Gibney et al. Philadelphia: University of Pennsylvania Press, 2008, 32.
10 Jullyette Ukabiala. "Slave Trade 'a crime against humanity'." *Africa Recovery* 15.3 (2001): 5.
11 Lee Taft. "Apology Subverted: the Commodification of Apology." *Yale Law Journal* 109.5 (2000): 1138.
12 Richard B. Bilder. "The Role of Apology in International Law and Diplomacy." *Virginia Journal of International Law* 46.3 (2006): 437.
13 Michel-André Horelt. *Rituals of Reconciliation. A Performance Based Approach to the Analysis of Political Apologies for Historic Crimes*. Munich: Ludwig-Maximilians-Universität, 2010. http://www.irmgard-coninx-stiftung.de/fileadmin/user_upload/pdf/MemoryPolitics/Work shop3/ HoreltEssay.pdf (21 February 2015).
14 Horelt. *Rituals of Reconciliation*, 5.

mony or reparations.[15] On the other hand, Aaron Lazare points to the symptoms of *pseudo-apologies:* vague or incomplete acknowledgements, the use of the passive voice, conditionality, questioning the damage which occurred, minimising the offence, expressing empathy without taking responsibility, apologising to the wrong party, and apologising for the wrong offence.[16] According to Dinah Shelton an apology, in order to be 'genuine', 'authentic', 'effective', should express the acceptance of responsibility without excuses, express sincere remorse or regret, and offer reparations as a future commitment. If not, it could be just a ritualised form of 'politeness discourse', or an expression of sorrow, compassion, or regret for events which are not deemed to be the speaker's responsibility.[17]

Apologies are usually entrusted only a secondary role in restorative justice, as material compensations enjoy primacy.[18] Apologies are sometimes dismissed as "cheap reconciliation", unable to change actual power relations.[19] If material compensations are not provided, victims might be asked "to become reconciled to loss",[20] thus enshrining injustice through a rights-based "politics of distraction". In fact, although restitution is a necessary element, apologies are also vital to reconciliation, since remembrance is linked to group and individual identity. Injustice always involves disrespect [21] while "apology is intrinsically an act of respect", [22] potentially able to restore the human worth and dignity of victims.

---

[15] Matt James. "Wrestling with the past: Apologies, Quasi-Apologies and Non-Apologies in Canada." *The Age of Apology: Facing up the Past.* Eds. Mark Gibney et al. Philadelphia: University of Pennsylvania Press, 2008, 137–153.
[16] Aaron Lazare. *On Apology.* Oxford: Oxford University Press, 2004, 8–9.
[17] Nicholas Tavuchis. *Mea culpa: A Sociology of Apology and Reconciliation.* Stanford: Stanford University Press, 1991, 16.
[18] See for instance the UN International Law Commission's Draft Articles on Responsibility of States for Internationally Wrongful Acts, adopted in 2001. UN Doc A/56/589 (2001).
[19] State-driven strategies of reconciliation usually de-emphasise restitution, and emphasise repair forms conducive to state-building. As Gibney and Roxstrom argue, "forgiveness often perpetuates the power imbalances that led to past violence, especially when the process is state-dominated". Mark Gibney and Erik Roxstrom. "The Status of State Apologies." *Human Rights Quarterly* 23 (2001): 935.
[20] Andrew Rigby. *Justice and Reconciliation: After the Violence.* Boulder: Lynne Rienner, 2001, 142.
[21] Bernard Boxill. "Morality of Reparation." *Social Theory and Practice* 2 (1972): 118.
[22] Trudy Govier and Wilhelm Verwoerd. "The practice of public apology: a qualified defense." *Saskatchewan Law Review* 65 (2002): 157.

Public apologies and their limitations

In the definition put forward by Thompson, a political or public apology is "a public act, carried out by the appropriate official, that acknowledges and takes responsibility for an injustice committed (or allowed) by officers of the state and commits governments to avoiding such injustices in the future".[23]

Bilder identifies several reasons for states to offer public apologies: (a) to follow the belief that apologising is the right thing to do; (b) to preserve or restore the image and reputation for decency and respect for legal and moral norms, a strong asset in international society; (c) to signal a change in position on the legality and appropriateness of a conduct, in the hope that apologising will help to establish or reinforce the desired international norms and customs; (d) to preserve the other party's honour and avoid risking escalations (thus including political calculation and expediency); (e) to escape retribution or retaliation by de-escalating the conflict; (f) to comply with external requests, e.g. ICJ sentences, without the need for any authenticity, or even under full external coercion in an act of purposeful humiliation, a possible source for further resentment; (g) to perform a public relations gesture towards a third party, directed at a domestic or international audience other than the state or people wronged, and designed to win public approval. [24]

Similar reasons exist for not giving collective apologies: (a) to avoid acknowledgement of the wrongs; (b) to avoid future liability, as apologies may be construed as an admission of responsibility; (c) to avoid creating a precedent; (d) to avoid weakening supported norms; (e) to save domestic honour, fearing domestic political costs; (f) to respond to a lack of incentives: e.g. in case of asymmetries of power, lack of possible retaliation, or no interest in maintaining good relations.[25] As such, apologies work as a signal: the apologiser is giving the victim an entitlement to trust that such things are true. [26]

Apologies may constitute the symbolic act able to break a cycle of violence involving two nations. But, to be successful, "the stage must be set by a process of negotiation and reconciliation".[27] Reconciliation has been defined, by Hayner, as "rebuilding relationships today that are not haunted by the conflicts and ha-

---

23 Thompson. "Apology, Justice, and Respect: A Critical Defense of Political Apology", 36.
24 Bilder. "The Role of Apology in International Law and Diplomacy", 464.
25 Ibid, 464.
26 Thompson. "Apology, Justice, and Respect: A Critical Defense of Political Apology", 32.
27 Ibid, 43.

treds of yesterday". [28] As in any response to a 'large scale evil', apologies entail unavoidable tensions and lack of tidiness with which those involved must come to terms. They include a trade-off between justice for victims and national healing.[29]

Starting from several empirical cases, scholars such as Thompson have drafted an ideal type of a successful political apology. This requires, firstly, memorability. An apology is an event that is supposed to constitute a watershed in the history of inter-community relations; it thus needs thorough preparation, adequate ceremony, and consequent actions. Secondly, the participation of both victims and wrongdoers (or their representatives) is necessary in order to reach a common understanding of the injustice by building a common narrative of the past, endorsing the content and context of the apology, and negotiating on subsequent acts of reparation. Thirdly, a clear commitment is needed, binding for future governments and citizens, to avoid a repetition of such injustices. This may be done by offering financial compensation or by embedding the new narrative in the official history of the nation through textbook revisions, plaques and monuments, exhibitions and commemoration days. A consensual parliamentary vote and the deliverance by an official above party politics, usually the head of state, may also help depoliticise the issue. Although this ideal-type may be very restrictive, even incomplete apologies may have positive effects, as "a general practice of apologies encourages nations to be aware of the harm they can do to outsiders". [30]

Nevertheless, political apologies also face important limitations. Firstly, how can polities take responsibility for wrongs committed by their predecessors? It is a challenge to understand and justify how contemporary actors may be able to apologise for historical abuses, as the historical gap blurs the responsibility link. [31] The issue may be solved when considering that structured groups, such as states, have decision-making processes and can act as agents.[32] As argued by Thompson, a state as a structured organisation is "an agent in its own rights,

---

[28] Priscilla Hayner. *Unspeakable Truths: Confronting State Terror and Atrocity.* New York: Routledge, 2001, 161.
[29] Jeff Corntassel and Cindy Holder. "Who's Sorry Now? Government Apologies, Truth Commissions, and Indigenous Self-Determination in Australia, Canada, Guatemala and Peru." *Human Rights Review* (2008): 4.
http://www.corntassel.net/CorntasselHolder.pdf (21 February 2015).
[30] Thompson. "Apology, Justice, and Respect: A Critical Defense of Political Apology", 43.
[31] Melissa Nobles. *The Politics of Official Apologies.* Cambridge: Cambridge University Press, 2008.
[32] Trudy Govier. *Forgiveness and Revenge.* London: Routledge, 2002. Ch. 5.

whose existence transcends the lives of the individuals who make it up", and should therefore take responsibility for its past deeds.[33] Apologies are deemed valid when there is an institution with a historical continuity, be it a church, a party, or a state.[34] Nevertheless, several other problems remain. On the one hand, according to standard theories of responsibility, the participation in committing an injustice is necessary for liability. Therefore it remains unexplained how distant-past wrongdoings may give current members of a polity the entitlement to apologise. Given that no individual consent is required in state membership, as opposed to private organisations, citizens have no moral duty to accept responsibility. On the other hand, always according to standard theories of responsibility, one needs to be a victim of injustice to be entitled to receive reparation. It remains unexplained how successors of victims may be entitled to forgive for the original crime and not only for the consequences that still directly affect them. [35]

Secondly, how can a state be remorseful or contrite? For Govier, groups have collective emotions: as they can forgive, they may also be able to apologise.[36] Nevertheless, the presence of collective remorse is contested in several cases of political apologies, where the expediency is apparent. The distance between interpersonal and institutional apologies blurs the relevance of the moral component of apology. In fact, the mediation of apologies by the public sphere and the media renders them problematic in terms of sincerity and authenticity. Apologies may be given in reaction to requests rather than voluntarily; public mediation may impede the genuine expression of emotion; and apologies may be finally driven more by interests and 'face-saving' strategies.[37] To answer to these issues, Tavuchis underlines that the authentic communication of sorrow may be merely perfunctory in many-to-many apologies, if not simply ruled out by the necessity of delegation.[38] The main function of collective apologies is therefore not sorrow as sincerity, but putting things on a public record, through a "public endorsement of the rules of conduct".[39] According to Digeser, intending

---

[33] Thompson. "Apology, Justice, and Respect: A Critical Defense of Political Apology", 37.
[34] Max Clark and Gary Allen Fine. "'A' for Apology: Slavery and the Discourse of Remonstrance in Two American Universities." *History and Memory* 22.1 (2010): 82–83.
[35] Thompson. "Apology, Justice, and Respect: A Critical Defense of Political Apology", 36–37.
[36] Govier, quoted in Thompson. "Apology, Justice, and Respect: A Critical Defense of Political Apology", 35.
[37] Jones."Apology Diplomacy: Justice for All?"
[38] Tavuchis. *Mea culpa: A Sociology of Apology and Reconciliation.*
[39] Bilder. "The Role of Apology in International Law and Diplomacy", 461–463.

apologies as a public act allows us to rule out the need for remorse.[40] The only remaining requirements for a genuine apology are taking responsibility for the past and offering a commitment for the future, conditions fulfilled by a transgenerational polity. For Thompson, "as an appropriate moral motivation, [it] may be enough that citizens recognise the moral importance to fulfil transgenerational obligations." [41]

Finally, how can states commit to avoid wrongdoings in the future? The issue has been underlined especially by realist scholarship, pointing to how states behave in their own interest and are not moral persons in the sense of acting consistently and responsibly over time. Nevertheless, it has to be recognised that states can and do take long-term commitments, a phenomenon that may again be explained through the lens of the 'transgenerational polity'. Through official acts of government (laws and treaties), their members pass on responsibilities and entitlements through generations for the sake of promoting political stability and individual security. [42]

A rational-choice analysis of reparation decisions

Different theories of International Relations (IR) allow one to make sense of the motivations of states for offering public apologies. According to a rational-choice approach to IR, apologising allows states to send signals about their intentions in the international anarchy, in order to reduce uncertainty and increase their material security. This rational-choice approach may be coupled with a constructivist approach, according to which states also look for ontological security, defined as "the desire to have a consistent sense of self and knowledge of [their] place in the world".[43]

Apologising may thus be understood as the result of a cost-benefit analysis. On the one hand, benefits include the re-establishment of diplomatic relations and the end of barriers to cooperation, thus enhancing material security, together with an accrued ontological security given by maintaining or projecting a certain image of self in the international community. On the other hand, the costs include both the monetary value of compensations and the political risk in terms of potential domestic reaction by a hostile audience, up to the level of threaten-

---

40 Peter E. Digeser. *Political Forgiveness*. Ithaca: Cornell University Press, 2001, 4.
41 Thompson. "Apology, Justice, and Respect: A Critical Defense of Political Apology", 40.
42 Ibid, 38–40.
43 Jones. "Apology Diplomacy: Justice for All?", 12.

ing politicians' own careers.[44] To solve this conundrum, several policies may be followed. A first one limits reparation to the symbolic side, excluding the possibility of financial compensation to reduce material costs. A second one foresees the use of a strategy of ambiguity to reduce the domestic political risks; this includes for instance the expression of empathy or regret without taking full responsibility for the facts.[45] On the basis of such factors it is possible to draw a typology of reparatory decisions, following Jones:[46]

	Low Costs	High Costs
Low Benefits	Only symbolic reparations	No reparations
High Benefits	Symbolic and material reparations	Ambiguous symbolic reparations

This chapter follows the static analysis approach provided for above. Nevertheless, the limitations of the approach should also be taken into consideration. In fact, reparation decisions are not static, as perpetrators happen to change their minds over time. This could be the consequence of either a change in foreign or domestic policy interests or a change in the normative environment. A normative change may be relevant in allowing for the vocalisation of victims' demands, and in reducing the domestic political costs. On the one hand, it may open up spaces for the vocalisation of demands by previously disempowered victims, for instance by women and minorities after the diffusion of norms of gender equality and minority protection. In this regard, the action of third states, international organisations and NGOs becomes relevant in putting forward the victims' demands and pressuring the perpetrators on reparative actions through bottom-up 'name and shame' actions, recommendations, sanctions, and legal actions. On the other hand, a normative change may help to reduce domestic political costs through the shift in public opinion caused by the internalisation of norms, thus lowering the likelihood of having to face strong domestic opposition. As argued by Nobles, reparations follow an ideological change in political elites through a top-down effect.[47]

The role of public apologies is still under-researched in Europeanisation theory. Magen and Morlino recall, among the four main gaps in knowledge

---
[44] Jennifer Lind. *Sorry States: Apologies in International Politics.* Ithaca: Cornell University Press, 2008.
[45] See above the symptoms of "pseudo-apologies" described by Lazare for further examples of ambiguities in apologies.
[46] Jones. "Apology Diplomacy: Justice for All?", 16.
[47] Nobles. *The Politics of Official Apologies.*

about the EU expansion-democratisation nexus, the lack of a literature focusing on external-internal linkages of democratisation, as well as on the interaction between external actors and domestic change processes. Apologies, as an inter- and trans-national phenomenon, fit in this research agenda.[48] The process of pre-accession adaptation is described as a major process of 'external governance'. Schimmelfennig and Sedelmeier outline three models of EU external governance and rules transfer, respectively based on external incentives or bargaining by rewarding, independent domestic lesson-drawing, and socialisation and learning. As the external incentives model maintains its main explanatory value for rule transfer in pre-accession countries, its main factors of compliance are the credibility of conditionality and the domestic cost of rule adoption. Rule transfer is found to be dependent on the context of conditionality (democratic versus *acquis* conditionality) and on country-specific conditions that influence the domestic costs.[49] The presence of recent historic legacies of conflict has been listed among the specific conditions that provide additional strategies for veto players and raise the costs of compliance, in particular for the current enlargement countries in the Western Balkans. In order to reach compliance in post-conflict situations, therefore, additional factors have to be present to redress the balance: an *endgame* situation with short-term, certain and relevant prospects of reward and sanction; non-prohibitive costs for the incumbent governments; and adequate levels of identification between the target government and society and the EU.[50]

There are two main factors which are peculiar to the Western Balkans and to their cycle of public apologies: the presence of legacies of the recent conflicts within collective memories, and their convergent foreign policy goal of achieving EU membership.

Firstly, it should be remembered that the states of the region are no older than 20–25 years: they came into being through the process of conflictual disaggregation of Yugoslavia – or, in the case of Albania, through the state anarchy of 1997–1998.[51] The conflicts of the recent past have left an important legacy in

---

[48] Amichai Magen and Leonardo Morlino. Eds. *International Actors, Democratization and the Rule of Law. Anchoring Democracy?* New York: Routledge, 2008, 11–12.
[49] Frank Schimmelfennig and Ulrich Sedelmeier. "Governance by conditionality: EU rule transfer to the candidate countries of Central and Eastern Europe." *Journal of European Public Policy* 11.4 (Aug 2004): 661–679.
[50] Frank Schimmelfennig. "EU political accession conditionality after the 2004 enlargement: consistency and effectiveness." *Journal of European Public Policy* 15.6 (Sept 2008): 918–937.
[51] Dorian Jano. "From 'Balkanization' to 'Europeanization': The Stages of Western Balkans Complex Transformations." *L'Europe en Formation* 349–350 (2008): 55–68.

collective memories. In their study, Georges Mink and Pascal Bonnard refer to the presence of 'seams' or 'veins' (*gisements*) of 'reactive memory',[52] stemming from legacies of conflicts within the collective memories of public opinions. These seams have the potential to be instrumentalised by political entrepreneurs to achieve legitimacy and popular mobilisation through historicising strategies. Incumbent governments thus face higher costs of compliance, and will be wary of apologising, wishing to avoid the risk of domestic political fallout.[53] The memories of recent conflicts are a factor raising the costs of public apologies. A first function of public apologies is thus also to signal progress in the reconciliation process, fuelled by civil society and external actors.[54] An apology becomes a viable political option only when its costs are non-prohibitive, i.e. "no serious political or legal repercussion"[55] should be expected. The presence of public apologies means that the risks associated were low enough for incumbent politicians to resort to it without fearing an existential threat to their own political careers.

Secondly, the Western Balkan countries are all candidate, or potential candidate, countries for EU accession, at least since 2003. The presence of a common foreign policy aim for these countries, together with EU conditionality on regional cooperation, has led their elites to develop a convergent foreign policy agenda. Their common goal is to ensure compliance with the *acquis* and with pre-accession conditions, and at the same time to depoliticise foreign policy in order to be able to respond positively to external demands without suffering domestic backlash. Their common foreign policy goal of EU accession is a factor raising the benefits of apologising. Moreover, apologies have the dynamic effect of reducing the conflict potential of reactive memories by fostering a consensus about the past and depoliticising collective memories, thus making it less easy for political entrepreneurs to exploit the legitimacy effect of historicising strategies. A second function of political apologies is thus to act as a catalyst for further change and reconciliation, by further reducing the domestic political costs

---

52 Georges Mink and Pascal Bonnard. *Le passé au Présent. Gisements Mémoriels et Actions Publiques en Europe Centrale et Orientale.* Paris: Michel Houdiard, 2010, 29.
53 Lind. *Sorry States: Apologies in International Politics.*
54 Reconciliation and regional cooperation have been buzzwords in the discourse of international actors in the Western Balkans since the Dayton Peace Agreements. The creation of regional fora, such as the Stability Pact for South East Europe (today's Regional Cooperation Council) helped diffuse and implement the concept, reaching the agenda of national governments. International conditionality on regional cooperation may be considered one of the factors fostering reconciliation up to the level when apologies became feasible political options.
55 Thompson. "Apology, Justice, and Respect: A Critical Defense of Political Apology", 31.

faced by governments in addressing foreign policy issues and enacting EU-fostered reforms.

In the Western Balkans, the presence of legacies of conflict raises the costs of apologising, while the countries' common foreign policy goal of EU accession raises its benefits. In Jones' typology of reparation decisions, the region thus falls into the case featuring both high costs and high benefits of reparations. As a result, it should be expected that the reconciliation process be punctuated by ambiguous apologies and symbolic reparations, in addition to the retributive justice delivered by the ICTY. Such a strategy of offering incomplete and partial restorative justice is rational because it allows countries to reap the benefits of reconciliation while permitting politicians to keep at bay the risk of domestic backlash. The next section, reviewing the process of apologising for Srebrenica and pointing to the role of external incentives and potential domestic backlashes in fostering a strategy of ambiguity, validates the theoretical framework introduced above.

Apologies for Srebrenica: a story in three acts

Three main apologies for Srebrenica have been uttered so far: the 2004 declaration of the Government of Republika Srpska, the 2010 resolution of the Serbian Parliamentary Assembly, and the 2013 apology by the President of Serbia, Tomislav Nikolić.

The three episodes, which are the main focus of this chapter, are not isolated; they find their place within the bigger picture of the cycle of public apologies that unfolded in the Western Balkans in general among former war enemies since the year 2000 and peaked in 2010. Starting with the atonement of Milo Đukanović for the role of Montenegrin soldiers in the siege of Dubrovnik, it continued with the exchanges between the new democratic leaders of Serbia and Croatia between 2003 and 2007, particularly after the election of Boris Tadić. Apologies in this first round remained partial and ambiguous in their acknowledgement of responsibilities, thus not achieving an effect of sincerity. Finally, in 2010, a new round of apologies was started by the new Croatian president Ivo Josipović and sustained by the need for Serbia to comply with EU expectations; the apologies of 2010 were deeper and more comprehensive, but also fostered stronger reactions and domestic opposition.

The 2004 declaration on Srebrenica of the government of Republika Srpska

The first apology for Srebrenica was uttered in 2004 by the government of Republika Srpska (RS), one of the two entities of Bosnia and Herzegovina. In the panorama of public apologies among Western Balkan states, it followed the early atonement of Milo Đukanović in the year 2000 for the siege of Dubrovnik, and the exchange in 2003 between Svetozar Marović, then president of the State Union of Serbia and Montenegro, and the president of Croatia Stipe Mesić. [56]

The apology by the RS government constitutes a *unicum* in the gamut of public apologies in the Western Balkans up to that moment. Firstly, it was the first time that regret was expressed not as a personal initiative of a head of state, usually a second-tier political figure as in the cases of Đukanović and Marović, but as an act of the governing executive body of the Serb-majority entity of Bosnia and Herzegovina. Secondly, it was also the first time that an act of apology touched upon the matter of the war in Bosnia, with its complications as a *new war*, in Kaldor's terms, with its blurring of the internal/international dimension.[57] Finally, it was the first time that an apology was extended over a matter, the Srebrenica massacre or genocide, which until that time had been the object of official attempts at revisionism or outright denial.[58]

In 2003, the international High Representative Paddy Ashdown fostered the setup by the government of Banja Luka of a Commission for Investigation of the Events in Srebrenica, to "establish the full truth on the events in and around Sre-

---

[56] For a more comprehensive analysis of public apologies among Western Balkan countries: Davide Denti. "Public Apologies in the Western Balkans: the Shadow of Ambiguity." *Public Apology Between Ritual and Regret. Symbolic Excuses on False Pretenses or True Reconciliation out of Sincere Regret?* Eds. Daniel Cuypers et al. Amsterdam: Rodopi, 2013, 61–91.

[57] The 2004 declaration of the RS government might seem a purely internal issue between one sub-state executive and one minority population living on its territory. In fact, the war-time links between Belgrade and the Bosnian Serb paramilitaries (as recognised by the ICTY and ICJ), as well as between the Srebrenica residents and the government of Sarajevo, allow us to consider it together with the other international apologies expressed in relation to war-time deeds in the region.

[58] Only two years before, in 2002, a controversy had followed the publication of the "Report about Case Srebrenica (first part)", authored by Darko Trifunović on behalf of the Republika Srpska Government Bureau for Relations with the ICTY. The report, denying the massacre and accusing the Red Cross of fabrication of the findings, was subsequently disowned by the Banja Luka authorities, and defined by the ICTY in the *Deronjić* sentence as "one of the worst examples of revisionism". International Criminal Tribunal for the former Yugoslavia (ICTY). *Prosecutor v. Miroslav Deronjić – Sentencing Judgement*. 30 March 2004, 69. http://www.icty.org/x/cases/deronjic/tjug/en/sj-040330e.pdf (21 February 2015).

brenica between 10th and 19th July 1995, aiming to establish lasting peace and build confidence in Bosnia and Herzegovina".[59] In its final report, released in October 2004, the Commission published a list of 8,371 names of missing or killed persons. The report also represented the first time that an official RS institution acknowledged that the massacre had taken place on such a scale, and that Serb militaries and paramilitaries were among its perpetrators.[60] The Srebrenica Commission report did not remain without consequences. Even before the text of the report was made public, the president of RS, Dragan Čavić, admitted on television that Srebrenica constituted a dark chapter of Serb history, and that the "massacre" of thousands of civilians by Serb paramilitaries effectively violated international law.[61] Soon afterwards, the RS government released an official apology on its website, stating that:

> The report clearly shows that enormous crimes were committed in the region of Srebrenica in July 1995.[62] [...] The Bosnian Serb Government shares the pain of the families of the Srebrenica victims, is truly sorry and apologises for the tragedy.[63]

The "objective scientific evidence" stemming from the report,[64] together with the need for RS not to see its international legitimacy obliterated as a polity built on genocide, may have been instrumental in convincing the government of Banja Luka to extend its apologies. The 2004 apology, as the previous ones in the region, remains a partial one, by not employing the term *genocide* and by not accepting full responsibility for the events. In the form that the RS government used, it looked more like a "regretful acknowledgement"[65] than a full apology. On the other hand, its importance can hardly be overstated: for the first time, a

---

[59] Government of Republika Srpska. *The Events in and around Srebrenica between 10th and 19th July 1995.* Banja Luka, 11 June 2004; Government of Republika Srpska. *Addendum to the Report of the 11th June 2004 on the Events in and around Srebrenica between 10th and 19th July 1995.* Banja Luka, 15 October 2004.

[60] Associated Press. "Bosnian Serbs Issue Apology for Massacre". *Bosnia Report* New Series No. 42. 11 November 2004. http://www.bosnia.org.uk/bosrep/report_format.cfm?articleid=1147&reportid=166 (21 February 2015).

[61] Tanja Topić. "Otvaranje najmračnije stranice." *Vreme* 1 July 2004. http://www.vreme.com/cms/ view.php?id=384060 (21 February 2015).

[62] Suad Smajić. "O jeziku mržnje i dvostrukog smisla." *Slobodna misao* 4 (2005): 46.

[63] Associated Press. "Bosnian Serbs Issue Apology for Massacre"

[64] Sheri Fink. "Serbs' Overdue Apology Delivers Hope for Humanity." *Detroit Free Press* 22 December 2004. http://warhospital.net/serbs.htm (21 February 2015)

[65] Lisa S. Villadsen. "The Regretful Acknowledgment: a Dignified End to a Disgraceful Story?" *Public Apology Between Ritual and Regret. Symbolic Excuses on False Pretenses or True Reconciliation out of Sincere Regret?* Eds. Daniel Cuypers et al. Amsterdam: Rodopi, 2013, 229–248.

Bosnian Serb official institution recognised the scale of the massacre and the Serb involvement, extending apologies for it.[66]

The 2010 resolution on Srebrenica by the Serbian Parliamentary Assembly

The following years, between 2004 and 2007, saw a revival of public apologies between Serbia, Croatia and Bosnia, following the election of Boris Tadić as head of state in Serbia. Tadić apologised three times, in 2004, 2006,[67] and 2007,[68] repeatedly declaring: "I apologise to all those who suffered from crimes committed in the name of the Serb people".[69] Tadić's gesture bore strong relevance, since it was the first time that the primary political figure of Serbia apologised for war crimes. At the same time, Tadić's ambiguity strategy, to defuse raising too much controversy at home, included stressing the impossibility of making the whole Serbian people responsible for crimes of specific individuals who had to face prosecution in court, together with the need for all parties engaged in conflict to apologise to each other, since "the same crimes have been committed against the Serbs". This kind of utterance has been defined by Lind as a *non-apology apology*. The perception that it contained a moral equivalence among crimes hindered its reception in Bosnia as a true atonement for war crimes.

The next step came a few years later, in 2010, kick-starting a new cycle of political apologies on a higher qualitative level.[70] In December 2009, Serbia handed in its application for EU membership, and the authorities from Brussels

---

[66] As recalled by Fink, "this unified narrative is important, because conflicting historical memories are what ignite and drive many of the world's armed conflicts. In the Balkans, radically one-sided memories of World War II interethnic violence were used as justification to wage war and commit atrocities in the early 1990s."
[67] Humanitarian Law Center. "Predsednik Srbije Boris Tadić se prilikom prve posete BiH, 6. decembra 2006. godine u Sarajevu, izvinio u ime srpskog naroda." Zagreb, 6 December 2006. http://www.hlc-rdc.org/?p=13592 (21 February 2015).
[68] Humanitarian Law Center. *Transitional Justice in Post-Yugoslav Countries. 2007 Report.* Zagreb, 2007, 66–67. http://www.documenta.hr/dokumenti/trans_eng2007.pdf (21 February 2015).
[69] Lind. *Sorry States: Apologies in International Politics.*
[70] For an in-depth analysis of the 2010 apology of the Serbian Parliamentary Assembly, see Jasna Dragović-Soso. "Apologising for Srebrenica: The Declaration of the Serbian Parliament, the European Union and the Politics of Compromise." *East European Politics* 28.2 (2012): 163–179.

made it clear that, in order to be recognised as a candidate, Belgrade had to accept responsibility for war crimes and act consistently, ultimately resulting in the arrest and hand-over to the Hague tribunal of the last wartime fugitives.[71] For the Tadić administration, this was the opportunity to resume a long-standing societal and parliamentary debate, and bring it to a conclusion. In fact, a draft parliamentary declaration on Srebrenica had already been proposed in 2005 by a coalition of NGOs to counter the issue of genocide denial in Serbia itself. A counter-proposal put forward by Vojislav Koštunica's nationalist DSS party, though condemning the crime committed in Srebrenica, expressed revisionist attitudes towards established facts and figures, and aimed at diluting its relevance by referring to Serbs' victimhood narrative and the list of crimes against them since the Second World War. The debate subsided until the 2007 ICJ *Bosnian genocide* case, in which Serbia was cleared of direct responsibility but condemned for omission. Tadić tried to revive the project of the parliamentary declaration, but found no supportive majority. Finally, in 2009 the European Parliament (EP) itself passed a resolution on Srebrenica, demanding both full cooperation with the ICTY, and symbolic reparations, exerting a form of moral pressure on Belgrade. The same year, Serbia made a number of important steps towards European integration, including the entry into force of visa-free travel and of the interim agreement on trade attached to the Stabilisation and Association Agreement (SAA). In autumn, the Commission released a positive opinion in its annual Progress Report, and Serbia submitted its formal application for EU membership. At that moment, Tadić re-tabled for discussion the Parliamentary declaration on Srebrenica. His fragile coalition between Democrats and Socialists found support on the issue by the few Liberal Democrats, while the declaration was opposed by the splintered but still nationalist opposition of Radicals and Progressives, joined by diaspora Serbs.[72] The text of the declaration was not born out of a public-wide deliberation, but rather negotiated behind closed doors in order to secure enough support for the 31 March 2010 vote, thus representing fundamentally "an act of political compromise":[73]

> The National Assembly of the Republic of Serbia most severely condemns the crime committed against the Bosniak population in Srebrenica in July 1995 in the manner established

---

[71] Jones. "Apology Diplomacy: Justice for All?"
[72] Dragović-Soso. "Apologising for Srebrenica: The Declaration of the Serbian Parliament, the European Union and the Politics of Compromise", 167–170.
[73] Ibid, 172.

by the ruling of the International Court of Justice. [... It extends] condolences and apologies to the families of the victims since not everything was done to prevent the tragedy.[74]

The 2010 resolution of the Serbian Parliament differs from other cases of apologies by parliamentary acts in that it was not adopted consensually by the assembly. To the contrary, the resolution was the object of an intense political debate, and the majority was able to pass it only by a very narrow margin of two votes. The Radical Party, in opposition, denounced it as shameful, while victims' organisations did not feel satisfied and found it to be a case of "too little, too late".[75] Textually, the resolution does not explicitly refer to Srebrenica as genocide, but ambiguously condemns the crime in its definition by the ICJ – i.e. as genocide, though without explaining the ICJ's evaluation – thus with an implicit recognition but without having to resort to the still unpalatable G-word.[76] It thus constituted a difficult exercise in reaching an equilibrium between breaching the state of denial of many among the Serbian political elite and public opinion about the war crimes, and risking causing a counterproductive domestic political backlash. Nevertheless, in addition to its vagueness on the scale of the tragedy and on the identity of its perpetrators, the declaration does not refrain from attempting to relativise the crime by referring, in its fourth paragraph, to the expectation that other legislatures from the region will follow by condemning and apologising for the crimes committed against the Serbs.[77]

The assessment of the apology by the analysts was mixed. On the one hand, Marko Attila Hoare downplayed it as "mealy-mouthed" and as aiming "to pacify European public opinion", "calculated to say enough to be acceptable to the EU",[78] though "probably the most that its authors could have pushed through

---

[74] National Assembly of the Republic of Serbia. *Declaration of the National Assembly of the Republic of Serbia Condemning the Crime in Srebrenica*. 31 March 2010. http://www.parlament.gov.rs/upload/archive/files/eng/pdf/2010/deklaracija%20o%20sre brenici%20ENG.pdf (21 February 2015).

[75] Mirza Velagić. "Serbia's Insincere Apology."*Congress of North American Bosniaks* 24 April 2010. http://www.bosniak.org/serbias-insincere-apology/ (21 February 2015).

[76] Helsinki Committee to Defend Human Rights in Serbia. "Srebrenica Resolution Opens a Public Debate in Serbia." *Helsinki Bulletin* 58. February 2010. http://www.bosnia.org.uk/news/news_body.cfm?newsid=2693 (21 February 2015).

[77] Dragović-Soso. "Apologising for Srebrenica: The Declaration of the Serbian Parliament, the European Union and the Politics of Compromise", 172.

[78] Robert Marquand. "War Crimes: Is Serbia's Srebrenica Apology Genuine?" *Christian Science Monitor* 31 March 2010. http://www.csmonitor.com/World/Europe/2010/0331/War-crimes-Is-Serbia-s-Srebrenica-apolo gy-genuine (21 February 2015).

parliament".⁷⁹ On the other hand, Ivan Vejvoda noticed how a landmark resolution by the Serbian legislature might mark a turning point towards reconciliation, a sign that Serbian institutions are taking stock of the work of intellectuals in the previous decade.⁸⁰ According to Tim Judah, the resolution was remarkable as "it makes it still harder to insist that the massacre never happened or that the number of victims has been grossly inflated." Despite its limitations, and given the deep polarisation in the Serbian parliament and public opinion, according to Judah, it was "a lot better than nothing" and "that the resolution was proposed at all is an achievement".⁸¹ As highlighted by Dragović-Soso, the parliamentary declaration was more "an instrument of foreign policy", aimed at the EU audience in order to foster Serbia's bid, rather than part of a longer-term process of value transformation and coming to terms with the past, which still had to mature within Serbian society.⁸² When applying Jones' typology of apologies, it is evident how the parliamentary declaration fits the case of a situation with high stakes with regard to both the potential benefits and the potential costs of apologising, giving rise to a spurious apology, one limited to the symbolic side and marked by multiple ambiguities, but still endowed with positive effects.

The 2013 apology by the President of Serbia, Tomislav Nikolić

The resolution of the Serbian Parliament in 2010 was followed by a renewed cycle of apologies between Serbia and Croatia, fostered by the election as head of state in Zagreb of the Social Democrat Ivo Josipović who, in the words of Slavenka Drakulić, "in the first year of his presidency has visited more mass graves and apologized more than anybody else".⁸³ Josipović apologized in front of the Bosnian Parliament by saying: "I deeply regret that Croatia, with its policies in the 1990s, contributed to that [conflict]".⁸⁴ He then visited

---

79 Marko Attila Hoare. "How to Apologise". *The Henry Jackson Society* 30 May 2010. http://greatersurbiton.wordpress.com/2010/05/31/how-to-apologise/ (21 February 2015).
80 Marquand. "War Crimes: Is Serbia's Srebrenica Apology Genuine?"
81 Tim Judah. "Serbia's Honest Apology." *The New York Times* 1 April 2010. http://www.nytimes.com/2010/04/02/opinion/02judah.html (21 February 2015).
82 Dragović-Soso. "Apologising for Srebrenica: The Declaration of the Serbian Parliament, the European Union and the Politics of Compromise", 165.
83 Slavenka Drakulić. "A few 'easy' steps towards reconciliation." *Baltic Worlds* 13 May 2011. http://balticworlds.com/towards-reconciliation/ (21 February 2015).
84 "Josipovic apologizes for Croatia's role in war in Bosnia." *Croatian Times* 15 April 2010.

the site of the Sijekovac killings, in order to pay homage to the Serbian victims of the Bosnian conflict as well. Finally, in November 2010 Josipović organised a joint visit with Boris Tadić to Vukovar, paying homage to the Croatian and Serbian victims of the killings in Ovcara and Paulin Dvor.[85] The Vukovar commemoration constitutes the most comprehensive act of atonement so far related to the wars of the 1990s; analyzed against Thompson's ideal-type,[86] it may be said to include memorability, victims' participation, and commitment for the future.[87] It also fostered regional reconciliation, as Bakir Izetbegović joined the party once again by apologising, a few days before Tadić's visit to Vukovar, "for every innocent person killed by the *Armija BiH*".[88] After it, though, the process subsided, and it took almost three years before a new apology was offered.

The third time an apology was uttered for Srebrenica, it came from the President of the Republic of Serbia, Tomislav Nikolić, a former vice-president of the nationalist Serbian Radical Party (SRS) of Vojislav Šešelj. After having lost four consecutive presidential elections between 2000 and 2008, Nikolić broke with Šešelj and founded the Serbian Progressive Party (SNS), with which he won the 2012 presidential election.

Nikolić's first steps as a President were marked by a series of gaffes: in an interview with the FAZ, he discussed his radical and Chetnik past, and was quoted as saying that a Greater Serbia was his "unrealized dream", since the international borders of Croatia and Bosnia were now definitely settled, and that "Vukovar was a Serb city and Croats have nothing to go back to there".[89] Soon after, Nikolić sparked even more controversy by declaring at the Montenegro television that "there was no genocide in Srebrenica. In Srebrenica, grave war crimes were committed by some Serbs who should be found, prosecuted and punished. [...] It is very difficult to indict someone and prove before a court that an event qualifies as genocide." He also declined to attend the annual Srebrenica commemoration, as Tadić had done in the past: "Don't always ask the

---

http://www.croatiantimes.com/news/General_News/2010-04-15/10325/Josipovic_ apologizes_for_Croatia%B4 s_role_in_war_in_Bosnia (21 February 2015).
85 "Tadić i Josipović izrazili izvinjenje i žaljenje." *Danas.rs* 4 November 2010.
http://www.danas.rs/danasrs/politika/tadic_i_josipovic_izrazili_izvinjenje_i_zaljenje_.56.html?news_id=202984 (21 February 2015).
86 Thompson. "Apology, Justice, and Respect: A Critical Defense of Political Apology", 42–43.
87 Again in Drakulić's words: the event "really did look impressive: two heads of state demonstrating good intentions, symbolically closing the vicious circle of war".
88 Drakulić. "A few 'easy' steps towards reconciliation."
89 Michael Martens. "Die Serben durften nicht entscheiden, wo sie leben wollen." *Frankfurter Allgemeine Zeitung* 19 May 2012. http://www.faz.net/aktuell/politik/ausland/wahl-in-serbien-die-serben-durften-nicht-entscheiden-wo-sie-leben-wollen-11750937.html (21 February 2015).

Serbian president if he is going to Srebrenica, my predecessor was there and paid tribute. Why should every president do the same?"⁹⁰

One year later, and merely one week after the April 2013 "First agreement on the normalisation of relations" between Serbia and Kosovo reached in Brussels by the Prime Minister Ivica Dačić and his counterpart Hashim Thaçi, the discourse of Nikolić changed substantially. Interviewed by the Bosnian state television BHRT, Nikolić reiterated the argument that everything that happened during the war, including Operation *Oluja*, had the features of genocide, but then added:

> I am on my knees because of that, here I'm on my knees and begging for a pardon for Serbia because of the crime committed in Srebrenica. I apologise for all crimes committed by any individual in the name of our state and our people.⁹¹

As in the previous case, this apology, too, refrains from the direct use of the term *genocide*. The Serbian leadership, in fact, refuses to be considered as the only responsible for it, seeing instead the Serbs also as victims of acts of ethnic cleansing and genocide (thus the reference to *Oluja*).

On the other hand, Nikolić's apology appears to be very important due to the personal past of the Serbian President as a member of the SRS, a party which has always held a nationalist and irredentist agenda, even opposing Milošević for being too moderate, and denying any wrongdoing by Serb forces during the conflict.⁹² Nikolić had also opposed the 2010 Parliamentary resolution on Srebrenica, as a member of the opposition to the Tadić administration. Finally, his latest unfortunate declarations as President-elect had prompted an "ice age"⁹³ in the relations of Serbia with Croatia and Bosnia.

---

90 Reuters. "Serbian president denies Srebrenica genocide." *Genocide Watch* 2 June 2013. http://www.genocidewatch.org/images/Serbia_12_06_02_Serbian_president_denies_Srebrenica _genocide.pdf (21 February 2015).

91 Dražen Remiković and Ivana Jovanović. "Analysts say Nikolic's Srebrenica apology is significant." *Southeast European Times* 29 April 2013. http://www.setimes.com/cocoon/setimes/ xhtml/en_GB/ features/setimes/features/2013/04/29/ feature-01 (21 February 2015).

92 As reminded by Nataša Kandić, one should "see his [Nikolić's] statements in conjunction with his own past". Kandić underlined the importance of the virtual kneeling gesture, in parallel to Willy Brandt's 1970 *Kniefall*, as "nobody has ever said anything like it in Serbia". "Bosnians are not enthusiastic about apology." *Deutsche Welle* 26 April 2013. http://www.dw.de/bosnians-are-not-enthusiastic-about-apology/a-16775294 (21 February 2015).

93 Predrag Šimic, quoted in Stefano Giantin. "Nikolic: "Belgrado s'inginocchia a Srebrenica"." *Il Piccolo* 26 April 2013.

One element that could have prompted the apology was the desire to improve Serbia's international relations, both bilaterally with Bosnia,[94] and multilaterally with the European Union.[95] On the one hand, according to Selim Šaćirović, the apology could "contribute to return of confidence between BiH and Serbia", thus helping both parties to overcome the past and build trust.[96] The personal past of Nikolić, though it casts shadows on the sincerity of the apology, seems relevant in terms of the capacity of the apology to commit to the non-repetition of similar acts in the future.[97] Moreover, it signals how the political majority in Serbia, the coalition of Socialists and Progressives, has adopted a stance on Europe and on regional reconciliation which follows closely the one of the previous alliance between Socialists and Democrats led by Tadić, the first to say "sorry" for Srebrenica and up to now the Serbian leader with the best relations with Zagreb.[98] At any rate, Nikolic's apology doesn't seem to have struck a

---

http://ilpiccolo.gelocal.it/cronaca/2013/04/26/news/nikoli-mi-inginocchio-a-srebrenica-1.6953442 (21 February 2015).

[94] Nikolić had recently been visited in Belgrade by two members of the tripartite Bosnian state presidency, Nebojša Radmanović and Bakir Izetbegović, while the third member, Zeljko Komšić, refused to follow, claiming that the Serbian President had offended the victims of the Bosnian war in his speech at the UN General Assembly on the role of international war crimes courts, in which Nikolić had described the Hague tribunal as an "inquisition". After the apology, Komšić commented that "this statement of President Nikolić will certainly contribute to the development of better relations between BiH and Serbia in the future. That kind of statement will surely relax things in the whole region". Remiković and Jovanović. "Analysts say Nikolic's Srebrenica apology is significant."

[95] According to Predrag Šimić, the apology could also have been aimed at ensuring that Serbia obtained a final date for the start of EU accession negotiations by the European Council of June 2013. Giantin. "Nikolic: "Belgrado s'inginocchia a Srebrenica"."

[96] Milorad Pupovać, president of the Independent Democratic Serbian Party (SDSS) of Croatia, noted that Nikolić's apology "is a confirmation of awareness of the severity of the crime that was committed, the responsibility which feel all those who represent the Serbian people, about the thing that the members of the Serbian people, or people who have performed some duties on behalf of the state of Serbia committed crimes against members of the Bosniak people", then expressed confidence that it might help improve relationships. Remiković and Jovanović. "Analysts say Nikolic's Srebrenica apology is significant."

[97] According to Fahrudin Kladičanin, co-ordinator at the Forum 10 academic initiative in Novi Pazar, "This is first time that Bosniaks in Serbia could hear such a thing from President Nikolić since they still see him as Šešelj's party member and it will, for sure, improve relations between Serbs and Bosniaks not only on Bosnia and Serbia, also through the whole region. This is, for sure, a step ahead for this authority and it should be respected." Remiković and Jovanović. "Analysts say Nikolic's Srebrenica apology is significant."

[98] Predrag Šimić, quoted by Giantin. "Nikolic: "Belgrado s'inginocchia a Srebrenica"."

full chord in Bosnia, where many judged it insincere and unreliable.[99] Nikolić also said that he would visit Srebrenica and make a donation to the victims,[100] but he did not attend the 2013 commemoration on 11 July, nor the one in 2014.

Finally, Nikolić's apology may also have had domestic politics motives, in response to the need for the Serbian President to regain control over public attention at a moment in which his Prime Minister and main coalition partner Ivica Dačić had come to the fore due to the Brussels agreement on Kosovo.

Conclusions: Sorry for Srebrenica? Apologies, ambiguities, and EU integration

Reconciliation among Western Balkan countries after the wars of the 1990s is an ongoing process involving the use of public apologies as a form of restorative justice to complement retributive efforts in bringing justice for crimes such as the Srebrenica genocide.

The apologies that have been extended up to now in relation to Srebrenica, in 2004, 2010, and 2013, appear to be incomplete and ambiguous. Such features, common to the wider cycle of apologies in the Western Balkan in relation to wartime crimes, reveal the presence not only of strong incentives to apologise, due to

---

[99] Al Jazeera reported the opinion of Emir Suljagić, a survivor of the Srebrenica massacre, activist and in 2014 Bosniak candidate for the Presidency of Bosnia and Herzegovina, according to whom Nikolić's behaviour was "duplicitous": "Mind you, we're dealing with a hard-line nationalist which let Kosovo go", noting also that Nikolić's apology is "one in a litany of presidential apologies in the Balkans". "Serbia president 'apologises' for massacre" *Al Jazeera* 25 April 2013. http://www.aljazeera.com/ news/europe/2013/04/ 2013425102523848273.html (21 February 2015).
The political activist Srđa Popović remarked that the apology was released "in the context of upco ming negotiations of Serbia with the EU. I don't believe that was meant in an honest way. It's merely political maneuvering and serves a political purpose". "Bosnians are not enthusiastic about apology." *Deutsche Welle*.
Also the association Mothers of Srebrenica criticised Nikolić, asking him to acknowledge the facts as a genocide. The association's president, Kada Hotić, recognised that "This statement is a big step forward and I welcome it, considering what the current president of Serbia use [d] to say before 10 or 20 years. However, he apologized on behalf of the crime, and not on behalf of genocide." Remiković and Jovanović. "Analysts say Nikolic's Srebrenica apology is significant."
[100] "Nikolić: Izvinjavam se za zločin u Srebrenici." *Novosti.rs* 25 April 2013. http://www.novosti.rs/vesti/naslovna/politika/aktuelno.289.html:431190-Nikolic-Izvinjavam-se-za-zlocin-u-Srebrenici (21 February 2015).

these countries' common foreign policy objective of EU membership, but also of high costs, due to the potential domestic backlash resulting from the legacies of the recent conflicts, with their stocks of reactive memories which may be used for popular mobilisation.

The rational-choice approach to reparation decisions employed in this chapter may help us understand the process of apologies for Srebrenica. It highlights how, in the presence of high benefits and high costs, apologies come accompanied by a strategy of ambiguity, allowing political actors to maximise the benefits of apologising while minimising the risk of domestic backlash.

Public apologies thus exert a double function. First, they are signals of an ongoing process of reconciliation, without which they would not be possible, as politicians would face prohibitive threats for their careers. Second, they are catalysts of additional change, since they help neutralise the conflict potential of reactive memories, thus further reducing domestic costs and allowing the process of reconciliation to continue. The process tracing of the three apologies given for Srebrenica validates this framework of analysis and helps to explain their ambiguous and partial nature.

References

Al Jazeera. "Serbia president 'apologises' for massacre", 25 April 2013. http://www.aljazeera.com/news/europe/2013/04/ 2013425102523848273.html (21 February 2015).

Associated Press. "Bosnian Serbs Issue Apology for Massacre". *Bosnia Report* New Series No. 42. 11 November 2004. http://www.bosnia.org.uk/bosrep/report_format.cfm?articleid=1147&reportid=166 (21 February 2015).

Bilder, Richard B. "The Role of Apology in International Law and Diplomacy." *Virginia Journal of International Law* 46.3 (2006): 433–473.

Boxill, Bernard. "Morality of Reparation." *Social Theory and Practice* 2 (1972): 113–123.

Clark, Max and Gary Allen Fine. "'A' for Apology: Slavery and the Discourse of Remonstrance in Two American Universities." *History and Memory* 22.1 (2010): 81–112.

Corntassel, Jeff and Cindy Holder. "Who's Sorry Now? Government Apologies, Truth Commissions, and Indigenous Self-Determination in Australia, Canada, Guatemala and Peru." *Human Rights Review* (2008): 4. http://www.corntassel.net/CorntasselHolder.pdf (21 February 2015).

Denti, Davide. "Public Apologies in the Western Balkans: the Shadow of Ambiguity." *Public Apology Between Ritual and Regret. Symbolic Excuses on False Pretenses or True Reconciliation out of Sincere Regret?* Eds. Daniel Cuypers et al. Amsterdam: Rodopi, 2013, 61–91.

Deutsche Welle . "Bosnians are not enthusiastic about apology." 26 April 2013. http://www.dw.de/bosnians-are-not-enthusiastic-about-apology/a-16775294 (21 February 2015).

Digeser, Peter E. *Political Forgiveness*. Ithaca: Cornell University Press, 2001.

Dragović-Soso, Jasna. "Apologising for Srebrenica: The Declaration of the Serbian Parliament, the European Union and the Politics of Compromise." *East European Politics* 28.2 (2012): 163–179.

Drakulić, Slavenka. "A few 'easy' steps towards reconciliation." *Baltic Worlds* 13 May 2011. http://balticworlds.com/towards-reconciliation/(21 February 2015).

Fink, Sheri. "Serbs' Overdue Apology Delivers Hope for Humanity." *Detroit Free Press* 22 December 2004. http://warhospital.net/serbs.htm (21 February 2015).

Giantin, Stefano. "Nikolic: "Belgrado s'inginocchia a Srebrenica"." *Il Piccolo* 26 April 2013. http://ilpiccolo.gelocal.it/cronaca/2013/04/26/news/nikoli-mi-inginocchio-a-srebrenica-1.6953442 (21 February 2015).

Gibney, Mark and Erik Roxstrom. "The Status of State Apologies." *Human Rights Quarterly* 23 (2001): 911–939.

Government of Republika Srpska. *The Events in and around Srebrenica between 10th and 19th July 1995*. Banja Luka, 11 June 2004. http://trial-ch.org/fileadmin/user_upload/documents/trialwatch/Srebrenica_Report2004.pdf (21 February 2015).

Government of Republika Srpska. *Addendum to the Report of the 11th June 2004 on the Events in and around Srebrenica between 10th and 19th July 1995*. Banja Luka, 15 October 2004. http://balkanwitness.glypx.com/srebr_final_e.pdf (21 February 2015).

Govier, Trudy. *Forgiveness and Revenge*. London: Routledge, 2002.

Govier, Trudy and Wilhelm Verwoerd. "The practice of public apology: a qualified defense." *Saskatchewan Law Review* 65 (2002): 139–162.

Hayner, Priscilla. *Unspeakable Truths: Confronting State Terror and Atrocity*. New York: Routledge, 2001.

Helsinki Committee to Defend Human Rights in Serbia. "Srebrenica Resolution Opens a Public Debate in Serbia." *Helsinki Bulletin* 58 (February 2010). http://www.bosnia.org.uk/news/news_body.cfm?newsid=2693 (21 February 2015)

Hoare, Marko Attila. "How to Apologise." *The Henry Jackson Society* 30 May 2010. http://greatersurbiton.wordpress.com/2010/05/31/how-to-apologise/(21 February 2015).

Horelt, Michel-André. *Rituals of Reconciliation. A Performance Based Approach to the Analysis of Political Apologies for Historic Crimes*. Munich: Ludwig-Maximilians-Universität, 2010. http://www.irmgard-coninx-stiftung.de/fileadmin/user_upload/pdf/MemoryPolitics/Workshop3/ HoreltEssay.pdf (21 February 2015).

International Court of Justice (ICJ). "Application of the Convention on the Prevention and Punishment of the Crime of Genocide (Bosnia and Herzegovina v. Serbia and Montenegro)" *Press Release* 8, 2007. http://www.icj-cij.org/presscom/index.php?pr=1897 &pt=1&p1=6&p2=1 (21 February 2015).

Humanitarian Law Center. "Predsednik Srbije Boris Tadić se prilikom prve posete BiH, 6. decembra 2006. godine u Sarajevu, izvinio u ime srpskog naroda." Zagreb, 6 December 2006. http://www.hlc-rdc.org/?p=13592 (21 February 2015).

Humanitarian Law Center. *Transitional Justice in Post-Yugoslav Countries. 2007 Report*. Zagreb, 2007. http://www.documenta.hr/dokumenti/trans_eng2007.pdf (21 February 2015).

International Criminal Tribunal for the former Yugoslavia (ICTY). *Prosecutor v. Radislav Krstić – Sentencing Judgement*. 19 April 2014. http://www.icty.org/x/cases/krstic/acjug/en/krs-aj040419e.pdf (21 February 2015).

International Criminal Tribunal for the former Yugoslavia (ICTY). *Prosecutor v. Miroslav Deronjić – Sentencing Judgement*. 30 March 2004. http://www.icty.org/x/cases/deronjic/tjug/en/sj-040330e.pdf (21 February 2015).

James, Matt. "Wrestling with the past: Apologies, Quasi-Apologies and Non-Apologies in Canada." *The Age of Apology: Facing up the Past*. Eds. Mark Gibney et al. Philadelphia: University of Pennsylvania Press, 2008. 137–153.

Jano, Dorian. "From 'Balkanization' to 'Europeanization': The Stages of Western Balkans Complex Transformations." *L'Europe en Formation* 349–350 (2008): 55–68.

Jones, Shannon. "Apology Diplomacy: Justice for All?" *Clingendael Discussion Papers in Diplomacy* 122 (2011): 3. http://www.clingendael.nl/publications/2011/20110900_cdsp_discussionpapersindiplomacy_122_jones.pdf (21 February 2015).

"Josipovic apologizes for Croatia's role in war in Bosnia." *Croatian Times* 15 April 2010. http://www.croatiantimes.com/news/General_News/2010-04-15/10325/Josipovic_ apologizes_for_Croatia%B4 s_role_in_war_in_Bosnia (21 February 2015).

Judah, Tim. "Serbia's Honest Apology." *The New York Times* 1 April 2010. http://www.nytimes.com/2010/04/02/opinion/02judah.html (21 February 2015).

Kaldor, Mary. *New and Old Wars: Organized Violence in a Global Era*. Oxford: Polity Press, 1999.

Lazare, Aaron. *On Apology*. Oxford: Oxford University Press, 2004.

Lind, Jennifer. *Sorry States: Apologies in International Politics*. Ithaca: Cornell University Press, 2008.

Magen, Amichai and Leonardo Morlino. Eds. *International Actors, Democratization and the Rule of Law. Anchoring Democracy?*. New York: Routledge, 2008.

Marquand, Robert. "War Crimes: Is Serbia's Srebrenica Apology Genuine?" *Christian Science Monitor*, 31 March 2010. http://www.csmonitor.com/World/Europe/2010/0331/War-crimes-Is-Serbia-s-Srebrenica-apology-genuine (21 February 2015).

Martens, Michael. "Die Serben durften nicht entscheiden, wo sie leben wollen." *Frankfurter Allgemeine Zeitung* 19 May 2012. http://www.faz.net/aktuell/politik/ausland/wahl-in-serbien-die-serben-durften-nicht-entscheiden-wo-sie-leben-wollen-11750937.html (21 February 2015).

Mink, Georges and Pascal Bonnard. *Le passé au Présent. Gisements Mémoriels et Actions Publiques en Europe Centrale et Orientale*. Paris: Michel Houdiard, 2010.

National Assembly of the Republic of Serbia. *Declaration of the National Assembly of the Republic of Serbia Condemning the Crime in Srebrenica*. 31 March 2010. http://www.parlament.gov.rs/upload/archive/files/eng/pdf/2010/deklaracija%20o%20srebrenici%20ENG.pdf (21 February 2015).

"Nikolić: Izvinjavam se za zločin u Srebrenici." *Novosti.rs*. 25 April 2013. http://www.novosti.rs/vesti/naslovna/politika/aktuelno.289.html:431190-Nikolic-Izvinjavam-se-za-zlocin-u-Srebrenici (21 February 2015).

Nobles, Melissa. *The Politics of Official Apologies*. Cambridge: Cambridge University Press, 2008.

Potočari Memorial Center website, http://www.potocarimc.ba/_ba/liste/nestali_a.php (21 February 2015).

Remiković, Dražen and Ivana Jovanović. "Analysts say Nikolic's Srebrenica apology is significant." *Southeast European Times* 29 April 2013. http://www.setimes.com/cocoon/

setimes/xhtml/en_GB/ features/setimes/features/2013/04/29/feature-01 (21 February 2015).

Reuters. "Serbian president denies Srebrenica genocide." *Genocide Watch*, 2 June 2013. http://www.genocidewatch.org/images/Serbia_12_06_02_Serbian_president_denies_Srebrenica_genocide.pdf (21 February 2015).

Rigby, Andrew. *Justice and Reconciliation: After the Violence*. Boulder: Lynne Rienner, 2001.

Schimmelfennig, Frank. "EU political accession conditionality after the 2004 enlargement: consistency and effectiveness." *Journal of European Public Policy* 15.6 (2008): 918–937.

Schimmelfennig, Frank and Ulrich Sedelmeier. "Governance by conditionality: EU rule transfer to the candidate countries of Central and Eastern Europe." *Journal of European Public Policy* 11.4 (2004): 661–679.

Smajić, Suad, "O jeziku mržnje i dvostrukog smisla." *Slobodna misao* 4 (2005): 46.

"Tadić i Josipović izrazili izvinjenje i žaljenje." *Danas.rs*. 4 November 2010. http://www.danas.rs/danasrs/politika/tadic_i_josipovic_izrazili_izvinjenje_i_zaljenje_.56.html?news_id=202984. (21 February 2015).

Taft, Lee, "Apology Subverted: the Commodification of Apology." *Yale Law Journal* 109.5 (2000): 1135–1160.

Tavuchis, Nicholas. *Mea culpa: A Sociology of Apology and Reconciliation*. Stanford: Stanford University Press, 1991.

Thompson, Janna. "Apology, Justice, and Respect: A Critical Defense of Political Apology". *The Age of Apology: Facing Up to the Past*. Eds. Mark Gibney et al. Philadelphia: University of Pennsylvania Press, 2008. 31–44.

Topić, Tanja. "Otvaranje najmračnije stranice." *Vreme* 1 July 2004. http://www.vreme.com/cms/ view.php?id=384060 (21 February 2015).

Ukabiala, Jullyette. "Slave Trade 'a crime against humanity'." *Africa Recovery* 15.3 (2001): 5.

UN International Law Commission's Draft Articles on Responsibility of States for Internationally Wrongful Acts, adopted in 2001. UN Doc A/56/589 (2001).

Velagić, Mirza. "Serbia's Insincere Apology." *Congress of North American Bosniaks* 24 April 2010. http://www.bosniak.org/serbias-insincere-apology/ (21 February 2015).

Villadsen, Lisa S. "The Regretful Acknowledgment: a Dignified End to a Disgraceful Story?" *Public Apology Between Ritual and Regret. Symbolic Excuses on False Pretenses or True Reconciliation out of Sincere Regret?* Eds. Daniel Cuypers et al. Amsterdam: Rodopi, 2013. 229–248.

Part 2: **Sites of Memory Transmission**

Sophie Oliver
The Spatial Choreography of Emotion at Berlin's Memorials: Experience, Ambivalence and the Ethics of Secondary Witnessing

> Even in the future, when we will have to do without direct encounters with witnesses, we need not lose our emotional involvement. People three or four generations removed from the Holocaust, and people without German roots, also feel deeply moved when they see the names of Holocaust victims written on their suitcases at Auschwitz, or when they stumble upon the ruins of the destroyed crematorium in the forsaken expanse of Birkenau, or when they read 'The Diary of Anne Frank' or watch the film 'The Pianist'. What we see time and again is that autobiographies, documentaries, feature films, interviews with survivors and visits to the former sites of horror can make past suffering accessible to young people and inspire them to open up their souls to it.
>
> Bundespräsident (German Federal President) Gauck, 27 January 2015[1]

On 30 August 2012, the German weekly *Die Zeit* carried the headline, superimposed onto a portrait of Adolf Hitler, "When will the past pass?"[2] The three-page article that followed was concerned with the dwindling significance of Holocaust remembrance for a new generation of Germans keen to shake off the burden of guilt; a generation of young people, of both German and immigrant descent, who are increasingly resistant to any form of identification with the dark past of their nation. Perhaps, writes the author of the article, this is just the logical consequence of the passing of time. In any case, he concedes with regret, one thing is clear: he will not be able to pass on to future generations the historical lesson or 'package from the past' [*Vergangenheitspäckchen*] that he once received, not with "the same content and weight."[3] The concern about how to preserve the memory and meaning of the Holocaust and other human tragedies in ways that may continue to instruct and serve as a warning to future generations is not a new one, but as the time when survivors and eyewitnesses will no longer be around to assist in these efforts draws nearer, it has become

---

[1] Speech of Joachim Gauck, President of Germany on Holocaust Remembrance Day, 27 January 2015. Online at http://www.bundespraesident.de/SharedDocs/Reden/DE/Joachim-Gauck/Reden/2015/01/150127-Bundestag-Gedenken.html (8 April 2015).
[2] "Wann vergeht die Vergangenheit?" *Die Zeit* No. 36. 30 August 2012.
[3] "Das Vergangenheitspäckchen, das ich einst bekommen habe, werde ich nicht mit exakt demselben Inhalt und demselben Gewicht weitergeben können." Bernd Ulrich. "Wer sind wir, heute?" *Die Zeit* No. 36, 2012, 2.

more urgent than ever. In response to this situation, many cultural memory practitioners are abandoning traditional forms of historical pedagogy in favour of new, experimental and *experiential* ways of (re)presenting the past.[4] Characteristic of this development is the move towards encouraging interactive, embodied and experience-based forms of reception, in particular at museums and memorials. Such experiential cultural memory models seek, through a range of innovative, multi-medial technologies and narrative strategies, to "transform bystanders and later generations into 'secondary witnesses'";[5] that is, to lead them beyond mere spectatorship towards the kind of active, empathic and ethical engagement more akin to witnessing. This trend has been observed at a number of so-called "memory museums"[6] as well as at "authentic" sites of trauma, such as the former Nazi concentration camps. The attempt to provide visitors to such sites with an authentic and engaging experience is frequently accompanied by what German historian Matthias Heyl describes as a "choreography of emotion." In line with this "choreography", he explains, specific affective responses to sites of historical trauma are either prescribed (sadness, empathy, a sense of injustice) or prohibited (indifference, amusement). Heyl views this phenomenon critically, arguing that attempts to direct visitors' behaviour and emotional responses can backfire, alienating rather than engaging audiences, particularly among the young.[7]

---

[4] The term "cultural memory" was developed by Jan and Aleida Assmann, and refers to the ways in which memory is exteriorised, objectified and transmitted through symbolic forms and objects, for example monuments, museums, libraries, archives, and other mnemonic institutions.
[5] Jens Andermann and Silke Arnold-de Simine. "Introduction: Memory Community and the New Museum." *Theory, Culture and Society* 29.3 (2012): 7.
[6] For a discussion of the meaning of this term see Silke Arnold-de Simine. "Memory Museum and Museum Text: Intermediality in Daniel Libeskind's Jewish Museum and WG Sebald's *Austerlitz*." *Theory, Culture, Society* 29.3 (2012): 15–16.
[7] "Durch die Sphäre der Befangenheit wird ein verdruckter Erwartungshorizont geschaffen, der signalisiert, dass die Gedenkstätte ein besonderer emotionaler Raum sei, die gegen Regelverstöße geschützt werden muss [...] Wir wissen aber, dass Drastik und Überwältigung ebenso dazu geeignet sind, Zugänge eher zu verschließen, wie wir um das Widerstandpotentiel Jugendlicher wissen, die sich – m.E. zurecht – dagegen wehren, wenn sie zum Objekt einer ‚Choreographie der Emotionen' von außen gemacht werden. Gerade die hohe soziale Erwünschheit gewisser emotionaler Reaktionen blockiert die emotionale Auseinandersetzung zuweilen." Matthias Heyl. *Mit Überwältigendem überwältigen? Auf die nationalsozialistischen Massen Verbrechen bezongene Gedenkstätten und Emotionen*. Keynote Speech at the Berlin-Brandenburgische Forum für zeitgeschichtliche Bildung 2012. http://lernen-aus-der-geschichte.de/Lernen-und-Lehren/content/10658 (8 April 2015).

This article builds upon Heyl's analogy of a choreography of emotion in order to consider, in a more literal sense, the ways in which memory spaces function – or are designed to function – to evoke emotional and ethical forms of reception in their interlocutors as part of an *embodied performance* of cultural memory. I examine visitor experiences at two well-known Holocaust memorial spaces that espouse an experiential and emotional approach to cultural memory: the Memorial to the Murdered Jews of Europe and the Jewish Museum, both in Berlin. At these sites, architectural space and form are the central props through and upon which the apparent authenticity of emotion and experience is choreographed. We have to do here, specifically, with a *spatial* choreography of emotion – one that is inspired, I suggest, by an ethics of reception based in empathy and affect. As with all choreographies, however, it is completed only by the presence and the movement of bodies. In this sense, all choreography is to some extent also an improvisation. It is the bodies of the visitors who come to the museum or memorial with their own experiences, attitudes and identities that complete the performance of remembrance; as we might expect, such encounters can produce unexpected and – to some – undesired responses. Nonetheless, supporters of memorial spaces such as the Jewish Museum Berlin and the Memorial to the Murdered Jews of Europe remain convinced of the power of experience and affect to engage audiences personally and ethically with the past and, especially, with the victims of historical trauma. Drawing on empirical observations of visitor experiences at these two memory spaces, this article explores some of the implications of the experiential turn in cultural memory, reflecting in particular upon the notion of ethical spectatorship within this context. I begin by providing some background on the emergence of experiential cultural memory practices, highlighting the influence of new approaches in museum pedagogy, particularly in relation to redefining the role of the visitor-spectators. In the second section of the paper, I examine in more detail the two Berlin-based sites, focusing on the ways in which the spatialities of each are designed so as to place an emphasis on affect, experience and open interpretation. Finally, I turn to visitors' own reflections on the sites in order to ask what the effects of this experiential approach within cultural memory practice might be. To what extent can visitors be said to fulfil (or perceive themselves to be fulfilling) the role implicitly attributed to them as participants of, or witnesses to, the cultural memory of historical trauma? Does the experiential approach provide a useful response to the threat of amnesia and moral disengagement that many see as being the future of Holocaust remembrance, or does it merely give rise to more ambivalence and forgetting?

The experiential turn in cultural memory practice: some background

> A hands-on experience of history – the DDR Museum is not an exhibition to regard [...] the visitor has to take part.[8]

> The German Emigration Center is full of state-of-the-art museum technology, beginning with the admission ticket, an iCard [...] Each iCard contains the story of an individual who either emigrated to the New World or found a new home in Germany. The iCard also activates many audio stations and interactive displays making a museum visit a thoroughly personal and emotional experience. Individual information and pictures enable identification with the actual person and invite visitors to become more involved with their story and, thus, the history.[9]

How does one engage publics in a past that for many seems less and less relevant to the present? The citations above, from the websites of the GDR Museum in Berlin and The Emigration Museum in Bremerhaven, northern Germany, illustrate the interactive and experiential approach taken in recent years by a number of institutions tasked with safeguarding the memory of important historical events. Both museums emphasise the use of interactive technology and active spectatorship as a means of providing visitors with an experience of the past that is personal, emotional and, as a result, engaging. The GDR museum, described on its website as "interactive, playful, vivid, entertaining and scientifically well-founded", promises visitors the "opportunity to experience the GDR everyday life yourself" and invites them to partake of such "authentic" experiences as driving in a simulator Trabi (Trabant, a car commonly produced in Soviet East Germany) and exploring a replica East German living room.[10] The concept at the German Emigration Museum, named European Museum of the Year in 2007, is similar: visitors are taken on an imagined journey, beginning in the "waiting hall" on a replica wharf of Bremerhaven – from which over 7.2 million emigrants departed for the New World in the nineteenth and twentieth centuries – and ending at Grand Central Station in New York. Even the physical discomfort of a voyage by boat is replicated, as one is made to walk through a swaying corridor, giving the feeling of "being at sea". If they choose, visitors may dress up in "historic emigrant clothing" and have a photograph taken as a keepsake. The *pièce de résistance*, however, is the state-of-the-art iCard with which each visitor

---

[8] DDR Museum Website. http://www.ddr-museum.de/en/museum/ (1 November 2012).
[9] Deutsches Auswanderer Haus Bremerhaven. http://www.dah-bremerhaven.de/en.museum.php#Museumstechnik (1 November 2012).
[10] DDR Museum Website. http://www.ddr-museum.de/en/museum/ (1 November 2012).

is presented before embarking on his or her journey. These electronic boarding passes bear the name and identity of someone who either emigrated from or immigrated to Germany, and can be used throughout the exhibition to activate information terminals, where visitors can learn more about the life of the person on their card.

The approach espoused by these museums is more than simply a means of attracting crowds; it also reflects a fundamental change in attitudes towards learning in museums and in the way visitors themselves are imagined. As Eilean Hooper-Greenhill observes, recent decades have seen a shift in museum pedagogy "from thinking about visitors as an undifferentiated mass public to beginning to accept visitors as active interpreters and performers of meaning-making practices."[11] This increasingly "democratic" approach to learning in museums has been described as part of the "New Museology", replacing the didactic ethos of Victorian museum culture with "more reflexive and multicultural approaches" in which museum experts "no longer disseminate knowledge to eager masses awaiting enlightenment" but rather "facilitate the active learning of diverse visitor groups."[12] The constructivist exhibition model developed by George E. Hein is a perfect example of this experiential approach; in it "learning is conceptualized as a process of experiencing the world and making sense of it in one's own mind within the context of one's own cultural background."[13] In other words, the visitor is no longer told what to think, but rather encouraged to come up with his or her own interpretation of the material presented. In many ways, this seems to be a liberating and entirely positive development, embraced by so-called memory museums as a means of renegotiating the codes and practices of the traditional history museum. As Silke Arnold-de Simine explains:

> These museums define themselves not just as sites of academic and institutional history but as spaces of memory, exemplifying a shift from a perceived authoritative master discourse on the past to the paradigm of memory which supposedly allows for a wider range of stories about the past.[14]

---

[11] Eilean Hooper-Greenhill. "Studying Visitors." *A Companion to Museum Studies*. Ed. Sharon MacDonald. Oxford: Blackwell Publishing, 2006, 363.
[12] Debbie Lisle. "Sublime Lessons: Education and Ambivalence in War Exhibitions." *Millennium – Journal of International Studies* 34 (2006): 845.
[13] Andrea Witcomb. "Interactivity: Thinking Beyond." *A Companion to Museum Studies*. Ed. Sharon MacDonald. Oxford: Blackwell Publishing, 2006. 352–361, 359. For Hein's own explanation of the constructivist model, see George E. Hein. "The Constructivist Museum." *Journal for Education in Museums* 15 (1995): 15–17.
[14] Arnold-de Simine. "Memory Museum and Museum Text", 15. This last claim, Arnold-de Simine suggests, needs to be critically interrogated.

In the context of museums dealing with the cultural memory of historical trauma, however, we might question whether such an open and tolerant approach is always desirable. Writing on war exhibitions, Debbie Lisle is critical of what she sees as New Museology's too liberal stance on what counts as truth. There may be cases, she suggests, where certain perspectives or interpretations may indeed quite rightly be considered *unacceptable*. Should we tolerate, for example, the perspective of Holocaust deniers or Neo-Nazis when creating the concept for a museum on the Second World War? By seeking to correct the restrictive, top-down didactics of the Victorian model, Lisle argues, New Museology has allowed today's curators "to avoid difficult decisions about truth, objectivity and bias by invoking the norms of diversity, equality and tolerance"; in this sense, she suggests, inclusivity may have the effect "of *closing down* critical space rather than opening it up to diversity."[15]

And yet, to say that New Museology adopts a more open pedagogical approach is not to assume that new museums act without intentions or desired effects. In many cases, the range of appropriate responses is set even before visitors arrive. At sites of Holocaust remembrance, in particular, the question to ask may not be whether in some cases it is preferable for museums to adopt a clear moral stance, as Lisle suggests, but rather whether this is ever even avoidable. The majority of visitors to such sites will already have a clear idea of what is expected of them, being to some extent already influenced by the codes and expectations that determine how one "ought" to respond to Holocaust narratives. It would, moreover, be naïve to imagine that experiential exhibition models do not produce specific *intended* effects of their own. As Arnold-de Simine notes:

> The key feature of all the memory museums is that they encourage visitors to empathise and identify with individual sufferers and victims, as if 'reliving' their experience [...] Aiming principally to achieve an emotional impact, memory museums provide people with an experience and confront them with a moral imperative – which more often than not places them at odds with their self-proclaimed objective of self-reflexivity.[16]

According to Andrea Witcomb, dialogic exhibition spaces such as those we have been discussing "use the full range of creative arts [including interactivity] to

---

15 Lisle. "Sublime Lessons", 850. Hooper-Greenhill says something similar in her book *Museums and the Shaping of Knowledge*, when she writes that "the total experience (in living history or interactive exhibits), the total immersion (in gallery workshops and events) can have the function, in the apparently democratized environment of the museum marketplace, of soothing, of silencing, of quieting questions, of closing minds." Eilean Hooper Greenhill, *Museums and the Shaping of Knowledge*. New York: Routledge, 1992, 214.
16 Arnold-de Simine. "Memory Museum and Museum Text," 16.

construct a highly immersive, experiential environment" in order to create an "aesthetic where there is a space for poetic, affective response."[17] Thus, while visitors may not be told in so many words what to think, the immersive and experiential nature of the exhibits will likely function in such a way as to influence how they *feel* within the museum or memorial space. The theory is that engaging the emotions through bodily activity makes for more effective and memorable learning than is achieved through traditional "look but don't touch" didactic approaches, in part because of the immediacy and apparent authenticity of affect.[18] As a teacher in a study conducted by Eilean Hooper-Greenhill into school pupils' learning experiences at museums comments: "Emotional response is the catalyst [for learning] because it's real."[19] Affect, it is suggested, increases our sense of *moral* engagement because it provides a sense of personal connection to the subject matter at hand; as Hooper-Greenhill explains: "emotions are personal; they are our way of claiming something as our own. An involvement without emotion is distant, unengaged, essentially *uninvolved*."[20] A learning encounter that is experiential, embodied, and emotional can, she suggests, be formative in a long-lasting and deep – even ontological – sense: "tacit learning shapes subjectivities."[21] In this light, it seems particularly suited to the kind of learning that many cultural memory spaces purport to provide. And yet, it is precisely this type of emotional coercion that critics such as Matthias Heyl find problematic. In the context of the cultural memory of historical trauma, the experiential approach reflects not only the pedagogical but also the moral or ethical priorities of the institutions involved. Emotion is seen as a catalyst for moral transformation; its choreography through interactive exhibits, personal narratives and other devices is thus more than a simple attempt to educate visitors about the past, it seeks to implicate each individual within the sphere of responsibility implied by the duty of remembrance. Nowhere is this more evident than at sites of Holocaust remembrance.

---

17 Witcomb. "Interactivity: Thinking Beyond," 359.
18 As Hooper-Greenhill puts it: "The conscious processes of verbal experience, which involve speaking, reading, listening, are not enough to engender true learning; the feeling processes, which are largely unconscious, must also be engaged and the way to do this is through bodily action. The research data shows the power of active bodily engagement to generate enjoyment, knowledge, understanding and enhanced self-confidence." Eilean Hooper-Greenhill. *Museums and Education: Purpose, Pedagogy, Performance*. London and New York: Routledge, 2007, 171.
19 Hooper-Greenhill. *Museums and Education*, 175.
20 Ibid.
21 Ibid, 179.

The spatial choreography of emotion: architecture and embodied experience at Holocaust memorials and museums

The United States Holocaust Memorial and Museum in Washington offers one of the most well- known examples of a memory museum that combines interactive and narrative elements in order to provide visitors with an experiential encounter with the cultural memory of historical trauma. A much debated 'immersive' prop used by the museum are the 'identity cards' with which visitors are presented on entering. An accompaniment to the permanent exhibition, these small booklets describe the experiences of someone who lived in Europe during the Holocaust and are designed to "help visitors to personalize the historical events of the time."[22] Interactive elements such as this, combined with other details of exhibition design – the inclusion of individual photographs of victims, and of replicas of original artefacts, for example – go a long way to creating the type of emotive and engaging experience that, according to the museum website "with unique power and authenticity [...] teaches millions of people each year about the dangers of unchecked hatred and the need to prevent genocide." A major part of the museum's effectiveness lies not only in the objects and artefacts presented, however, but in the space in which they are housed. From the outset, the architectural design of the space privileged an emotional understanding of the Holocaust, and was tailored to provide visitors with an affective experience appropriate to the gravity of the subject matter. As the architect James Ingo Freed explains:

> I felt intuitively that this was an emotional building not an intellectual building [...] I don't believe that you could ever understand the Holocaust with the mind. You have to feel it.[23]

> It is not meant to be an architectural walk, or a walk through memory, or an exposition of emotion, but all of this. I want to leave it open as a resonator of emotions. Odd or quiet is not enough. It must be intestinal, visceral; it must take you in its grip.[24]

---

[22] United States Holocaust Memorial Museum Division of Education online. *Resources for the Classroom: Identification cards.* http://www.ushmm.org/education/foreducators/resource/pdf/idcards.pdf (19 September 2012).
[23] James Ingo Freed. "The United States Holocaust Memorial Museum." *Assemblage* 9 (1989): 59, 65.
[24] Ingo Freed. "The United States Holocaust Memorial Museum," 73.

In order to heighten the experience, Freed sought to produce in visitors a feeling of separation and alienation from the city they were in, to mark both spatially and acoustically that they were entering a different realm: "We disorient you, shifting and re-centering you three times, to separate you emotionally as well as visually from Washington."[25] In addition to this spatial separation of visitors from their normal, "outside" lives, the museum's architectural form – and its manipulation by the exhibition designers – makes use of movement to direct or choreograph visitors' bodies in ways that provoke particular physiological and emotional effects. As Edward Linenthal explains:

> The feel and rhythm of the space and the setting of mood was important. Appelbaum [the head of the design team] identified different qualities of space that helped to mediate the narrative: constrictive space on the third floor for example, where the visitors enter the world of the camps, the space becomes tight and mean, heavy and dark.[26]

Appelbaum himself has commented that he sought to recreate for visitors the feeling of flux and movement that existed during the years of exile and persecution under the Nazi regime. This inclusion of an embodied and emotive experience of movement was, he explains, central to the empathy-based pedagogy of the museum:

> We realised that if we followed those people under all that pressure as they moved from their normal lives into ghettos, out of ghettos into trains, from trains to camps, within the pathways of the camps, until finally to the end...[i]f visitors could take that same journey, they would understand the story because they will have experienced the story.[27]

This emphasis on the movement of visitors' bodies, and on the haptic and sensory aspects of visitor experience as catalysts for empathic affect, marks the United States Holocaust Memorial Museum out as one of the earliest attempts to enact what I am calling the *spatial* choreography of emotion. Its innovative design prefigures similar architectural approaches at Holocaust museums and memorials built around the world, including the Memorial to the Murdered Jews of Europe and the Jewish Museum in Berlin. Both are similar to the Washington museum in that they enact what is first and foremost an *architectural* experience. As we shall see, in these memory spaces, the material aspects of the

---

25 Ibid, 65.
26 Edward T. Linenthal. "The Boundaries of Memory: The United States Holocaust Museum." *American Quarterly* 46.3 (1994): 408.
27 Ralph Appelbaum. "For the Living." WETA-TV (PBS) transcript, roll 128, t-27, 3–4, cited in Linenthal. "The Boundaries of Memory," 410.

architectural design and the space itself, in which visitors move, speak, and breathe, are at the core of the experience offered to the public.

The Jewish Museum

Even before the official opening of Berlin's Jewish Museum in 2001, more than 350,000 visitors queued to visit the empty building designed by Polish born architect Daniel Libeskind, securing the status of the new museum as a major architectural highlight in the city's ever evolving urban landscape. Originally intended as an annex to the existing city museum, Libeskind's design altered the very parameters of the architectural competition launched by the city planners: not only has the Jewish Museum gained its own, fully independent identity, but its own extension in the form of an academy and research centre has recently opened across the street. Libeskind's proposal was – in the words of James Young – a "spatial enactment of a philosophical problem", namely, "how does a city 'house' the memory of a people no longer at 'home' there?"[28] His response to this problem drew on resources well beyond the anticipated confines of architectural design: a broken Star of David, plotted on a map of pre-war Berlin; an unfinished opera; an essay by Walter Benjamin and a list of the names of Jewish inhabitants of the city deported to concentration camps.[29] The title of the proposal, "Between the Lines", referred to what Libeskind described as "two lines of thinking, organisation, and relationship. One is a straight line, but broken into many fragments; the other is a torturous line, but continuing indefinitely."[30] Between these two lines, as between the architectural lines of the museum, there emerges a series of voids, indicating the absence of Jewish life in Berlin since the Shoah.[31] The unique spatiality of Daniel Libeskind's design – cold empty spaces bordered by jagged edges and irregular, leaning concrete walls, the angular, zinc clad exterior punctured by a series of gashes or slits – provides both a literal and metaphorical representation of absence and discontinuity. Simultaneously on the verge of becoming and of unbecoming, the building was to serve – in Libeskind's own words – as "an emblem where the not visible has made itself apparent as a void, an invisible." In line with the New Museology approach de-

---

28 James E. Young. "Daniel Libeskind's Jewish Museum in Berlin: The Uncanny Arts of Memorial Architecture." *Jewish Social Studies* 6.2 (2000): 10, 1.
29 Daniel Libeskind. *The Space of an Encounter.* London: Thames and Hudson, 2001, 26–27.
30 Libeskind. *The Space of an Encounter*, 23.
31 Arnold-de Simine. "Memory Museum and Museum Text," 22.

scribed above, Libeskind placed spectator *experience* at the core of his philosophical concept: "The idea is very simple: to build a museum around a void that runs through it, a void that is to be experienced by the public."[32] For Libeskind, the design of this museum offered an opportunity to rewrite the museum script, including the role played by visitors. "The museum form itself", he asserted, "must be rethought to transcend the passive involvement of the viewer."[33] A key stage in this process, and an important side effect of Libeskind's deconstructive design, has been to usurp the didactic structures of the traditional exhibition space, thereby destabilising visitors' expectations. As James Young explained in 2000:

> Instead of merely housing the collection, this building seeks to estrange it from the viewer's own preconceptions. Such walls and oblique angles, [Libeskind] hopes, will defamiliarize the all-too-familiar ritual objects and historical chronologies.[34]

The museum's exhibits have in many ways become secondary to the spatial topography of the building itself, transforming it into a *memorial* space that troubles the very historical narratives it holds, and forces visitors to think differently about what a museum *does*. According to Naomi Stead, the Jewish Museum Berlin proposes a complex overlapping of museum, memorial and monument: "the museum as archive, for the collection and display of historical objects, the museum as memorial, for the provocation of memory in its visitors, and the museum as monument, the physical embodiment of memory."[35] And yet, the Jewish Museum is not a Holocaust memorial, even if it is frequently mistaken for one. As the deputy director of the museum Tom Freudenheim stated in 2001: "We've been very assertive about not being a Holocaust Museum. The Holocaust is inescapable here anyway, since the building has a Holocaust Tower and Libeskind's architecture has all kinds of suggestive issues, if you want to read the building in a certain way [...] It's a very important and a critical part of [the] story and we're not trying to downplay or underplay it or push it away, but it isn't the whole story of the history of the Jews in Germany."[36] The "story" that

---

32 Daniel Libeskind. "Between the lines." *Daniel Libeskind: Erweiterung des Berlin Museums mit Abteilung Judisches Museum*. Ed. Kristin Feireiss. Berlin: Ernst & Sohn, 1992, 63.
33 Libeskind. *The Space of an Encounter*, 29.
34 Young. "Daniel Libeskind's Jewish Museum," 17.
35 Naomi Stead. "The Ruins of History: allegories of destruction in Daniel Libeskind's Jewish Museum." *Open Museum Journal* 2 (2000): 7.
36 Tom L. Freudenheim, Gautam Dasgupta, and Bonnie Marranca. "Berlin's New Jewish Museum: An Interview with Tom Freudenheim." *Journal of Performance and Art* 65 vol. 22.2 (2000): 42.

the museum exhibition would like to tell, critic Peter Chametzky suggests, is one of German-Jewish contributions to intellectual, scientific and artistic life; a story of "assimilation and cooperation" that might be used to "promote a qualified tolerance of cultural diversity in contemporary Germany – to define the German national narrative as one that can be inclusive of religious and ethnic difference."[37] This narrative, of course, runs contrary to the message communicated through the building's architectural voice. Indeed, there is a marked difference in mood between the two floors of the museum – the upper floor housing the permanent exhibition, with its often cheerful celebration of German-Jewish culture (epitomised, perhaps, in the vending machine offering kosher Haribo sweets), and the lower floor, which visitors explore first. This lower space is made up of three intersecting windowless "axes" or corridors. The Axis of Exile, with its uneven and ascending floor, leads outside to the Garden of Exile, and is framed by increasingly narrow, slanting walls. The Axis of Continuity forms a path connecting the old building of the museum with the staircase leading up to the exhibition levels. It is interrupted or cut across by the Axis of the Holocaust, which itself leads to the dead end of what has become known as the "Holocaust Tower": an unheated, twenty-four metre tall void lit only by a small opening in the top corner of the space. This "voided void"[38] echoes the other empty, unheated and unlit voids that run vertically through the new building, and which refer, according to Libeskind, "to that which can never be exhibited when it comes to Jewish Berlin History: Humanity reduced to ashes."[39]

One of the most common readings of this spatial design, beyond an analysis of its possible metaphorical meanings, is to emphasise its emotional impact upon visitors. The museum building is said to provoke an "emotional and psychological disturbance in the visitor" akin to a shattering of the ego.[40] Its architecture, it is argued, wants to invoke a "feeling of disorientation and irritation",[41] it destabilizes visitors, "somatically inducing feelings of displacement, emptiness, loss."[42] Observations within the space, as well as many visitors' own accounts of the museum, would seem to support this analysis. A sense of disorientation is visible on faces and in body language, as visitors wonder which path

---

[37] Peter Chametzky. "Not What We Expected: The Jewish museum Berlin in Practice." *Museum and Society* 6.3 (2008): 227.
[38] Libeskind. *The Space of an Encounter*, 29.
[39] Daniel Libeskind, citied on Jewish Museum Berlin Website, http://www.jmberlin.de/main/EN/04-About-The-Museum/01-Architecture/01-libeskind-Building.php (1 November 2012).
[40] Stead. "The Ruins of History," 10.
[41] Arnold-de Simine. "Memory Museum and Museum Text," 24.
[42] Chametzky. "Not What We Expected," 220.

they are supposed to take, which axis should come first. On one occasion, I observed a man asking one of the museum guides for directions, only to be told that in this lower level, there is no direction: each must decide for him or herself which way to walk around the exhibit. Other visitors reflected critically upon the order in which they had decided to view the space: coming out of the "Holocaust Tower" one Frenchman commented to his group: "It's difficult. It's the end. We should have done that at the end." The result, for many, is a sense of unfamiliarity and apprehension expressed in a cautious and uncertain step, and the frequent looking around to locate companions. As one visitor expressed it:

> The ground floor is very uncomfortable – all these empty rooms, highlighting the curves and sharp angles. You feel unsure, unconfident and fearful. You need to do some efforts to go further, every step seems to be difficult, you feel a balance disorder.[43]

Visitor books – which are in general completed after visitors have been through the permanent exhibition on the upper level – refer again and again (though by no means *always*) to the experiential or emotional effects of the building. Comments such as: "The Void Monument – I cried", and "L'architecture fait vivre une réele histoire [the architecture brings history to life]" seem to confirm, at least partially, the interpretation of the museum as "an experiential space [which] tries to generate visceral reactions and emotionally as well as psychologically disturbing effects of disorientation in museum visitors."[44] The emotional disturbance experienced by visitors has been interpreted by some scholars as a form of re-enactment or re-living of the process of mourning. As Stead puts it:

> The museum is able to function as a memorial without conventional monumentality, since each visitor 'performs' the commemoration as a function of his or her passage through the space. The museum is thus 'worked through' in a choreographed process analogous to Freud's work of mourning.[45]

---

43 The visitor accounts cited in this article were collected over a period of two years between 2010 and 2012, through various methods, including informal interviews, an online survey and an examination of visitors' own written accounts of their experiences in visitor comment books at the sites and on online blogs. In some cases, as here, I have drawn from student essays written for the course 'Testimony and its Reception in 20th Century Literature, Art and Film' that I taught at the University of Potsdam in the Summer Semester of 2012.
44 Arnold-de Simine. "Memory Museum and Museum Text," 21. Arnold-de Simine lists this experiential reading of the museum as one of three possible readings, the two other being metaphorical (the museum as metaphor that it is the visitor's responsibility to interpret) and allegorical (the museum as emblem).
45 Stead. "The Ruins of History," 14.

The Jewish Museum Berlin takes on an "antimonumental monumentality" for Stead, to the extent that it privileges the individual experience of each museum visitor as part of a "performance" of mourning and commemoration.[46] The emphasis here is upon the notion of active spectatorship; the idea, central to the New Museology approach, that interpretation is open. This concept is clearly expressed on an information panel at the bottom of the stairs as one enters the lower floor. Citing Libeskind, the panel instructs visitors about the architectural concept: "What is important is the experience you get from it. The interpretation is open." This assertion of openness and inclusion does not go unappreciated by visitors, as the following comment indicates:

> I really liked being a part of the monument – that my own feelings symbolised something, that they meant something. I could really experience the installations with (almost) all of my senses. This kind of experience was very personal because certainly every person thinks about the same things in a different way.[47]

And yet, despite claims of openness, there are elements of the lower floor of the Jewish Museum that act in ways that most certainly guide or direct visitors' emotions. Even if, arguably, the architectural experience may be open to interpretation, the museum's display practices seem to counteract this endeavour, cleaving, in David A. Ellison's words "to a more conventional style at odds with the building's larger claims to auratic abstraction."[48] An example of this occurs at the entrance to the Garden of Exile, where an information panel makes clear the intended effects of the space. Another citation from Libeskind informs visitors about the sensations a stroll through the forty-nine columns on slanting ground will evoke in them, and about the interpretation they should make of the experience: "One feels a little sick walking through it. But it is accurate, because that is what perfect order feels like when you leave the history of Berlin." Small prompts such as this make clear the intended effects of the museum space and point, however subtly, to the choreography of emotion at work there.

---

46 Ibid, 10.
47 Extract from a student essay, written for the course "Testimony and its Reception in 20th Century Literature, Art and Film", Potsdam, 2012.
48 David A. Ellison. "The Spoiler's Art: Embarassed Space as Memorialisation." *The South Atlantic Quarterly* 110.1 (2011): 92.

The Memorial to the Murdered Jews of Europe

> The memorial's design is experience-based, insofar as it aims to create a particular emotional experience among visitors who walk through the vast field of stelae [...] It is intended to elicit a somatic, corporal form of memory, based not primarily on reflection but on emotional experience.[49]

Like the Jewish Museum Berlin, the Memorial to the Murdered Jews of Europe has been described by scholars as an experiential memorial space in which emotion is privileged over intellectual engagement with historical facts. Opened to the public in 2005, after more than a decade of debate and controversy,[50] the memorial occupies a large plot in the centre of Berlin, between Brandenburg Gate and Potsdamer Platz. It was designed by New York based architect Peter Eisenman (originally in collaboration with sculptor Richard Serra), and consists of an undulating field of 2,711 concrete stelae, which visitors may enter and exit from any angle. Given that Libeskind once studied under Eisenman, it is not surprising that this memorial should possess the same kind of "auratic abstraction" often associated with the Jewish museum. While criticised by some, the abstract elements of the design – there is little signage, and, if one fails (as many do) to visit the information centre underneath, nothing to indicate the intended purpose of the memorial – reflect both Eisenman's own conceptual struggle with the problematic of aestheticizing the Holocaust, and his stated desire to leave the site open to all uses and interpretations. As he famously commented: "You can't tell them what to do with it. If they want to knock the stones over tomorrow, honestly, that's fine. People are going to picnic in the field. Children will play tag in the field. There will be fashion models modeling there and films will be shot there. I can easily imagine some spy shoot 'em ups ending in the field. What can I say? It's not a sacred place."[51] Not a sacred or "authentic" place, (though building, as Irit Dekel suggests, literally and figuratively, on the palimpsest of Berlin's historical memory, including Goebbel's headquarters

---

[49] Kirsten Harjes. "Stumbling Stones: Holocaust Memorials, National Identity, and Democratic Inclusion in Berlin." *German Politics & Society* 23.1 (2005): 142.

[50] These debates and the process of commissioning the memorial are well documented elsewhere. See, for example James Young. "Germany's Holocaust Memorial Problem – And Mine." *The Public Historian* 24.4 (2002): 65–80.

[51] "How long does one feel guilty? SPIEGEL Interview with Holocaust Monument Architect Peter Eisenman"*Spiegel Online International*, 5 September 2005. http://www.spiegel.de/international/spiegel-interview-with-holocaust-monument-architect-peter-eisenman-how-long-does-one-feel-guilty-a-355252.html (1 November 2012).

and Hitler's bunker nearby[52]), the memorial does not stand for anything. It is not intended to be read as a symbol; it is, Eisenman has somewhat cryptically explained, "what Immanuel Kant calls the *Ding an sich*. It is a Thing; it is there [...] you cannot represent that which defies description."[53] And yet, it is clear from Eisenman's comments elsewhere that he did have a specific effect in mind when he designed the memorial. In an interview for *Die Zeit*, Eisenman explained that he did not wish to represent the Holocaust (in any case for Eisenman an impossible and flawed task), but rather to produce an experience of uncertainty for visitors: "They should ask: what is this? Where am I?" Even more striking (and precise) is his assertion that at the memorial, "the cognitive experience should give way to the emotional".[54] Eisenman, then, wanted the memorial to provoke an affective experience for visitors, causing them to question themselves and the very process of remembrance and memorialisation itself. He has to a large extent been successful in this aim. As Hanno Rauterberg wrote in his comments accompanying a dedicated photo essay about the site, the Memorial to the Murdered Jews of Europe is a space that cannot be fully captured through the eyes, it is not a memorial to be *looked at*, but must rather be experienced in three and even four dimensions. This is not a landscape of remembrance [*Erinnerungslandschaft*], he suggests; what has been created is a landscape of *experience* [*Erfahrungslandschaft*].[55] The "experience" offered by this space is sensory and *embodied;* visitors walk through and interact with the Field of Stelae, get lost within it, while all the time absorbing the sounds, textures and shadows it – and its other visitors – produce. For Kirsten Harjes, this kind of design departs from traditional memorial models in that it offers "a form of memory that is more tangible, tactile, and authentic", a memorial in which "the visitor emotionally and physically participates in the memory".[56] As at the Jewish Museum, a walk through this memorial is designed to be disorienting: narrow spaces, cold concrete, and uneven floors give one the sensation

---

52 Irit Dekel. "Pan-topia: Exposing the Palimpsest of Meanings at the Holocaust Memorial, Berlin." *History and Theory: The Protocols Bezalel Academy of Art and Design* 14 (2009). http://bezalel.secured.co.il/zope/home/en/1252746792 (1 November 2012).
53 Peter Eisenman. Interview(s) with Johan Åhr. Johan Åhr. "Memory and Mourning in Berlin: On Peter Eisenman's Holocaust-Mahnmal." *Modern Judaism* 28.3 (2005): 208, 284.
54 "Was ist noch Kritisch?" [Interview with *Die Zeit* and Peter Eisenman led by Thomas Assheuer, Hanno Rauterberg, Ullrich Schwarz] *Zeit Online*, 1 January 2001. http://www.zeit.de/2001/05/200105_eisenman-intervi.xml (1 November 2012).
55 Hanno Rauterberg. "Baustelle des Gedenkens." *Holocaust Mahnmal Berlin*. Baden: Lars Müller Publishers, 2005, 14.
56 Harjes."Stumbling Stones: Holocaust Memorials, National Identity, and Democratic Inclusion in Berlin," 142.

of being lost, unsure and uncertain on one's feet. Visitor accounts of the site indicate that a number of people experienced rather strong – and often disturbing – emotional responses, using words such as 'claustrophobic', 'confusing', 'oppressive' and 'trapped' to describe how they felt.[57] One visitor admits: 'I was not exactly scared, but I remember that it felt strange and eery [sic]. I was so relieved when I saw one of my friends again because the situation made me feel alone and disoriented.'[58] Reported physiological responses included goose pimples, increased heart rate and general feelings of tension.[59] In travel blogs describing the memorial, words such as 'eerie', 'chilling', 'sobering', 'unsettling', 'isolated' and 'alone' appear over and over again, with one woman describing the concrete stelae of the memorial as 'looming menacingly', adding that she 'emerged again with relief' on the other side of the memorial. Another blog writer stresses the unexpected feeling of loneliness within the otherwise busy public space:

> I walked deep into the middle and with each uneven step I seemed to descend from where I had started at street level. I could no longer see the horizon; all I could see were gray stones surrounding me, towering over me. Under my feet was a grid pattern which seemed to simulate the larger grid I was lost in. I looked up to the sky for some orientation, but the indistinct, overcast sky provided no texture for me. From the screams and laughter in the distance I knew I wasn't alone, but for that moment I felt alone, completely and utterly alone.[60]

These types of affective and even physiological response are welcomed by Eisenman, who despite his stated desire to leave the memorial open to all interpretations and interactions, confessed: "I have heard people say they were in awe and felt a sense of speechlessness; their hands got moist, and I am pleased with these kinds of reactions."[61] And yet, simple observation on any day of the week will prove that Eisenman was correct in his prediction; the memorial is different things to different people. For young children with little previous knowledge of the Holocaust, it is a joyous playground. For a number of my respondents the experience was barely affective at all. For the author of the follow-

---

[57] These responses were collected by the author between 2010 and 2012 through an online survey entitled "Experiences of Memory".
[58] Extract from a student essay, written for the course 'Testimony and its Reception in 20th Century Literature, Art and Film', Potsdam, 2012.
[59] Response to the survey "Experiences of Memory".
[60] *Pillar Perspectives Blog* 7 June 2012. www.lonelyplanet.com/travelblogs/67/158425/Pillar+Perspectives+-+Holocaust+Memorial+Berlin?destId=359364 (31 October 2012).
[61] Åhr. "Memory and Mourning in Berlin," 285.

ing travel blog, the Memorial was simply another stop on a long list of tourist attractions, equal in interest and importance to the site of a celebrity faux-pas:

> We saw the Brandenburg Gate, Parliament House, the hotel where Michael Jackson dangled his baby over the balcony, the Holocaust Memorial and other buildings.[62]

Similarly, at the Jewish Museum, it would be inaccurate to say that all, or perhaps even most visitors were deeply emotionally moved by the space, or, if they were, that they necessarily interpreted this as a form of remembrance or commemoration of Holocaust victims. Even for those who did report signs of emotional unsettlement, we might question the cause or source of their apparently affective experiences – were these visitors simply feeling what they thought they *should* feel? Was their account of the experience influenced by what they thought I, as a researcher, wanted to hear? In other words, shouldn't we treat the notion of authenticity with suspicion, even, or especially when used in relation to emotions? As important as these questions are, I would like to set them aside for now; let us for the sake of argument accept that at least *some* visitors do genuinely experience emotional unsettlement at these sites. The question still remains: what is the effect of all this? Does such affect enable visitors to better understand and respond with empathy to the suffering of victims, and does it encourage them to re-evaluate their role within the landscape of cultural memory?

Constructing chronotopes of witnessing: Experience, emotion and transformation

> The [United States Holocaust Memorial] Museum needs to elicit in its visitors an imaginary identification – the desire to know and to feel, the curiosity and passion that shape the postmemory of survivor children. At its best, it would include all of its visitors in the generation of postmemory. The Museum's architecture and exhibits aim at just that effect; to get us close to the affect of the event.'[63]

Marianne Hirsch's suggestion that *all* visitors to the United States Holocaust Memorial Museum might in some sense adopt, through their experience of the space, the role of carriers of memory in a way similar to the children of survivors,

---

[62] Angela and Nicole MacCaster. "Berlin." *Travel Blog*. http://www.travelblog.org/Europe/Germany/Berlin/Berlin/blog-64781.html (1 November 2012).
[63] Marianne Hirsch. *Family Frames: Photography, Narrative, and Postmemory*. Cambridge: Harvard University Press, 1997, 249.

reflects a belief – also held to a certain extent by the museum designers – that providing visitors with an embodied, emotional experience will *involve* them in a way that exceeds mere unattached spectatorship and leads them more towards the position of (secondary) witnesses. A similar assumption could be and has been made about the possible impact of our two Berlin-based memory spaces. Memorial spaces such as these are, as Andrew Gross has commented, designed to "*act out* the trauma of the Holocaust as architecture; walking through them is supposed to be a step towards *working through* that trauma as feeling and experience."[64] Both aim to engage their interlocutors on an embodied, emotional and *ethical* level: it is not only (or not at all) about leaving with a more accurate knowledge of the facts of the Holocaust; indeed, at the Holocaust Memorial, many visitors overlook or decide not to explore the information centre at all. Rather, the aesthetic encounter with the memorial space itself is conceived as a moment of "witnessing"; a unique and *corporeal* experience, characterised by intense and often unsettling affect that, it is alleged, provides a deeper understanding of the other's trauma. That this kind of empathic affect might possess ethical or transformative potential is acknowledged by psychologist Martin Hoffman and, to a lesser extent, Dominick LaCapra in their separate work on 'empathic distress' and 'empathic unsettlement'. Both concepts adopt a broad definition of empathy in terms of its manifestation as affect. Empathic unsettlement or distress can accommodate a range of emotions from discomfort to fear or sadness, to anger and a sense of injustice. For LaCapra, empathic unsettlement consists in "being responsive to the traumatic experience of others, notably of victims" and involves "a kind of virtual experience through which one puts oneself in the other's position while recognizing the difference of that position."[65] According to LaCapra, opening oneself to empathic unsettlement is pedagogically useful because "it complements and supplements [the] empirical research and analysis" of traditional historiography by helping us to "understand traumatic events and victims".[66] For Hoffman, empathic distress may also serve to motivate pro-social attitudes and behaviour, thus transforming passive spectators into active, ethical witnesses. Empathic distress becomes a form of witnessing, he suggests, "when it becomes so intense and penetrates so deeply into one's motive system that it changes one's behaviour beyond the immediate situation", inspiring one to act on behalf of suffering others in both

---

64 Andrew Gross. "Holocaust Tourism in Berlin: Religion, Politics, and the Negative Sublime." *Journeys: The International Journal of Travel and Travel Writing* 7.2 (2006): 76.
65 Dominick LaCapra. *Writing History, Writing Trauma*. Baltimore: John Hopkins University Press, 2001, 78.
66 Ibid, 78.

general and specific ways.⁶⁷ The potential for empathy to promote witnessing attitudes has also been explored by E. Ann Kaplan in her work on atrocity images.⁶⁸ Kaplan cites a particularly poignant passage from Susan Sontag's *On Photography*, in which Sontag describes how deeply moved and *altered* she had been after viewing images of the Bergen-Belsen and Dachau concentration camps for the first time: "Nothing I have seen – in photographs or in real life – ever cut me as sharply, deeply, instantaneously. Indeed it seems plausible to me to divide my life into two parts, before I saw those photographs (I was twelve) and after."⁶⁹ Despite Sontag's own critical reflections upon the viewing of atrocity photographs, it is clear that in some sense her early encounter with what are by now iconic images of suffering constituted a "breaking point" in her understanding of the world – one that may well have initiated her lifelong political engagement with human suffering and its representation. Indeed, this is a convincing example of a witnessing attitude emerging from a personal experience of empathic distress after a mediated encounter with the suffering of others. For Kaplan, witnessing involves "feeling so shocked by suffering that one is moved to act."⁷⁰ "In witnessing", she writes, "we understand empathy's potential social impact, especially when it is deeply and enduringly felt"⁷¹ – as in the case of Susan Sontag's experience. But witnessing is not the only possible outcome of empathy, as Kaplan is careful to explain. Indeed, there are cases where too much affect or the "wrong" type of empathy may work against ethical or political engagement. Kaplan uses the term "empty empathy" to describe "the transitory, fleeting nature of the empathic emotions that viewers often experience; [when] what starts as an empathic response gets transformed into numbing by the succession of catastrophes displayed before the viewer."⁷² In other words, she suggests, overexposure to (re)presentations of suffering and empathic or affective *over-arousal* can in fact limit our capacity for pro-social behaviour. There are cases, she notes, when "the empathic response to an image of catastrophe [is]

---

67 Martin L. Hoffman. "Empathy, Justice, and the Law." *Empathy: Philosophical and Psychological Perspectives*. Eds. Amy Coplan and Peter Goldie. Oxford: Oxford University Press, 2011, 236–7.
68 E. Ann Kaplan. "Global trauma and public feelings: Viewing images of catastrophe." *Consumption Markets and Culture* 11.1 (2008): 3–24; "Empathy and Trauma Culture: Imaging Catastrophe." *Empathy: Philosophical and Psychological Perspectives*. Eds. Amy Coplan and Peter Goldie. Oxford: Oxford University Press, 2011, 255–76.
69 Susan Sontag. *On Photography*. New York: Anchor Doubleday, 1989, 19–20.
70 Kaplan. "Empathy and Trauma Culture," 257.
71 Ibid.
72 Ibid, 256.

so strong and so painful that the individual turns away, or thinks distracting thoughts, unable to endure the feelings aroused."[73] In this case, not only does too much empathy have a paralysing effect, disabling the observer's capacity for pro-social action, but the experience of empty empathy itself becomes a form of harm or violence against *spectators*, disempowering them and, in some cases, leaving them traumatised themselves.

> The trouble with images that arouse empty empathy is the passive position such pictures put the viewer in [...] they do not move the viewer to action. They rather make one feel hopeless.[74]

Some visitor accounts of our two Berlin memorials seem to support this view. In one woman's account, the experience of affect and empathic unsettlement is accompanied by over arousal and paralysing feelings of dejection and hopelessness. For this woman, the Jewish Museum represented the culmination of a series of affect-filled cultural memory experiences in Berlin that resulted in a kind of ethical *disempowerment:*

> While all of the historical information we took in was incredible, it took an emotional toll on my husband and I. There's just no way that you can tour Berlin's Nazi sites and museums without coming to the conclusion that most Germans were culpable in the rise of Hitler and the majority carried out his fanatical and genocidal policies without question. In the Jewish Museum cafeteria, I covered my face with my hands. "So basically, most humans are evil", I said to him. "Pretty much", he replied.[75]

My own personal response to the Jewish Museum was similar. Visiting it for the first time, I found myself gradually overwhelmed by the space; my discomfort in the museum was palpable and culminated in my viewing of an installation by Menashe Kadishman. Kadishman's work is made up of hundreds of metal faces laid on the floor in one of the "voids" that are so central to the architecture of the museum. These faces are meant to represent, I assumed, the Jewish victims of the Holocaust, and are laid out in such a way that visitors can walk over them. On witnessing this performance of interactive spectatorship, I experienced a very physical feeling of nausea. The effect of empathic unsettlement for me was that I left the memorial space immediately, unable to continue my tour of the museum and its exhibits. And yet, I am still writing and thinking

---

73 Ibid.
74 Ibid, 268.
75 "Berlin: Third Reich Site."*Chris Around the World: A travel journalist's tips from the road.* http://caroundtheworld.com/2010/12/01/berlin-third-reich-sites/ (9 March 2012).

about the experience today, years later, just as the woman in my previous citation wrote and reflected upon her experience after the event.

There is some evidence that the Holocaust Memorial, while often emotionally or physically distressing to visitors, also served to increase the sense of understanding and ethical engagement of some respondents, either by providing them with the physical and temporal space to reflect or by prompting a recognition of the responsibility of visitors to abstain from certain forms of behaviour, with the ensuing a motivation to act upon that recognition by confronting other visitors:

> Being in Berlin and visiting the memorial brought all of my latent feelings and emotions about the Holocaust into very sharp focus [...] My visit to Berlin was a whirlwind of activity; visiting the Memorial provided me with a moment of calm. [76]

> I generally remember that it was always very intense moments walking through the memorial. The slight loss of orientation, the disconnection to what happens outside the memorial when diving into it and the quietness are encouraging emotions and thoughts. Apart from these feelings I always felt anger and frustration about people running around, shouting without any signs of reflection. I was often tempted to confront them to think about what they do and where they are doing it.[77]

Some visitor accounts of the memorial clearly indicated a progression from empathic distress to a subsequent process of reflection and even ethical engagement, both in relation to the Holocaust as the original event, and to the commemorative function of the memorial. This is especially evident in the following blog entry:

> The vibe I am getting at the site was – LOST. A frustrating sentiment I am sure that every Jew experienced during the Holocaust. Then another vibe was – PANIC. I don't know but I just felt hysteria. And lastly – WHY. I mean why the murder? It did not have to happen, right? I believe that art only speaks to you when you let it, and it's very special when it does.[78]

Other accounts – both solicited and unsolicited – focus on the impact and behaviour of other visitors. For some, children playing hide and seek among the stelae was disturbing and disrespectful; for others it was something positive, "a sign that the memorial was engaging the imagination of the visitor, reaching

---

[76] Response to the survey "Experiences of Memory".
[77] Response to the survey "Experiences of Memory".
[78] "Holocaust Memorial Berlin." *Dutched Pinay Travel Diaries.* http://misst2000ph.blogspot.de/2012/04/holocaust-memorial-in-berlin.html (1 November 2012).

out to them on different levels, the emotional as well as the intellectual."[79] Interaction with other visitors was in some cases even viewed as an indicator of the existence of a community bound by a shared burden of remembrance: "Through encountering other spectators, we consider not only the space but ourselves as spectators and as individuals that share a history."[80] In the case of the following blogger, not only does the experience of empathic unsettlement encourage reflection or confrontation with major ethical and social questions, it also provides a source of personal catharsis.

> I'm a little tired and I know that reflected in the bell-bottom of each of my tears are some slight visions and reflections of more immediate personal heartaches of (maybe) missing home and (certainly) family who my heart is missing now and from the past as I begin this huge journey. My body has seized the opportunity; found its excuse to let it all leak out a little bit.[81]

In all of the cases I am citing here, it is impossible to know in concrete terms if and how these visitors' experiences altered their subsequent behaviour, beyond encouraging them to reflect and speak about the memorial spaces. As Susannah Radstone has warned, there is a danger that the processes of traumatic identification encouraged by sites such as these may come to replace more traditional, and perhaps more effective modes of political engagement.[82] And yet, it does seem plausible to suggest that the visitors cited have undergone some kind of transformation as a result of their experiences. If we can speak of a witnessing moment, then this moment occurs, I would argue, not in the experience of affect or unsettlement, but in the decision to reflect upon this experience with others. Many who visit these sites do chose to write or speak about their experience, or to post photographs and short films of their visits online. The sharing network *You Tube* is replete with such videos – from extracts of a tourist's amateur holiday film to recordings of complex dance choreographies performed within the memorial space. Such online testimonials are often intended to educate or inform others who may not be able to visit the sites – one blogger, for example, published a post dedicated to encouraging those who visit Berlin to engage

---

[79] "Friday photo – Children at the Holocaust memorial in Berlin. 17 April 2009" *Heather on her Travels*.http://www.heatheronhertravels.com/ (1 November 2012).
[80] Extract from a student essay, written for the course "Testimony and its Reception in 20th Century Literature, Art and Film", Potsdam, 2012.
[81] *Berlin: History, blisters and wide open spaces.* http://www.travbuddy.com/travel-blogs/41672/Berlin-History-blisters-wide-12, (1 November 2012).
[82] Susannah Radstone. "Memory Studies: For and Against." *Journal of Memory Studies* 1.1 (2008): 34. Cited in Arnold de Simine. "Memory Museum and Museum Text," 18.

with its Holocaust history. Of the three sites she recommends, the two she describes most fervently are the Jewish Museum and the Memorial to the Murdered Jews of Europe.

Conclusion

The Memorial to the Murdered Jews of Europe and the Jewish Museum in Berlin construct a spatial aesthetics in which affective experiences of empathic distress are encouraged via complex interactions of space, form and the movement of bodies. Whether this spatial choreography of emotions will necessarily promote a deeper understanding of trauma and ethical engagement in visitors is by no means a given; indeed, empirical research seems to suggest that visitor responses are as much characterised by ambivalence as they are by empathy or concern. Even when empathy or affect is present, it can have the effect of alienating or paralysing visitors, rather than encouraging them to become engaged politically. When something akin to ethical witnessing or transformation does occur, it usually takes the form of an act of reflection or working through: visitors "bear witness" publically, either through conversation and debate with friends and colleagues or, often, through the use of digital media. A short look at the many and varied comments such digital testimonies inspire demonstrates the extent to which such forms of (inter)active engagement with cultural memory can accord memorial visits with an "afterlife", the potential influence of which is limitless. In all cases, however, it is crucial to acknowledge the significance of that which visitors themselves bring to the aesthetic encounter with the memorial space. Their previous knowledge, expectations and experiences will all have an effect on their experience. For it is they who participate in and perform the choreographic moment – sometimes supporting, sometimes challenging the narrative of the space. Indeed, I would suggest, it may be precisely this spectatorial ambivalence, this possibility for unconditioned and *unchoreographed* responses that provides such memorial spaces with the potential to produce moments of ethical reception or witnessing. Historical memory, like personal memory, is neither stable nor a-political; it cannot guarantee consensus or unity, whether on the macro level of national and transnational politics, or on the micro level of individual encounters with ever-expanding cultural memory practices. In some ways, both the Memorial to the Murdered Jews of Europe and the Jewish Museum Berlin offer an eloquent response to Adorno's critique about poetry after Auschwitz; neither tries to represent the Holocaust in a way that draws a line under the past in any redemptive sense, instead they testify to the impossibility of doing so.

Perhaps it is in this act of witnessing against the possibility of a final, redemptive testimony that visitors to both sites can most ethically partake.

Acknowledgements

My thanks go especially to the students who took part in my course 'Testimony and its Reception in 20th Century Literature, Art and Film', at the University of Potsdam, in the summer of 2012. And also to the Alexander von Humboldt Foundation, who by granting me a fellowship enabled this research to take place. Finally, I thank Professor Aleida Assmann of the University of Konstanz for her guidance and advice.

References

Andermann, Jens and Silke Arnold-de Simine. "Introduction: Memory Community and the New Museum." *Theory, Culture and Society* 29.3 (2012): 3–13.

Arnold-de Simine, Silke. "Memory Museum and Museum Text: Intermediality in Daniel Libeskind's Jewish Museum and WG Sebald's *Austerlitz*." *Theory, Culture, Society* 29.3 (2012): 14–35.

Bernd, Ulrich. "Wer sind wir, heute?" *Die Zeit, No.* 36, 30 August 2012.

Chametzky, Peter. "Not What We Expected: The Jewish Museum Berlin in Practice." *Museum and Society* 6.3 (2008): 216–245.

DDR Museum Website. http://www.ddr-museum.de/en/museum/ (1 November 2012).

Dekel, Irit. "Pan-topia: Exposing the Palimpsest of Meanings at the Holocaust Memorial, Berlin." *History and Theory: The Protocols Bezalel Academy of Art and Design* 14 (2009). http://bezalel.secured.co.il/zope/home/en/1252746792 (1 November 2012).

Deutsches Auswanderer Haus Bremerhaven. http://www.dah-bremerhaven.de/en.museum.php#Museumstechnik (1 November 2012).

Ellison, David A. "The Spoiler's Art: Embarassed Space as Memorialisation." *The South Atlantic Quarterly* 110.1 (2011): 89–100.

Freed, James Ingo. "The United States Holocaust Memorial Museum." *Assemblage* 9 (1989): 58–79.

Freudenheim, Tom L., Gautam Dasgupta, and Bonnie Marranca. "Berlin's New Jewish Museum: An Interview with Tom Freudenheim." *Journal of Performance and Art* 65 vol. 22.2 (2000): 39–47.

Gauck, Jaochim. Presidential Speech on Holocaust Remembrance Day, 27 January 2015. http://www.bundespraesident.de/SharedDocs/Reden/DE/Joachim-Gauck/Reden/2015/01/150127-Bundestag-Gedenken.html (8 April 2015).

Gross, Andrew. "Holocaust Tourism in Berlin: Religion, Politics, and the Negative Sublime." *Journeys: The International Journal of Travel and Travel Writing* 7.2 (2006): 73–100.

Harjes, Kirsten. "Stumbling Stones: Holocaust Memorials, National Identity, and Democratic Inclusion in Berlin." *German Politics & Society* 23.1 (2005): 138–151.

Hein, George E. "The Constructivist Museum." *Journal for Education in Museums* 15 (1995): 15–17.

Heyl, Matthias. *Mit Überwältigendem überwältigen? Auf die nationalsozialistischen Massen Verbrechen bezongene Gedenkstätten und Emotionen*. Keynote Speech at the Berlin-Brandenburgische Forum für zeitgeschichtliche Bildung 2012. http://lernen-aus-der-geschichte.de/Lernen-und-Lehren/content/10658 (8 April 2015).

Hirsch, Marianne. *Family Frames: Photography, Narrative, and Postmemory*. Cambridge: Harvard University Press, 1997.

Hoffman, Martin L. "Empathy, Justice, and the Law" *Empathy: Philosophical and Psychological Perspectives*. Eds. Amy Coplan and Peter Goldie. Oxford: Oxford University Press, 2011. 230–249.

Hooper-Greenhill, Eilean. *Museums and Education: Purpose, Pedagogy, Performance*. London and New York: Routledge, 2007.

Hooper-Greenhill, Eilean. "Studying Visitors." *A Companion to Museum Studies*. Ed. Sharon MacDonald. Oxford: Blackwell Publishing, 2006. 362–376.

Hooper Greenhill, Eilean. *Museums and the Shaping of Knowledge*. New York: Routledge, 1992.

Kaplan, E. Ann. "Global trauma and public feelings: Viewing images of catastrophe." *Consumption Markets and Culture* 11.1 (2008): 3–24.

Kaplan, E. Ann. "Empathy and Trauma Culture: Imaging Catastrophe." *Empathy: Philosophical and Psychological Perspectives*. Eds. Amy Coplan and Peter Goldie. Oxford: Oxford University Press, 2011. 255–76.

LaCapra, Dominick. *Writing History, Writing Trauma*. Baltimore: John Hopkins University Press, 2001.

Libeskind, Daniel. "Between the lines." *Daniel Libeskind: Erweiterung des Berlin Museums mit Abteilung Judisches Museum*. Ed. Kristin Feireiss. Berlin: Ernst & Sohn, 1992.

Libeskind, Daniel. *The Space of an Encounter*. London: Thames and Hudson, 2001.

Linenthal, Edward T. "The Boundaries of Memory: The United States Holocaust Museum." *American Quarterly* 46.3 (1994): 406–433.

Lisle, Debbie. "Sublime Lessons: Education and Ambivalence in War Exhibitions." *Millennium – Journal of International Studies* 34 (2006): 841–862.

Radstone, Susanna. "Memory Studies: For and Against." *Journal of Memory Studies* 1.1 (2008): 31–39.

Rauterberg, Hanno "Baustelle des Gedenkens." *Holocaust Mahnmal Berlin*. Ed. Peter Eisenmann, Baden: Lars Müller Publishers, 2005, 11–16.

Sontag, Susan. *On Photography*. New York, Anchor Doubleday, 1989.

Spiegel Online. "How long does one feel guilty? SPIEGEL Interview with Holocaust Monument Architect Peter Eisenman." *Spiegel Online International* 5 September 2005. http://www.spiegel.de/international/spiegel-interview-with-holocaust-monument-architect-peter-eisenman-how-long-does-one-feel-guilty-a-355252.html (1 November 2012).

Stead, Naomi. "The Ruins of History: allegories of destruction in Daniel Libeskind's Jewish Museum." *Open Museum Journal* 2 (2000): 1–17.

United States Holocaust Memorial Museum Division of Education online. *Resources for the Classroom: Identification cards*. http://www.ushmm.org/education/foreducators/resource/pdf/idcards.pdf (19 September 2012).

Witcomb, Andrea. "Interactivity: Thinking Beyond" *A Companion to Museum Studies*. Ed. Sharon MacDonald. Oxford: Blackwell Publishing, 2006. 353–361.

Young, James E. "Daniel Libeskind's Jewish Museum in Berlin: The Uncanny Arts of Memorial Architecture." *Jewish Social Studies* 6.2 (2000): 1–23.

Young, James E. "Germany's Holocaust Memorial Problem – And Mine." *The Public Historian* 24.4 (2002): 65–80.

Zeit Online. "Was ist noch Kritisch?" [Interview with *Die Zeit* and Peter Eisenman led by Thomas Assheuer, Hanno Rauterberg, Ullrich Schwarz] *Zeit Online*, 1 January 2001. http://www.zeit.de/2001/05/200105_eisenman-intervi.xml (1 November 2012).

Åhr, Johan. "Memory and Mourning in Berlin: On Peter Eisenman's Holocaust-Mahnmal." *Modern Judaism* 28.3 (2005): 283–305.

Birga U. Meyer
The Universal Victim – Representing Jews and Roma in a European Holocaust Museum

Although the Holocaust is being commemorated throughout Europe, the idea that its memory has a common European form is usually denied. Scholars argue either that each nation state has its own form of national commemoration or that national differences override any common European memory. However, the research on which this denial is based rarely takes more than one nation state into account and, where it does, it emphasizes the distinctiveness of national elements. Following Daniel Levy and Natan Sznaider, I believe that the memory of the Holocaust is comprised by local, national, European and even global elements simultaneously.[1] The binary distinction between a national and European memory, however, positions one form of memory against the other so that the ways that they combine and interact are no longer visible.

In this article, I will analyze the representation of Jewish and Roma victims as one crucial component within Holocaust representations.[2] Examining the permanent exhibition at the Holocauszt Emlékközpont/Holocaust Memorial Center (HDKE) in Budapest, I ask how this exhibition constructs a narrative about the victims through pictorial and textual representations and explore the extent to which these representations build on an imagined concept of victimhood. The HDKE is a particularly striking example of museum representations, because it stands within the traditions of so-called Holocaust museums and references international Holocaust commemoration while also explicitly countering the dominant right-wing discourse about the Holocaust in Hungary.

---

[1] Daniel Levy and Natan Sznaider. *Erinnerung im globalen Zeitalter: Der Holocaust.* Frankfurt/M.: Suhrkamp, 2007. 26–28. The term global is misleading as it suggests unity within memory constructions both in the western and in the non-western world dominated by the West. For a critique on the claim that Holocaust memory is global, see Jeffrey C Alexander. "On the Social Construction of Moral Universal: The 'Holocaust' from War Crime to Trauma Drama." *European Journal of Social Theory* 5.1(2002): 5–85, 59.

[2] Aiming to identify European, national and regional elements and their interrelations in Holocaust representations, my dissertation analyzes permanent exhibitions in history museums in Hungary, Austria and Italy. Historical culture and memory can be analyzed by turning to their cultural products. Klas-Göran Karlsson. "The Holocaust as a Problem of Historical Culture." *Echoes of the Holocaust. Historical Cultures in Contemporary Europe.* Eds. Klas-Göran Karlsson and Ulf Zander. Lund: Nordic Academic Press, 2003, 9–57, 32.

Framing the image of victims in the Holocauszt Emlékközpont exhibition in Budapest: between European and national commemoration

After the Hungarian parliament decided in March 2002 to establish the HDKE, the centre was quickly set up in a former Orthodox Synagogue in a small side street of the 9th district in Budapest.[3] It opened on 15 April 2004 with a temporary exhibition on the Auschwitz-Album, including, in addition to this exhibit, a hastily put together one on the persecution of the Roma.[4] A permanent exhibition curated by Judit Molnár then opened in April 2006.

The centre does important work to commemorate the Holocaust, facilitate reflection on and stimulate more research about it. The exhibition itself addresses the issues of the Hungarian perpetrators, portrays Hungarian society as responsible and holds it accountable. The Holocaust is treated as an important topic for Hungarians in general instead of as a separate one relevant only to Jewish communities. The narrative spans the period from 1920 to 1945 and thus deals with both the time before and after the German occupation in 1944. It treats the Holocaust as a historic period of its own merit instead of comparing it to the crimes committed during Communism. Last but not least the exhibition is dedicated to both the Jews and Roma persecuted in Hungary, which thereby expresses empathy and solidarity with these victims of the Holocaust.[5] Hence, the centre counters a dominant, right-wing discourse that idealizes the Horthy area, externalizes responsibility, downplays the Holocaust by comparing it to the Communist crimes and denigrates its victims.[6]

---

[3] On its founding see Brigitte Mihok. "Erinnerungsüberlagerungen oder der lange Schatten der Geschichtsverzerrung." *Ungarn und der Holocaust. Kollaboration, Rettung und Trauma.* Ed. Brigitte Mihok. Berlin: Metropol, 2005, 157–168, 163.
[4] The exhibition about the Roma was put together by the Romedia Foundation, the Roma Press Center and the Roma Ethnographic Collection three weeks before. János Bársony and Ágnes Daróczi. *Pharrajimos: The Fate of the Roma During the Holocaust.* Budapest: Idebate Press, 2008, iv.
[5] Opening panel "What is the Holocaust", Section 1.
[6] A good overview of the dominant discourse can be found in Randolph L. Braham. "Hungary and the Holocaust: The Nationalist Drive to Whitewash the Past." *The Treatment of the Holocaust in Hungary and Romania during the Post-Communist Era.* Ed. Randolph L. Braham. New York: Columbia University, 2004, 1–43; Éva Kovács and Gerhard Seewann, "Ungarn. Der Kampf um das Gedächtnis." *Mythen der Nationen. 1945 – Arena der Erinnerung.* Ed. Monika Flacke. Berlin: Deutsches Historisches Museum, 2004, 817–845.

The HDKE's critique of the dominant discourse is unusual for Hungary and for Hungarian museum representations of the Holocaust.[7] What the centre presents reflects the international shift within Holocaust historiography towards perpetrator history and the representation of the suffering of the victims as tragedy. The HDKE's architecture and design cite internationally acclaimed Holocaust commemorations seen in Washington, Jerusalem and Berlin.[8] Both historiography and references to international museum sites align the HDKE with acclaimed Holocaust museums, secure its position as a valid site for Holocaust commemoration and accredit its narrative. At its outset, then, the HDKE is positioned between the Hungarian national discourse on the Holocaust and international scholarship and commemoration of it. Scholars usually applaud the initiative to commemorate the Holocaust in Hungary, but the location and design of the centre have received criticism, as have inconsistencies within the exhibition and the fact that the museum fails to represent the period after 1945.[9]

The simultaneous presence of international and national Holocaust commemoration continues in the exhibition design and the narrative presented. The exhibition, found in the basement of the centre, develops its narrative through widely accepted strategies for historical displays. It consists of three hierarchical layers. The first presents the main narrative, the second personalizes it and the third provides supplementary information about it. The main narrative is conveyed via text, illustrated with images. The text is the crucial element for conveying the main message about the base content and ensuring that the objects

---

[7] The most well-known representation of the Holocaust in Hungary is the one in the Terror House, which denigrates Holocaust history. Regina Fritz and Katja Wezel. "Konkurrenz der Erinnerungen? Museale Darstellung von diktatorischen Erfahrungen in Ungarn und Lettland." *Aufarbeitung der Diktatur – Diktat der Aufarbeitung? Normierungsprozesse beim Umgang mit diktatorischer Vergangenheit*. Ed. Katrin Hammerstein. Göttingen: Wallstein, 2009, 233–246. Representation in the National Museum, the Military Museum and the small Holocaust Museum in Hódmezővásárhely are equally problematic. The Jewish Museum or the Glass House also present alternative stories to the dominant discourse.

[8] Regina Fritz and Imke Hansen. "Zwischen nationalem Opfermythos und europäischen Standards. Der Holocaust im ungarischen Erinnerungsdiskurs." *Universalisierung des Holocaust? Erinnerungskultur und Geschichtspolitik in internationaler Perspektive*. Ed. Jan Eckel and Claudia Moisel. Göttingen: Wallstein, 2008, 59–85, 80.

[9] Criticism on the location, the choice of the synagogue and the architecture of the centre has been voiced by many. For a good overview see Mihok. "Erinnerungsüberlagerungen oder der lange Schatten der Geschichtsverzerrung," 164. Among others Regina Fritz's diverse works criticize the exhibition. For example Regina Fritz. "Wandlung der Erinnerung in Ungarn. Von der Tabuisierung zur Thematisierung des Holocaust." *Zeitgeschichte* 6 (2006): 33, 303–317, 312.

on display are understood accordingly. A main text panel, which also holds one photo or material object indexical to the theme, introduces each of the eight sections. Longer text panels then further explicate the content, illustrated by several photos, documents and sometimes film images. The main narrative is personalized through family histories and biographical panels on the side.[10] Five families, four Jewish and one Roma, are presented on TV-screens in most rooms.[11] In the videos, a narrator tells the family stories alongside moving and still images so that text (in this case spoken) again features prominently. The visitor can find supplementary content on the touch screens and on the less central panels. The touch screens in part include the same text, photos and documents shown in the main exhibition area but also provide additional information and more photos or documents. The most important supplements here are video interviews of survivors speaking on the theme established in a room.

The narrative begins with the presentation of a relatively calm good time before the Holocaust, covers discrimination and expropriation and reaches a climax with the mass murders. It ends with a description of the liberation of the concentration camps and the war-trials in Hungary. In this, the exhibition follows accepted Holocaust historiography, which usually highlights the same stages of before, during and after the persecution. The national narrative about the Holocaust in Hungary is presented within this frame, for example by discussing discrimination through turning to the Horthy Regime and its antisemitic laws. The broader European narrative thus runs alongside the national one. As is the case in most exhibitions, the perpetrators and their actions define the exhibition outline. The whole exhibition is thus structured through the perpetrator perspectives.[12]

The visitor encounters a tragic story of the victims. Since tragedy has become the general mode of Holocaust representation, this is no surprise.[13] While the texts and photos make the tragedy overt, the exhibition design foreshadows it. The visitor steps into a dark and gloomy ambiance dominant throughout the ex-

---

[10] The biographic panels, hung on the side and in smaller font, present a famous victim and parallel her or him with a Hungarian with a similar story. For example Anne Frank is paralleled with Lilla Ecséri. Panel "Anne Frank" and "Lilla Ecséri", Section 4.
[11] Sections 7 and 5 do not present family stories.
[12] Holtschneider first analyzed this for the Holocaust exhibition at the Imperial War Museum. K. Hannah Holtschneider. *The Holocaust and Representations of Jews. History and Identity in the Museum*. London/New York: Routledge, 2011, 31.
[13] Jeffrey C. Alexander brilliantly analyzes the presentation of the Holocaust as tragedy. Alexander. "On the Social Construction of Moral Universal: The 'Holocaust' from War Crime to Trauma Drama."

hibition space. Except for the white seventh Section, the walls, floor and ceiling of the exhibition are painted black. The panels are grey with the occasional use of orange to highlight individual texts or panels. Yellow spotlights cast limited light onto the panels. Along the walls, white neon lights have been inserted into horizontal lines that lead the visitor from one room to the next and not only provide light for walking and a sense of direction but also symbolize Jewish life lines, running out towards the end of the exhibition. Sad melancholic music runs on repeatedly and fills the whole exhibition with sound. The fixed walkway that the visitor has to follow forms a circle from the courtyard, through the exhibition, into the renovated synagogue and either out to the memorial wall or to the café and the museum bookstore. The linear structure, where beginning middle and end are clearly defined, suggests that the visitor has encountered the complete story of the Holocaust in Hungary – which displays loss and sadness, climaxes in mass murder and ends with the commemoration of the dead.

Sadness and loss, the death of the victims, are absolute at the HDKE. The story here diverges from other European victim representations, which do address life after 1945. All exhibition elements emphasize the death of the victims, be it the walkway, the design, the frame, the images or the textual narrative. The victims die and disappear and no longer challenge post-war society.[14] This is in part due to the specific history of the Holocaust in Hungary, where most Jews, especially those in the countryside, were killed. For Roma another story would need to be told, as a larger group survived.[15] In both groups, however, people survived and returned to Hungary where they faced serious difficulties. The absoluteness of death depicted at the HDKE excludes those who returned, however, and hinders the reflection on post-war Jewish and Roma life in Hungary. The exhibition also fails to address the attitude of the general population towards the survivors, the difficulties to reestablish Jewish communities, the ongoing perse-

---

[14] The exhibition represents survivors on the touch screens, in biographic panels and through family stories. Compared to the stories of the dead, who are given more space, a more prominent place and whose stories are repeated, the stories of survival remain marginal. The final text states that "the hundreds of thousands who had been murdered could not be brought back to life" and "the few who did survive 'continued dying' after the liberation even though '100,000 deportees had returned home' ". The opening panel "Liberation and calling into account", Section 8; the panel "The fate of Hungarian Jews and Roma"; Touch screen "The fate of Hungarian Jews and Roma", Section 8.

[15] As research on the Roma is still fragmentary, reliable numbers are hard to establish. An estimated one in three died. János Bársony. "Hungarian Pharrajimos, the Unexplored Territories of the Roma Holocaust and Its Aftereffect." *The Holocaust in Hungary: A European Perspective*. Ed. Judit Molnár. Budapest: Balassi Kiadó, 2005, 404–417, 410–411.

Fig. 1: Neon lights in the permanent exhibition of the Holocaust Memorial Center in Budapest.

cution of the Roma, the question of memory, and continuing Antisemitism and Racism in post-war Hungary.[16]

---

[16] Fritz and Hansen. "Zwischen nationalem Opfermythos und europäischen Standards. Der Holocaust im ungarischen Erinnerungsdiskurs," 81.

Defining Jews – the representation of Jewish victims at the HDKE

Before becoming the mostly dead victims, Jews first are first constructed as a coherent group.[17] Taking both text and photos into account, it becomes evident that Jews living in Hungary are defined as a group whose main characteristics are national belonging, modernity, urbanity and a bourgeois culture and self-understanding. The exhibition presents them as carriers of the capitalist enterprise in Hungary and as such, they are shown as beneficial to the nation.[18] The text says that Jews made significant contributions to the economy, to culture, to science and to the arts in Hungary.[19] It states that they mostly spoke Hungarian and self-identified as Hungarians. Accordingly, the curator emphasized their national belonging, so-to-speak nationalizing all Jews, primarily by adding Hungarian before the word Jew, labeling them as compatriots or by nationalizing names and places.[20] Including Jews within the nation, the museum makes a conscious reference to the dominant discourse in Hungary that questions whether Jews are to be regarded as Hungarian or to be excluded from the national body. Questioning national belonging was essential in the antisemitic discourse in the early nineteenth century and continues to be important today.[21] That Jews are presented as

---

[17] For the most part, this is accomplished through the panel "The Jews in Hungary", through the touch screens "Jews and Roma in Hungary", "Our Compratiots" and through the family histories, all presented in Section 1.

[18] This is emphasised for example when the text on economic exclusion states that "Hungarian Jews as a group were among the most successful in Europe. Due to their early participation in capitalist development, they occupied strong positions in industry, commerce and banking. An especially great number of Jewish individuals chose economic, intellectual, scientific and artistic careers." Touch screen "Deprived of Property. The Pauperization and Despoilment of Hungarian Jews, 1920–1944", Section 3.

[19] See for example the photos on the touch screen labeled "Our compatriots", Section 1. Here the Jews and Roma who contributed to Hungarian society are shown and their profession or contributions listed.

[20] Panel "Jews in Hungary", Section 1; Touch screen "Our compatriots", Section 1; Opening panel "Responses", Section 7. Nationalization even extends to foreign land, in particular to Auschwitz-Birkenau, described as "The largest cemetery in Hungarian history", Opening panel "Deprived of Life", Section 6. This references the speech that Dr. Bálint Magyar, the Minister of Education, made in Auschwitz on 14 April 2004. Magyar Nemzeti Múzeum. *The Citizens Betrayed – In Memory of the Victims of the Hungarian Holocaust.* Budapest: MNM, 2006, 19.

[21] Fritz and Hansen. "Zwischen nationalem Opfermythos und europäischen Standards. Der Holocaust im ungarischen Erinnerungsdiskurs." 64. Aside from proposing an alternative interpretation, this implicitly affirms the projection that Jews might pose a problem to the nation

beneficial to the nation further situates their persecution as tragedy, suggesting that capitalist, scientific and cultural development was lost through it.[22]

While nominally denying that Jews were a coherent group, the curator has constructed one nonetheless.[23] The group's homogeneity is based on the omission of those who do not fit into the above categories. Not discussed in their own right are religious Jews, especially of Orthodox faith, the Yiddish speaking communities and women. Gestured towards but less significant are working class Jews and those of rural communities. It is striking how little Orthodox Jewry is addressed explicitly.[24] Omitted in the main text and unmarked in most images, Orthodox Jewry does appear in the story of the Galpert-Ackermann family, which followed the Orthodox faith. However, alluding to a dichotomy between traditional and modern, the exhibition implicitly devalues the Orthodox faith.[25] Overall, both the Neolog and Orthodox faiths are treated as private and individual matters.[26] Consequently, the museum does not address the impact that the persecution had on practicing Jews, the desecration of the synagogues and scriptures and discrimination based on religion.[27]

Gender as a social category is also not discussed. Leaving gender unmarked, the exhibition presents a classic perspective, relegating women to the private or

---

if they are not Hungarian. A perceived danger posed by those who did not opt for complete assimilation is defused. István Deák. "Anti-Semitism and the Treatment of the Holocaust in Hungary." *Anti-Semitism and the Treatment of the Holocaust in Postcommunist Eastern Europe*. Ed. Randolph L. Braham. New York: Columbia University, 1994, 99–124.

22 This suggests the problematic notion that the Holocaust was tragic due to the value of the victims.

23 The exhibition states that "The Jewish population of Hungary was diverse both culturally and socially." But this is not represented in the exhibition, Panel "The Jews in Hungary", Section 1.

24 I am grateful to Dr. Katalin Pécsi who directed my attention to the imbalanced representation of Orthodox Jews in the exhibition.

25 Words such as 'old', 'traditional', 'strict' or 'ancient rules' are positioned as a binary to a modern, less religious life, which is described in more positive terms and characterized as integrated and accepted. For example the "Galpert-Ackermann family" and the "Singer family", Section 1.

26 In the rare cases where religion is represented, it is a private matter of the individual. Where Jewish communities appear, only the Neolog movement is gestured towards and its contribution to integration is the reason why. This can be seen in the panel dedicated to the Rabbis Lipót Löw and Immánuel Löw. Lipót Löw is shown to have modernized the synagogue service and is highlighted for delivering his speeches in Hungarian. His son Immánuel Löw is said to have been a "symbolic figure for the integrated Jews". Panel "Lipót Löw and Immánuel Löw", Section 2.

27 An exception is the video showing the history of Antisemitism in which religious hatred against Jews is the main topic. Video "History of Antisemitism" after Section 3.

social sphere and men to the public realm. Men are the active agents of capitalist Hungary while women appear at their side – this is most evident in the wedding videos shown in Room one.[28] The different status between men and women is visible but naturalized and thus inscribed as ahistorical. Different experiences of men and women during their persecutions vanish and the Holocaust is largely imagined through a male perspective. This remains true, even if, as I will show later, the victims are largely presented as passive, helpless women.

Visible but less central are notions of class and the differences between urban and rural structures. Barely representing working class environments, the exhibition focuses on middle class and upper class Jews. They are the ones who contributed to the nation, and they appear in most texts, images and objects.[29] However, all class backgrounds are touched upon in the family stories.[30] Again, emphasis is on the upper and middle classes; however, the difference that class affiliation made for the persecution is indicated in all sections.[31] The countryside is part of the main narrative, but the large disparity between rural and urban structures in Hungary remains obscure. The impact of rural structures in Hungary on the persecution, the large percentage of Jews in some villages and the proximity between perpetrators and their victims remain hidden.

This exclusion of gender and religion and the less prominent discussion of class and rural structures mean that conflicts between Jews and non-Jews and within the Jewish communities themselves remain hidden. The personal lives of Jews – their origin, gender and class, their faith and values, their social and economic positions, all of which affected the victims and their perception of the persecutions – disappear in the narrative. Individuality is taken away, plurality denied and Jews are merged into a homogenous group of people.

It is this homogenous group that is victimized as the exhibition continues. Jews as active agents, as presented in Section one, disappear and instead become objects in the story of their persecution. From Section two onwards, they at best react to, but mostly silently endure, the measures against them. As the

---

28 Wedding video, Section 1.
29 A sense of bourgeois belonging is produced not only via text. The objects shown are all associated with a higher or middle class, for example books or binoculars. The photos show people with typical bourgeois professions such as doctors, lawyers or journalists.
30 The Hatvany-Deutsch, Chorin and Weiss families belong to the upper class, the Braun-Wechsler and Singer family to the middle class and the Galpert-Ackermann family to the working class. Their working class background is mentioned, but as the family story continues, it becomes less central to their fate. Working poor are represented through the Roma family.
31 See, for example, family histories in "Deprived of Property", Section 3.

narrative unfolds, Jews are talked about, the exhibition addresses what has been done to them, while their own thoughts, actions, and feelings are hardly represented.[32] A central dilemma in Holocaust representations is that this was the goal of the persecutors: to dehumanize and objectify the victims. In result many primary sources from the Holocaust do so as well, given that they were produced by the perpetrators. Holocaust commemorations thus often strive to give a name and a story to individual victims in order to restore their humanity to them. To represent the Holocaust through a narrative structured through perpetrator actions and through primary sources made by them mirrors the objectification which was the goal of the Holocaust, and also cements these sources as all-encompassing. To instead represent the victims with agency, even if agency only means that the people targeted had their own opinions, values and specific reactions to the violence (that they had a life of their own) helps to present them as human. To reflect on the objectification of the Holocaust and its reflection in the primary sources and today's representations can counter the perpetrators' success in eradicating the individual traces, a success which unfortunately still last today, as the examples mentioned above show.

The HDKE tries to counter the objectification it presents but relegates the counter-elements to a peripheral position. The most obvious counterpoints are the video interviews of survivors and the responses of Jews described in Section seven.[33] In the interviews, Jews tell their own stories. These remain subjective even when told in a descriptive tone. The voice, speech acts, facial expressions and the fact that there is a first-person narrator make it a subjective and active account. Unfortunately, there is no information on the survivors or their stories aside from the brief segments presented. Shown on the touch screens as one of many elements next to photos, documents and texts, they are presented as add-ons, as extra information. In the hierarchy of the exhibition, the videos rank low. They are not central to the narrative, which works equally well without them. Furthermore, the videos are cut in such a way that the survivor narrates

---

[32] For a critique of this display mode see Mieke Bal. *Double Exposures. The Subject of Cultural Analysis.* London/New York: Routledge, 1996.

[33] The family stories are intended to personalize persecution. But due to the representational mode, the family members remain objects of the measures discussed in the third person. A few biographies deviate from this, for example the one of Miklós Nyiszli, who managed to survive serving Mengele's staff. The panel describes how he survived due to a mixture of luck and cleverness. Panel "Miklós Nyiszli", Section 6.

what is discussed in the section, so that the accounts are merely there to provide subjective illustrations of the main narrative of the exhibition.[34]

The seventh Section presents the Jewish councils, the Kasztner group and the Zionist Youth groups.[35] Jewish responses to their own persecution, left out elsewhere in the exhibition, are addressed here, but more as an afterthought.[36] While the groups described are still talked about, their members are juxtaposed to "the overwhelming majority of Jews" who "received the increasing persecution passively".[37] This imagined passive majority best expresses the lack of agency the exhibition constructs for the victims. Individual agency is limited to a few particularly brave people. The exhibition further differentiates these few. The Jewish Council's members are heavily criticized and the display even goes so far as to undermine them, explaining they have "usually made the wrong decisions".[38] The Kasztner group is shown to have been faced with the dilemma of saving some by sacrificing others.[39] The exhibition narrative portrays individual agency as a complicated and critical matter, at times even making people complicit in the persecution. The reactions of Jews leave the main narrative of the persecution untouched. Clearly an exception to the persecution, the curators relegate agency to the side. Thus while certain elements work against the objectification of the Jews, they are less important than, or an explicit exception to, the objectifications.

Depicting Jews– photos in museum displays

The objectification of Jewish victims is particularly striking in the visual material provided. The photographs in Section one are mainly private photos taken by Jews to represent themselves. They show economic activities, family portraits or passport images of the individuals in question. In most museums, private pho-

---

[34] This is the same for interviews shown at the Imperial War Museum. Holtschneider, *The Holocaust and Representations of Jews*, 69.
[35] The seventh Section also covers individuals who helped Jews and members of the *Sonderkommando*, who resisted their persecution.
[36] Design and location of the section communicate that the reactions are less central. The section reverses the color scheme and is presented at the very end of the exhibition.
[37] Touch screen "The Responses of the Persecuted – What They Knew, Why They did not Resist", Section 7.
[38] Panel "Dilemmas: the Jewish Council", Section 7.
[39] Panel "Dilemmas: the Kasztner Group", Section 7.

tos claim to personalize and individualize the macro narrative.[40] At the HDKE most private photos instead define Jews as Jews. The people serve as examples of group characteristics. The personal photo then disappears from Section two onwards. From then on the photos of victims encountered in the exhibition can be roughly divided into photos showing discriminatory practices, such as exclusion, humiliation and robbery, and photos capturing the more violent stages of the persecution from forced labor to ghettoization and deportation to mass murder. Most common are photos showing groups of people. It is not the individual, the family or circle of friends the photo portrays, but the people who were victimized together.

Research has shown that museums mostly use perpetrator images and photos taken by complicit spectators, closely followed by images taken by the allies after the liberation.[41] At the HDKE this is also true, with only very few exceptions.[42] Because the photographer did not have to hide, these photos are direct, clear and centered. They present a classic perspective and show the victim who best serves the intended message. The victim is in the centre, framed by the perpetrators, who are, in turn, framed by spectators or the landscape.[43] Since these photos are often sharp and of high quality, the museum can edit, enlarge, cut and transfer them to a different carrier with relative ease. This makes the perpetrator and liberator photos a seemingly first choice to use.[44] Pictures taken by those complicit with the perpetrations are, however, deeply problematic.[45] All

---

[40] This fails, as photos become mute when removed from the private context in which they are otherwise read. Holtschneider. *The Holocaust and Reprentations of Jews*, 58.
[41] Ibid, 29.
[42] The most prominent exception is the photo of inmates burning bodies taken by the *Sonderkommando* in Auschwitz-Birkenau. Photos of people witnessing the persecutions who are not complicit with the perpetrators are shown on the touch screens.
[43] Klaus Hesse. "Bilder lokaler Judendeportationen. Fotografien als Zugänge zur Alltagsgeschichte des NS-Terrors. " *Visual History. Ein Studienbuch.* Ed. Gerhard Paul. Göttingen: Vandenhoeck & Ruprecht, 2006, 149–168, 156.
[44] The few photos taken by the victimized and people who considered the perpetration a crime, on the contrary, are often blurred, unclear, out of focus and the object might not be positioned in the centre. Being considered a "bad" photo in the traditional sense, these photos have been largely ignored within museum displays. Georges Didi-Hubermann. *Images in Spite of All. Four Photographs from Auschwitz*. Chicago/London: University of Chicago Press, 2008.
[45] Images that reproduce the gaze of the perpetrators are complicit because the photographer participated in the discrimination against the victims and legitimized the actions by clicking the shutter. Susan Sonntag. *On Photography.* New York: Anchor Books, 1989, 10–12. According to Cornelia Brink photos of spectators or the allies equally represent the gaze of the perpetrators and so are also complicit. Cornelia Brink. *Ikonen der Vernichtung. Öffentlicher Gebrauch von Fotografien aus nationalsozialistischen Konzentrationslagern nach 1945*. Berlin: Akademie, 1998,

photographs present a perspective which is spatially and temporally specific. They do not show historical reality, but a fragment in need of contextualization, critical examination and interpretation. What a photo communicates depends on its historical context and upon the present situation in which it is used and perceived.⁴⁶ Despite this, photos tend to be seen as supporting a claim of authenticity and suggest past reality. Photos complicit with the perpetration, then, claim to show the persecution directly, head on and to depict its full reality. Taken from the perspective of the perpetrators, however, they only reveal the perpetrator perspective and reproduce it. If not outright antisemitic, complicit photos are at least removed from the victim, and they present that victim without empathy or solidarity, regarding it as the perpetuator's object. They reproduce a strategy of victimization through showing only the victims' persecution and not what happened before or after. The victims have no agency.

Such photos fit well into an authoritative narrative told from the perpetrators' perspective that mirrors the chronology of persecution. While the ideological baggage of perpetrator images is well known, museum exhibitions usually do not address this issue and display practices with a different perspective remain rare.⁴⁷ The photos are not used as an artifact in need of contextualization and interpretation, but simply as illustrations of the intended narrative. Where captions are provided, they define what is seen in the picture or give additional information not directly related, instead of providing information on the photo and its context.⁴⁸

---

218. I believe this needs to be given a more complex interpretation as spectators and allies did use different image strategies. For an introduction to this discussion, see Tim Cole. *Traces of the Holocaust. Journeying in and out of the Ghettos*. London: Continuum, 2011, 92.

46 John Tagg. *The Burden of Representation. Essays on Photographies and Histories*. Minneapolis: University of Minnesota Press, 1988.

47 Central questions have already been asked in the classic article on perpetrator photos by Sybil Milton. "Images of the Holocaust – part I." *Holocaust and Genocide Studies* 1 (1986): 1, 27–61; Sybil Milton. "Images of the Holocaust – part II." *Holocaust and Genocide Studies* 1 (1986): 2, 193–216.

48 Criticism on illustration is given by Janina Struck. *Photographing the Holocaust. Interpretation of the Evidence*. New York: I.B. Taurus & Co Ltd., 2004, 51; Thomas Thiemeyer. *Fortsetzung des Krieges mit anderen Mitteln. Die beiden Weltkriege im Museum*. Paderborn: Ferdinand Schöningh, 2010, 303.

Depicting victims – the photos from the Auschwitz-Album at the HDKE

Iconic images of the Holocaust are used in several European museums, cropped, enlarged or edited differently and with different captions and annotations.[49] At the HDKE, the photos from the Auschwitz-Album are a prime example.[50] They constitute a rare pictorial source for the handling of Hungarian deportees in Auschwitz-Birkenau. The photos from the Album, almost certainly taken by two SS members in charge of the identification office in the main camp, are among the most reproduced photos of the Holocaust worldwide.[51]

The HDKE uses the photos from the Auschwitz-Album in several sections, but it is in Section six, where the exhibition narrative reaches its climax, that they are shown most. This part of the exhibition mainly discusses the violence of the Arrow Cross in Hungary and the concentration camp system. The photos from the Auschwitz-Album are part of a video entitled "A Day in Auschwitz". The video is shown on five middle-sized TV-screens, hung next to each other along a long wall with barbed wire painted on it. The room is filled with dramatic, sad, mourning music, punctuated with drums, which evoke a heartbeat. The video features a stream of photos interrupted by short telegram-style titles. It begins by stating the location as "Auschwitz-Birkenau" and informing the viewer that it is "May 26, 1944 morning". Within the video, the visitor then sees several photos of the victims before their selection at the ramp, and is told that this is a "Hungarian Jewish transport from Beragszász".[52] Photos from the ramp are then shown under the heading "Before lining up", with photos from the selection process under the caption "Selection: life is at stake", and photos of those declared unfit for work under "Doomed to die". Towards the end of the video peo-

---

49 On iconic images see Brink. *Ikonen der Vernichtung*. Iconic images are transnational as they easily transcend national borders. Other photos along side iconic ones share the same iconic markers, for example showing a cattle car or railroads.
50 Serge Klarsfeld. *The Auschwitz album: Lili Jacob's album*. New York: Beate Klarsfeld Foundation, 1980. It is still considered the best edition of the album.
51 Gideon Greiff. "The 'Auschwitz Album'. The Story of Lili Jacob." *The Auschwitz Album. The Story of a Transport*. Ed. Israel Gutmann and Bella Gutterman. Jerusalem/Oświęcim: Newton Ltd, 2002, 71–86. On the album's reception see Struck. *Photographing the Holocaust*, 100–119; Yasmin Doosry. "Vom Dokument zur Ikone: Zur Rezeption des Auschwitz-Albums." *Representations of Auschwitz. 50 Years of Photographs, Paintings, and Graphics*. Ed. Yasmin Doosry. Oświęcim: Auschwitz-Birkenau State Museum, 1995, 95–104.
52 Berhovo in Czech. The area was annexed to Hungary in 1939, which is not clear in the installation at the HEK. Greiff. The "The 'Auschwitz Album'. The Story of Lili Jacob," 72.

ple in front of the gas chambers are shown under the title "The last seconds". Most photos have individual captions that provide extra information, such as "Crematoria in the background", "Dr. Mengele smoking" or "Zyklon B in barrel on the truck".[53] The captions indicate what is to be seen by stating that the photograph shows the "Selection" "men", "women and children", "Dwarfs" or "Hungarian Jews at Crematorium IV".[54] Some captions label the victims as "defenceless and humiliated".[55] While not all photos in the installation are from the Auschwitz-Album, all those showing victims are, except for the last one.[56] The last photo, shown on all five screens, is from the photos taken secretly by members of the *Sonderkommando* to prove the mass murder.[57] Cropped and enlarged, the blurred image shows how *Sonderkommando* members were forced to burn the bodies of the dead in ditches.[58] It is with this final photo that the video, lasting two minutes and thirty seconds, ends.

The video is one of the highlights of this section. Framed by an introductory panel on Auschwitz-Birkenau and presented with additional information on the concentration camps, the video takes up most of the space, alternating between Hungarian and English. While the overall video is the same when the victims are shown, different photos appear on each screen. The photos have clearly been

---

53 The information of the caption is highlighted in yellow within the photo.
54 While only some of the Album's captions are referred to in the video, the caption here follows the antisemitic perspective of the album, highlighting a supposedly unfit character amongst the deportees by singling out physically different people. For a discussion of the antisemitic ideology in the album, see Nina Springer-Aharoni. "Photographs As Historical Documents." *The Auschwitz Album. The Story of a Transport.* Ed. Israel Gutmann and Bella Gutterman. Jerusalem/Oświęcim: Newton Ltd, 2002, 87–97, 95.
55 Video "A day in Auschwitz", Section 6.
56 The photos from the album are also shown on the touch screen, this time in their original format but with different captions, including the photos of those declared fit for work. The touch screens "Deprived of Life. The Annihilation of Hungarian Jews at Auschwitz-Birkenau" and "Deprived of Life. Operation Höss", Section 6. The captions differ but do not contextualize the photos.
57 For an extensive discussion of the photos from the *Sonderkommando*, see Didi-Hubermann. *Images in Spite of All.*
58 The photo was taken through a window, of which the frame is still visible in the original image. Used as an icon, this window frame is usually cropped and the part where the bodies are burned enlarged. Struck. *Photographing the Holocaust*, 112–113. Three of the four photos taken by the resistance in the *Sonderkommando* are shown on the touch screen. Only for the photo of the women is some context provided. Its caption reads "Photograph taken by the resistance movement in the camp: when the dressing rooms were full, the victims had to undress in front of Crematorium V". The touch screen "Deprived of Life. The Annihilation of Hungarian Jews at Auschwitz-Birkenau", Section 6.

Fig. 2: Video installation *A day in Auschwitz* in the permanent exhibition of the Holocaust Memorial Center in Budapest.

edited, most evident when a different frame than in the original is chosen or parts highlighted in the photo. The camera zooms in on single aspects within photos or pans over them. Every visitor will see at least parts of this video, as one has to walk by the screens to get to the next section. It provides movement and captures the visitor's attention through the dramatic display mode. Each of the photos would merit a closer look, but inserted into a tight and fast-paced narrative, the significance of the individual photo is lost. The composition of different photos on each screen means that emphasis is laid on their resemblances rather than their individuality. Clearly, this presentation takes excess of meaning and agency from the photos.[59]

The photos in the video are not contextualized beyond the descriptions I outlined above. The video does not reveal who took the photographs, when they

---

59 On excess of meaning see Susan Pearce. "Objects as meaning; or narrating the past." *Objects of Knowledge*. Ed. Susan Pearce. London: Athlone Press, 1990, 134–135. On the agency of the photo Horst Bredekamp. *Theorie des Bildakts*. Frankfurt/M.: Suhrkamp, 2010.

were taken or for what reason. As for the persons depicted, their history after 1945 remains unknown, at least at this point. Their role within the video is to illustrate its narrative. A later, less central panel provides a brief history of the Album, focusing on Lili Meier, an inmate who found the Album after her liberation from Dora-Mittelbau and recognised her Rabbi, members of her family and herself in the photo. She first kept the album for herself, but donated it to Yad Vashem in 1980. The panel tells her story and that of the Album. It states that two SS men took the photos, describes what they show and lists them as "the most important pictorial documents of the mechanism of extermination at Birkenau".[60] Even in this panel, the accompanying photos are not marked as deriving from the Album and it is not possible to identify them anywhere in the exhibition through the information provided. The museum does not address the problems these photographs pose in presenting the perpetrator perspective.

Using the photos from the Auschwitz-Album, the video sums up the narrative on Jewish victims shown at the HDKE. The video functions at the level of generalizations, which the "A day in Auschwitz" already indicates. The day depicted is an example of a typical day in Auschwitz-Birkenau and the victims portrayed represent the typical victims arriving. As their individual stories are not told – albeit known in part– they appear to have no history.[61] Since we see them going to their death – neither those declared fit for work are shown nor is Lili Meier – they equally have no future. They arrive from a collection camp which has not been contextualized; they are selected at the ramp and go to their death to be burned in ditches in the last gruesome image.[62] Here the HDKE depicts the victims in the same vain as the SS men: as degraded objects of a well-ordered, highly organized and efficient persecution.[63]

This, the video claims, is what the victims looked like. The majority of victims shown are women, children and the elderly. Younger women and men are not represented. The women, often with many children, stand and wait, walk along a given path or pause and gaze at the camera. They do as they are told.

---

60 Panel "Lenke Jakab (Lili Jákob)", Section 6. The naming of Lili Meier with the family name she had while living in Capartho-Ruthenia rather than with the name she took through her marriage in the U.S., effectively integrate her into the Hungarian nation.
61 Many of the people have been identified. See Israel Gutmann and Bella Gutterman. *The Auschwitz Album. The Story of a Transport.* Jerusalem/Oświęcim: Newton Ltd, 2002.
62 The visitor also learns nothing about the largely Orthodox and Yiddish-speaking communities in Carpatho-Ruthenia.
63 The SS men who took the photos wanted to portray the victims as having no individuality, as Yasmin Doosry convincingly shows. Doosry. "Vom Dokument zur Ikone: Zur Rezeption des Auschwitz-Albums,"102.

The old men stand in groups, equally awaiting their fate. The caption qualifies them as Hungarian Jews, defenseless and humiliated, indicating how the photos are to be decoded. Since photos are silent, it appears as if the victims were also defenseless and humiliated – even though the ramp and the waiting areas were full of sound. The victims remain silent even though some have their mouths open in the photos, as if in the act of speaking. The music hides this unusual silence, drawing attention away from it. Reflecting on silence in a setting of constant noise is difficult. The victims do not speak to the visitor or to each other. This silence is essentialised through the statement "Most of the Jews who were declared unfit for work, stripped naked, silently entered the gas chamber they thought was a shower."[64] Again, the silent, passive passage to death is a metaphor that deeply affects how we imagine the Holocaust victim.

The victims represented in this display are helpless, inactive, silent and uniform. Their bodies are subjected to the perpetrators and the people are represented as objects. Instead of as specific evidence, the photos in the exhibition generalize concentration camp victims, who are characterized through their victimhood. They are the universal European victim, imagined when the Holocaust is remembered within Europe.[65] The HDKE draws on this figure, which, as a template, can be filled with further messages. The template is broad and flexible and is adapted to the national discourse. At the HDKE, the national discourse surfaces mainly where the national belonging of the victims is addressed. The Jews shown are Hungarians, from Hungary, who silently and passively went to their deaths.

Non-universal victims – Roma: the Other on display

The passive, silent and dead victim is a current archetype in Holocaust representations.[66] One dilemma with it is that other victims often cannot compete; they cannot qualify as the universal, passive and dead victim. The HDKE only addresses one other victim group in detail: the Roma.[67] The stories of

---

64 Touch screen "Deprived of Live. The Annihilation of Hungarian Jews at Auschwitz-Birkenau", Section 6.
65 Levy and Sznaider. *Erinnerung im globalen Zeitalter*, 228.
66 Ibid.
67 Other victim groups are named in passing. The opening panel in Section one states that the Nazis murdered "millions of Poles, Russians and people of other nationalities in Europe besides

their persecution in Hungary are not homogenous and cannot be told in the same way as that of the Jews. They are not silent, not passive and the representation does not offer identification with them. In the end it is their agency as the unknown and foreign Other which sets them apart most, disqualifying them as universal victims. While included in the display, a closer look at their representation shows that they are not seen in their own right. Sadly, the presentation also reiterates racist stereotypes. The effect is that the Roma appear as the marginalized Other, the victim named but not accounted for. Their suffering is shown, which is exceptional in Hungary, but empathy with the Roma remains limited.

The information provided about Roma at the HDKE is cursory and fragmented. A text states that they on the one hand lived in Hungary since the fourteenth century and that other Roma moved there from Romania in the middle of the nineteenth century. However, specific information on the different groups of Roma and their migrations, their cultural backgrounds and their distinct histories is not provided.[68] While the text outlines that most lived in permanent settlements and spoke Hungarian, others are portrayed as nomads. The Hungarians are said to have "welcomed" them or held them "in high esteem".[69] The curator does not address how Roma identified with respect to the Hungarian nation and does not presented Roma as part of Hungarian society. The Roma and the non-Roma population are consistently differentiated. Due to this, Roma are set up as the counterpart to Hungarian citizens. National belonging of Roma is questioned through an emphasis on the Roma migration to Hungary, their lack of integration into and their exclusion from Hungarian society. From Jews, who are portrayed as part of the Hungarian society, the Roma are Othered also. Contrary to the Jews, Roma do not belong and are not beneficial to the nation.[70]

Jews, in addition to large numbers of Gypsies, homosexuals, mentally ill patients, Jehovah's witnesses as well as the political and religious opponents of Nazism." Opening Panel "What is the Holocaust?", Section 1. These groups are listed again in Section six where Soviet prisoners of war and resistance fighters are added. Panel "Auschwitz-Birkenau" Section 6. Mentally ill people are talked about in Section 5, but only with respect to German policies against them. Panel "Deprived of Dignity: Europe", Section 5. And touch screen "Deprived of Human Dignity. Deprived of Dignity in Europe" under "The Reich before the war", Section 5.

68 Brigitte Mihok. *Vergleichende Studie zur Situation der Minderheiten in Ungarn und Rumänien (1989–1996) unter besonderer Berücksichtigung der Roma*. Frankfurt/M.: Lang, 1999, 150–151.

69 Panel "Roma in Hungary", Section 1.

70 According to the exhibit they might have become beneficial, had it not been for the Holocaust. The Bogdán-Kolompár family is presented as ascending from the working poor to the working and possibly even to the lower middle class. "Bogdán-Kolompár Family", Section 1. Es-

While officially holding an equal place within the narrative, Jews take centre stage and the exhibition relegates Roma to the periphery. The amount of space devoted to them is significantly smaller and the placement less prominent. Where told, their stories are presented after the Jewish ones, almost as an afterthought, or added onto the Jewish experiences.[71] Less care seems to have been taken in putting the panels on Roma together, as seen most obviously in the video interview with Roma women, who are simply described as "Roma in Auschwitz". All other interviews were conducted for the exhibition and names are provided for all.[72] Roma, the exhibition suggests, were victims of the Holocaust but ones that are more marginal. Their specific narratives of persecution and liberation are silenced or, through the add-on narratives, their stories are equated with those of Jewish victims. The visitor might assume that she or he has been informed about the Roma, whilst in fact being left with a very incomplete and disjointed image. This marginalization becomes extremely problematic in the commemoration at the memorial wall. Constructed according to the Jewish tradition, the HDKE devotes no separate space for the remembrance of Roma victims.[73] The dedication to the Roma uttered in Section one, becomes shallow here, if it had not already been so.

In addition to this marginalization and as a key part of the process of Othering, the exhibition iterates racist stereotypes about Roma. While the text states that Roma were diverse, Roma are in fact divided into two groups: settled and

---

tablishing the Holocaust as a barrier for integration ignores the fact that racism in Hungary was also an effective hindrance to this.

71 In Sections 3 and 7, Roma are not mentioned at all. In the second, fifth and eighth sections, they are not part of the main narrative and, for example, appear only on the touch screen and in the family story. In Sections 4 and 6, where they are part of the main narrative, their stories are told after those of the Jews, have significantly less space and are placed in less visible parts of the room. Where Roma experiences are added after the Jewish ones, the text states, in one or two sentences, that Roma suffered under the same or similar conditions. The opening panel, "Deprived of Human Dignity", Section 5, panel "Everyday Humiliations", Section 5. A similar approach is chosen in Section 8. Jews and Roma are talked about together at the start of the text that then continues including the Roma nominally, but addressing those deported for forced labour, the residents of the ghettos, the survivors, and the forced military labourers, groups commonly associated with Jews and not Roma. Touch screen "Liberation and calling into account. The fate of Hungarian Jews and Roma", Section 8.

72 Touch screen "Deprived of Freedom. The persecution of Roma", Section 4; Touch screen "Deprived of Life. Massacre of the Roma", Section 6. The interviews with the Roma were conducted at different times and have a very different setting.

73 The memorial wall uses the Jewish tradition to name the dead. Fritz and Hansen. "Zwischen nationalem Opfermythos und europäischen Standards. Der Holocaust im ungarischen Erinnerungsdiskurs," 79.

"vagrant".[74] Making this distinction, the narrative turns mostly to Roma without permanent settlement. They are described as people who "clung to their nomadic way of life and permanently lived in tribal, clannish circumstances".[75] The language used implies a backward orientation of the Roma who continued to living as nomads. This combines with a continuous representation of dirty clothes, of Roma sitting on the ground, of children with uncombed hair and poor clothing. The photos on display evoke an ethnographic iconography of Roma as the dirty Other. That this image, still dominant today, is in itself racist and violent is not clarified in the exhibition.[76] A settled life appears as the norm, while the vagrant one is problematic, to say the least. Furthermore, Roma are shown to beg, make music, and work as seasonal laborers or as rural artisans. Not contextualizing these professions within the racist limitations Roma experienced, they appear as inherent characteristics of Roma and not as historically specific social positions.

The exhibition clearly states that local authorities, executive forces, Germans and Arrow Cross members persecuted Roma.[77] The policies against Roma remain unclear, however. The exhibition states that officials had resentments against them while at other times the opposite is said.[78] Officials appear to have mostly

---

[74] The Roma are defined as the two groups in Section one, mainly on the panel "The Roma in Hungary" and the touch screen "Jews and Roma in Hungary", Section 1. The word vagrant already expresses a negative evaluation of nomadic life as it depends on its binary opposite, settled.

[75] Touch screen "Jews and Gypsies in Hungary. The Roma in Hungary", Section 1.

[76] This is different when mass murder is described. Lice, diseases and epidemics clearly result from the concentration camp system and ghettos and thus are not shown as inherent characteristic of Roma.

[77] As for the murder of the Roma during the Holocaust, the perpetrators that are most addressed are the Germans and the Arrow Cross Members. At this point Hungarian gendarmes are mentioned in one sentence only. "Hundreds of them [Roma] were shot into mass graves by Arrow Cross thugs and gendarmes at Szolgaegyháza, Várpalota, Lajoskomárom, Nagyszalonta, Lengyel and other places." Panel "The massacre of the Roma", Section 6.

[78] This is due to the diversity of Roma persecution in Hungary but that is not made clear. The exhibition states that Roma lived in uncertainty and were dependent on the "good or ill-will of the local authorities". This suggestion of both positive and negative attitudes side by side relativizes the real hatred Roma almost always experienced. A little later the same panel states that "The occasional bitterly anti-Gypsy views and suggestions of low-level public officials and local civilians were usually not supported by competent authorities in the Ministry of the Interior", suggesting that racism happened just occasionally and came from the lower, less competent groups. Panel "The persecution of Roma", Section 4. Similar statements can be found in the panel "The massacre of the Roma" Section 6.

overreacted, using "forced efforts".[79] It is not clear whether the attempted "integration into Hungarian society" might have been acceptable had it not been for the force with which it was applied.[80] Not only is the fact that regional officers targeted Roma, in and of itself, problematic, but that this went too far. Gesturing vaguely towards racism as the reason for unjust brutality, the exhibition does not mention it explicitly. When racism against Roma is described words such as "sometimes" or "occasionally" are often added.[81] Still, that discrimination and violence was directed against Roma, taking their rights, dignity and life, is clearly conveyed in the exhibition – an exception in Hungary today.

Conclusion

The main problem with the representation of Jewish and Roma victims at the HDKE is the authoritative narrative through which the stories are imparted. Claiming to present a full, inclusive account hides the museum's construction of victimhood and the characteristics displayed appear as factual truth. The pictorial evidence displayed, for example from the Auschwitz-Album, is used as illustration rather than being presented as evidence. Contextualization about the genesis of the photos is missing, as well as their history and role within the discourse about the victims. Not utilizing the photos for what they could communicate, the exhibition uses them instead to construct an authoritative narrative about victimhood. The Jews and Roma presented are objects spoken about and inserted into a narrative structured through the persecution. The representation establishes the Jewish victims as the typical, universal victims of the Holocaust. In this imagination, the Jewish victims are a passive, helpless and humiliated group, depicted through the perpetrators' gaze. Deviations from this presentation remain marginal at best. This archetypical victim is so dominant that other victims are expected to have similar characteristics and are evaluated accordingly. If other victims, here the Roma, fail to show these imagined characteristics – due to their own unique history – they are less relevant. As a result, their persecution is not told in its own right and the Roma are marginalized once more.

This presentation is not unique to the HDKE or even to Hungary. The Holocaust itself is a European event, its historiography clearly has a global dimen-

---

79 Panel "The Roma in Hungary", Section 1.
80 Ibid.
81 Panel "The persecution of Roma", Section 4.

sion, and the primary sources from it are available throughout the world. Museum techniques equally do not end at the national border. This produces representations common in Europe, following European and even global trends, in which specific configurations of how to conceptualize the Holocaust develop. The construction of agency, for both the perpetrators and the victims, are templates available for the museum representation, the universal victim being one of them. European representations provide a general frame in which the specific story of the nation is then presented. Displaying a national narrative is in itself a European feature. The narrative about the imagined victim is told via the national narrative and this hides its European character. The European frame, for example the construction of a helpless and passive victim, is broad. Each institution can apply it to the national discourse and interpret it according to the specific national context. European and national discourse may merge, depending on the specific museum and its political position. Accordingly, both national discourse and institutional evaluation of it determine how the victims are invested with meaning beyond the universal template. The nationalization of the Jews as Hungarians is for example unique at the HDKE. By nationalizing the Jews as Hungarians, the HDKE explicitly positions itself against the perspective dominant in Hungary that excludes Jews from the nation. As a result, the representation of the victims of the Holocaust in the HDKE is neither European nor national, but a representation in which European, national and institutional elements transformed into a new hybrid narrative.

The HDKE counters a conservative and right-wing interpretation of the Holocaust. This is exceptional among the few institutions that address the Holocaust in Hungary. Nonetheless, the HDKE presents an authoritative exhibition in a problematic display mode that even repeats racist stereotypes. While common in Europe, this display mode needs to be evaluated and improved. A first step would be to allow diverse subject positions, plural perspectives and transparent interpretations. The individual victim needs a voice that is differentiated from the speech act of the curators and tells the victim's own, personal story. Choosing a multi-faceted narrative instead of a linear story, would reveal different views, conflicts, debates and blank spots. Pluralizing the story, it would also make historical interpretations visible. The interpretive frame could explicate the evidence from the Holocaust, enabling the visitor to conduct historical analysis. The process of contextualizing and then interpreting evidence would reveal the limitations of primary sources and consequently our ability to define history. To communicate the limits of perpetrator photos makes the one-sided construction of victimhood transparent. To know how a photo of a victim came into being, how violent this depiction was and still is, is crucial in order to display and view them as partial and very limited representations of the people victi-

mized. Showing and viewing them with this in mind might even bestow some
dignity back onto the people shown in the photos and restore agency to them.

References

Alexander, Jeffrey C. "On the Social Construction of Moral Universal: The 'Holocaust' from
  War Crime to Trauma Drama." *European Journal of Social Theory* 5.1(2002): 5–85.
Bal, Mieke. *Double Exposures. The Subject of Cultural Analysis.* London/New York: Routledge,
  1996.
Bársony, János, and Daróczi, Ágnes. *Pharrajimos: The Fate of the Roma During the Holocaust.*
  Budapest: Idebate Press, 2008.
Bársony, János. "Hungarian Pharrajimos, the Unexplored Territories of the Roma Holocaust
  and Its Aftereffect." *The Holocaust in Hungary. A European Perspective.* Ed. Judit Molnár.
  Budapest: Balassi Kiadó, 2005. 404–417.
Braham, Randolph L. "Hungary and the Holocaust: The Nationalist Drive to Whitewash the
  Past." *The Treatment of the Holocaust in Hungary and Romania during the
  Post-Communist Era.* Ed. Randolph L. Braham. New York: Columbia University, 2004.
  1–43.
Bredekamp, Horst. *Theorie des Bildakts.* Frankfurt/M.: Suhrkamp, 2010.
Brink, Cornelia. *Ikonen der Vernichtung. Öffentlicher Gebrauch von Fotografien aus
  nationalsozialistischen Konzentrationslagern nach 1945.* Berlin: Akademie, 1998.
Cole, Tim. *Traces of the Holocaust. Journeying in and out of the Ghettos.* London: Continuum,
  2011.
Deák, István. "Anti-Semitism and the Treatment of the Holocaust in Hungary." *Anti-Semitism
  and the Treatment of the Holocaust in Postcommunist Eastern Europe.* Ed. Randolph L.
  Braham. New York: Columbia University, 1994. 99–124.
Didi-Hubermann, Georges. *Images in Spite of All. Four Photographs from Auschwitz.*
  Chicago/London: University of Chicago Press, 2008.
Doosry, Yasmin. "Vom Dokument zur Ikone: Zur Rezeption des Auschwitz-Albums. "
  Representations of Auschwitz. 50 Years of Photographs, Paintings, and Graphics. Ed.
  Yasmin Doosry. Oświęcim: Auschwitz-Birkenau State Museum, 1995. 95–104.
Fritz, Regina, and Katja Wezel. "Konkurrenz der Erinnerungen? Museale Darstellung von
  diktatorischen Erfahrungen in Ungarn und Lettland. " *Aufarbeitung der Diktatur – Diktat
  der Aufarbeitung? Normierungsprozesse beim Umgang mit diktatorischer Vergangenheit.*
  Ed. Katrin Hammerstein. Göttingen: Wallstein, 2009. 233–246.
Fritz, Regina and Imke Hansen. "Zwischen nationalem Opfermythos und europäischen
  Standards. Der Holocaust im ungarischen Erinnerungsdiskurs. " *Universalisierung des
  Holocaust? Erinnerungskultur und Geschichtspolitik in internationaler Perspektive.* Eds.
  Jan Eckel and Claudia Moisel. Göttingen: Wallstein, 2008. 59–85.
Fritz, Regina. "Wandlung der Erinnerung in Ungarn. Von der Tabuisierung zur Thematisierung
  des Holocaust. " *Zeitgeschichte* 6 (2006): 33, 303–317.
Greiff, Gideon. "The 'Auschwitz Album. The Story of Lili Jacob." *The Auschwitz Album. The
  Story of a Transport.* Ed. Israel Gutmann, and Bella Gutterman. Jerusalem/Oświęcim:
  Newton Ltd, 2002. 71–86.

Gutmann, Israel, and Bella Gutterman. *The Auschwitz Album. The Story of a Transport.* Jerusalem/Oświęcim: Newton Ltd, 2002.

Hesse, Klaus. "Bilder lokaler Judendeportationen. Fotografien als Zugänge zur Alltagsgeschichte des NS-Terrors." *Visual History. Ein Studienbuch.* Ed. Gerhard Paul. Göttingen: Vandenhoeck & Ruprecht, 2006. 149–168.

Holtschneider, K. Hannah. *The Holocaust and Representations of Jews. History and Identity in the Museum.* London/New York: Routledge, 2011.

Karlsson, Klas-Göran, and Ulf Zander. *Echoes of the Holocaust. Historical Cultures in Contemporary Europe.* Lund: Nordic Academic Press, 2003, 9–57.

Klarsfeld, Serge. *The Auschwitz album: Lili Jacob's album.* New York: Beate Klarsfeld Foundation, 1980.

Kovács, Éva, and Gerhard Seewann. "Ungarn. Der Kampf um das Gedächtnis." *Mythen der Nationen. 1945 – Arena der Erinnerung.* Ed. Monika Flacke. Berlin: Deutsches Historisches Museum, 2004. 817–845.

Levy, Daniel, and Natan Sznaider. *Erinnerung im globalen Zeitalter: Der Holocaust.* Frankfurt/M.: Suhrkamp, 2007.

Mihok, Brigitte. "Erinnerungsüberlagerungen oder der lange Schatten der Geschichtsverzerrung." *Ungarn und der Holocaust. Kollaboration, Rettung und Trauma.* Ed. Brigitte Mihok. Berlin: Metropol, 2005. 157–168.

Mihok, Brigitte. *Vergleichende Studie zur Situation der Minderheiten in Ungarn und Rumänien (1989–1996) unter besonderer Berücksichtigung der Roma.* Frankfurt/M.: Lang, 1999.

Milton, Sybil. "Images of the Holocaust – part I." *Holocaust and Genocide Studies* 1 (1986): 1, 27–61.

Milton, Sybil. "Images of the Holocaust – part II." *Holocaust and Genocide Studies* 1 (1986): 2, 193–216.

Pearce, Susan. "Objects as meaning; or narrating the past." *Objects of Knowledge.* Ed. Susan Pearce. London: Athlone Press, 1990. 134–135.

Sonntag, Susan. *On Photography.* New York: Anchor Books, 1989.

Springer-Aharoni, Nina. "Photographs As Historical Documents." *The Auschwitz Album. The Story of a Transport.* Ed. Israel Gutmann, and Bella Gutterman. Jerusalem/Oświęcim: Newton Ltd, 2002. 87–97.

Struck, Janina. *Photographing the Holocaust. Interpretation of the Evidence.* New York: I.B. Taurus & Co Ltd., 2004.

Tagg, John. *The Burden of Representation. Essays on Photographies and Histories.* Minneapolis: Universtiy of Minnesota Press, 1988.

Thiemeyer, Thomas. *Fortsetzung des Krieges mit anderen Mitteln. Die beiden Weltkriege im Museum.* Padaborn: Ferdinand Schöningh, 2010.

Andrej Kotljarchuk
The Memory of the Roma Holocaust in Ukraine: Mass Graves, Memory Work and the Politics of Commemoration

> Blood and screaming at Babi Yar!
> There are thousands of graves over disadvantaged and persecuted victims
> No granite stones on the graves of murdered Roma.
>
> Mikha Kozimirenko, Romani–Ukrainian poet (1938–2003)

Thousands of Soviet Roma were killed in 1941–1944 by Nazi *Einsatzgruppen* and local collaborators. They were almost never deported to extermination camps, but instead their bodies were left at the scenes where these crimes were committed. In the protocols of the Soviet *Extraordinary Commission for Investigation of War Crimes,* the Roma were often counted as murdered civil citizens, without specifying their ethnicity. Despite the existence of a small number of accounts identifying the victims of these murders as Romani, the Roma part of the Holocaust history is still little known in post-Soviet space.[1]

In 1976 an official memorial at Babi Yar was erected in Kyiv on the location of the largest massacre during WWII of Eastern European Jews and Roma. However, the Soviet leadership discouraged placing any emphasis on ethnic aspects of this tragedy. The Nazi policy of extermination of Roma was neglected; the war was depicted as a tragedy for all Soviet peoples.[2]

The discussion of the Romani identity cannot be isolated from the memory of the genocide during WWII, which makes the struggle over the past a reflexive landmark that organizes the politics of commemoration.[3] There are 47,000 Roma

---

[1] This study was supported by the Foundation for Baltic and East European Studies (Sweden) and Södertörn University as a part of the research project "The Roma Genocide in Ukraine 1941–1944: History, memories and representations". The author wishes to thank Piotr Wawrzeniuk, David Gaunt, Anders Blomqvist (Södertörn University), Matthew Kott (Uppsala University), Mikhail Tyaglyy (Ukrainian Centre for Holocaust Stuidies), Barbara Törnquist-Plewa (Lund University) and anonymous reviewers for their comments and suggestions on prior drafts.
[2] Alaina Lemon. *Between two fires Gypsy performance and Romany memory. From Pushkin to Postsocialism.* Durham: Duke University Press, 2000, 148.
[3] Adam Bartosz. *Tabor Pamieci Romow.* Tarnow: Regional Museum of Tarnow Press, 2003; Elena Marushiakova and Vesselin Popov. "Holocaust and the Gypsies. The Reconstruction of the Historical Memory and Creation of New National Mythology." *Beyond Camps and Forced Labour. Current International Research on Survivors of Nazi Persecution.* Eds. Johannes-Dieter Steinert and Inge Weber-Newth. Osnabrück: Secolo, 2006, 805–826; Slawomir Kapralski. "Symbols

in contemporary Ukraine.⁴ The Roma minority is often associated with poverty and crime, which has in turn converted it into a marginalized social group.⁵ In 1991 the government of independent Ukraine allowed the establishment of new memorials at Babi Yar that specifically identified the ethnicity of victims. A Jewish memorial was built in the same year.⁶ A Roma memorial is still under construction. In addition, about 20 monuments to victims of the Roma genocide have been erected in Ukraine during the last ten years. However, dozens of Roma mass graves remained unmarked and in need of elementary preservation and commemoration. The controversial battles over commemoration of WWII and the Holocaust in Ukraine make this process much more complicated;⁷ and scholars still do not have a clear picture of what is going on with post-Soviet politics of commemoration of the Roma genocide.

Sources

The author has used a wide range of sources. Among them are media publications, protocols of the *Extraordinary Commission for Investigation of War Crimes (ChGK)*, articles of local historians, and photos. Most of the material for this article was collected during field research in 2010 and 2012. In September 2010 the author, together with colleagues from the French centre *Yahad-In Unum* and Södertörn University, participated in field research in Volhynia. In July–August 2012 an independent expedition to Kyiv, Poltava, Vinnitsa, Sumy and Chernihiv regions was carried out. Field work included interviews with witnesses of geno-

---

and Rituals in the Mobilisation of the Romani National Ideal." *Studies in Ethnicity and Nationalism* 12.1 (2012): 64–81; Andrej Kotljarchuk. "World War II Memory Politics: Jewish, Polish and Roma Minorities of Belarus."*The Journal of Belarusian Studies* 1.7 (2013): 7–40.
4 All-Ukrainian census 2001.
5 Oleksandr Belikov. "Derzhavna politika stosovno tsygan Ukrainy: istoria i suchasnist." *Naukovi zapiski. Zbirnik prats molodikh vchenikh ta aspirantiv*. Kyiv: National Academy of Sciences, 2008, 24–56.
6 Tatiana Evstafieva. "K istorii ustanovleniya pamiatnika v Bab'em Yaru." *Evreiskii obozrevatel*. 11 (30 June 2002).
7 Jeff Mankoff. "Babi Yar and the struggle for memory, 1944–2004." *Ab Imperio* 2 (2004): 393–415; Rebecca Golbert. "Holocaust Sites in Ukraine: Pechora and the Politics of Memorialization." *Holocaust and Genocide Studies* 18.2 (2004): 205–233; Wilfried Jilg. "The Politics of History and the Second World War in Post-Communist Ukraine." *Jahrbücher für Geschichte Osteuropas* 54.1 (2006): 50–81; Omer Bartov. *Erased: vanishing traces of Jewish Galicia in present-day Ukraine*. Princeton: Princeton University Press, 2007; Aleksandr Burakovsky. "Holocaust remembrance in Ukraine: memorialization of the Jewish tragedy at Babi Yar." *Nationalities Papers* 39.3 (2011): 371–389.

cide, local experts and agents of memory. The field research also included geographic and photographic investigation of memory objects. Simultaneously expositions in local museums were investigated.

Aims and theoretical framework

The purpose of the present study is to analyze the Soviet and contemporary politics of memory regarding the Roma Holocaust in Ukraine with the focus on memorials and mass graves. The principal questions are:
- What role does Ukraine's past dependence on the Soviet period play in the contemporary politics of the memory of the Roma genocide in Ukraine?
- What are the causes of the active memorial work in contemporary Ukraine regarding the Roma Holocaust mass graves?
- Who are the agents of memory?
- What external and internal factors play a role in this segment of the memory policy?

These questions acquire a special interest in a comparative perspective. In Russia, there are no monuments in the places of the mass executions of Roma that indicate the ethnicity of the victims. Belarus has only three such sites.[8] At the same time more than twenty monuments have been raised over the past ten years on the places of Roma massacres in Ukraine. What kind of agents of memory are behind the numerous constructions of new memorials in Ukraine? Roma communities? The authorities? Ukrainian NGOs? Political parties? The European Union? Foreign funders?

The theoretical model for this article is based on the concept of "sites of memory" developed by Pierre Nora and Lawrence Kritzman. They argue that memory shapes the future by determining our attitude to the past, emphasising that crystallised memories are extremely powerful factors in the mobilization of an ethnic group and the strengthening of their identity. The sites of memory, considered by these scholars very broadly (that is, as images on banknotes or in movies), are an extremely powerful factor in the consolidation of a nation and

---

8 Andrej Kotljarchuk. "Palityka pamiaci u suchasnai Belarusi. Memaryialy druhoi susvetnai vainy i etnichnyia menshastsi krainy." *ARCHE* 2 (2013): 173–194.

mobilization of ethnic groups. The process of inclusion of an ethnic minority's collective memory into a national context takes place through sites of memory.[9]

The authorities are not interested strictly in history but in memory, which always has a strongly engaged political meaning. In this regard, it is important to trace the history of sculptural projects for public monuments that did not secure the approval of the authorities (in other words, failed the contest) and were never implemented. While history belongs to humanities, the science that associated with a critical understanding of past events through source criticism, memory is coupled with contemporary politics and the dedicated creation of a historical myth capable of uniting different ethnic and social groups in society.

Memorial politics crystallise in sites of memory, amongst which the most influential ones are monuments, because the physical space of memory is created through them, connecting a historical event, a remembrance day and the participants in the ceremony.[10] The memorial gives sacral meaning to the landscape, which "helps to create the national iconography of a contemporary state".[11] In a democratic state, memory politics are a common action field for the authorities and civil society that, in turn, have important leverage (independent media etc.). In a totalitarian state, the government has a virtual monopoly over public memory, deciding what to remember and what to forget. In such states, the inscription on a public monument must always be approved by the authorities and is the ultimate, canonised and embedded in concrete viewpoint of the official stand on events of the past.

The idea of raising monuments to the dead did not originate with WWII, but no other war has given birth to so many. A typical war memorial gives the following information: a short description and chronology of tragic events, the number or list of victims, information about the criminals and words addressed to the victims' descendants. Not only is the sculptural group important, but also the place chosen by the authorities for the monument (a central or marginal point of the cultural landscape). The language or languages of the monument play a

---

9 Pierre Nora and Lawrence Kritzman. *Realms of memory: rethinking the French past.* 1. New York: Columbia University Press, 1996; *Realms of memory: rethinking the French past.* 2. New York: Columbia University Press, 1997.
10 Nurit Schleifman. "Moscow's Victory Park: A Monumental Change." *History and Memory* 13. 2 (2001): 5–34; Benjamin Forest and Juliet Johnson. "Unravelling the Threads of History: Soviet-Era Monuments and Post-Soviet National Identity." *Annals of the Association of American Geographers* 92.3 (2002): 524–547; Henry Pickford. "Conflict and Commemoration: Two Berlin Memorials." *Modernism modernity* 12.1 (2005): 133–173.
11 Michaela Schäuble. "How History Takes Place: Sacralized Landscapes in the Croatian-Bosnian Border Region." *History and Memory* 23.1 (2011): 24.

major role. Thus, a language that the majority of the population does not understand refers to the ethnic meaning of the site of memory, even when ethnicity cannot be guessed directly. In most cases, an inscription in the language of a minority is accompanied by an inscription in the official language, which in the Post-Soviet monuments is Ukrainian.

The Soviet period, 1942–1991

The author believes that the comprehensive analysis of contemporary Ukrainian memory politics is not possible without an examination of the Soviet period. The theory of 'path dependence' is suitable for the analysis of contemporary memory politics with respect to WWII. In accordance with this theory, the scope and limitations of new politics (including memory politics) are determined by the political choices made or results attained much earlier by the previous political regime.[12]

Information in the Soviet WWII media about the Nazi extermination of Roma was minimal. Roma were not mentioned (unlike Jews) in the well-spread widely-disseminated note on Babi Yar announced by Soviet Foreign Minister Vyacheslav Molotov on 6 January 1942.[13] One can agree with Karel Berkhoff that the absence of significant foreign or domestic political factors was a main reason for the almost complete silence on the part of the Soviets about the killings of Roma by Nazis. He points out that "in the eyes of the Kremlin, Gypsies, who actually were subject to the same mass extermination as Jews [Stalin did know about Roma in 1943], had no political value".[14]

However, in some wartime publications the Soviet media stressed that the extermination of Roma by the Nazis was motivated exclusively by racial goals. In June 1944, the front correspondent of the leading military newspaper, *Krasnaya Zvezda* Ilya, Konstatinoskii published an article about the forced deportation to Transnistria of Romanian Roma by the regime of Ion Antonescu and also about their mass death on the Ukrainian steppes.[15] 29 August 1944 the largest

---

[12] Stefan Hedlund. *Russian Path Dependence*. London: Routledge, 2005.
[13] "Nota narodnogo komissara inostrannykh del SSSR tov. V. M. Molotova ot 6 ianvaria 1942 goda." *Nurnbergskii process. Sbornik materialov.* Moscow: Gosudarstvennoe izdatel'stvo iuridicheskoi literatury, 1954, 515–516.
[14] Karel Berkhoff. "Pogolovnoe unichtozhenie evreiskogo naseleniya. Holocaust v sovetskikh SMI, 1941–1945." *Holocaust i suchasnist'* 1.7 (2010): 116.
[15] Ilya Konstatinovskii. "Zemlia Moldavii." *Izvestia* 137.8439 (10 June 1944): 3.

Soviet newspaper, *Izvestia,* argued that the systematic destruction of Roma by Nazis was racially motivated: "With particular sadism and cruelty the Germans shot Gypsies, including women and children living in Vyborg, Pushkino and Novorzhev districts. All of them were shot just for the fact that they were Gypsies".[16]

After the war the exceptional nature of the systematic extermination of the Roma people was not recognised by the Soviet state. Soviet historians had created a huge historiography of what they termed the *Great Patriotic War,* without using the word Holocaust or the expression the genocide of Jewish and Roma peoples. The Soviet totalitarian regime kept silent about many aspects of the war. In addition to the Holocaust, there was little mention of crimes by Soviet partisans, the history of the non-Soviet Ukrainian partisan resistance, and the mass collaboration with the Nazi regime on the part of Russians and Ukrainians. During the Soviet era, the Nazi genocide of Roma was muted. The victory was seen to be achieved by all Soviet people, and the war was depicted as a tragedy for all Soviet peoples. Ignoring the ethnic background of the victims, the authorities persistently used a vague concept of "peaceful Soviet citizens" (*mirnye sovetskie grazhdane*). The key note of Soviet memory politics was heroisation. For Soviet leaders, this war was first of all a war of heroes: soldiers, partisans and members of the underground resistance. Thus hundreds of Roma and Jewish mass graves have remained unmarked or marked by simple, anonymous obelisks. Without having a public space, the collective memory of the Roma genocide continued, mainly in oral form in Romani family circles.[17]

The Soviet policy of forgetting can be described by the formulation of Karl Jaspers, who called the silence surrounding the Nazi past in Europe "aggressive".[18] Those who tried to break taboos on memory were repressed. For example, in 1968 engineer Mikhailo Kochubievsky was arrested in Kyiv for talking with people in Babi Yar. Kochubievsky argued that "Babi Yar is not just a site for a nameless massacre of victims of fascism, but the largest place of genocide of the Jewish people".[19] The struggle of the Jewish community and

---

[16] "Soobshchenie Chrezvychainoi Gosudarstvennoi Komissii po ustanovleniu i rassledovaniu zlodeianii nemetsko-fashistskikh zakhvatchikov i ikh soobshchnikov." *Izvestia* 205.8507 (29 August 1944): 3.

[17] Michael Stewart. "Remembering without Commemoration: the Mnemonics and Politics of Holocaust memories among European Roma." *Journal of the Royal Anthropological Institute* 10.3 (2004): 561–582.

[18] Gilad Margalit. *Germany and its gypsies: a post-Auschwitz ordeal.* Madison: University of Wisconsin Press, 2002, 176.

[19] Mikhail Mitsel. "Zapret na uvekovechivanie pamiati kak sposob zamalchivania Holocausta." *Holocaust i suchasnist'* 1.2 (2007): 14.

Soviet intelligentsia for recognition of the Jewish genocide led to some compromise with the government. In many cases (but not in Babi Yar), the inscription on the monuments in Russian during the Soviet era was translated into Yiddish. The letters of the Hebrew alphabet left no doubt about the ethnic origin of the victims.[20]

The lack of an educated Roma elite and the poor integration of Roma into Soviet society did not give Roma a chance for any recognition of their tragedy. Unlike the Jews, the Roma people did not have a political and cultural diaspora outside the Soviet Union or an independent state representing their ethnic community. The *Great Soviet Encyclopaedia* briefly informed its readers that "during the Second World War in 1939–45 twenty thousand Gypsies were brutally exterminated by the Nazis in Central and Eastern Europe".[21] However, the number of victims was underestimated. In addition, the Soviet Union was not mentioned, and Nazi-occupied territory was not, according to the *Great Soviet Encyclopaedia*, a place of the massacre of Roma people. By 1991 there was not a single monument to the genocide of Roma in the Soviet Union. In contrast, by 2013, 113 places of mass extermination of Roma were identified on the territory of Ukraine;[22] and 27 mass graves in Belarus.[23] However, dozens of mass graves remain unknown or unmarked, many of which were destroyed in the course of construction and agriculture.[24]

Ukraine's past dependence and contemporary problems of commemoration

Memorialization of the victims of the Nazi genocide of the Roma in Ukraine faces a number of objective obstacles related to the Soviet period. One of the main problems of contemporary memory politics is the depersonalisation of the vic-

---

20 Mordechai Altshuler. "Jewish Holocaust Commemoration Activity in the USSR under Stalin." *Yad Vashem Studies* 30 (2002): 221–240.
21 Tatiana Ventsel. "Tsygane." *Bolshaya Sovetskaya Enciklopedia*. 28. Moscow, 1978, 606–607.
22 *Peresleduvannia ta vbivstva romiv na terenakh Ukrainy u chasi druhoi svitovoi viini. Zbirnik dokumentiv ta spohadiv.* Ed. Mikhail Tyaglyy. Kyiv: Ukrainian Centre for Genocide Studies, 2013. Table 2.
23 Kotljarchuk. "Palityka pamiaci u suchasnai Belarusi," 173–194.
24 Andrej Kotljarchuk. "Natsistskii genotsid tsygan na territorii okkupirovannoi Ukrainy: rol' sovteskogo proshlogo v sovremennoi politike pamiati." *Holocaust i suchasnist*. 1.12 (2014): 24–50.

tims of the Roma genocide. The Roma traditionally avoid contact with the authorities, and the official data and the real number of the Roma can differ greatly.

The number of Roma in 1941 on what is today the territory of Ukraine is unknown. The Soviet census of 1939 gives a figure of 10,443 Roma in Soviet Ukraine. However we know that the official census and the actual number of Roma differ significantly. For example, the All-Ukrainian census of 2001 counted 14,000 Roma in Transcarpathia. At the same time, the regional tax registration office listed 25,720 Roma in Transcarpathia, which is 55 per cent of all Ukrainian Roma.[25] This of course makes no sense. The situation prior to WWII was even more complicated. The 1939 Soviet census did not include the Roma population in the Crimea, which became part of Ukraine in 1954. In addition, this census did not account for Roma in territories occupied by the Soviet Union during WWII: Polish Western Ukraine, Romanian regions of Northern Bukovina and Southern Bessarabia; and Transcarpathia, which before the war was an autonomous part of the Czech Republic and during the war was occupied by Hungary. These regions, which were settlement areas of the Roma population, were merged into Ukraine as a result of WWII.

Most Ukrainian Roma were nomadic before WWII and had no passports, and they avoided any contact with the authorities, including the census scribes. All this greatly complicates all possible calculations. Aleksandr Kruglov in his quantitative study of Roma genocide victims in Ukraine states that there were about 20,000 Roma on the territory of today's Ukraine at the beginning of WWII. The total number of victims among the Ukrainian Roma is estimated by him to be 19,000–20,000, of whom more than half were Romanian Roma deported to southern Ukraine.[26] It should be also noted that agricultural and warm climate Ukraine was a traditional place for the summer migration of North-Russian, Belarusian and Baltic Roma agricultural workers.[27] Researchers of the Roma genocide also point out that a significant number of mass graves of nomadic Roma remain unknown. Often the only witnesses were the perpetrators themselves.[28] Due to the lack of reliable statistics on the size of the pre-war Romani population in the Soviet Union, Poland, Romania, and the Czech Republic, any exact figure

---

25 *Materialy mizhnarodnoi tsyhanoznavchoi konferentsii Romy Ukrainy iz minulogo v maibutne.* Kyiv: Justinian, 2008, 13.
26 Aleksandr Kruglov. "Genocide tsygan v Ukraine 1941–1944: statistiko-regional'nyi aspect." *Holocaust i suchasnist'* 2.16 (2009): 86–113.
27 Ibid.
28 Nadezhda Demetr and Nikolai Bessonov, and Niklolai Kutenkov. *Istoriya tsygan – novyi vzgliad.* Voronezh: IPF, 2000. 217.

of victims is questionable. A recent study estimates the number of the Roma genocide victims on the territory of Ukraine to vary from 26,000 to 62,500, with the likely figure to be in excess of about 40,000.[29]

De-personification of victims is another problem for memory work on the Roma Holocaust. It also highlights the difference between the memory of the Jewish and the Roma tragedy. The Jewish community already in the war years had made an effort to document the tragedy of Babi Yar.[30] Some testimonies were published by Soviet war correspondents already during the war.[31] The report *Black Book*, which was prepared by Vasily Grossman and Ilya Ehrenburg, was banned in the Soviet Union. However, in 1946, it was published in the USA and has been available to Western scholars and Soviet dissidents.[32] In 1991, in Kyiv, the first memory book of the Jewish victims of Babi Yar was published. The first list of Jewish victims of Babi Yar was already prepared during the Soviet period and included more than 7000 names.[33] A new list published later contains more than 14,000 names.[34] The names of Roma victims of Babi Yar still are unknown.

A number of other factors distinguish the memory work in the Jewish and Roma tragedies. Unlike the Jews, the Roma to a great extent lack their own cultural landscape. If today the Jewish Holocaust is remembered, not only through monuments but also through deserted synagogues, the former Jewish ghettos and cemeteries, the Roma do not have any such cultural markers. With the genocide, almost all their physical space of memory was destroyed.

In addition, Ukrainian Roma have names and surnames which are typical for the local population (Ukrainian, Polish, Russian, Hungarian and Romanian). The role of anthroponymy is important. When the protocols of the Soviet *Extraordinary Commission for Investigation of War Crimes* (ChGK) do not specify the ethnic origin of the victims, it is still possible to identify Jewish victims by analysing names. This is impossible in case of Roma victims.

---

29 Andrej Kotljarchuk. "Nazi Genocide of Roma in Belarus and Ukraine: the significance of census data and census takers." *Etudes Tsigane* 1 (2015).
30 Jeff Mankoff. "Babi Yar and the struggle for memory, 1944–2004," 393–415; Arno, Lustiger. *Stalin i evrei: Tragicheskaia istoriya Evreiskogo antifashistskogo komiteta i sovetskikh evreev.* Moscow: Rosspen, 2008.
31 Aleksandr Avdeenko and Petr Olender. "Babi Yar." *Krasnaya Zvezda* 274.5645 (20 November 1943): 3; Vasily, Grossman. "Doroga na Berlin." *Krasnaya Zvezda* 38.6026 (15 February 1945): 3.
32 *The Black Book: the Nazi crime against the Jewish people*. Published by the Jewish Black Book Committee, New York: Duell, Sloan and Pearce, 1946.
33 Ilya Zaslavskii. Ed. *Kniga Pamiati. Imena pogibshikh v Bab'em Yaru*. Kyiv: Oberih, 1991.
34 Ilya Levitas. Ed. *Babi Yar: Kniga pamiati*. Kyiv: Stal, 2005.

In most cases, the Roma were executed at sites, which were chosen by the Nazis for the extermination of the Jewish population, POWs and partisans. Such sites were usually classified by the *Extraordinary Commission for Investigation of War Crimes* and marked. None of the monuments, however, referred to the Roma victims of genocide. In post-Soviet Ukraine in many such places new monuments have been erected that this time emphasise the ethnicity of the genocide victims. For example the new Roma memorials at Babi Yar, Pirohova Levada, Koziatyn, Ostroushki and Odessa were designed on this basis.

A further difference between Jews and Roma in Ukraine is that, unlike Ukrainian Jews, Roma are not a homogeneous ethnic group. The Romani community of Ukraine is divided into a number of cultural and religious groups. Among them are Protestants, Orthodox Christians, Muslims, and Catholics. There are more than ten dialect groups of Roma in Ukraine, each using different Romani dialects as well as different languages in everyday life (Ukrainian, Russian, Romanian, Hungarian, Slovak, etc). Relations between different groups of Roma are not always close.[35] Until 1956 the majority of Ukrainian Roma were nomadic. This means that often the emotional (family) link between the Roma community and local Holocaust mass graves is missing. This is precisely the situation in Torchyn, Ostroushki, Vilshanka and many others places. For instance an unknown group of Roma were killed by Nazis near the west Ukrainian town of Torchyn. However, the local Romani community is represented today by Romanian Roma, the survivors and descendants deported to southern Ukraine. They lived after the war in Transnistria and moved to Torchyn in 1956 after the Soviet *Act of Settlement of all Nomadic Gypsies*. As a result the Roma of Torchyn remember well the mass deaths of their deported ancestors in southern Ukraine, but know nothing about the local massacre, which were observed during field studies (interviews recorded in the author's archives). This situation is typical. Coupled with the lack of educated strata among the Roma, this means that the Ukrainian Roma themselves cannot usually be active agents of memory. This is why, in contrast to the Jewish situation, the localization of mass graves and initiatives to raise monuments have come mostly from the non-Romani NGOs and the Ukrainian government.

According to the 2004 resolution of the Ukrainian parliament, an International Remembrance Day of the Holocaust of the Roma is held annually on 2 Au-

---

35 Lev Cherenkov. "Tsyganskaya dialektologiya v Ukraine. Istoriya i sovremennost." *Materialy mizhnarodnoi tsyhanoznavchoi konferentsii Romy Ukrainy iz minulogo v maibutne*. Kyiv: Justinian, 2008: 161–172.

gust and local authorities have to erect memorials on the places of mass executions in order to commemorate the genocide.[36] As a result more than 20 monuments commemorating Roma victims of the Nazi genocide have been erected in Ukraine since 2005.

The case of Babi Yar (or Babyn Yar in Ukrainian, means Old Woman's Ravine) is considered to be the single largest massacre in the history of the Holocaust and has become a central symbol of the Nazi genocide on the occupied Soviet territory. While in some regions of Ukraine the active process of commemoration of Jewish and Roma Holocaust mass graves is going on, in the capital conflict over memory continues.[37]

Babi Yar is a chain of seven deep ravines in the north-western suburb of Kyiv. There on 29–30 September 1941, nine days after the German occupation of the city began, more than 33,000 Jewish civilians were exterminated by the Nazis in two days of mass killings. Near Babi Yar the Lukianivka railway goods station is situated and Jewish victims who were forced to assemble there believed that the Nazis were going to deport them from Kyiv to another place. The total number of people murdered in Babi Yar between 1941 and 1943 (Jews, Roma, Soviet POWs and underground fighters, the mentally ill, Ukrainian nationalists, civilians) is estimated to be about 100,000.[38] Executions of Roma in Babi Yar by the Nazis continued until the liberation of the city by the Red Army in November 1943.[39] According to Anatoly Kuzntesov the mass killings of Jews and Roma caused alarm among the ethnic Ukrainian majority. "Jews kaput, Gypsies too, and then Ukrainians, then come you" – was a popular saying in Kyiv during the war.[40]

During the war the Jewish tragedy of Babi Yar was reported in Soviet media.[41] The massacre of Jews was mentioned in a diplomatic note by Foreign Minister Vyacheslav Molotov on 6 January 1942 entitled *On the widespread robbery, devastation of the population, and the atrocities of the German authorities on*

---

36 On the night of 2 August 1944 the so-called *Zigeunerlager* in Auschwitz-Birkenau was eliminated by the Nazis. In 2002 this day was proposed by the Council of Europe as *International Roma and Sinti Genocide Remembrance Day*.
37 Burakovsky. "Holocaust remembrance in Ukraine." 371–389; Ingmar Oldberg. "Both victims and perpetrators. Ukraine's problematic relationship to the Holocaust." *Baltic worlds* 4.2 (2011): 40–43.
38 Karel Berkhoff. *Babi Yar: Site of Mass Murder, Ravine of Oblivion*. Washington: United States Holocaust Memorial Museum, 2012.
39 Aleksandr Kruglov. *Sbornik dokumentov i materialov ob unichtozhnenie natsistami evreev Ukrainy v 1941–44*. Kyiv: Institut Judaiki, 2002, 78.
40 Anatoly Kuznetsov. *Babi Yar. Roman-dokument*. Frankfurt am Main: Posev, 1970, 157.
41 Mankoff. "Babi Yar and the struggle for memory, 1944–2004," 393–415.

the occupied territories of the Soviet Union, and published in 1942 by the leading newspaper Pravda.[42] Nation-renowned war correspondents Vasily Grossman, Aleksandr Avdeenko and Petr Olender also published testimonies about the mass killings of Jews in Babi Yar in 1943–1945.[43] However, the mass murder of Roma in Babi Yar was not mentioned.

On 29 February 1944, Soviet media published the *Extraordinary Commission for Investigation of War Crimes in Kyiv*, a report led by Nikita Khrushchev. The Commission's report did not specify the ethnicity of the victims and muted the racial character of the mass killings, noting that: "In Babi Yar over 100,000 Soviet citizens were killed, women, children and old folk".[44] The decision of the Communist Party's leadership to ignore the racial and genocidal nature of the massacre in Babi Yar was crucial for the Soviet policy of forgetting the Jewish and Romani Holocausts. The decision was taken despite the Soviet leadership's knowledge of the results of investigation by *Extraordinary Commission for Investigation of War Crimes*, which contained detailed information on the mass murder of Roma in Babi Yar. A major witness, a professor at the Kyiv Institute of Forestry Ivan Zhitov, stated that the Germans killed Roma in Babi Yar three months after the Jewish massacre, meaning at the end of December 1941.[45] A local woman, L. I. Zavorotnaya-Grigurno stated that "Roma were shot at the Babi Yar massacre later than the Jews". She stated that "during the war she saw several gypsy wagons with people drove past her house by Nazis towards Babi Yar". One of the witnesses, N. Tkachenko, claimed to see Romani clothes left after the killings in Babi Yar.[46] Until 1991 none of the testimonies were available for research, making it impossible to study the mass murder of Roma in Babi Yar. However, despite the lack of available written sources, the extermination of

---

42 "Nota narodnogo komissara inostrannykh del SSSR tov. V. M. Molotova ot 6 ianvaria 1942 goda." *Nurnbergskii process. Sbornik materialov*. Moscow: Gosudarstvennoe izdatel'stvo iuridicheskoi literatury, 1954, 504–517.
43 Avdeenko and Olender. "Babi Yar." 3; Grossman. "Doroga na Berlin," 3.
44 "Soobshchenie Chrezvychainoi Gosudarstvennoi Komissii po ustanovleniu i rassledovaniu zlodeianii nemetsko-fashistskikh zakhvatchikov i ikh soobshchnikov o razrusheniyakh I zverstvakh sovershennykh nemetsko-fashistskim zakhvatchikami v gorode Kyive." *Izvestia* 50.8352 (29 February 1944): 3.
45 "Svidetel'stvo zhitelei goroda Kieva khudozhnika Nikolaya Adrianovicha Priakhova i professora Ivana Nikolaevicha Zhitova i drugikh o massovykh rasstrelakh v Bab'em yaru." *Central State Archive of the supreme power and administration of Ukraine* (TsDAGO). Fond R- 4620, opis 3, sprava 243a, list 38.
46 Vitalii Nakhmanovich. "Rasstrely i zakhoroneiya v raione Bab'ego Yara vo vremia nemetskoi okkupatsii goroda Kyiva 1941–43." *Babi Yar: chelovek, vlast', istoriya. Dokumenty i materialy*. Kyiv, 2004, 84–163.

Roma in Babi Yar was a well-known oral history for the residents of post-war Kyiv. In the famous book *Babi Yar: A Document in the Form of a Novel* (1966) Anatoly Kuznetsov, who grew up in Kyiv noted:

> The fascists hunted Gypsies as if they were game. I have never come across anything official concerning this, yet in the Ukraine the Gypsies were subject to the same immediate extermination as the Jews ... Whole tribes of Gypsies were taken to Babi Yar, and they did not seem to know what was happening to them until the last minute.[47]

In April 1945 *Pravda* informed the Soviet people about the decision of the government of Ukraine to build in Babi Yar a memorial and a museum "to the memory of ten of thousand residents of Kiev".[48] Despite the announcement there were no monuments in Babi Yar until 1976 and the site was unmarked until 1966. Thus, 19 September 1961 Yevgeny Yevtushenko, the renowned Russian poet, published the epic *Babi Yar* in *Literaturnaya gazeta*, the leading periodical of the Union of Soviet Writers. The poem, whose first line is "Over Babi Yar there are no monuments" became a strong public protest against the government's refusal to recognise Babi Yar as a Holocaust site.[49] In March 1963 at a meeting with Soviet writers Nikita Khrushchev, the leader of the country and the former head of Ukraine and the ChGK on Babi Yar, devoted special attention to Yevtushenko's poem. According to Khrushchev "the author of the poem showed an ignorance of historical facts, he believes that the victims of Nazi atrocities were only the Jews, in fact there [in Babi Yar] were murdered many Russians, Ukrainians and other Soviet people of various nationalities".[50]

In 1966 Anatoly Kuznetsov's documentary novel, *Babi Yar,* was published in the Soviet Union in censored form in the monthly literary magazine *Yunost'*. Moreover, the next year the novel was printed in 150,000 copies by the Komsomol publishing house *Molodaya gvardiya*.[51] It should be note that fragments concerning the genocide of Roma were kept in the text. The novel was highly criticised by the leading Soviet newspaper *Izvestia*,[52] and both the book and the monthly literary magazine were confiscated from all Soviet libraries. The totalitarian regime ordered the silencing of the tragedy of Roma, an order which was

---

47 Anatoly Kuznetsov. *Babi Yar. A documentary novel*. New York: The Dial Press, 1967.
48 "Pamiatnik pogibshim v Bab'em Yaru." *Pravda* (3 April 1945): 3.
49 Zvi Gitelman. "Politics and the historiography of the Holocaust in the Soviet Union." *Bitter legacy: confronting the Holocaust in the USSR*. Ed. Zvi Gitelman. Bloomington: Indiana University Press, 1997, 20.
50 "Rech' tovarishcha N. S. Khrushcheva." *Pravda* 89 (10 March 1963): 1, 4.
51 Anatoly Kuznetsov. *Babi Yar. Roman-dokument*. Moskva: Molodaya gvardiya, 1967.
52 P. Troitskii. "Po stranitsam zhurnalov." *Izvestia* 19.15413 (20 January 1967): 5.

carefully followed by Soviet officials, historians and media. Moreover the Soviet leadership, who long sought to monopolise the collective memory of the war, left Babi Yar out of the official war narrative, and even sought to eradicate the site of memory physically. On 13 March 1961 as the result of an accident at the Kurenivka brick factory near Babi Yar, the dam securing the loam pulp failed after rain, releasing large volumes of pulp down to Babi Yar.

On 29 September 1966 on the 25th anniversary of the tragedy, an unauthorized rally in Babi Yar was held for the first time in the Soviet era. The participants demanded the recognition of the Jewish genocide and the construction of a monument at Babi Yar. The rally was attended by famous Soviet writers and dissidents among them Viktor Nekrasov, Boris Antonenko-Davidovich, Ivan Dziuba, Petr Yakir, Sergei Paradzhanov, Vladimir Voinovich and Sergei Dovlatov. However, the Roma tragedy was not discussed.[53] Soviet authorities gave in to the pressure of civil society and in 1966 a foundation stone was placed in Babi Yar with the inscription in Russian: "There will be erected a monument to the Soviet people – victims of fascist crimes in the period of temporary occupation of Kyiv in 1941–1943". Finally in 1976 a typically Soviet monument in heroic style was erected at the Babi Yar site with the inscription in Russian: "Soviet citizens, POWs, soldiers and officers of the Red Army, were shot here in Babi Yar by German Fascists".[54] Despite the silence on the Holocaust, the memorial legitimised the practices of memory. Every year, on 29 September the monument has been visited not only by Jews but also by local Roma. It was during these years that the Romani tradition was born to bring to the monument the photos of relatives murdered by the Nazis.[55] This practice continues to this day. By this ceremony the Roma community is trying to overcome the problem of de-personalization.

The Soviet policy of forgetting complicated the contemporary documentation of the Roma genocide. The result of this long-term government policy was the depersonification of victims of the Roma genocide. As a result, it remains unknown when, how many, and what groups in Babi Yar of Roma were killed. Roma of Kyiv state that their relatives were shot in Babi Yar in 1941.[56] The archival sources support their testimonies. In 1937, a Romani craft cooperative, *Trudnatsmen*, was established in Kurenivka near Babi Yar that united 27 Roma families. In 1941 an administrative building for the Romani cooperative was situated in Babi Yar in the former NKVD shooting range. There is no evidence about the existence of Ro-

---

53 Rafail Nakhmanovich. "Babi Yar-1966: kak eto bylo." *Maidan* 28 September 2006.
54 Tatiana Evstafieva. "Babi Yar vo vtoroi polovine XX veka." *Babi Yar: chelovek, vlast', istoriya. Dokumenty i materialy.* Kyiv: Vneshtorgizdat, 2004, 187–206.
55 Kotljarchuk. "Natsistskii genotsid tsygan na territorii okkupirovannoi Ukrainy," 24–50.
56 Ibid, 24–50.

mani craft cooperative in Kyiv after WWII.[57] However, neither scholars nor Roma of Kyiv are able to compile a list of the victims.

With glasnost and perestroika, new interpretations developed in Ukraine regarding the significance of the Roma and Jewish victims of the Nazi occupation. The Soviet monopoly on memory ended and the significance of the Roma genocide underwent a substantial change. After the collapse of the Soviet Union, the government of independent Ukraine allowed in 1991 the establishment of a new memorial at Babi Yar, specifically identifying the victims as Jewish and Roma. In 1989 the Soviet monument was completed; however, the plaques in Yiddish and Russian only provided information about the Jewish genocide. On September 29, 1991 on the 50th anniversary of the tragedy, the Jewish memorial *Menorah* was opened in Babi Yar. In 1992, a monument to Ukrainian nationalists was erected. For the last decade a number of monuments have been built in Babi Yar devoted to the memory of murdered children, the mentally ill, POWs, Soviet underground fighters, Orthodox priests, and Ukrainian nationalists, *Ostarbeiters*, Dynamo Kyiv football players and victims of the Kurenivka accident of 1961. As a result a competition of victimhood was created in Babi Yar. The Roma memorial is still under construction.

In 1995, an initiative to erect a Roma monument in Babi Yar was taken by the sculptor Anatoly Ignashchenko (1930–2011). One of the most famous Ukrainian sculptors and half-Roma by origin, Ignashchenko is the producer of more than 200 monuments around the world. He was also the chief-sculptor of a Soviet monument in Babi Yar. Ignashchenko admitted that an idea to raise a monument at Babi Yar came to him after talking with Romani activists Mikha Kozimirenko and Vladimir Zolotarenko.[58] In 1996 Ignashchenko produced a model of the monument, which was a gypsy wagon made of wrought iron. The author came up with an original solution to overcome the de-personification of victims. He attached to the tent photo frames in which relatives are encouraged to insert photos of victims. The inscription on the monument was completed both in Ukrainian and Romani: "To the memory of Roma exterminated by the Nazis in 1940–1945. We remember!"

Roma activists, students and members of the Catholic Community in Kyiv participated in fundraising for the monument and in volunteer work in Babi Yar. The monument was completed, and the ground prepared in 1997. However, in the end, the raising of the monument was forbidden by City architect Serhij

---

57 State Archives of the City of Kyiv (DAMK). Fond R-1, opis 1, sprava 10715.
58 Vladimir Platonov. "Babiy Yar: Tragedia o tragedii." *Zerkalo Nedeli* 39 (1997); Serhii Yarmoluk. "Kvitok do Romanistana." *Den'* 30 May 1998; Natalia Zinchenko. "Baron i kosmos." *Aratta* 17 February 2009.

Babushkin with the motivation that it did not fit with the general design of the Babi Yar memorial. As a result the monument was transported to western Ukraine and awarded to the town of Kamyanets-Podilsky.

On 29 September 1999 at the cost of Roma organizations a simple foundation stone was put in Babi Yar with an inscription in Ukrainian: "In this place will be build a memorial to the victims of the Roma Holocaust". On the night of 4 July 2011, a few weeks before the International Day of the Roma Holocaust, a foundation stone dedicated to the Romani victims was vandalized. On 13 July 2011 the Roma Congress of Ukraine sent an open letter of protest to Prime Minister Mykola Azarov, who was the chair of the committee for the 70th anniversary of Babi Yar. Roma called for an end to "the discrimination of their memory by the state" and required the inclusion of Romani representatives in the committee and dialogue with the government regarding the construction of a memorial in Babi Yar.[59] In 2012 a new foundation stone was built on the same site, this time sponsored by the state. A new inscription in Ukrainian appeared: "In memory of the Roma who were shot in Babi Yar". Romani activists point out the inscription can be interpreted as a final version of the monument. Romani activists are outraged by the fact that they have been waiting almost 25 years for a memorial in Babi Yar while a number of other memorials have been built during this period of time.[60] Monuments dedicated to various groups of victims are scattered in different places in Babi Yar at a considerable distance from each other. There is neither a central memorial for all groups of victims, nor a museum. The existing public map of Babi Yar is not easily accessible and to find the Roma memorial stone is rather difficult.

The creation in 2007–2012 of the public agency the *National Historical Memorial Preserve Babyn Yar* is an important stage in the Ukrainian politics of memory.[61] This agency is responsible for the development of the memorial site. The staff of The National Preserve organizes a ceremony on the International Day of the Roma Holocaust and informs the public about the Remembrance Day on their Webpage. On 12 April 2012 the "Concept of development of the National Historical Memorial Preserve" was approved by the Ukrainian government. The

---

59 "Romi vimahaut'vid Azarova vshanuvaty i ikhni Holocaust." *Ukrains'ka Pravda* 13 July 2011.
60 Kotljarchuk. "Natsistskii genotsid tsygan na territorii okkupirovannoi Ukrainy," 24–50.
61 *Decree 308 of the Cabinet of Ministers of Ukraine On the establishment of Memorial Reserve Babyn Yar*, 1 March 2007. http://www.kby.Kyiv.ua/komitet/ru/documents (22 October 2014); *Decree 258/2010 of the President of Ukraine Viktor Yushchenko about the National status of Memorial Preserve Babyn Yar*. http://www.kby.Kyiv.ua/komitet/ru/documents (22 October 2014).

Fig. 1: Romanis at the foundation stone in Babi Yar on the International Roma Genocide Remembrance, 2012. Photo by Andrej Kotljarchuk.

curator of a new memorial project is Larysa Skoryk.[62] She is a renowned architect and a producer of *Bykivnia Graves* – a National memorial dedicated to the victims of Stalin's terror.

Despite all the conflict over the past, Babi Yar is step by step becoming a national pantheon of all the groups of Nazi victims. Today this place is regularly attended by Romani activists, official Ukrainian and foreign delegations. The Roma tragedy of Babi Yar is well represented in the media space of Ukraine. A simple Google search gives over 15 thousand references to the phrase "Babi Yar and Roma" in Ukrainian. However when in August 2001, Pope John Paul II visited Babi Yar he did not mention the Nazi atrocities committed against the Romani victims of the genocide in his speech. Actually the ex-president of Ukraine, Viktor Yushchenko, is the only head of state who frequently mentioned

---

62 *Official website of Larysa Skoryk.* http://www.skoryk.net.ua/sakralna-arhitektura-monumenty/babyn-yar (22 October 2014).

the Roma tragedy of Babi Yar and issued a special statement on the memory of the Nazi genocide of Roma people.[63]

Recent trends in commemoration politics

Andrii Portnov argues that humanization is the basic strategy of contemporary Ukrainian memory politics regarding WWII, a switch from the memory of heroes to the memory of the suffering of ordinary people.[64] Topics prohibited during Soviet times such as the Holocaust, the Ukrainian Insurgent Army (UPA), and the Ukrainian-Polish ethnic cleansings in Volhynia became themes for public debates. In 2003, 60 years after the ethnic cleansing in Volhynia, 59 prominent Ukrainian intellectuals wrote an open letter "Open Wound of Volhynia". Public debates were initiated and on 11 July 2003, the presidents of Poland and Ukraine, Aleksander Kwasniewski and Leonid Kuchma, inaugurated in the village of Pavlivka/Poryck the first monument of reconciliation.[65]

New trends created opportunities for inclusion of the Roma collective trauma into the national context. The 2004 parliament's resolution certainly gave a powerful impetus to the memory work. In particular the parliament instructed the "Cabinet of Ministers of Ukraine, together with local authorities to identify mass graves and to investigate Hitler's ethnocide of Roma during WWII, in order to commemorate deported and executed representatives of this national minority".[66] Indeed, since 2005 the Ukrainian government has supported a number of Roma Holocaust memory projects.[67]

Another strong argument for the intensification of memory work is the integration of Ukraine into the EU.[68] The European Commission against Racism and Intolerance (ECRI) continuously monitors the implementation of the 2004 parliamentary resolution in order to determine the extent of actual implementation of

---

63 "Address of the President of Ukraine Viktor Yushchenko devoted to the International Day of the Roma Holocaust." *Forum Natsii* 8.87 (2009): 11–12.
64 Andrii Portnov. "Uprazhneniya s istoriei po-ukrainski." *Ab Imperio*. 3 (2007): 13.
65 Yaroslav Hrytsak. *Strasti za natsionalizmom*. Kyiv: Krytyka, 2004, 126–137; Alexander Osipian. "Ethnic Cleansings and Memory Purges: The Ukrainian-Polish Borderland in 1939–1947 in Modern Politics and Historiography." *Ab Imperio* 2 (2004): 297–328.
66 "Resolution 2085–IV of the Verkhovna Rada of Ukraine on the International Day of the Roma Holocaust."*Vidomosti Verkhovnoi Rady Ukrainy*. 2 (2005): 65.
67 Tatiana Gabrielson. *Propaganda of Romani Culture in Post-Soviet Ukraine*. Unpublished PhD dissertation. The University of Texas at Austin. 2006, 127–132.
68 Anders Nordström. *The interactive dynamics of regulation: exploring the Council of Europe's monitoring of Ukraine*. Stockholm: Stockholm University Press, 2008, 221–229.

the program of commemoration of the Roma genocide.⁶⁹ Ukraine is a member of the EU program "Roma Decade 2005–2015". Following many European countries, Ukraine abandoned the official use of the word 'Gypsies' in favour of the more politically correct name 'Roma'. As known this term was recommended by the First World Congress of Roma in London in 1971. Today Ukraine is the only country in post-Soviet space that has replaced the official nomenclature, using 'Roma' in official documentation and media. Substantial support to commemoration projects in Ukraine has been given by foreign institutions, in particular the German Federal Foundation for Remembrance, Responsibility and the Future, the Friedrich Ebert Foundation and the George Soros Foundation "Renaissance". The Soros Foundation has a special *Roma of Ukraine Program*, which has supported exhibitions on the memory of the Roma genocide, scientific conferences, and publication of documents. In order to overcome the de-personification problem the Romani organization of Odessa signed in 2011 an agreement with the oblast archives of Odessa. The intended result of the cooperation is to produce a memory book with a list of Romanian Roma deported to Transnistria. A number of scientific conferences on the genocide of Roma people held in Ukraine was organized by the *Ukrainian Centre for Holocaust Studies*, which also accumulated a considerable bibliography.⁷⁰ Recently the *All-Ukrainian Association of Teachers of History* published with the financial support of the EU a textbook for secondary schools. A chapter of the textbook is about the Nazi genocide of Ukrainian Roma. As usual the link between the Nazi genocide, Axis powers and Ukrainian collaborators is missing and all responsibility is placed exclusively on the Germans.⁷¹

There is one more difference between the memorialization of Roma and Jewish mass graves. Monuments to the Jewish Holocaust are usually funded from abroad with the assistance of local Jewish communities. The Roma Holocaust memorials as a rule are initiated and funded by Ukrainian NGOs and local organizations. In Vilshanka (Poltava region), it was the local Cossack organization; in Pirohova Levada (Pyriatyn, Poltava region) – a local historical association, district authorities and private persons; in Kozatyn (Vinnitsa region) – a local veteran's organization, the Communist Party of Ukraine, the municipality, a subsidiary of the Ukrainian Railways; in Ostroushki (Sumy region) – the village administration and private persons. The contemporary memorial work is carried

---

69 *Stan dotrimannia Ukrainoiu evropeiskikh standartiv z prav i svobod ludyny.* Kyiv: Verkhovna Rada Press, 2010, 163–164.
70 Kotljarchuk. "Natsistskii genotsid tsygan na territorii okkupirovannoi Ukrainy," 24–50.
71 Petro Kendzior, Ed. *Razom na odnii zemli. Istoriya Ukrainy bogatokul'turna.* Lviv: ZUKTs, 2012.

out by a wide variety of different mainly non-Roma actors. Only three out of twenty memorials were initiated and partly funded by Romani organizations. New memorials on the places of mass executions of Roma are often motivated by the example of the capital. Thus, at the opening ceremony of 2011 in Ostroushki the deputy head of Sumy oblast Oleg Boyarintsev said: "the place where they were killed, thousands of our countrymen should be known by everyone in the Sumy region. Ostroushki is our Babi Yar".[72]

Fig. 2: The Cossacks of Lubny and the author at Roma Holocaust Memorial Cross in Vilshanka (Lubny district). 2012. Photo by Vadim Udod.

Today Ukraine shares with Germany the honorary first place in Europe regarding the number of Roma genocide memorials. However, a number of problems remain. Not all local authorities have implemented the 2004 decision of parliament. There are a number of regions (for example Crimea) where the International Day of the Roma Holocaust does not give a rise to any commemoration efforts. On 2 August the central TV channels of Ukraine did little to recall the

---

72 *Official News Portal of Sumy region.* http://sumyinfo.com (22 October 2014).

tragedy of the Roma people. Some new genocide memorials (for example in Malyn and in Kopyli) despite the available data include no reference to the victims of Romani origin. As Michael Tyaglyi states the genocide of Roma is still considered by the researchers as "a second-class genocide which is located on the periphery of contemporary Ukrainian historical research".[73]

Differences at the local level are significant but inexplicable. In Mykolaiv, Odessa and Lutsk regions, exhibitions dedicated to the genocide of Roma were held, International Remembrance Day celebrated and new memorials erected. In Mykolaiv the local authorities involved non-Romani pupils in the memory work.[74] At the same time in the eastern autonomous republic of Crimea, occupied in 2014 by Russia, despite many identified mass graves of Roma victims, there are still no monuments on places of mass executions indicating that the victims are of Roma origin and the Remembrance Day is not celebrated.

An acute problem is that a large number of Roma genocide mass graves remain unmarked. They are situated in remote rural areas (for example in Kysylyn, Lutsk region), which was not mentioned by the *Extraordinary Commission for Investigation of War Crimes*. Because of the privatization and high cost of agricultural lands, only memorialization can preserve unmarked graves from destruction. Today many mass graves are preserved by the owners of lands representing the older generation– the last witnesses of the genocide. That is the case in Ratne.

Conclusion

Post-Soviet Ukraine is a region of dynamic politics of the commemoration of the victims of the Roma Holocaust. The country is actively constructing a unifying model of collective memory capable of integrating all minority groups into a single national project. It is important to stress that the Roma Holocaust memorials are being built in both in the Western and Eastern parts of the country.

The major reasons for the intensification of memory work on the Roma Holocaust in Ukraine are:
– A new official strategy regarding the memory of WWII.

---

[73] Mikhailo Tyaglyy. "Babyn Yar yak mistse masovogo vynishchennia ukrainskikh romiv: typova model?" *Unpublished paper presented on the international conference Babi Yar: mass killings and its memory.* Kyiv, 25 October 2011.

[74] Olena Hrynevich. "Romi Ukrainy i Mikolaevshchyna." *Naukovi zapiski. Zbirnik prats molodikh vchenikh ta aspirantiv.* Kyiv: National Academy of Sciences, 2008, 136–145.

- A higher level of democratization in comparison with neighbouring Russia and Belarus.
- A process of integration into the EU, leading to some adjustments of the Ukrainian memory politics to comply to European standards.

The revising of the Soviet myth of WWII opened the once closed floodgates of memory. Fast-paced memorialization of the Roma genocide confirms the fact that the realignment of Soviet history around new narrative axes is taking place in the memory politics of today's Ukraine. For a long time the Roma minority was not included in Ukrainian nation building. The commemoration of the Roma Holocaust has the possibility to change this situation, boosting the inclusion of Roma in contemporary Ukrainian society. In the situation of the absence of a native Romani state, common territory, language, culture and religion, a shared memory of the genocide brings together different groups of Roma, mobilizing their national movement. As Slawomir Kapralski points out:

> Romani Holocaust is already the main element of the Roma identity and the centre piece of their historical memory. Through the rituals of remembrance Roma focus on their common past in order to create a better future.[75]

The problems related to commemoration of the genocide of the Roma on the territory of Ukraine are limited, as this study confirms, mainly by the 'path dependence' factor and not by deliberately discriminatory politics towards the Roma minority.

References

Achim, Viorel. *The Roma in Romanian history.* Budapest: Central European University Press, 2004.
Adam, Zeikan and Elena Navrotska. *Bilii kamin' z chornoi kativni. Holocaust romiv Zakarpatti*, Uzhhorod: Uzhorods'ka miska drukarnia, 2006.
"Address of the President of Ukraine Viktor Yushchenko devoted to the International Day of the Roma Holocaust." *Forum Natsii* 8.87 (2009): 11–12.
All-Ukrainian census of 2001. http://2001.ukrcensus.gov.ua (22 October 2014).
Altshuler, Mordechai. "Jewish Holocaust Commemoration Activity in the USSR under Stalin." *Yad Vashem Studies* 30 (2002): 221–240.
Avdeenko, Aleksandr and Petr Olender. "Babi Yar." *Krasnaya Zvezda* 274.5645 (20 November 1943): 3.

---

[75] Kapralski. "Symbols and Rituals in the Mobilisation of the Romani National Ideal," 77.

Babi Yar: Kniga pamiati. Ed. Ilya Levitas. Kyiv: Stal, 2005.
Bartosz, Adam.*Tabor Pamieci Romow*. Tarnow: Regional Museum of Tarnow Press, 2003.
Bartov, Omer. *Erased: vanishing traces of Jewish Galicia in present-day Ukraine*. Princeton: Princeton University Press, 2007.
Belikov, Oleksandr. "Derzhavna politika stosovno tsygan Ukrainy: istoria i suchasnist." *Naukovi zapiski. Zbirnik prats molodikh vchenikh ta aspirantiv.* Kyiv: National Academy of Sciences, 2008. 24–56.
Berkhoff, Karel. *Babi Yar: Site of Mass Murder, Ravine of Oblivion*. Washington: United States Holocaust Memorial Museum, 2012.
Berkhoff, Karel. "Pogolovnoe unichtozhenie evreiskogo naseleniya. Holocaust v sovetskikh SMI, 1941–1945." *Holocaust i suchasnist'* 1.7 (2010): 62–122.
Bessonov, Nikolai. *Tsyganskaia tragediia 1941–1945. Fakty, dokumenty, vospominaniya. Vooruzhennyi otpor*. Sankt Petersburg: Shatra, 2010.
Bessonov, Nikolai. "Tsygane SSSR v okkupatsii. Strategii vyzhivaniia." *Holocaust i suchasnist'*. 2:6 (2009): 17–52.
Björklund, Bengt. "Romska massgravar i Ukraina." *E Romani Glinda*. 5 (2010): 12–18.
Burakovsky, Aleksandr. "Holocaust remembrance in Ukraine: memorialization of the Jewish tragedy at Babi Yar." *Nationalities Papers* 39.3 (2011): 371–389.
Cherenkov, Lev. "Tsyganskaya dialektologiya v Ukraine. Istoriya i sovremennost." *Materialy mizhnarodnoi tsyhanoznavchoi konferentsii Romy Ukrainy iz minulogo v maibutne*. Kyiv: Justinian, 2008: 161–172.
Decree 308 of the Cabinet of Ministers of Ukraine On the establishment of Memorial Reserve Babyn Yar, 1 March 2007. http://www.kby.Kyiv.ua/komitet/ru/documents (22 October 2014).
Decree 258/2010 of the President of Ukraine Viktor Yushchenko about the National status of Memorial Preserve Babyn Yar. http://www.kby.Kyiv.ua/komitet/ru/documents (22 October 2014).
Demetr, Nadezhda, Nikolai Bessonov and Niklolai Kutenkov. *Istoriya tsygan – novyi vzgliad*. Voronezh: IPF, 2000.
Do 70-rokovin tragedii Babynogo Yaru. Dokumental'na vystava. Kyiv: Derzhavna Arkhivna Sluzhba Ukrainy, 2011.
Evstafieva, Tatiana. "Babi Yar vo vtoroi polovine XX veka." *Babi Yar: chelovek, vlast', istoriya. Dokumenty i materialy*. Ed. Tatiana Estafieva and Vitalii Nakhmanovich. Kyiv: Vneshtorgizdat, 2004. 187–206.
Evstafieva, Tatiana. "K istorii ustanovleniya pamiatnika v Bab'em Yaru." *Evreiskii obozrevatel."* 11 (30 June 2002).
Forest, Benjamin and Juliet Johnson. "Unravelling the Threads of History: Soviet-Era Monuments and Post-Soviet National Identity." *Annals of the Association of American Geographers* 92.3 (2002): 524–547.
Frydman, Aleksandr. "Neviadomy genocide: znischenne belaruskikh tsyhanou u 1941–1944." *ARCHE*. 2 (2004): 2–13.
Gabrielson, Tatiana. *Propaganda of Romani Culture in Post-Soviet Ukraine*. PhD dissertation. The University of Texas at Austin. 2006, 127–132.
Gitelman, Zvi. "Politics and the historiography of the Holocaust in the Soviet Union." *Bitter legacy: confronting the Holocaust in the USSR*. Ed. Zvi Gitelman. Bloomington: Indiana University Press, 1997. 14–43.

Golbert, Rebecca. "Holocaust Sites in Ukraine: Pechora and the Politics of Memorialization." *Holocaust and Genocide Studies* 18.2 (2004): 205–233.
Grossman,Vasily. "Doroga na Berlin." *Krasnaya Zvezda* 38.6026 (15 February 1945): 3.
Hedlund, Stefan. *Russian Path Dependence*. London: Routledge, 2005.
Holocaust i suchasnist'. Special issue on the history of Roma Holocaust. 2.16 (2009).
Hrynevich, Olena. "Romi Ukrainy i Mikolaevshchyna." *Naukovi zapiski. Zbirnik prats molodikh vchenikh ta aspirantiv*. Kyiv: National Academy of Sciences, 2008. 136–145.
Hrytsak, Yaroslav. *Strasti za natsionalizmom*. Kyiv: Krytyka, 2004.
Istorichnyi ta etnokulturnyi rozvitok tsygan (roma) Ukrainy. Donetsk, 2006.
Jilg, Wilfried. "The Politics of History and the Second World War in Post-Communist Ukraine." *Jahrbücher für Geschichte Osteuropas* 54.1 (2006): 50–81.
Kalinin, Valdemar. *Zagadka baltiiskikh tsygan*. Minsk: Logvinov, 2005.
Kapralski, Slawomir. "Symbols and Rituals in the Mobilisation of the Romani National Ideal." *Studies in Ethnicity and Nationalism* 12.1 (2012): 64–81.
Kendzior, Petro, Ed. *Razom na odnii zemli. Istoriya Ukrainy bogatokul'turna*. Lviv: ZUKTs, 2012.
Ilya Zaslavskii Ed. *Kniga Pamiati. Imena pogibshikh v Bab'em Yaru*.. Kyiv: Oberih, 1991.
Konstatinovskii, Ilya. "Zemlia Moldavii." *Izvestia* 137.8439 (10 June 1944): 3.
Korsun, Ivan. "Tsyganskaya doroga. Vospominaniya." *Holocaust i suchasnist'*. 2.6 (2009): 172–210.
Kotljarchuk, Andrej. "World War II Memory Politics: Jewish, Polish and Roma Minorities of Belarus."*The Journal of Belarusian Studies* 1.7 (2013): 7–40.
Kotljarchuk, Andrej. "Palityka pamiaci u suchasnai Belarusi. Memaryialy druhoi susvetnai vainy i etnichnyia menshastsi krainy." *ARCHE* 2 (2013): 173–194.
Kotljarchuk, Andrej. "Natsistskii genotsid tsygan na territorii okkupirovannoi Ukrainy: rol' sovteskogo proshlogo v sovremennoi politike pamiati." *Holocaust i suchasnist* 1.12 (2014): 24–50.
Kotljarchuk, Andrej. "Nazi Genocide of Roma in Belarus and Ukraine: the significance of census data and census takers." *Etudes Tsigane* 1 (2015).
Kruglov, Aleksandr. "Genocide tsygan v Ukraine 1941–1944: statistiko-regional'nyi aspect." *Holocaust i suchasnist'* 2.16 (2009): 83–133.
Kruglov, Aleksandr. *Sbornik dokumentov i materialov ob unichtozhnenii natsistami evreev Ukrainy v 1941–44*. Kyiv: Institut Judaiki, 2002.
Kuznetsov, Anatoly. *Babi Yar. A documentary novel*. New York: The Dial Press, 1967.
Kuznetsov, Anatoly. *Babi Yar. Roman-dokument*. Moskva: Molodaya gvardiya, 1967.
Kuznetsov, Anatoly. *Babi Yar. Roman-dokument*. Frankfurt am Main: Posev, 1970.
Lemon, Alaina. *Between two fires Gypsy performance and Romany memory. From Pushkin to Postsocialism*. Durham: Duke University Press, 2000.
Levitas, Ilya. "Nerazgadannye tainy Bab'ego Yara." *Evreiskie vesti/*, 17.18 (1993).
Lustiger, Arno. *Stalin i evrei: Tragicheskaia istoriya Evreiskogo antifashistskogo komiteta i sovetskikh evreev*. Moscow: Rosspen, 2008.
Mankoff, Jeff. "Babi Yar and the struggle for memory, 1944–2004." *Ab Imperio* 2 (2004): 393–415.
Margalit, Gilad. *Germany and its gypsies: a post-Auschwitz ordeal*. Madison: University of Wisconsin Press, 2002.

Marushiakova, Elena and Vesselin Popov. "Holocaust and the Gypsies. The Reconstruction of the Historical Memory and Creation of New National Mythology." *Beyond Camps and Forced Labour. Current International Research on Survivors of Nazi Persecution.* Eds. Johannes-Dieter Steinert and Inge Weber-Newth. Osnabrück: Secolo, 2006. 805–826.

Materialy mizhnarodnoi tsyhanoznavchoi konferentsii Romy Ukrainy iz minulogo v maibutne. Kyiv: Justinian, 2008.

Mitsel, Mikhail. "Zapret na uvekovechivanie pamiati kak sposob zamalchivania Holocausta." *Holocaust i suchasnist'* 1.2 (2007): 9–30.

Muzychenko, Yaroslava. "Tsigans'ke gore." *Ukraina moloda* (9 August 2008).

Nakhmanovich, Rafail. "Babi Yar-1966: kak eto bylo." *Maidan* (28 September 2006).

Nakhmanovich, Vitalii. "Rasstrely i zakhoroneiya v raione Bab'ego Yara vo vremia nemetskoi okkupatsii goroda Kyiva 1941–43." *Babi Yar: chelovek, vlast', istoriya. Dokumenty i materialy.* Ed. Tatiana Estafieva and Vitalii Nakhmanovich. Kyiv, 2004. 84–163.

Nora, Pierre and Lawrence Kritzman. *Realms of memory: rethinking the French past.* 1. New York: Columbia University Press, 1996; *Realms of memory: rethinking the French past.* 2. New York: Columbia University Press, 1997.

Nordström, Anders. *The interactive dynamics of regulation: exploring the Council of Europe's monitoring of Ukraine.* Stockholm: Stockholm University Press, 2008.

"Nota narodnogo komissara inostrannykh del SSSR tov. V. M. Molotova ot 6 ianvaria 1942 goda." *Nurnbergskii process. Sbornik materialov.* Moscow: Gosudarstvennoe izdatel'stvo iuridicheskoi literatury, 1954. 504–517.

Official website of Larysa Skoryk. http://www.skoryk.net.ua/sakralna-arhitektura-monumenty/babyn-yar (22 October 2014).

Ofitsinsky, Roman. "Romi i prymusova prats ana Zakarpatti 1939–1944." *Romologia: istoria ta suchasnist'.* Ed. Roman Ofitsinsky. Uzhhorod: Lira, 2013, 76–82.

Oldberg, Ingmar. "Both victims and perpetrators. Ukraine's problematic relationship to the Holocaust." *Baltic worlds* 4.2 (2011): 40–43.

Osipian, Alexander. "Ethnic Cleansings and Memory Purges: The Ukrainian-Polish Borderland in 1939–1947 in Modern Politics and Historiography." *Ab Imperio* 2 (2004): 297–328.

"Pamiatnik pogibshim v Bab'em Yaru." *Pravda* (3 April 1945): 3.

Peresleduvannia ta vbivstva romiv na terenakh Ukrainy u chasi druhoi svitovoi viini. Zbirnik dokumentiv ta spohadiv. Ed. Mikhail Tyaglyy. Kyiv: Ukrainian Centre for Genocide Studies, 2013.

Jerzy Dębski and Joanna Talewicz-Kwiatkowska. Ed. *Prześladowania i masowa zagłada Romów podczas II wojny światowej w świetle relacji i wspomnień..* Warszawa: Romski Instytut Historyczny, 2008.

Pickford, Henry. "Conflict and Commemoration: Two Berlin Memorials." *Modernism modernity* 12.1 (2005): 133–173.

Pirohova Levada. Narysy. Kyiv: Prosvita, 2012.

Platonov, Vladimir. "Babiy Yar: Tragedia o tragedii." *Zerkalo Nedeli* 39 (1997).

Portnov, Andrii. "Uprazhneniya s istoriei po-ukrainski." *Ab Imperio* 3 (2007): 93–138.

"Rech' tovarishcha N. S. Khrushcheva." *Pravda* 89 (10 March 1963): 1, 4.

"Resolution 2085–IV of the Verkhovna Rada of Ukraine on the International Day of the Roma Holocaust."*Vidomosti Verkhovnoi Rady Ukrainy.* 2 (2005): 65.

"Romi vimahaut'vid Azarova vshanuvaty i ikhni Holocaust." *Ukrains'ka Pravda,* 13 July 2011.

Schäuble, Michaela. "How History Takes Place: Sacralized Landscapes in the Croatian-Bosnian Border Region." *History and Memory* 23.1 (2011): 23–61.

Schleifman, Nurit. "Moscow's Victory Park: A Monumental Change." *History and Memory* 13. 2 (2001): 5–34.

Stan dotrimannia Ukrainoiu evropeiskikh standartiv z prav i svobod ludyny. Kyiv: Verkhovna Rada Press, 2010.

Stauber, Roni and Raphael Vago. "The Politics of Memory: Jews and Roma Commemorate their Persecution."*The Roma: A Minority in Europe. Historical, Political and Social Perspectives*. Eds. Roni Stauber and Raphael Vago. Budapest: Central European University Press, 2007. 117–132.

Stewart, Michael. "Remembering without Commemoration: the Mnemonics and Politics of Holocaust memories among European Roma." *Journal of the Royal Anthropological Institute* 10.3 (2004): 561–582.

"Soobshchenie Chrezvychainoi Gosudarstvennoi Komissii po ustanovleniu i rassledovaniu zlodeianii nemetsko-fashistskikh zakhvatchikov i ikh soobshchnikov o razrusheniyakh I zverstvakh sovershennykh nemetsko-fashistskim zakhvatchikami v gorode Kyive." *Izvestia* 50.8352 (29 February 1944): 3.

"Soobshchenie Chrezvychainoi Gosudarstvennoi Komissii po ustanovleniu i rassledovaniu zlodeianii nemetsko-fashistskikh zakhvatchikov i ikh soobshchnikov." *Izvestia* 205. 8507 (29 August 1944): 3.

Sumyinfo. Official News Portal of Sumy region. http://sumyinfo.com (22 October 2014).

"Svidetel'stvo zhitelei goroda Kyiva khudizhnika Nikolaya Adrianovicha Priakhova i professora Ivana Nikolaevicha Zhitova i drugikh o massovykh rasstrelakh v Bab'em yaru." Central *State Archive of the supreme power and administration of Ukraine (TsDAVO)*. Fond R- 4620, opis 3, sprava 243a, list 38.

The Black Book: the Nazi crime against the Jewish people. Published by the Jewish Black Book Committee, New York: Duell, Sloan and Pearce, 1946.

Troitskii, P. "Po stranitsam zhurnalov." *Izvestia* 19.15413 (20 January 1967): 5.

Tyaglyy, Mikhail. "Nazi occupational policies and the mass murder of the Roma in Ukraine." *The Nazi genocide of the Roma. Reassessment and Commemoration*. Ed. Anton Weiss-Wendt. New York-Oxford: Berghahn Books, 2013. 120–152.

Tyaglyy, Mikhailo. "Babyn Yar yak mistse masovogo vynishchennia ukrainskikh romiv: typova model?" *Paper presented on the international conference Babi Yar: mass killings and its memory*. Kyiv, 25 October 2011.

Ventsel, Tatiana. "Tsygane." *Bolshaya Sovetskaya Enciklopedia/*. 28. Moscow, 1978. 606–607.

Yarmoluk, Serhii. "Kvitok do Romanistana." *Den'*, 30 May 1998.

Zajava Ministerstva kultiry Ukrainy z nagodi Mizhnarodnogo dnia Holocaustu romiv. 2 August 2013. http://mincult.kmu.gov.ua (22 October 2014).

Zimmermann, Michael. *Rassenutopie und Genozid: die nationalsozialistische 'Lösung der Zigeunerfrage'*. Hamburg: Christians, 1996.

Zinchenko, Natalia. "Baron i kosmos." *Aratta*, 17 February 2009.

Part 3: **Local and Marginal Memory**

Anna Wylegała
Forced Migration and Identity in the Memories of Post-War Expellees from Poland and Ukraine

Although it is difficult to speak about a common European memory, during the twentieth century many communities in Europe were subjected to certain universal experiences, which in some cases might have resulted in similar (yet not shared) memories. Such experiences include the mass and forced population transfers which occurred during and immediately after the Second World War. Millions of Europeans lost their home countries and had no other choice but to re-establish their identities in another place and under different socio-political circumstances. Historians and demographers have attempted numerous comparative analyses of these events[1]; however insufficient attention has been devoted to the way forced migration is remembered in collective memory, and to how it has shaped the identities of the expelled. There is also a noticeable shortage of studies comparing these memories and the different and/or similar ways they function among groups of exiles from different countries.

Therefore, I would like to attempt a comparative analysis of the memories of exiles from Poland and Ukraine. My study is based on empirical data collected from two small, local communities: Krzyż, a German town that became part of Poland, and Zhovkva, a Polish town that was integrated into Soviet Ukraine. Due to the qualitative nature of this analysis and the complexity of social circumstances in specific cases, I believe that a study with a local focus presents more opportunities for in-depth conclusions.[2] Despite differences in pre-war history, the post-war situation of exiles is similar in both of the communities chosen.

Krzyż was a German town before the War, inhabited by Germans as well as an assimilated Jewish minority, but the latter were deported towards the end of the 1930s. The town lay near what at that time was the Polish border. After the war the Polish border was moved west, and Krzyż lost almost all of its popula-

---
[1] See, e.g. the German historian Philipp Ther's comparative study: Philipp Ther. "The Integration of Expellees in Germany and Poland after World War II: A Historical Reassessment." *Slavic Review* 55 (1996): 779–805.
[2] For an example of analysing collective memory by juxtaposing two case studies, see Małgorzata Melchior's study about the cultural differences between neighbouring villages with different histories: Małgorzata Melchior. "Przeszłość jako czynnik zróżnicowań kulturowych dzisiaj – przypadek dwóch sąsiadujących wsi." *Kultura i Społeczeństwo* 4 (1996): 109–118.

tion – the Germans either fled from the coming front in 1945, or were forcibly relocated to Germany within the first year after the end of the War. The largest group of Krzyż's new inhabitants consisted of "repatriates"[3] from the former Eastern Borderlands of Poland (referred to hereafter as the Borderlands), while the remainder included groups of Poles who had lived on the other side of the border near Krzyż before the War, and settlers from Greater Poland and Central Poland.

Zhovkva lay within the borders of the 2nd Polish Republic before the war, and was a multinational and religiously heterogeneous Borderland town: its population consisted of comparable numbers of Jews, Poles and Ukrainians. The war deprived Zhovkva of its Jews and some of its Poles; most of the survivors of the Holocaust and the remaining Poles left for Poland after 1945, when the area was finally included in the Soviet Union. Due to post-war Soviet repressions, which in large part targeted sympathisers of the underground Ukrainian independence movement, the town also lost many of its Ukrainian inhabitants. The new population of Zhovkva consisted of Ukrainians deported from Poland in the years 1944–46, arrivals from Eastern Ukraine and other Soviet Union Republics, as well as Ukrainian migrants from nearby Galician villages.

The situation of the forced migrants in both Krzyż and Zhovkva was very difficult: both the Poles being "repatriated" to Poland and the Ukrainians "returning" to Great Ukraine had lost their homes and regional homelands, and were forced to adjust to new social, political and cultural circumstances. They also had to participate in the reconstruction of social relations with the other groups of settlers, all within the framework of undemocratic political systems.

The aim of this article is to analyze the way in which forced relocation is remembered by expellees now living in Krzyż and Zhovkva. I would also like to determine whether, despite the respective differences in historical trajectories and political circumstances, these memories share any similarities. When differences are found, I will attempt to explain them. Further, I would like to consider how these memories affected the post-migrational reshaping of identity. In my analysis of the phenomenon of forced relocation I will discuss its various stages: the journey itself (and an evaluation of its causes); the ensuing first stage of cultural and material adaptation (first impressions, settling down, economic arrangements), as well as psychological adaptation related to living in a new place (the emotions accompanying the entire process). Due to my interest in the reconstruction of identity among forced migrants I will also consider the be-

---

[3] Due to the ideological connotations of this word, I will always use it in parenthesis, along with the phrase "reclaimed lands".

ginning steps of long-term processes of social integration within a new community. Although I will analyze the accounts of particular members belonging to each group, i.e. instances of individual and biographical memory, I agree with Halbwachs that the memory of each individual is by its very nature social, or at least its individuality is grounded in a social framework.[4] Collective memory provides, as Kaja Kaźmierska suggests, a certain type of "code" that is necessary for interpreting ones' personal biographical experience and transforming it into an element of identity that is congruent with the culture of memory within which the individual functions.[5] With these principles in mind, I treat my analysis, from a theoretical point of view, as a search for the collective within the individual, and as an attempt to explain the mutual connections between these two realms.

The data collected in Krzyż and Zhovkva include over 150 interviews recorded with individuals from various groups of inhabitants and their families; however for the purposes of this article I selected only the interviews with the oldest generation of forced migrants: the "repatriates" from the Borderlands living in Krzyż and the Ukrainians resettled from Poland in Zhovkva. The interviews were conducted as biographical narratives. Those from Zhovkva were recorded in Ukrainian.

Forced resettlement

The Journey

The Journey is the point of departure for the entire experience of forced resettlement, and for the migrants it marks the beginning of a trajectory that robs them of the control they had previously had over their lives.[6] In his study of post-war processes of social integration in Lubomierz in the "reclaimed lands", Zdzisław Mach compared migration to a ritual of passing. Utilising van Gennep's classic theory, Mach underlined three phases of migration: the phase of separation (exclusion), the liminal (marginal) phase, and the phase of aggregation (inclusion).[7]

---

[4] Maurice Halbwachs. *On collective memory.* Chicago (IL): The University of Chicago Press, 1992.
[5] Kaja Kaźmierska. *Biografia i pamięć. Na przykładzie pokoleniowego doświadczenia ocalonych z Zagłady.* Kraków: Nomos, 2008.
[6] Fritz Schütze, and Gerhardt Riemanan. "'Trajectory' as basic theoretical concept for analyzing suffering and disorderly social processes." *Social Organization and Social Process. Essays in Honour of Anselm Strauss.* Ed. David R. Maines. New York: De Gruyter, 1991, 333–358.
[7] Zdzisław Mach. *Niechciane miasta. Migracja i tożsamość społeczna.* Kraków: Universitas, 1998.

For forced migrants, leaving their family homes constitutes a very clear beginning of the phase of separation, an experience of exclusion. What the tales of the "repatriates" who came to Krzyż and Zhovkva have in common is the emotional recollection of the journey itself as long and arduous:

> We went to Ukraine. It was 1946, the end of February, beginning of March. It was very cold. They gave everyone two carts, to each family, so that we could go in these carts, and we went. To the station in Uhnow. There' a train station two kilometres from Uhnow, they took us there ... They took us to Ternopil province, to Berezhany, that's a nice county town – Berezhany ... There was a whole host of people there, with animals if someone had taken any, with little children – with everything, horses and livestock. They unloaded us on the sidetrack. I was still a little boy but I remember that mum wrapped me up in a shawl because it was very cold, with fierce wind and horrible weather. We spent a month in that backwater. (Z., m., b. 1934)[8]

> We sang "Lulajże Jezuniu" [a Christmas carol] in boxcars in Lubań Śląski. And, ma'am, and we discovered in Lubań that my father's family was living in Legnica. So back we went from Lubań to Legnica. No food, no – well, there was drink, because there was water, but no food. Frozen potatoes and onions for Christmas, because we didn't have anything when we came from Russia, you know, we barely had clothes. That was life, it wasn't so easy. (K., m., b. 1930)

What differentiates the Polish interviews from the Ukrainian ones is the length and amount of detail in the narratives about the journey. One can find long descriptions in almost every Polish account, with variations depending on the author's narrative skill and the level of emotionality involved. The stories of Poles from the Borderlands abound in tales of the makeshift nature of everyday life during the weeks of forced train transportation: cooking outside during stops and various ways of acquiring food. In the Ukrainian accounts lengthy descriptions of the journey are much more rare, with the deportation itself often receiving only a token description:

> How did it look? Well, they gave us carts, then there was a train in Lubaczów, so we got on the train... We got to the train in carts, they packed us in the train and we went. We got here... how far is it from Rawa, not too far, some 30 kilometres. We got here and father was already waiting, and he somehow picked us up, and we stayed here. (Z., f., b. 1923)

Why these descriptions are brief is easy to understand, considering the fact that most of the Ukrainian migrants coming from Poland (with the exception of those

---

[8] The reader can find information concerning the respondent and the town in which the interview was conducted beneath every quotation: Z. stands for Zhovkva; K. for Krzyż; m. for male; f. for female; and b. for year of birth.

who first went to Eastern Ukraine) travelled several dozen, or at most a little over 100, kilometres to Zhovkva; the deportees from the Borderlands, on the other hand, had to travel several hundred, and in some cases in excess of a thousand, kilometres. Although in post-war conditions even a small distance could translate into a long journey, the discrepancy in distances travelled becomes apparent in the Poles' vivid memories of their exodus.

The Polish descriptions are lengthier, adorned with more detail, and weave more threads. Many of these threads, which appear in the majority of the Polish interviews (e. g. separation from the family, getting lost during the train journey), are not present in Ukrainian interviews at all. There are several reasons for this situation: first of all, the Polish "repatriates'" journey was not only longer but it also abounded in various events and adventures. In addition, the Poles' awareness of the distance they travelled contributed to a stronger sense of finding oneself in a threshold situation, with an increased sense of danger and uncertainty, as evidenced by the following quote:

> Finally we had to go. And it was like this – we lost all we had, all that my mother and father had worked for throughout their lives. I was 15 years old when we left Czortków ... This very moment was awfully heavy. We all cried, and everything was so... The children didn't know why we were crying so they cried as well. It was horrible, I mean, can you understand – all your life's belongings, it's like watching it all burn, and maybe even worse than that, because if it actually burned it would've been gone. But we had to leave everything behind, whatever you set your eyes upon, you were leaving it behind. It was truly horrible. (K., f., b. 1930)

An additional factor differentiating the Polish and Ukrainian narratives is the collectively shaped narrative moulds, which are dependent on the language and culture in which they are rooted. Harald Welzer describes these moulds as the second most significant, next to experience, of the "material out of which biographies are constructed".[9] What today shapes the biographical narratives of the former inhabitants of the Polish Borderlands – a factor that is missing in the case of the Ukrainians – is the collective retelling of the memories of forced migration, which began to take place in Poland as early as the 1970s due to more lenient censorship policies.[10] Popular culture, although controlled by the

---

[9] Harald Welzer. "Materiał, z którego zbudowane są biografie." Transl. Magdalena Saryusz-Wolska. *Pamięć zbiorowa i kulturowa. Współczesna perspektywa niemiecka.* Ed. Magdalena Saryusz-Wolska. Warszawa: Universitas, 2009, 39–58.

[10] An analysis of the image of the "repatriate" in Polish popular culture, on the basis of press releases and editorials, is offered by Maria Tomczak in: Maria Tomczak. "Obraz osadników w

government, broke with previous political taboos against mentioning the relocations. One of the best examples of this practice is the film *Sami Swoi* (*All Friends Here* or *Our Folks*). A brief period of thaw in Polish politics allowed for an at least partial release of Borderland narratives. In Ukraine similar expression was impossible until the beginning of the 1990s. Due to the possibility of emotional release in Poland, the stories told today by "repatriates" from Krzyż include humorous elements, which show that years of "retelling" have created some distance between the storytellers and their traumatic experience:

> We were riding all together, sleeping on some straw, which was padded, and if someone had mattresses they slept on mattresses ... [laughter] There was this tub in our car. You know the type, round, made out of wooden planks, used for laundry back in the day [laughter]. And there was this older lady, and she'd been affluent, but then they took her estate and she was impoverished. And I won't forget [laughter], how she stirred in her sleep on the straw, and somehow climbed into that tub. And she's sitting in the tub and can't get out [laughter]. And she's mumbling to herself, but we can all hear her: "Lord, oh Lord, what has it all come to. There I was, sleeping in fine duvets and now I'm going to Poland in a tub" [laughter] Everyone in the car was laughing. So she climbed out and went on normally. (K., f., b. 1915)

How strongly biographical memory is shaped not only by the experiences of a given individual, but also by the way he or she communicates with other actors in social roles, and by the influence of factors such as the media, is evidenced by the fact that in several narratives from Krzyż the reader can find direct references to the protagonists of the film *Sami Swoi*. The interviewees use scenes appearing in the film to describe their personal experience; it can only be speculated whether such scenes have become a part of the reality of their memories:

> And so we arrived in Poland – without a clue, we didn't really know where. We just went where the place was, where they pointed us to. We travelled for three weeks. We left our home, Kazimierz, I will remind you, in 1946 on the 4th of March, from the station... the station... it was... the Oszmiana station, because it was a ways from Oszmiana. And then they drove us around, just like that, in those boxcars, to be sure. Three... three weeks we travelled west, to get here. Just like... just like in the film, like Karguls and Pawlaks, that's how we travelled, with those cows. (K., f., b. 1922)

---

prasie i publicystyce polskiej." *Ziemie Odzyskane 1945–2005. 60 lat w granicach państwa polskiego*. Ed. Andrzej Sakson. Poznań: Instytut Zachodni, 2006, 45–58.

Coercion and agency

What strongly differentiates Polish and Ukrainian memory is the matter of responsibility for the forced resettlement and the place of the individual within the context of larger historical events. Both the Poles and the Ukrainians recall the transfers as acts of repression, forced upon them and inflicted by someone from the outside. However, this coercion varies in character and constitutes a different threat to the identity of the Poles and the Ukrainians. For the latter group, the transfers are more often remembered as acts of direct violence – Ukrainian narratives feature the brutality of Polish and Soviet troops as well as the helplessness and fear for one's life present among the migrants.

> But the most important thing was that the Poles used brute force to make us leave. Because at first they just told us to go, there was a soviet committee prepared, and to resettle... Folk didn't go, because why would they leave whatever they had, their fields and whatnot, and go somewhere, no-one even knew where... Later though, when they started killing, things became unbearable, folk had to leave. They were forced to... (Z., m., b. 1929)

Poles speak rather about voluntary "repatriation", although they frequently emphasise that, in fact, there was no real choice – there were threats of repression, hostile Ukrainians, or simply the need to be where Poland was. In particular this last factor is entirely absent from Ukrainian narratives. It is visible here how strongly the civic and patriotic stances of the inhabitants of the Borderlands were shaped by the experience of living in the Second Polish Republic, in their own country. The Ukrainians were deprived of such an experience, with "Greater Ukraine" being far more of an abstraction to them than a new Polish state was to the Borderlanders.

> In 1945, as a result of treaties signed, the eastern parts of Poland were incorporated into the USSR. They sold us out in Potsdam and earlier in Yalta! Unfortunately, eastern Poland was now a part of the USSR and we were given a choice – sign up for soviet citizenship or leave. Obviously, we didn't even think about it – we chose the latter ... Of course, on the one hand we felt regret, the experience of being driven out of our homeland – because we were driven out, there's no treaty here, a treaty is a piece of paper, while the people were driven out. We were forced to go away, there were no other possibilities. What, were we supposed to sign up as Russian citizens, us being Poles? You couldn't just do that, simply change, or as the Ukrainians said, switch sides. (K., m., b. 1929)

As a matter of course, the patriotic motivation is remembered alongside coercion – direct or indirect. Words such as "decree", "evacuation" and "population transfer" are used. However, such opinions are decidedly fewer, and they usually appear in a political context – everything is happening because Poland no longer exists in the interviewee's homeland.

For the Ukrainians then, a population transfer is always synonymous with deportation, and for Poles it is more of a forced migration. While such differences in the interpretation of the event of resettlement are slight, they do have a significant influence on the possibility of rebuilding one's identity in the new place of residence. The Poles retain a degree of agency in the mechanism of the forced transfer, which allows them to ascribe meaning to their loss and their lack of choice, thus helping them to partly neutralise the destructive influence of these circumstances. The Ukrainians are deprived of their homeland and their home through deportation, without receiving anything in return. The Poles who leave do so because they are forced to; however they are also making a decision: they choose between staying at home and living in the USSR, being potentially threatened with repressions in the future, and between the necessity of leaving home to be allowed to live in Poland. Despite the poignancy of the situation, this choice allows them to keep or construct a sense of individual agency, of which the Ukrainians are deprived from the very beginning.

Both the Poles and the Ukrainians point to the guilty parties responsible for their plight. Ukrainian migrants most often blame the Poles and the Soviets in equal measure. However, for many Ukrainian respondents the blame does not rest on any particular group, and is not even a category essential for the experience of deportation. Impersonal phrasing is a characteristic feature of their narratives, and sometimes, as in the case of the following quotation, the migrants are unable to select words appropriate for describing what they lived through; they either do not know such words, or their understanding of what happened is insufficient for a categorised description.

> They resettled us. (And when was that, during the war still?) In 1945. When the war ended, there was this Polish... I don't know what to call this, it was like they [people] went away. (And you were forced to do this? They told you to go?) They forced us, the whole family. Many Ukrainians here left. (Could you take your animals and everything?) We took everything, they put us on trains, and we all went like animals. The animals went and we did. (Z., f., b. 1922)

The common denominator for all the Polish narratives is the conviction that the Soviets are to blame for the loss of the respondents' homelands. Sometimes they are called Ruskies, sometimes Soviets, at other times they appear as "reds" or "communists". Occasionally, other groups share the blame: in the case of respondents originally from contemporary Ukraine, the Ukrainians. In the case of interviewees more interested in, or knowledgeable about, the political situation at the end of the war, it is the Allies, who "sold Poland out". Of particular interest is that even in the case of uneducated respondents, with rural backgrounds, the impersonal phrasing so characteristic for the Ukrainian descriptions never appears in Polish accounts. There is no indication of an inability among the Poles to situate themselves within the larger context of forced resettlement as part of a greater political process. Once again, it is clear how advantageous the years of working with the memory of this specific experience – in families, in the local community, and, especially after 1989, in public discourse – proved for the Polish inhabitants of the Borderlands. The Polish respondents have no trouble with clearly judging their past, because they have done it numerous times before. In comparison, the Ukrainians, who were deprived of similar opportunities, seem lost and helpless in the face of their own, untold experience.

Chaos and rebuilding

Adaptation

After arriving at their new place of residence both the Ukrainians and the Poles faced the necessity of gradually reorganising their lives, especially on its most basic, everyday level. Many respondents speak about the difficulties of finding a house or apartment, of wandering from one homestead to another, and of weeks of waiting at the train station for promised help. The reluctance to live in someone else's house is also mentioned – people who had just been expelled from their own homes were often offered the homes of those who had met a similar fate:

> We arrived here, in Zhovkva. And spent, what, three weeks at the train station, on the platform? So they chased us all around the place. We went to Dobrosyn, folks from Dobrosyn were taken away to Siberia? and these young girls had stayed. They cried and wandered around that house where we were supposed to go... "I don't want this house, it is full of tears", said I. (Z., f., b. 1921)

> When we arrived here in Krzyż it was early Spring. There were still no leaves on the trees. We didn't have a place to live because German women were still living in these here houses. So they put us in the school, or where the school is now. Before the war the place had been a hospital, or during the war. That's where the repatriates lived, in rooms with several families in them. That's how it was. How long did we live there? A couple of weeks to be sure, and only then people went out to look for places where they could stay ... When we were a bit bigger, me and J. [interviewee's sister] would always ask our father why he had chosen the run-down shack he did ... And he always said: "There were still German women with children living everywhere", he would say, "and I'm not one for forcing them out." (K., f., b. 1940)

The deported were at the mercy of their new authorities, who were often indifferent to the plight of the newcomers. To this day, their accounts contain bitterness and the conviction that they were betrayed by the authorities and left without help. The "repatriates" in both towns also harbour grudges against other groups of settlers, chiefly those who lived near Zhovkva and Krzyż before the war. The inhabitants of Krzyż who came from the Borderlands complained that it was the "Poles from Poland" who had the easiest time settling in the abandoned German town, primarily by shamelessly looting property intended for the deportees. The deportees from Zhovkva resented the fact that, in contrast to the economic migrants from villages near Zhovkva, who "came for the Polish and Jewish estates", they were forced to obtain everything through hard labour:

> We stayed outdoors for three weeks in Poland, here in Krzyż. There, ma'am, on Marchlewski street stood this, this big barn, and we stayed in that barn for three weeks, before we got an apartment, because everything was already taken by "Poles". But it wasn't taken by Poles, it was taken by thieves ... And we stayed until we got this place, in this here house. (K., f., b. 1929)

Although adaptation in both cities was made even more difficult by wartime damage, the situation of Krzyż's new citizens was far worse. The town, which had been 50% demolished by the Soviets, took a long time to recover, and the necessity of participating in the process of rebuilding constituted an additional burden for many. However, in numerous accounts, the post-war rebuilding of Krzyż is portrayed as a patriotic and lofty deed, generating energy and the most positive of emotions, instrumental in cementing the new community:

> When we arrived, we had to start from scratch. Firstly – for example I remember that us scouts, we cleared the debris, because here, where the John Paul II park is now located, there was once a town square, and it was completely ruined, so we – the youth – cleared the debris, and we took the bricks to some square, and it was said that these bricks would be used to rebuild Warsaw. That was a grand aim: all of society was building its capital city. That was the slogan. But then it turned out that the bricks went to Drawsko village [near Krzyż], and elsewhere, to other construction sites, and all this public effort was wasted. The enthusiasm was great, people wanted to do a lot of things, but nobody controlled it, and that's what happened to the public effort ... Of course, the people were not discouraged, because it was a time of need. So we cleared the debris, and maybe the bricks weren't used for some lofty purpose, but there was some order, and you were doing something. (K., m., b. 1928)

Despite knowing that such lofty ideals often diverged from dreary reality, for many interviewees the participation in the rebuilding of a city to which they were tied for life became a constructive experience, both for their own identities and for creating bonds among Krzyż's new inhabitants. In comparison to Zhovkva, the inhabitants of Krzyż gained striking advantage from rebuilding their town after the war. In the minds of the Poles, the memory of the difficulties associated with the first period of adaptation is balanced by the joy of rebuilding their homeland – both locally and, on a larger scale – ideologically. The building blocks for this ideological homeland consisted of the bricks from Krzyż that were supposed to go to Warsaw. Even if these building blocks were wasted because the bricks were pilfered, the public effort cemented a common bond and gave the inhabitants of Krzyż the strength stemming from a sense of agency and of the ability to change the surrounding reality, if only on a local scale.

The new population of Zhovkva had no such experience. Although also recovering from the passing of the front, Zhovkva suffered much less, and this was certainly a positive factor. Yet, paradoxically, the lack of need for extensive rebuilding in a material sense translated into a lack of the community-bonding experience that arises from rebuilding in a material sense. This in turn led to yet another lost opportunity to create a sense of community. In addition, while the people of Krzyż were united in the hope of forging a new reality (although not on the level of politics) in the first period of post-war restoration, the totalitarian regime enforced upon the inhabitants of Zhovkva a passiveness that was the only assurance of relative safety.

Fear

A very important element of the memory of forced resettlement consists of the fear experienced during the first days in the new town. The tales of the first impressions of Krzyż and Zhovkva sound almost apocalyptic even today. The reality which the migrants encountered at the end of their journey was shocking and frightening, primarily due to the still-prevalent wartime violence that permeated the towns. For many of the Krzyż and Zhovkva "repatriates", the first human being encountered in the town was a machine gun toting soldier (usually a Soviet), and the first sight – bodies strewn across the streets. Regardless of whether these bodies belonged to UPA guerilla fighters executed by the Soviets (in Zhovkva) or slain Germans (in Krzyż), they made a shocking impression on the newcomers.

The first weeks in both towns resembled living in a minefield – in a figurative, socio-political, and literal sense. Krzyż was a classic example of the Polish "Wild West in the Reclaimed Lands", with all the entailing lawlessness and violence; Zhovkva witnessed the painful consequences of the raging conflict between the UPA and the Red Army. The memory of the first period of adaptation is thus pervaded by a sense of danger; in secondary literature concerning the post-war situation in the "reclaimed lands", this sense is enumerated as among the primary factors influencing the instability of settlement.[11] The danger stemmed from the martial nature of everyday life – the Red Army governed both towns immediately after the war, and this was painfully palpable each day. The settlers from Krzyż and Zhovkva remember the gunfights, brawls and havoc caused by Red Army soldiers.

> And when we already got to Zhovkva, just in the evening, there was a light drizzle... Further away was a grain silo, and we were closer to here, and the silo was guarded. We arrived... The first night – nothing, the second night – shooting. We didn't know what was happening, we had got out of the frying pan and into the fire... And those bandits that guarded the grain had some laughs and started shooting, scaring people... (Z., m, b. 1929)

> The most troublesome for the railway were the Ruskies, because they came through here, either going from Berlin or to Berlin, since there is a junction here. Things happened at the station, but I didn't go there since I was young. When I went anywhere, then it was either with dad or mum, always under some protection. I was afraid of them, very afraid ... You'd prefer to avoid them at a distance, never deal with them. (K., f., b. 1930)

A specific type of fear felt upon arrival was fear of the authorities. In the narratives from Krzyż, fear was usually exceeded by animosity, sometimes mingled with contempt; the new communist authorities had their powerbase outside Poland, and were thus considered unwanted and dangerous, but at times also ridiculed. In the accounts of the people from Zhovkva there is no irony or ridicule. It is clear from the interviews that in Krzyż the authorities were a real threat only to those who actively opposed them, while in Zhovkva everyone was potentially in danger, guilty or not. The migrants from Poland came under particular suspicion in post-war Zhovkva, partly due to having relatives abroad. One can imagine the magnitude of the fear inspired by the Soviet government, considering the fact that the oldest generation of interviewees is still today too frightened to speak about their opinions of the regime. It can only be deduced from vague hints that the declared stance of not caring about politics is, in fact, a manifestation of a still-existing fear.

> What I'm saying is, we've never dabbled in any politics, at all, and that's why we were able to survive, no-one's ever touched us. No one gave us any medals, and no one locked us up

---

11 Jędrzej Chumiński. "Czynniki destabilizujące proces osadnictwa we Wrocławiu (1945– 1949)." *Studia nad procesami integracji i dezintegracji społeczności Śląska*. Ed. Władysław Misiak. Wrocław: Wydawnictwo Uniwersytetu Wrocławskiego, 1993, 55–78; Macin Zaremba. *Wielka Trwoga. Polska 1944–1947. Ludowa reakcja na kryzys*. Kraków: Wydawnictwo Znak, Institute of Political Studies PAN, 2012.

in any prisons. Because there were some that got involved... these Ruskies that they've sent here... Say one of them saw Lenin, so what, he'd go to work for the regional committee... Nope, we did our work on the side, we did everything on the side. (Z., f., b. 1928)

The memories of the first moments in both Krzyż and Zhovkva are characterised by an extreme sense of insecurity, even in one's own home. The interviewees recount their constant fear of being attacked – by Germans, Ukrainian nationalists, Muscovites, the Red Army, or "regular" bandits. The fear was not limited to outside threats, but also included neighbours.

> We were afraid. At first we didn't want to go out. They took some of our families to Osieczno village. The clearings were empty. We were near the road. We went through the forest. There was nothing but forest for 11 kilometres. We stopped for the night. There was no light, no lamp, nothing. And the Germans were still around. The next day: "We're going back!" (K., f., b. 1922)

> I still remember how they walked around near our house. They were wrapped up in cloaks and wore huge trench-coats. Their hands were hidden. Over there, where our garden is now, near the forest, they always came out of the woods and wandered in our orchard. As soon as it got dark they would be in our orchard. And we would immediately lock ourselves in the house, like that. (So you were afraid of them?) Of course we were afraid. Because who knows who these people are, and what's out there? (Z., f., b. 1944)

Both fragments illustrate the level of fear, but also the mutual distrust – the settlers, strangers to each other, were afraid of a sort of undefined "others". They did not want to check who was wandering through their garden at night. On the one hand, living among other people was a guarantee of safety, offering protection from the Germans and guerillas hiding in the woods; on the other hand, even the neighbours could prove to be dangerous. The fear of the new neighbours suggests the level of animosity that became one of the most important factors impeding, and often halting, the process of building a new community. In the majority of the narratives, everyone who does not belong to a narrowly-defined group of "us" is a potential enemy. In such cases, the stories about various "bandits" are accompanied by a sense of alienation and loneliness, of being able to rely only on oneself. In time, such feelings combined with the perceived, constant hostility of one's surroundings can result in an inward retreat, a conscious withdrawal from the community, as in the case of the woman quoted below.

> All sorts of things happened here. They told us: "You didn't want to work so you came here." The locals were very aggressive. They called us names. You don't know... I can't explain... There was a period here when all the Greek-Catholic churches were closed down and turned into Orthodox churches. Some people didn't want that... All sorts of things happened. People were so angry. The locals were all Banderovtsy. But there were others here...

the Krasnopaganshchiks, the Red Army, those who... It was terrifying. But I'm telling you, we didn't get involved in anything, we didn't see anything, not a thing. (Z., f., b. 1928)

The burden of animosity

Establishing new relations with other migrants was also an important challenge faced by the settlers. After the war both towns included a mixture of various groups, as well as individuals, whose wartime stories were far too divergent and unique to provide mutual understanding based on a common plight. All of these people were faced with the necessity of establishing new relations with each other.

In the memories of both groups of migrants, the Ukrainians and the Poles, the difficulty of beginning to build relations with locals who lived in the communities surrounding Krzyż and Zhovkva is particularly apparent. The dominant motif in the tales of the "repatriates" is negativity, and above all, the lack of help and basic human compassion. Situations in which the migrants were refused a symbolic glass of water or milk by the better-off locals are still painful to recall.

> We were [treated] like dogs, ma'am. My sister-in-law had a baby of seven months when she came here, and she had no milk, nothing. There was no goat, no one here had a goat yet. We only earned enough for one later. We bought an old goat, to get milk. Ma'am, when we came to Drawsko, three kilometres on foot, I remember walking as well, they drove us off with dogs, like that: "Go, go away, go, there's no milk for you." That's how it is you know, this is still with us, it stayed with us. (K., f., b. 1929)

The lack of understanding on the locals' part, along with their accusations that the "repatriates" came to Krzyż/Zhovkva in order to take the German/Polish estates, are also strongly remembered. The migrants were offended by the accusations of greed that illustrated a complete lack of understanding of their tragic plight, and by being treated like foreigners by their fellow countrymen.

> Well, anyway, these weren't... We weren't greeted or accepted like friends. Rather like foes, which was the unexpected part, because not only were we deprived of our homes, it turned out that we came here to steal and that we were the enemy. Because we came from across the Bug you see, so I say, after I gathered up the courage, I say: "Lady, do you even know where the Bug is? I'm not from across the Bug, I'm from across the San. And do you know where that is? No, and where's the Bug? No, then what are you going on about, what's that about being from across the Bug, is it supposed to be something worse? And where are you from?" Afterwards I had to speak like this, because they treated us like nobodies, the locals. (K., f., b. 1930)

> (And when you came here, to Zhovkva, in '45, how were you received? Did they treat you like locals, or like outsiders?) Like outsiders! "Shits", they said. These locals didn't accept us. (Local Ukrainians?) Local Ukrainians, local folks, not one bit, no! ... (But you spoke the same language...) Yup. In the beginning they didn't accept us. I don't know why they didn't. Did they understand that we were forced to leave? They said we came for the Polish houses, Polish land. (Z., f., b. 1928)

A difficult memory, still thriving among the "repatriates", is a feeling of being inferior due to their economic situation. Both the Poles from the Borderlands in Krzyż, and the Ukrainians from Poland in Zhovkva formed a kind of economic sub-class[12] in their new towns. From the start, they were not only objectively poorer than the settlers from Greater Poland and Central Ukraine, but more importantly, unlike the locals, they could not count on the support of their families. In addition, their poverty, combined with cultural differences and the fact that most of the "repatriates" came from rural areas, inspired the locals to brand them with the humiliating tag of "hicks".

> And that stung me, when we came there, to Poland, it was our Poland as well! But when we arrived here, in the west... Also here in Poznań province, the people weren't really honest either. They called us "Ukrainians"... And what could you do? Tough luck. People didn't understand how it was ... Because we did, in fact, arrive poor. What could we have had? You couldn't take everything, only the things you could carry, nothing more ... They had everything prepared for them, but we've had to leave everything behind. So they should have understood that this was not right. They laughed that we arrived in paper bags. That's what you could hear, it was unpleasant. But you didn't pay attention, because what could you do, you had to keep on living ... We were always the ones who were worse. (K., f., b. 1930)

The respondents who were at least in their teens when they experienced resettlement are now able to contextualise their past emotions, and search for a rational explanation for the locals' behaviour. Those who were only children at the time are left with a painful sense of wrongdoing, which still causes negative emotions.

> They greeted us with irritation, they called us "shits". (Why?) Shits, meaning that we came from a "Shit-hole". We had these neighbours, who were rich. There were two girls there, like me and my sister, from the same year. So we would come over to their house to play. We lived in poverty. And they had white bread. For us, mum would bake bannocks, she fed

---

12 Ther. "The Integration of Expelees"; Volodymyr Kitsak. "Deportovanii z Polshchi ukraintsi: rezultaty pershoho etapu vhodzhennia v socium ta ekonomichnoho prystosuvannia u 1944–47 rr." *Ukraina-Polshcha: istorychna spadshchyna i suspil'na svidomist'*, vol. 2: *Deportatsii 1944–1951*. Lviv: Natsional'na Akademia Nauk Ukrayny, Instytut Ukrainoznavstva im. I. Krypiakevycha, 2007.

us as best she could. So over at their place L., the rich girl, would sometimes give us some bread, and we ate... [with trembling voice]. Our parents wouldn't stand it, they always yelled at us for it. (Z., f., b. 1944)

The theme above of objective differences between the "repatriates" and other settlers is present in interviews from both towns, but in very different forms. In Zhovkva, mutual judgements are vague, lacking in detail, and usually limited to a simple (although very confident) statement that the others were "different". Based on the interviewees' accounts, it is impossible to determine what the differences between the Ukrainians from Poland and those living near Zhovkva were. One reason for this might be that – apart from the Orthodox creed shared by some of the settlers from the Chełm region – the objective differences between these two groups in Zhovkva were factually minuscule, and ethnographic in character at most. The other reason might be that the image of the migrant from Poland did not become a part of shared memory in Ukraine; it was not filtered through mass culture like the image of the "repatriate" from the Eastern Borderlands was in Poland. The inhabitants of Zhovkva branded each other with names suggesting foreignness, but the social imagination did not aid them in creating a topos of the migrant as someone with definite traits. The situation was different in Krzyż. Firstly, the objective differences between the settlers from the Borderlands and the other settlers were definitely great. Additionally, the shared narratives about the forced migrations created clear images of the Borderland-repatriate and the "settler from the Central" (the aforementioned film "Sami Swoi" provides examples of both), which shaped the biographical memories of the inhabitants of Krzyż *ex post*. According to Kaja Kaźmierska, biographical memory is fused with the shared memories of the community which a person inhabits, and the latter provide context for the former, at the same time enabling the interpretation of one's own experience.[13] It is because of the richness of this context that the images of the "repatriate" and the "Centralak" ("Centralite") feature so strongly in the interviews with the inhabitants of Krzyż.

In summary, although both the Poles and the Ukrainians struggled with similar problems after arriving in their new towns, a closer look at their accounts reveals significant differences in the situations of the settlers from each group – as well as on their outlook on rebuilding their identities. The first difference concerns the period of difficulties associated with the initial stage of adaptation. Fear and mutual distrust permeate the memories recounted by the Polish and Ukrainian settlers in a similar fashion; however, in the Polish narratives these feelings are swiftly replaced by tales of a gradual befriending by initially hostile

---

13 Kaźmierska. *Biografia i pamięć*.

people, and an equally gradual creation of a relatively stable and safe life in a new political reality. The Ukrainian narratives show that the fear of the communist regime was a part of everyday life long after the "repatriates" from the Borderlands began to feel free to tell each other political jokes in Krzyż. In Zhovkva, on the other hand, the distrust of other people which was the product of that fear, long continued to paralyse the process of social bonding. This had significant consequences for the issue that interests me, namely the rebuilding of identity. To say that a prolonged, intense experiencing of fear has a negative impact on the psyche is a truism. Yet a factor of equal importance is the fact that in a post-migrational period, when recent migration is potentially stigmatising, prolonged fear leads to the migrants' eschewing all attempts to establish a new identity, which prevents the trauma from being addressed. As a result, the difficult experience of a break in the continuity of one's identity can become too powerful to overcome.

The post-migrational reconstruction of identity

Homesickness

If we compare the journey itself to the separative phase of the migrational rite of passage, then the first period of adaptation becomes the liminal phase, a time of crossing, in which the individual is suspended – they have not severed their bonds with the old reality, nor have they established a connection with the new one. For nearly all of the interviewees, the most important emotion associated with this period is an overbearing feeling of homesickness. The respondents recall that for a notable period of time after their arrival they lived in the past, focussing on what they had left in their previous homes, rather than on their present lives.

> We reminisced, of course. Mum always did, because she was a Lviv lifer, constantly going on about Lviv, living in Lviv, Lviv songs... Mum always reminisced. In any case, when we came here in the beginning, in 1945, everyone said that this was temporary. Initially, we all thought that the Americans would come again and that there would be world war three and that we would return to our homes. This lasted for a long time, no-one believed that we would have to stay here ... So mum was fixed on the idea, it kept her going. (K., m., b. 1928)

Although homesickness was a universal emotion among the migrants from Krzyż and Zhovkva, the Poles and the Ukrainians were in fact longing for different things. The settlers from the Borderlands speak mostly about their hometown or village, about land understood as a "small fatherland", but also about the specific type of Polish identity unique to the Borderlands region, which they did not manage to bring west. It seems that their tragedy lay in the forced interruption of the coherence and integrity of their – borrowing a term from Stanisław Ossowski – "ideological and private homeland".[14] The force of this homesickness and its destructive influence on the functioning of settlers in their new hometown is evidenced by the accounts of people who never got over the loss of their old homes, never grew accustomed enough to their new homes to call them their own. In their cases, the process of adapting to life's new conditions failed, the migration led to a defeat, particularly on the level of personal identity. Even if these interviewees acclimated themselves to their new geographical and cultural conditions, they never managed to reach the phase of aggregation, the stage of identity assimilation.

> You still wish you could return to your home. I would like to see it one more time before I die, but I certainly won't... These days I can't go very far. My husband would go with me, if he had come from the east, but he's from around here, so he never felt the urge. The children also got used to this place ... Only I keep collecting what I can, whatever souvenirs I can, so that the children, and then the grand-children might know how it was. Difficult memories. It's hard to forget, we were too big. We remember everything. If I had been younger, I wouldn't remember so much, it wouldn't hurt me so much. But here I am, walking around, walking down the streets in Czortków, and often I feel as if I'm back home, in the east. (K., f., b. 1930)

The Ukrainians deported from Poland were homesick as well, but for them home meant their family's land, farmed by past generations, and homesteads surrounded by safe and familiar neighbourhoods. Sometimes they sorely missed the people they had left in their old country, from whom they became separated by the border for many years. The differences between the feelings of homesickness experienced by the Polish and Ukrainian deportees are amply illustrated by their stories of trips to their old countries, which they undertook in the 1990s. Both the Poles and the Ukrainians realise during their visits that there is nothing left for them in their old homelands. The Ukrainians claim, with a sense of disappointment, that their relatives who avoided deportation became Polonised; the Poles on the other hand complain that they cannot find *their place*, which in the case of the interviewee quoted below means firstly his native village, which was razed, and secondly, in a metaphorical sense – the Polish Border-

---

14 Stanisław Ossowski. "Analiza socjologiczna pojęcia ojczyzny." *Dzieła*, vol. 3, Warszawa: PIW, 1967, 201–226.

lands, which no longer exist in the shape remembered by the exiled "repatriates".

> At first, everybody wanted to [go]. I went as well, a couple of times, to my old place, to, uh, Lubaczów ... Well, it seems fine, but what's there for us...? Well, they have, their children are already Poles. You understand, they're no longer Ukrainians. My younger [sister] married a Pole, so they're Polonised, that's that .... You can't do anything about it. Let them be Poles then, if they remain friends with the Ukrainians, if they agree, if there's... Well, what can you do. (Z., f., b. 1928)

> So I went ma'am, I've been to Dubno, I've been to Ptyt, I went to see that little church. The Ukrainians burned that church down, there's nothing left but a cross. The church is burnt. It's gone. So recently I went to Volhynia, and God forbid, when I saw all of this, pure horror, you want to, you wanted to cry ... So now I can't say how they could've done this. Where our home, where our estate stood, not only ours, but also where those Ukrainians lived, the grand landowners, there's no trace of any of it, ma'am. I searched for my place, where my pa had his cottage, the cottage, the barn, the pens. I searched for it all. So I say to myself, maybe I'll find a stone, maybe a piece of wood, but no. There was nothing. They levelled it all. (K., m., b. 1930)

The complexity of the differences between Polish and Ukrainian homesickness appears amplified in the migrants' reaction to the necessity of finally accepting their loss: the Ukrainians are able to accept it, albeit with bitterness and regret; the Poles cannot.

Uncertainty and temporariness

The second strongest emotion, further reinforcing liminality and the suspension of the first period after arriving in Krzyż and Zhovkva, is the sense of temporariness and instability. In part, it is a natural extension of the same homesickness that caused the people to hope for a swift return to their former home and that prevented them from accepting the change in their lives. Another factor that contributed to the persistence of these emotions was the belief that the post-war political reality was not final, and that all it took was a small change in global politics and the borders would change again. Nearly all of the migrants claim that they were convinced for a very long time that their stay in Krzyż or Zhovkva was not permanent.

> When repatriation came, no-one believed that it would be permanent, either there, in the east, or here. Many people believed that it was just a pause, to calm everyone down and stop the war. When we arrived here there was this rumour going around for, I don't know, two years, that we wouldn't stay long, that in a couple of months, or a year at

> most, we would return east. ... Some folks even kept on to their property there, to have a place to go back to. (K., m., b. 1931)

> And what were the attitudes among the people? "We'll stay here for a year. We won't stay here for long." (You thought you'd be coming back?) Yes, that we'd return. (That you'd return to Lubaczów?) Yes. There was this policy back then that they'd come back to their homes, the owners, that they'd be able to punish you somehow. That caused fear. I gave up on that house, I told you about that Polish woman. ... Then I bought it officially, legally, and I'm not afraid of anyone here. (Z., m., b. 1917)

As the second quotation illustrates, the sense of temporariness was often combined with the fear that the previous owners of the newly occupied houses would return. Despite the authorities' copious efforts to convince the settlers that such a threat was unrealistic, the migrants were afraid that their new homes might turn out to be only temporary living quarters. A recurring theme within this context is the striving for "legalising" or "securing" the new property by gathering the necessary documentation, or simply by purchasing the property, foregoing the state as an intermediary.

A careful analysis of the Zhovkva and Krzyż deportees' narratives shows that temporariness and uncertainty constituted a comparable burden only during the initial stage of adaptation. For the Ukrainian migrants, these feelings were swiftly superseded by fear and the general despondency associated with the repressiveness of the Soviet political system. For the deportees from the Borderlands, the situation was different, and it seems that the lasting sense of instability associated with their new surroundings had more long-term consequences. There were two essential causes for this. Firstly, after the war the Polish migrants were convinced, to a far greater degree than the Ukrainian migrants, that a turn in international politics would return the lost eastern territories to Poland. The people had high hopes for Władysław Anders,[15] the Polish government in exile in London, and waited for the Allies to "snap out" of their mind set regarding Poland. The interviewees from Krzyż speak about listening to Radio Free Europe, participating in anti-government organisations and the general spirit of resistance present among the inhabitants of the "reclaimed lands" who came from

---

[15] Władysław Anders – Polish military, general and politician. After the Soviet invasion of Poland in 1939 he was imprisoned by the Soviets, and after the Sikroski-Majski treaty in 1941 he was released and formed the Polish Army in the Soviet Union (consisting of Polish citizens deported to the USSR in 1939–1941). Finally, the so called Anders Army left USSR and fought alongside the Western Allies, capturing Monte Cassino. After the establishment of the communist government in Poland Anders stayed in exile, as most of his soldiers. Immediately after the war, many Poles hoped for his comeback and fight against the communist rule in Poland.

the Borderlands. It seems that this stubborn hope was the result of the status that their lost Borderlands homeland held in their minds: it was, as I mentioned before, not only personal, but also integral to the ideological, "grand" homeland. In the post-war period, the Ukrainians did not have an exiled political representation on a comparable scale to Poland; therefore the Ukrainian deportees had a harder time hoping for a change originating from abroad. In addition, the bloody conflict between the Ukrainian independence underground and the Red Army, which took a heavy toll on the civilian population, caused many deportees to simply hope for stability and peace – at all costs.

The second cause lies in the character of post-war propaganda in Poland and Ukraine. Whilst in the Ukrainian SRR the subject of any border changes after the war was usually avoided, the propaganda in the People's Republic of Poland made the return of the "reclaimed lands" one of its leading themes. On the one hand, the settlers were being convinced that the Western and Northern Territories had always belonged to Poland. On the other hand, the fear of the Germans was fuelled and exploited, and the spectre of German vengefulness was constantly brought up.[16] In principle, this was a means of procuring the loyalty of the new inhabitants of these lands: the settlers were supposed to be thankful to the communist authorities for guarding the western border and providing them with safety. The narratives from Krzyż show the strength of the combined influence of the state-spread fear of the Germans' return and the hope of reclaiming the Borderlands cultivated by the "repatriates". The interviewees from Krzyż speak about the years of living in a state of readiness to leave and waiting for "Anders[17] to arrive on a white horse", about their intentional refusal to set down roots in the new town. This refusal had two aspects – the aspect of personal identity and the communal aspect. On the level of identity, it stalled psychological adaptation, making it impossible to accept the finality of migration and the lack of the option to return. On the social level, it negatively impacted the formation of a new community, also in its most basic, material sense: for many years after the war, the deportees from the Borderlands did not renovate the houses and estates left by the Germans, and did not construct new buildings. This phenomenon is perfectly conveyed by the following quotation from a respondent born near Nowogródek (presently in Belarus): why invest in something that is "not ours", without being certain that it will become ours?

---

16 Andrzej Sakson. "Procesy integracji i dezintegracji społecznej na Ziemiach Zachodnich i Północnych Polski po 1945 roku." *Pomorze – trudna ojczyzna? Kształtowanie się nowej tożsamości 1945–1995*. Ed. Andrzej Sakson. Poznań: Instytut Zachodni, 1996, 131–154.
17 See note 15.

Yes, everyone thought that they would go back. Not only that, I worked in construction. And when I went to work in 1960 in Krzyż, no-one was building anything. "Because it's not ours". Who wanted to live here? Just the railway workers, due to this junction, and then the factories. But to get too attached to Krzyż – not really. Only in the beginning of the 60s did things budge a little. And later, what with the plots of land, towards the end of those 60s, people really started building. So you could say that when I went to work they started building, in 1963. (K., f., b. 1942)

Foreignness and cultural adaptation

The third important challenge for rebuilding the identities of the deportees was the necessity of adapting to new cultural and geographical conditions and the associated feeling of foreignness, as well as the difficult relations with the still-remaining Polish population in Zhovkva and the German population in Krzyż. Once again, the interviews conducted in Krzyż and Zhovkva suggest that these problems affected both groups of settlers to a very uneven degree. The sense of foreignness does not appear strongly in accounts about the first moments in Zhovkva, and neither does contact with the Poles. This is easy to understand when one remembers that the Ukrainians deported from Poland largely had not witnessed the departure of Polish inhabitants of the town. The urban landscape of Zhovkva was also hardly very different from what the Ukrainians, who had previously lived tens of kilometres away, had been used to previously. The type of architecture, the furnishings, the way of farming or organising a workshop were all similar, and the natural environment remained largely the same. Hence, the process of cultural adaptation does not form a separate thread in the narratives from Zhovkva.

The town that the new inhabitants of Krzyż arrived in, in addition to being still dangerous due to military activity, was tangibly and painfully foreign – and therefore even more threatening. Not only was the space, still saturated with an entirely foreign German atmosphere, the people were foreign as well – for the migrants, very often the first people encountered in Krzyż after the railway workers were Germans. Both the physical space and the German population who had a negative attitude towards the Polish settlers made the newcomers uneasy.

> Everything seemed strange to us here. The signs were still in German everywhere at the train station. (K., f., b. 1915)

> Father went to town here in Krzyż and I jumped into the street. Today this is Staszic street. I don't know what it was called back then, but I do know that there was a German woman in a window and when she saw me she yelled: "Polnische Schweinerei!" That's how she greeted me here – there were still some Germans around. I'm not very surprised by her reaction,

because they were being expelled – we knew how it was – but still, it was an unpleasant event. "First time in Krzyż – I think to myself – that's some greeting." (K., m., b. 1929)

After the first difficult contact it was necessary to establish some sort of relations with the Germans. In many cases, the Polish settlers shared apartments with them for several months, and they also worked together. The relationships between the former and current owners varied – some were steeped in animosity, others were formally proper, and others still were cordial and resulted in contact being maintained via mail for many years. These latter relationships favoured working on one's memory and identity, by enabling the transfer of local know-how and by reducing the sense of being an intruder in a new place. Far more important than the direct, yet short-lived, contacts with Germans was the matter of adapting to life in a post-German cultural milieu. The foreignness of the natural environment, economy, material culture and climate was a significant barrier to adaptation for many of the interviewees in Krzyż.[18] Aside from the difficulties associated with settling down, the foreignness redefined cultural adaptation as a wholesale process of changing one's symbolic universe.[19] The German cultural and geographical landscape was a hostile, alien environment for the embittered and unhappy deportees from the Borderlands, requiring the additional efforts of assimilation and discovery. The vast majority of the interviewees remember the process as a sorrowful experience. Many of these people are prone to idealising their original homeland at the expense of the unwanted, "not our" reality in which they were forced to live after the war; this is especially true for those who never got to see their homeland again. In the east "everything was better", from land through housing up to the very air; contrary to the insinuations of getting rich off of German estates, honest people lost out on the resettlement, in a material sense.

> How can you even compare the soil in Volhynia to the soil over here. Over there, when you plant wheat, you get a head this big, and over here? This wheat doesn't have a head. Over there, there's land and there's wealth. This place was so wild, nothing would grow, so, we hadn't any horses or even a cow or anything, yea, we wanted to go back. (K., f., b. 1935)

---

[18] For an example of a discussion on this matter, see Andrzej Brencz, who employs the collective category of a "cultural landscape". Andrzej Brencz. "Oswajanie niemieckiego dziedzictwa kulturowego. Z badań etnologicznych na Środkowym Nadodrzu." *Wokół niemieckiego dziedzictwa kulturowego na Ziemiach Północnych i Zachodnich.* Ed. Zbigniew Mazur. Poznań: Instytut Zachodni, 1997, 191–216.

[19] I employ the terms 'cultural adaptation' and 'symbolic universe' as they are understood by Józef Niżnik in: Józef Niżnik. *Symbole a adaptacja kulturowa.* Warszawa: Centralny Ośrodek Metodyki Upowszechniania Kultury, 1985.

> Different buildings. Back home there were no brick houses, there were wooden houses. These were beautiful homes, really beautiful, and all of them topped with red tiles, plate and red tiles. But they were nice buildings, and they were very well-kept buildings, over there a householder cared for his house. And over here, we came and everything was just bricks and bricks, we couldn't get used to it. Over there you could leave a sausage or something lying around, and that sausage could lay there for a week and it wouldn't turn white, wouldn't spoil. Here you put it in the fridge and it's completely off in a week. Everywhere there's this humidity, well maybe not humidity, but the air is different, humid, back there the air was dry. (K., f., b. 1934)

An additional barrier to rebuilding identity and social life in a post-German town was the strong, negative sentiment that persisted after the war towards everything that was German. The new environment that the settlers were forced into was not only alien, unwanted and unknown – it was primarily hostile, because it reminded one about the recent horrors of war. The interviewees from Krzyż remember their dislike of everyday items, German books, signs on buildings and even church furnishings.

> There was a hostile tendency in the people towards German things, tools, even German buildings. We have a church here that was constructed in 1774. It was an Evangelical church. Inside, there was an altar and two rows of benches. ... We had to renovate the church, we had to rebuild some parts. In 1945 and 1946 people came here from my parts, from Stanisławów province, also known as Kołomyja, from Tarnopol province, Volhynia, Belarus, Lithuania, as well as Krakow, Warsaw and Poznań provinces. There was this gathering of people and everyone was against these German appliances, these German remainders, even if it was antique architecture, no-one cared. (K., m., b. 1934)

The German "patina", as all German material heritage was called by the propaganda of the People's Republic of Poland, reminded the new inhabitants of Krzyż for a very long time that they were foreigners in the town. This was an obvious obstacle for social and psychological adaptation.

Conclusions

An analysis of the material collected allows for the claim that, despite the different historical contexts and cultures of memory in Poland and in Ukraine – both past and present – the experience of forced resettlement is universal enough to enable one to find shared traits in the narratives told about it today. I believe that these traits are best called, drawing upon Harald Welzer and his associates, the topoi of memory.[20] Examples of the topoi present in the narratives of both groups of deportees include: the journey, the fear of strangers, a sense of temporariness, poverty. The emotional similarity of the recounted experiences is in some cases striking: if, as an experiment, one were to remove the factual elements from the accounts and switch the quotes around their significance would remain equally authentic.

At the same time, the biographies of individual interviewees and the cultures of memory which they inhabit, affix the topoi in diverse narrative structures, and in various cultural "shells" – causing them to function differently. Thus, in the Polish accounts the topoi of the journey and homesickness take the leading roles, while the Ukrainian accounts are centred around the fear of strangers (and especially of the authorities) and poverty. There are also issues which appear only in the narratives of one of the groups – e. g. the extended sense of temporariness and the fear of the Germans' return in the memories of the Poles.

Analysing the narratives of the Polish and Ukrainian migrants also illustrates how hard, and at the same time how varied – due to the political, social and cultural contexts – the post-migrational processes of rebuilding identity really were. What constituted an opportunity for one group was often a burden or an insignificant factor for the other. For the Polish interviewees, the largest barrier to adaptation was their relationship with their own homeland (its status as an integral part of their ideological homeland), as well as the lingering, postwar sense of temporariness and uncertainty, amplified by objective cultural differences between their old and new homes. For the Ukrainian deportees, the factors which most destabilised the process of rebuilding identity included the repressiveness of the political system and the ensuing fear and lack of trust, which also delayed the formation of social bonds in Zhovkva. It appears that, in an initial balance of opportunities and dangers for the reconstruction of identity immediately after the migration, the Ukrainians faced slightly better odds – primarily because of the similarities between their old and new homelands, and the nature of their relationship with the former. In the end however, the conditions became roughly even. Although the Polish deportees got off to a worse start, these initial conditions were later replaced by better opportunities for reworking traumatic experiences: a relative (in comparison to the Ukrainians) ideological liberty, and the easier formation of new social structures.

---

20 Harald Welzer, Sabine Moller and Karoline Tschuggnall. "'Dziadek nie był nazistą'. Narodowy socjalizm i Holokaust w pamięci rodzinnej." Transl. Paweł Masłowski. *Pamięć zbiorowa i kulturowa. Współczesna perspektywa niemiecka*. Ed. Magdalena Saryusz-Wolska. Warszawa: Universitas, 2009, 351–410.

References

Brencz, Andrzej. "Oswajanie niemieckiego dziedzictwa kulturowego. Z badań etnologicznych na Środkowym Nadodrzu". *Wokół niemieckiego dziedzictwa kulturowego na Ziemiach Północnych i Zachodnich*. Ed. Zbigniew Mazur. Poznań: Instytut Zachodni, 1997. 191–216.

Chumiński, Jędrzej. "Czynniki destabilizujące proces osadnictwa we Wrocławiu (1945–1949)". *Studia nad procesami integracji i dezintegracji społeczności Śląska*. Ed. Władysław Misiak. Wrocław: Wydawnictwo Uniwersytetu Wrocławskiego, 1993. 55–78.

Halbwachs, Maurice. *On collective memory*. Chicago (IL): The University of Chicago Press, 1992.

Kaźmierska, Kaja. *Biografia i pamięć. Na przykładzie pokoleniowego doświadczenia ocalonych z Zagłady*. Kraków: Nomos, 2008.

Kitsak, Volodymyr. "Deportovanii z Polshchi ukraintsi: rezultaty pershoho etapu vhodzhennia v socium ta ekonomichnoho prystosuvannia u 1944–47 rr". *Ukraina-Polshcha: istorychna spadshchyna i suspil'na svidomist'*, vol. 2: *Deportatsii 1944–1951*. Lviv: Natsional'na Akademia Nauk Ukrainy, Instytut Ukrainoznavstva im. I. Krypiakevycha, 2007.

Mach, Zdzisław. *Niechciane miasta. Migracja i tożsamość społeczna*. Kraków: Universitas, 1998.

Melchior, Małgorzata. "Przeszłość jako czynnik zróżnicowań kulturowych dzisiaj – przypadek dwóch sąsiadujących wsi". *Kultura i Społeczeństwo* 4 (1996): 109–118.

Niżnik, Józef. *Symbole a adaptacja kulturowa*. Warszawa: Centralny Ośrodek Metodyki Upowszechniania Kultury, 1985.

Ossowski, Stanisław. "Analiza socjologiczna pojęcia ojczyzny". *Dzieła*, vol. 3, Warszawa: PIW, 1967. 201–226.

Sakson, Andrzej. "Procesy integracji i dezintegracji społecznej na Ziemiach Zachodnich i Północnych Polski po 1945 roku". *Pomorze – trudna ojczyzna? Kształtowanie się nowej tożsamości 1945–1995*. Ed. Andrzej Sakson. Poznań: Instytut Zachodni, 1996. 131–154.

Schütze, Fritz and Gerhardt Riemanan. "'Trajectory' as basic theoretical concept for analyzing suffering and disorderly social processes". *Social Organization and Social Process. Essays in Honour of Anselm Strauss*. Ed. David R. Maines. Berlin/New York: De Gruyter, 1991. 333–358.

Ther, Philipp. "Integration of Expellees in Germany and Poland after World War II: A Historical Reassessment". *Slavic Review* 55 (1996): 779–805.

Tomczak, Maria. "Obraz osadników w prasie i publicystyce polskiej". *Ziemie Odzyskane 1945–2005. 60 lat w granicach państwa polskiego*. Ed. Andrzej Sakson. Poznań: Instytut Zachodni, 2006. 45–58.

Welzer, Harald. "Materiał, z którego zbudowane są biografie". Transl. Magdalena Saryusz-Wolska. *Pamięć zbiorowa i kulturowa. Współczesna perspektywa niemiecka*. Ed. Magdalena Saryusz-Wolska. Warszawa: Universitas, 2009. 39–58.

Welzer, Harald, Sabine Moller and Karoline Tschuggnall. "Dziadek nie był nazistą". Narodowy socjalizm i Holokaust w pamięci rodzinnej'. Transl. Paweł Masłowski. *Pamięć zbiorowa i kulturowa. Współczesna perspektywa niemiecka*. Ed. Magdalena Saryusz-Wolska. Warszawa: Universitas, 2009. 351–410.

Zaremba, Macin. *Wielka Trwoga. Polska 1944–1947. Ludowa reakcja na kryzys*. Kraków: Wydawnictwo Znak, Institute of Political Studies PAN, 2012.

Inge Melchior
Forming a Common European Memory of WWII from a Peripheral Perspective: Anthropological Insight into the Struggle for Recognition of Estonians' WWII Memories in Europe

Meelis, a medical doctor born in Estonia in 1922, shows me a small, black box. When he opens it, I see a piece of dry mud. "I had the possibility to go to the place where my parents were killed. [...] I brought some mud from that place [...], and here is the mud. [...] This is one of the relics with which I live." The mud is all Meelis has left in memory of his mother. Both his parents were killed in 1942 by agents of the NKVD, the secret police of the Soviet Union, responsible for much of the political repression under the rule of Stalin. After probing my stance towards World War II (WWII), Meelis reveals that the particular NKVD agent who killed his mother was a Jew. It is obvious that he does not feel completely comfortable telling this story to a Western European:

> Meelis: I don't know whether you want to hear this, or whether you are not allowed to listen to this at all, but among those who committed crimes against humanity were also Jews.
> I: Yes this is very...
> Meelis: But we don't speak about it!
> I: ... this is a very difficult topic, but...
> Meelis: This is a very difficult topic, but I think, that you don't dare to... I am afraid, that you don't dare to listen to what I am telling you.
> I: No, I...
> Meelis: Because then they can immediately accuse us of anti-Semitism.
> I: Yes some people do that.
> Meelis: Yes some people, but in the world is such general sentiment. In Estonia one is caught in this question, but this is considered undesirable. Thus, for you I am now an undesirable person, a suspicious type, about whom you should inform the Estonian defence police.

Meelis has formed a clear conceptualization of how Western Europeans remember WWII: for "them", the Holocaust is politically a very sensitive question, which one is not allowed to speak about in ways that mention Jews as *perpetrators* of crimes against humanity. In Estonia, Meelis implies, people's experiences are different from those of Western Europeans since many Estonians suffered from Soviet, rather than Nazi repression. However, Estonians lack the sort of clear-cut and incontestable interpretation of WWII that has been formulated in Western Europe.

Until the late 1980s, historiographies of WWII were mainly national undertakings; every nation-state singled out its own victims and heroes.[1] This began to change in the 1990s. The Soviet Union fell and the European Union (EU) changed from an economic union into a more political one. The Balkan war awakened horrific memories of WWII, and brought these memories back to the European stage. Moreover, an EU decision on restitution of Holocaust era assets was pending at that time, which too raised new debates. In this *trans*national context, the meaning of the Holocaust changed from being merely a question of Jews and Germans to being a question of humanity: it became a universal symbol of human rights violations.[2] These discussions have resulted in a European institutionalization of WWII memories: common commemoration days and even common accounts in history textbooks.[3]

This aim of institutionalizing a common evaluation of Europe's past has not come without problems. In 2004, several post-Communist countries – such as Estonia – entered the European Union, where people have other historical experiences: most of them suffered not just from Nazi regimes but also from Communist regimes. This led for example to a political clash of memories in 2005, when European countries commonly celebrated 60 years after the end of WWII.[4] The Baltic presidents argued that for them WWII did not end in 1945, but only in 1991 with the fall of the Soviet Union. The Estonian and Lithuanian presidents decided not to attend the commemoration. This lack of a mutual understanding of WWII memories in Europe was all the more sensitive for the Baltic people because the commemoration was held in Moscow: Western Europe and Russia were collectively commemorating WWII in a ceremony from which the Baltic States felt excluded.

---

[1] Tony Judt. "The past in another country: myth and memory in post-war Europe." *Memory and power in post-war Europe.* Ed. Jan-Werner Müller. Cambridge: University Press, 2002, 157–183.
[2] Bernhard Giesen. *Triumph and trauma.* London: Paradigm Publishers, 2004, 48–54; Daniel Levy and Natan Sznaider. "Memory Unbound: The Holocaust and the Formation of Cosmopolitan Memory." *European Journal of Social Theory* 5.1 (2002).
[3] Konrad Jarausch and Thomas Lindenberger. "Contours of a critical history of contemporary Europe: a transnational agenda." *Conflicted memories: Europeanizing contemporary history.* Eds. Konrad Jarausch and Thomas Linderberger. New York / Oxford: Berghahn Books, 2007.
[4] Maria Mälksoo. "The Memory Politics of Becoming European: The East European Subalterns and the Collective Memory of Europe." *European Journal of International Relations* 15.4 (2009). See also: Eva-Clarita Onken. "The Baltic States and Moscow's 9 May Commemoration: Analysing Memory Politics in Europe." *Europe-Asia Studies* 59.1 (2007).

International Relations' scholar Maria Mälksoo has argued that this decision of the Baltic presidents to voice their conflicting perspective on WWII memories is part of the politics of becoming European.[5] She argues that the Baltic States, as new EU members, do not feel 'fully European', and their different WWII memories also prevent them from becoming so. The decision not to attend the 9 May 2005 commemoration is therefore both a search for recognition of their different WWII memories and a way to resist the hegemonic 'European WWII memory'. In other words, although the decision reflected a spirit of independence, it actually expresses feelings of insecurity. The central question of this chapter goes beyond these memory politics. It concerns how *ordinary* Estonians perceive these transnational encounters between different 'mnemonic communities'.[6] What are the emotions of ordinary Estonians as regards European memory disputes? An understanding of European WWII memories in Estonians' everyday lives can provide new insight in these types of insecurities, which often come with life in a globalizing world.

Since the fall of the Soviet Union in 1991, Estonia has increasingly become part of this globalizing world due to the opening of borders, new communication technologies and the increased mobility of people, things and ideas. This process also includes growing intercultural dialogue, which, as several social scientists have argued, has often gone hand in hand with the growth of insecurity. According to Anthony Giddens, people who live in a 'post-traditional society' can no longer take their own traditions and histories for granted, but have to defend them vis-à-vis the alternatives.[7] In a similar vein, Zygmunt Bauman has argued that the increasing encounters between people with different frames of reference have brought about more ambivalent and volatile identities, values and social structures, which come at the expense of a sense of security.[8] In traditional societies, people "tended to belong to a community by default. Nobody challenged their group membership [...]".[9] Therefore, people just knew which/whose cultural 'rules' to adhere to.

---

[5] Mälksoo. *The Memory Politics of Becoming European.*
[6] Eviatar Zerubavel. "Social Memories: Steps to a Sociology of the Past." *Qualitative Sociology* 19.3 (1996): 289.
[7] Anthony Giddens. *Modernity and self-identity.* Cambridge: Polity, 1991. As a sidenote, those alternatives have of course always existed but were not that visible previously.
[8] Zygmunt Bauman. *Liquid modernity.* Cambridge: Polity, 2000.
[9] Thomas Hylland Eriksen. "Human security and Social Anthropology." *A World of Insecurity: Anthropological Perspectives on Human Security.* Eds.Thomas Hylland Eriksen, Ellen Bal and Oscar Salemink. London/New York: Pluto Press, 2010, 8.

Such insecurity could be seen in the intercultural encounter between Meelis and me, where the 'rules' were not that obvious. In telling me his story, Meelis was very cautious and insecure. Should he tell me the story about his murdered mother according to the 'Estonian rules' or according to what he sees as my 'Western European' frame of reference? Not choosing the 'right rules' might result in misunderstanding on my side (for example silencing him by calling him an anti-Semite), which would be extremely painful for him. The interesting question is why Meelis invoked WWII as a topic of discussion in the first place; he ignored my questions and took the lead to start a dialogue on WWII. The insecurities invoked in ordinary Estonians by contemporary European WWII memory disputes and WWII analogies (Nazism versus Communism, Jewish victimhood versus Estonian victimhood, etc.) will be the focus of this chapter. Its (relatively) recent accession to the EU and the contested WWII memories in Estonia make Estonia the perfect lens through which to explore this issue.

Methodological reflection

In order to understand everyday encounters with 'European WWII memory' from the Estonians' point of view, I conducted in total two years of in-depth ethnographic field research (four brief periods and one long period between August 2007 and August 2012). From April 2010 to April 2011, I lived in Tartu (100,000 inhabitants), a cultural and university city of Estonia, where I attended commemorations, participated in cultural events, went folk dancing twice a week, and visited people in their homes. Most data have been collected within informal networks that developed from these events and that grew more extensive throughout my fieldwork. I have both conducted interviews (with an interview guide and recorder) and participated in more spontaneous informal conversations (where I made notes and transcribed them afterwards).[10] It might go without saying that the ethnographic data I gathered is not representative for the whole Estonian population, not in the least because I only focused on Estonian speakers and left the Russian speaking population – about 25% of the total population – out of my research. However, I did participate in the activities of a *wide range* of informal social networks in Estonian society: 'memory activists', 'young intellectuals' and people from the countryside.

---

10 All data was gathered in the Estonian language. The quotes in this article have been translated by the author.

Meelis belongs to the group 'memory activists': active citizens who contribute to the production of memory.[11] I met these informants mainly through commemorations, which many of them attend and/or organize. Tartu's memory activists, mainly male and between the ages of 40 and 95, can be characterized by their devotion to contribute to historical justice and contemporary society. Some of them had been political prisoners of the Soviet regime. Others were active participants in the anti-Soviet resistance in the 1980s. Others only joined the 'group' after 1991, convinced of the importance of remembrance and of the development of Estonians' knowledge about their history as a small and young nation-state. Although these memory activists have a fairly extreme view of society, in general their convictions are shared by a large part of society since they are rooted in the Singing Revolution of the late 1980s and early 1990s. Their active contribution to the regaining of state independence in 1991 is also why their claims are taken rather seriously by political officials and their narratives are generally not contested in the media; for instance, their request to institutionalize a 'Freedom Fighters' commemoration day, or to officially recognize the Estonian men who fought in WWII in the German army. A slightly related group with which I spent much time consists of the 'victims of history': Estonians who were repressed (mostly deported to Siberia) during the Soviet period and who have organized themselves into a group they call 'Memento'.[12] Compared to the memory activists, those in this group see the importance of remembering as more personal (in terms of a mourning process) and less political.

Through my contacts in Tartu University, I have also participated in and observed an informal network of more highly educated, mainly young Estonians: young intellectuals. Most of them grew up in a city (Tallinn or Tartu) during the period of the 'Singing Revolution': the anti-Soviet demonstrations in the late 1980s and the rebuilding of the Estonian nation-state in the 1990s. Their education makes them critical citizens, aware of the power of memory politics and nationalism. At the same time, their upbringing in a nation-state in the making creates a sense of patriotic duty, which comes with the notion that independence is not something to take for granted. I met a particular part of this group through my participation in Estonian folkdance classes. In that context I collected my data mostly through observation and participation, rather than conversations.

---

11 I borrowed this concept from: James W. Booth. "Kashmir Road: Some Reflections on Memory and Violence." *Millennium – Journal of International Studies* 38.2 (2009).
12 Website of the organization of repressed: http://www.memento.ee/.

Another group that can be distinguished among my informants is people from the countryside. The memories of the Soviet period (and with them of WWII) I have encountered in the south-Estonian village are completely different from those of my informants in Tallinn or Tartu. In these cities, the concept of 'rupture' is very prevalent the discourse about the Soviet period (thus the 'naturalness' of the Estonian period and the 'unnaturalness' of the Soviet period are emphasized).[13] In the countryside, on the other hand, stories express nostalgia about the Soviet period, and thus criticize contemporary Estonian society.[14] In order to understand these stories as well, I lived for two months in the countryside (May–June 2011). Because my countryside informants felt less represented in the 'Estonian memory discourse', they had a certain distance towards Estonian memories of WWII – and with that the possibility for a more critical (or even opposing) stance.

Of course it is possible to distinguish even more subgroups among my informants, and obviously, the groups distinguished here are not homogenous either. The distinction here is only made to serve as a way to give insight into the variety of stories that I have included in my analyses. This variety is not only important for methodological but also for theoretical reasons. My focus is not solely on Estonians who have a particular historical experience – in other words, who have lived through a particular historical period. Thus, when I speak of 'memories' in this chapter, I refer not only to 'autobiographical memory' or 'individual memory',[15] but also to 'post-memory' or 'vicarious memory'.[16] The latter two be-

---

[13] For an extensive elaboration on the 'rupture' discourse in Estonia, see: Ene Kõresaar. *Memory and History in Estonian Post-Soviet Life Stories*. Tartu, Estonia: Tartu University, 2004. (PhD thesis)

[14] A comparable argument is made based on the case of Lithuania investigated by anthropologist Neringa Klumbyte. "Memory, Identity, and Citizenship in Lithuania." *Journal of Baltic Studies* 41.3 (2010).

[15] Different terms are used to distinguish between the memories that individuals have and the memory that is passed on within communities. For example, French sociologist Maurice Halbwachs distinguishes between 'autobiographical memory' –the memory of events during one's own lifetime – and 'historical memory' – the memory of an event that happened before one's lifespan and which is passed on through historical records: Jeffrey K Olick. "Collective Memory: The Two Cultures." *Sociological Theory* 17. 3 (1999): 335. What Halbwachs means by 'autobiographical memory' is similar to what Aleida Assmann means by 'individual memory': Aleida Assmann. "Four Formats of Memory: From Individual to Collective Constructions of the Past." *Cultural History and Literary Imagination*. Eds. Christian Emden and David Midgley. Oxford: Peter Lang, 2002.

[16] 'Post-memory' is a concept introduced by Marianne Hirsch in "The Generation of Postmemory." *Poetics Today* 29.1 (2008): 103 – 128. 'Vicarious memory' refers to a rather similar phenomenon, a term used by Jacob J Climo. "Memories of the American Jewish Aliyah: Connecting the

long to the category of 'collective memory' and entail specifically the memory of people who did not live through a particular historical event, but who identify closely with those who did. As members of the same 'mnemonic community', they have been socialized through family memories, political memories and/or cultural memories.[17] Members of a mnemonic community not only share a history, they also share what Jan Assmann calls 'mnemohistory'; that is, they are not "concerned with the past as such, but only with the past as it is remembered".[18] Applying this understanding of memory, not only do my old informants have memories of WWII, but those in their twenties do as well.

This focus on memory beyond the political and autobiographical levels requires in-depth anthropological fieldwork; it is not sufficient to study media representation and memory politics, and to read biographies of or do interviews with cultural/political figures and 'survivors'. In this study it was thus important to form a diverse social network and invest in forming long-term relationships of trust. The beginning of my fieldwork showed that it is difficult to get beyond the 'official' history discourse during a first interaction. Especially since I am a Western European researcher, people felt the need to explain first – or sometimes even defend –why *Estonians* remember WWII differently from Western Europeans. Building trust thus proved essential for moving beyond that official representation; first I had to prove that I was not judgmental towards Estonian historiography. Ethnographic data is obviously gathered in 'dialogue'; reflection on this dialogue has given me direct insight into the fears and insecurities that come to the fore in an intercultural dialogue, where one party perceives the other to have different memories. The ethnographic method has also allowed me to follow the stories of my informants, rather than my own assumptions. Especially in the context of a chapter like this, which deals with contested collective memories and memories ascribed to certain groups, anthropological fieldwork makes it possible to go beyond only comparing and contrasting 'European memory' with 'Estonian memory', and to consider different perceptions and emotions *within* mnemonic communities as well.

In order to be able to place the perceptions and emotions of my informants in the broader context of society, I also make use of survey data from the survey 'I, the world and the media' (*Mina, Maailm ja Meedia*). These data were gathered

---

Individual and Collective Experience." *Social Memory and History: Anthropological Perspectives*. Eds. Jacob J Climo and Maria G Cattell. Oxford: Altamira Press, 2002, 118.
17 Zerubavel. *Social Memories*; Assmann. *Four formats of memory*.
18 Jan Assmann. "From 'Moses the Egyptian: The Memory of Egypt in Western Monotheism' and 'Collective Memory and Cultural Identity'." *The Collective Memory Reader*. Eds. Jeffrey K Olick, Vered Vinitzky-Seroussi and Daniel Levy. Oxford: University Press, 2011, 209.

by the department of Journalism and Communication of Tartu University from among a representative sample of the Estonian population (N = 1583, N of ethnic Estonians = 1076). The survey was conducted in 2003, 2005, 2008 and 2011. In this chapter I use the most recent data (the same questions were also posed in 2005). The quantitative data provided a means of contextualizing the in-depth and personal (ethnographically gathered) stories about WWII in contemporary everyday life.

Estonia's (contested) WWII history

The beginning of the Estonian history of WWII goes back to 23 August 1939, when Stalin and Hitler signed the Molotov-Ribbentrop Pact and divided Europe into two spheres of influence. Estonia was allocated to the Soviet Union. After Hitler's attack on Poland, the Soviet Union began the establishment of military bases and the stationing of Soviet troops in the three Baltic States. Estonia was *de facto* incorporated into the Soviet Union on the 17 June 1940, the same day that France surrendered to Germany. The Soviet Union took over all political decision making.[19] Those who were seen as a danger to the new regime were arrested, deported, imprisoned or even shot. In this first Soviet occupation, Estonia lost 94,000 people, of which 40,000 had fled the country and 54,000 were mobilized, executed or deported.[20]

In the summer of 1941, the front moved into Soviet Russia, and Estonia fell under German rule. This time, Jews and Communists had to fear for their lives. Since only 1200 Jews had remained in Estonia by the beginning of the war, the territory was already declared *Judenfrei* in January 1942. During the German occupation, which lasted until 1944, Estonia lost 7798 of its citizens by execution or perishing in prison camps: 70% of them Estonians, 15% Russians and 12% Jews.[21] An additional 100,000 Estonians fled to the West at the end of the German occupation when the Soviet army again approached Estonian territory.[22] When the German army surrendered in 1944, Estonia was *re*incorporated into

---

[19] Jaak Kangilaski, Virve Kask, Kalev Kukk, Jaan Laas, Heino Noor, Aigi Rahi-Tamm, Rein Ratas, Anto Raukas, Enn Sarv and Peep Varju. "The white book: losses inflicted on the Estonian nation by occupation regimes 1940–1991." Ed. Riigikogu Estonian State Commission on Examination of the Policies of Repression, the Government of the Republic of Estonia and Ministry of Justice. Republic of Estonia: Estonian Encyclopaedia Publishers, 2005, 10–12.
[20] Toivo U Raun. *Estonia and the Estonians*, Stanford: Hoover Press, 2001, 154.
[21] Kangilaski. *The white book*, 29.
[22] Raun. *Estonia and the Estonians*, 166.

the Soviet Union. This time the Soviet occupation would last until 1991. Being a strategically located and small population, Estonia suffered many losses in WWII. In total, Estonia lost 23.9 percent of its pre-war population (271,200 out of 1,136,400), of which almost one third (about 81,000 Estonians) died – including victims of the Soviet deportations and genocides and of the German deportations and the Holocaust.[23]

Two subjects in Estonian WWII historiography are controversial in the current European context: (1) the interpretation of the Estonian men who joined the German army as freedom fighters, (2) the absence of a Holocaust memory. To understand contemporary historiography, it is important to take a closer look at how these two themes were interpreted in the official history that was promoted during the Soviet period. In Soviet historiography, the Soviet victory in the defeat over Nazism was very central. The Soviet soldier was the hero of WWII and the liberator of Europe, and fascism was the undisputed evil.[24] The German soldier was thus the henchman of evil. Hence, the Estonian men who had joined the German army were said to been brainwashed by the Germans: they were fighting against their 'own' (Soviet) army. They were portrayed as criminals and a threat to the Estonian Soviet Socialist Republic (ESSR) that was finally restored and they had therefore to be removed from society. Many of them were imprisoned in Siberia. The question of the Holocaust was not discussed in Soviet historiography.[25] The Soviet citizens were said to have suffered the most of all people in WWII, and therefore, the number of Soviet Jews killed was hidden in the total number of Soviet losses. Fascism was portrayed as the ultimate enemy of Communism, not of the Jewish population.

After Estonia regained its independence in 1991, history was drastically rewritten, with the idea – as new Prime Minister Mart Laar put it – 'to give the people back their history'.[26] It was a complete mirror version of the Soviet history, and based – especially in the beginning – on very personal stories. These personal accounts were believed to contain the historical truth that had managed to

---

23 Kangilaski. *The white book*.
24 Siobhan Kattago. "Agreeing to disagree on the legacies of recent history: memory, pluralism and Europe after 1989." *European Journal of Social Theory* 12 (2009). See more on the interpretation of WWII in Russia: Amir Weiner. "The Making of a Dominant Myth: The Second World War and the Construction of Political Identities within the Soviet Polity." *Russian Review* 55.4 (1996).
25 Karel C. Berkhoff. *Motherland in Danger: Soviet Propaganda During World War II*. Harvard: Harvard University Press, 2012.
26 Mart Laar. "When will Russia say 'sorry'?" *The Wall Street Journal*. Tallinn, 2004. Quoted in: Ene Kõresaar, ed. *World War II and Its Aftermath in Estonian Post-Soviet Life Stories*. Amsterdam/ New York: Rodopi, 2011, 3.

stay unpolluted from the Soviet lies. For these reasons, Estonia's new history was an emotional, nationalistic story about suffering during the Soviet period. WWII was not seen as a separate period in itself, but rather as the beginning of the Soviet occupation. The war years only began to be questioned at the end of the 1990s, when negotiations about EU accession started. The EU and NATO voiced their concerns about Estonia's policies toward the Russian minority and about Estonian historiography: the history of the Russian Estonians had to be (more) included, WWII and the Soviet period needed to be disentangled, Estonian collaboration and Jewish victimhood had to be investigated.[27]

From a Western European perspective on WWII – which by the end of the 1990s had shifted from a focus on the *guilt* of the perpetrators to the *collective responsibility* of people to prevent injustice from repeating itself[28] – the Estonian way of dealing with the past was criticized as lacking in self-reflection. From a historical perspective, though, it is not so surprising that Estonian veterans have been thanked by Estonian officials for their struggle for independence while in German uniforms. Nor is it surprising that the Holocaust is lacking from Estonians' 'collective memory'. With regards to the former, these men had been requested in 1944 by former Estonian Prime Minister Jüri Uluots to join the German army to defend their home country against the approaching Red Army and not to fight for the Nazi ideology. As relates to the latter, Jews were a very small ethnic minority in Estonia, their WWII story was absent from the official Soviet historiography, and in the stories that circulated in close circles of trust, the focus was on the suffering during the Soviet rather than the German occupation.[29] Despite these historic reasons, the question remains whether European societies generally should be able to acknowledge the suffering of other people than one's own in the name of liberal and democratic values, as was decided at the Stockholm Conference in 2000.[30]

---

[27] Doyle E. Stevick. "The Politics of the Holocaust in Estonia: Historical Memory and Social Divisions in Estonian Education." *Reimagining Civic Education: How Diverse Societies Form Democratic Citizens.* Eds. E. D. Stevick and B. A. U. Levinson. Lanham. Maryland: Rowman & Littlefield Publishers, 2007.
[28] Bernhard Giesen. *Triumph and trauma*, 141–153.
[29] Stevick. *The politics of the holocaust in Estonia.*
[30] See for more information on the discussion of the Stockholm Conference: Levy and Sznaider. *Memory unbound.*

The perceived superiority of the Western European memories of WWII

At the Stockholm Conference in 2000, representatives of 46 nations came together to discuss education, remembrance and research on the Holocaust: to make "the commemoration of the Holocaust a foundation myth of the European Union".[31] Scholars have argued that in practice though, rather than having *a* European memory, Europe is divided into different 'mnemonic communities': 'Western Europe' and 'Eastern Europe', 'Central Europe' and 'Russia'.[32] Although these categories are simplifications that do not exist in reality (in other words, Ideal types), they *may* exist in people's perceptions.[33] In the stories of my informants, both a 'Western European' and an 'Estonian' memory of WWII *do* exist, as social constructs that are "real in their consequences".

From my very first encounter with Estonian society, it was clear that Western Europeans are perceived as having different memories. First of all, Western Europeans are perceived as having no negative memories of Communism at all. For that reason, secondly, Western Europeans are seen to consider Hitler to be the cruelest dictator ever, not comparable to any other, not even to Stalin. This form of memory means that for Europe Germany was the main enemy in WWII, not Soviet Russia. Thirdly, the Jews are considered, according to my informants, *the* victims of the twentieth century in Western Europe, which leaves no room for the memory of other people who also suffered tremendously. Fourthly, Europe was considered to be liberated in 1945 when Nazi Germany was defeated. These are just four elements that return in the stories of literally all my informants as constituting understandings of WWII in Western Europe that are different from their own: this is what *they* (other Europeans) remember, but not what *we* (Estonians and other Baltic people) remember.

The Estonian 'memory activists' with whom I hung out a great deal, not only perceive Western Europeans as remembering differently *in content*, but also as *treating* the past differently. Firstly, people in Western Europe are perceived as being very politically correct, at the expense of the truth. The story of Meelis illustrates this with regard to the Holocaust: "Among those NKVD and KGB people

---

31 Malgorzata Pakier and Bo Strath. Eds. *A European Memory? Contested Histories and Politics of Remembrance*. New York/Oxford: Berghahn Books, 2010, 12.
32 Pakier and Strath. *A European Memory?*
33 See for Thomas' famous words on this: W. I. Thomas. "The definition of the situation." *Sociological Theory: A Book of Readings*. Eds. Lewis A. Coser and Bernard Rosenberg. New York: The MacMillan Company, 1970.

who actually committed crimes against humanity, mass murders, shootings, arrests, deportations, who sent people to camps, to death camps, many were Jews. But we are not allowed to stress this." In this context, Meelis and several other memory activists argue, political correctness precludes justice, since the perpetuators cannot be punished. Western European political correctness is thus perceived as sustaining and creating injustice, and this also holds for those Western European soldiers who are not commemorated because they died in Nazi uniforms: "In the West they do not dare to speak about their own history",[34] said one of the speakers on the annual commemoration of the Estonian men who fell on the eastern front in German uniforms.

Secondly, Western Europe is perceived as having a more individualistic than collectivistic approach towards history. There, "nationalism is a bad thing", Lembitu (memory activist, born 1943) explained, and Andres (memory activist, born 1941) added: for them "where they come from (their roots) becomes less important", because they are too involved in making money. The young intellectuals in my research are generally less critical about the political correctness and individualistic approach in Western Europe – as they understand it as part of the democratic value system they support – but they do agree with the memory activists that Western Europeans should make a greater effort to understand the specific historical situation of Estonia and its current status as a young and small nation-state.

In other words, European memories of WWII are perceived as based on 'historical memory' and a 'settled past', which has its strength in its openness towards individual interpretation and discussion, while at the same time taking a clear, incontestable moral stance. This stands in clear contrast with Estonian WWII memories, which are much more based on still unsettled, highly dynamic and diverse 'communicative memories'. This Western European memory of WWII and the way of dealing with the past are seen as hegemonic, as '*the* European' understanding of the past. 'European WWII memory' is not the sum of national memories, nor is it a 'new' memory; it is rather seen as the memory of the core member states imposed upon the 'extended European family' (the periphery). Before I can discuss how this difference in perceptions engenders feelings of insecurity among my Estonian informants, I first explore the perceived ambiguity and inferiority of Estonian memories of WWII.

---

34 Speech of a representative of the Estonian Legion Friends' Club at the Sinimäed commemoration, 31 July 2010.

The perceived ambiguity and inferiority of Estonian memories of WWII

Estonian collective stories of WWII are of course much closer to the emotional and family life of Estonians than are the collective WWII memories of Western Europeans. It is in the Estonian mnemohistory that the family memories of suffering during the Soviet era find meaning, and that relatives who fought in a German uniform are not accused of being fascists. At the same time, it is because this mnemohistory is much closer and people have more informal knowledge of local experiences, that Estonian memories are perceived as much more ambiguous, scattered and contradictory.

Firstly, in terms of historical experiences, the Estonian population was divided by the different relations with the forces fighting in WWII. Estonians as a people cannot be featured as having been on either 'the German side' or 'the Soviet side'. More than one in four ethnic Estonians (27.1%) reports having had an acquaintance or relative in the German army. One in three Estonians personally knows someone who was in the Soviet army (34.3%).[35] One in six Estonians (15.9%) had a loved-one fighting in both uniforms and having been torn apart by WWII's main sides.[36]

My Estonian language teacher Tiina (born 1970) once explained to me that: "My father was first in the German army, then in the Soviet one. This is completely normal for an Estonian man." Moreover, many families faced the fact that some relatives were fighting in or suffered by wearing the one uniform and others in/by the other. As is the case in the family history of former Prime Minister of Estonia Mart Laar, born 1960:

---

35 Since my ethnographic material concerns only ethnic Estonians, the data I have presented here are only valid for those who have identified themselves as 'Estonians' (N = 1076). In order to give the reader more context, I have analyzes as well of the total Estonian population (including Russian speakers, N= 1583)): 19.5% of the respondents knew someone who had fought in the German army (lower than the average among Estonian speakers) and 47.6% knew someone who had participated in the Soviet army (higher than the average among Estonian speakers).

36 It is important to note here that these figures do not present historical facts; not necessarily one in every four Estonians was in the German army. These figures say something about the present: they point towards memory rather than history. My point of departure here is that it does not matter to people's 'post-memory' whether someone in his/her family was *factually* in the German or Soviet army. What matters is whether they *believe* this to have been the case or not.

> [M]y grandfather was shot by the Nazis. Two of my great-uncles were sent to Siberian death camps by the Soviets. My father-in-law was deported to Siberia as a nine-year-old boy, where he struggled to survive against death by starvation. Unknown to him, his hopes of seeing his father alive again were in vain; his father was shot early in 1941 by the KGB in Moscow's Kirov prison for the crime of being an ordinary policeman in independent Estonia.[37]

Clearly, it is not possible to characterize Estonians as a people – and as a mnemonic community – as having been on or suffered by either the one or the other side.

Secondly, these kinds of family stories reveal contradictions in the Estonian narrative of WWII in terms of content. On the one hand, they imply that ordinary Estonians were forced by the regime in power – as *innocent victims* – to be on either one side or the other; in other words, it was not an *ideological* choice. On the other hand, it is commonly understood that the Estonian men in the German army *fought for the right cause* as 'freedom fighters'. These seeming contradictions exist in one and the same story. Sirje (a young intellectual, born 1982) explained to me back in 2008:

> Estonians were mobilized, forced to join the German army as they were forced to join the Soviet army. Of course, there were people who volunteered. But – as Estonians joined the German army – they were fighting for the liberty of their homeland – Estonia – not for the ideals of Nazi-Germany.

One of the ambiguities in the Estonian narrative of WWII thus lies in the crucial question: did Estonians *passively* endure the war or did they *actively* defend their home country? According to the survey data, 50.3% of ethnic Estonians agree with the first statement, 37.9% find it hard to say, and 11.7% agree with the second statement.[38] On the political level, these contradictory narratives coexist as

---

37 Laar. *When will Russia say 'sorry'?*
38 Respondents were asked whether they agreed more with statement A or statement B: A) Estonians who either fought on the German or Russian side should be treated equally as having been forced by the occupant. (meaning Estonians passively endured WWII).
B) Estonians who fought on the German side fought for independence, those on the Russian side for the reestablishment of Soviet occupation. (meaning Estonians had an active role in WWII and fought for ideological reasons). People could answer: (1) I agree completely with A, (2) I agree more with A, (3) difficult to say, (4) I agree more with B, (5) I agree completely with B. Again, for the sake of the argument on ethnic Estonians I have left the Russian speakers out of the analysis. For the total population (N = 1583) the figures are as follows: 42.6% agrees more with A, 46.3% thinks that is hard to say (most favourable category for the Russian speakers

well and the question still lacks a clear answer. Despite these different historical interpretations, I should stress here though that my informants' stories are united in the belief that none of the Estonian men in the German army were fighting for the *wrong* cause.

Another paradox in the Estonian narrative in terms of content comes forward in the stories about which occupation was worse. To continue the story of Sirje, she argued: "Estonians had suffered a lot from the crimes committed by Red Army. For us, the deeds and the crimes of the Nazis and the Communists are BOTH "bad". But "Western Europe" isn't very eager to comprehend it."[39] [sic]

Sirje, among other informants, stresses that both occupations and dictators (Hitler and Stalin) were equally bad. At the same time, these same stories narrate that the German occupation was much less terrible. For instance, it is a common story that the German soldiers knocked on the door, asked for honey and bread, and gave something in return. They were polite, in contrast to the Russians, who rushed into the house, and just took what they wanted. Tiina, whose father had been both in the German and Soviet army, explained: "During my life I have always been told that the German period was not as bad as the Russian one. '42 and '43 were better than '44 and '45."

Thirdly, the way of dealing with WWII in Estonia is perceived as inconsistent and at times too timid, especially by memory activists. The Estonian state takes contradictory stances. On the one hand the Estonian men who served in the German army are thanked for their fight for their home country. On the other hand they are denied official acknowledgement as freedom fighters. Annika (born 1960), one of the memory activists, explains that state representatives were always present at the Sinimäed commemoration to honor the Estonian men who had lost their lives in WWII in German uniforms. After EU accession, Estonian officials suddenly did not dare to show up anymore. These memory activists would rather see the Estonian state straighten its back: defend the 'historic truth' against the Western European political correctness.

The young intellectuals in my research see the situation from a bit more nuanced perspective. On the one hand, they agree that it is a duty of Estonians to commemorate one's own victims and evaluate the Estonian soldiers in German uniforms from within their own historical circumstances. On the other hand, they acknowledge the importance of adjusting to the democratic values prevalent in Western Europe, meaning to pay tribute also to non-Estonian

---

to answer – the statements are clearly designed within the Estonian discourse and do not fit closely with the Russian mnemohistory), and 11.1% agrees more with B.
39 Personal email correspondence with Sirje in 2008.

WWII victims (such as Jews) and to take the sensitivity of the soldiers in German uniforms into account. Young intellectuals understand the difficult situation in which Estonian politicians find themselves, having to balance between the wishes and memories in Western Europe and in their own society.

My informants in the countryside, on the other hand, do not seem particularly concerned about the representation of Estonia's WWII history in Europe. They consider Europe to be far removed from their personal lives. In addition, they feel less national duty to present *one* 'Estonian (hi)story' to the outside world. As many of them do not see their personal experiences reflected, especially when it comes to the Soviet period, they generally feel some distance towards the 'national story'. Priit (born 1950) complains that Estonian politicians should rather take care of the representation of diverging historical experiences *within* Estonian society than within Europe.

After decades of political repression, in which an 'Estonian' WWII story was impossible, most of my informants (also those on the countryside) express the *need* for a nationally unifying rather than dividing memory of WWII. In practice, however, discussions on a common European memory of WWII provoke the heterogeneity of stances within Estonia.[40]

Emotions of insecurity

The perceived hegemony of a (Western) European memory and a sense of inferiority about the Estonian memory of WWII, challenges Estonians' feeling of group membership in the 'European family'. This situation has led to a sense of 'existential insecurity', often expressed in the stories of my informants in the form of two questions:[41] (1) Are we Estonians fully European? (2) How can we Estonians be European and also stay true to our Estonian traditions? This connection between the memory of WWII and European identity does not fall out of the clear blue sky. WWII was not a significant period in Estonian historiography in the early 1990s; all historical eras were subordinate to the traumatizing Soviet experience, which was number one of which one was trying to make sense.[42]

---

[40] Once more, I solely refer here to heterogeneity within the Estonian speaking part of the population, not paying attention to the Russian speakers at all. Other scholars such as Siobhan Kattago have focused on the ethnic differences when it comes to WWII memories. See Kattago. "Agreeing to disagree on the legacies of recent history."

[41] See Eriksen. *Human security and social anthropology*, 8, for more information on the relationships between globalization, identity and insecurity.

[42] Kõresaar. *World War II and Its Aftermath in Estonian Post-Soviet Life Stories.*

Only with negotiations for EU accession in the late 1990s, did WWII enter the public stage in Estonia.

It was in this same period that the Estonian people were 'returning to Europe' in their construction of a national identity, and away from Russia. For this reason, "West and East have been antipodes for Estonian-self-construction, reflecting the dichotomy of Europeanisation and Russification, goodies *versus* baddies".[43] Even those people I have spoken to who do not support Estonia's *political* integration into Europe, do not question that Estonia is *culturally* European (the antipode of 'Soviet'). This strong will to be European has led to a fear of not being acknowledged by other Europeans as 'fully' European; identification requires recognition by others.[44] The encounter with the (significantly different) experience and mnemohistory of WWII in Western Europe plays into this fear.

In this context, how can we understand the spontaneous invocation of WWII in informal conversations that I had with Estonians? The first time I encountered this was during fieldwork in 2007. The Bronze Soldier – a Soviet WWII memorial, of importance at that time to the Russian minority – had just been relocated from the city center to the outskirts. This led to violent riots in Tallinn and interethnic tensions grew in society generally. I wanted to understand what this relocation meant to ethnic Estonians. I have argued elsewhere that its meanings were closely related to feelings of uncertainty.[45] In several instances, I was answered by means of an analogy: what would you think if there were still statues of Hitler in The Netherlands? How would you feel if 30% of your population were Germans who had stayed after the war? In this analogy with WWII – comparing a Soviet soldier with Hitler, and the Russian minority with German occupiers – WWII serves as an interpretative 'anchor'. By invoking WWII, my informants could translate their feelings about the Communist period to my frame of reference of something similarly cruel (WWII). Moreover, to draw WWII analogies in such intercultural encounters created a dialogue, a first step away from insecurity by claiming a voice as Europeans.[46]

These emotions of insecurity about one's identity are very widespread in Estonia. Even young, more highly educated Estonians who have a relatively secure

---

[43] Eiki Berg. "Local resistance, national identity and global swings in Post-Soviet Estonia." *Europe-Asia studies* 54.1 (2002): 111.
[44] Jocelyn Maclure. "The politics of recognition at an impasse? Identity politics and democratic citizenship." *Canadian journal of political science* 36.1 (2003): 3–21.
[45] Inge Melchior and Oane Visser. "Voicing Past and Present Uncertainties: The Relocation of a Soviet World War II Memorial and the Politics of Memory in Estonia." *Focaal – Journal of Global and Historical Anthropology* 59 (2011).
[46] Maclure. *The politics of recognition at an impasse?*

position in society long for recognition within Europe. Katre (a young intellectual, born 1985) feels that Western Europeans have trouble understanding why the Soviet repression completely overshadows the cruelties of WWII for Estonians: "They do not know what it is not to have a state." This perceived misunderstanding is problematic in building a fruitful relationship between people:[47] If Western Europeans cannot understand our history, then how can we ever belong to the European family? This is not just because of having different historical experiences. Linda (a close relative of deportees, born in 1942) explains:

> Many [Western Europeans] do not know about the Soviet period and the deportations and about those politics. Many do not even know that Estonia exists. [...] If I am honest, I think they are not interested in what has happened here.

But there is more to this than a lack of knowledge and interest: will Estonians ever become equal partners of Western Europeans? This fear of having to adapt again to an 'other' whereas the 'other' is not prepared to adapt as well, was clearly apparent in one of my conversations with Kaie (born 1975), a history teacher living in Estonia's northern countryside. When I asked her about the idea of creating a common European history, she answered:

> I am curious whether that means that France is going to learn about Estonian history as well then. Did you learn anything in school about Estonian history? [..] It is just not fair. Why do we need to learn about France and England and The Netherlands, and no one is learning about us?

Again this raises the question: Do we really belong to Europe? In the case of Estonia – a small country with a strategic geopolitical location – this reveals not only insecurity about questions of belonging, but also about security as such. Can we trust Western Europeans in case of need? The 'return to Europe' in the 1990s was a way to secure Estonia's independence, to create allies in the West. The differences in WWII memories are however still in the way of complete trust. Not the least because the Russian mnemohistory coincides with the Western European one in the sense that fascism is seen by both as the biggest evil of WWII (Kattago 2009). With the relocation of the Bronze Soldier, not only Russian activists but also the Russian state drew upon this correspondence in mnemohistory, which excluded the Estonian point of view. During my fieldwork at that time, the fears were omnipresent: Will Western Europe support the decision of

---

47 See also Maclure. *The politics of recognition at an impasse?*

the Estonian state and with that, have respect for *our* historical experience? Linda expressed this view:

> At that time we were afraid that this turn would not stop, that Russians would take back power. This support [by the EU] showed that we are not alone. We were afraid that no one would care about us in Western Europe.

This fear reflected Estonia's historical experience of Western Europe not bothering to free the Baltic States from Soviet oppression at the end of WWII, which is still an open wound. The 'white boat' is an everyday expression that shows up from time to time in conversations of Estonians. It refers to an anticipated and expected salvation that might never come.

The second insecurity is closely related to the paradoxical question of how to belong to Europe without neglecting one's Estonian duties. This is exactly what happened in the conversation with Meelis: he felt he needed to adapt the story to my Western European frame of reference, and at the same time did not want to cause damage to the honor of his mother (and other compatriots whose story he felt he needed to put forward). To act upon one's local duties is considered very important in Estonia; it keeps the culture alive. According to Katre, this has to do with the realization that independence is not something that can be taken for granted: it has to be won again every day. The fear of extinction – being a people of only one million – is very real in Estonia. Peeter (born 1950), an Estonian chemistry professor, explained this feeling as follows:

> A small people are very much aware of the realistic situation that their culture can be destroyed in no time. We Estonians, all Estonians have this feeling. We just know from history that we can be overruled so easily. During the Soviet period so many small peoples died out. [...] [Our pride] is a defense mechanism. We realize how important it is for a small people to defend its culture, its values, its customs, its language, because this is what keeps us alive.

Andres agrees with Peeter and relates this to Estonians' relationship with Western Europeans:

> I think that European values start to gain ground [in Estonia] and that the individual is getting more important. But Estonia is small, so in order to protect and keep our culture, the community [*rahvas*] has to be at least as important as the individual.

These duties towards what is seen as 'real Estonian' – as *Estonian* experiences – are difficult to reconcile with the will to be European if the latter involves the need to respect a contradicting and 'foreign' mnemohistory of WWII. Ideally, therefore, Estonia would like to be a member of the European family *and* have its particular understanding of WWII recognized by the other members (which would allow them to 'keep' it). The feeling of misrecognition, which is central to the insecurity described above, "can inflict a grievous wound, saddling its victims with a crippling self-hatred. Due recognition is not just a courtesy we owe people. It is a vital human need".[48] Struggles for recognition are thus struggles over 'who we are', in order to enhance self-respect and dignity. They appropriate 'safe spaces' in which people can tell their life stories without being judged. In this reasoning, I argue that the invocations of WWII in many of my conversations with Estonians have been an attempt to create a dialogue. Through these dialogues, my interlocutors have appropriated a voice, which is a crucial step in the struggle for recognition. To be engaged in a dialogue is a way to get out of the position of passively enduring humiliation and thereby restore a bit of the lost self-respect.[49]

Concluding remarks on a common WWII memory from a peripheral perspective

The 'return to Europe' of Estonia has created insecurity in this tiny state in the north-eastern corner of Europe. Estonia had the image of being a 'western state' in the Soviet Union, but with the return to Europe it has become an eastern country on the periphery. The fear of not being acknowledged as 'fully European' and of not being equal partners in Europe has created an insecure feeling about Estonia's national identity. Since the historical experiences of WWII in Estonia are so different from those in Western Europe, debates about WWII evoke Estonians' fear of not belonging to the European family because of a lack of mutual understanding. In some other post-Communist countries such as Croatia, there actually is an anti-fascist discourse, which (ironically) makes WWII in those countries less of a significant marker of European belonging.

The story of Meelis is a clear example of an intercultural encounter where WWII is invoked to create a dialogue and to claim a voice for oneself. Meelis is in search of *inter*cultural recognition of the right to his family story: that his mother was an innocent victim and that he is allowed to blame the perpetrator, even though he was a Jew. A closer look at the everyday encounter with the idea

---

48 Charles Taylor. "The Politics of Recognition." *Multiculturalism: Examining the Politics of Recognition*. Ed. Amy Gutmann. Princeton: Princeton University Press, 1994, 25–26.
49 Axel Honneth. *The Struggle for Recognition: The Moral Grammar of Social Conflicts*. Cambridge: Polity Press, 1995, 164.

of a common European memory reveals that the invocation of WWII is not a conscious, rational decision; it is rather a response to emotions of insecurity and a way to make sense of one's contested personal stories.

Listening to such stories allows one to gain in-depth insight into emotions of insecurity and also helps one to better understand the WWII analogies invoked in Estonian politics. As in many other post-Communist countries, "the wheels of communicative memory are [still] turning" in Estonian society. Lacking a "coherent, condensed narrative of communism"[50] makes Estonian memory politics highly emotional.[51] In some cases, political decisions are based on the idea of increasing solidarity with the rest of Europe. But Baltic politicians increasingly dare to take a clear stance in which they defend their 'national memories', for instance in 2005, when the Estonian and Lithuanian president decided not to attend the 60th anniversary over the defeat of Nazism. At that time, they drew an analogy between the experience of Soviet repression in the Baltic States and the tragedies of WWII in the rest of Europe. Maria Mälksoo has argued on the basis of foreign policy speeches that "Polish and Baltic calls for equal remembrance of their pasts emerge as an essential part of their individuation process as European, of their becoming *a European subject.*"[52]

Analogies between Soviet terror and WWII terror create dialogue and dialogues are a first step in the direction of mutual understanding. Dialogue can lighten the burden of insecurity; an insecurity which life in a globalizing world inevitably brings along.

Acknowledgements

I would like to thank Prof. Pál Nyiri and Dr. Freek Colombijn (VU University Amsterdam) for their comments on an earlier draft of this chapter, and also Jeroen Moes (EUI, Florence) for proofreading this chapter. I am indebted as well to the participants of the conference '*Towards a Common Past? Conflicting Memories in*

---

50 Éva Kovács. "Communism and after: The cynical and the ironical – remembering Communism in Hungary." *Regio: Minorities, politics, society* 1 (2003): 156.

51 I thus disagree with Jarausch and Lindenberger, who describe the Baltic States as being "marked by anti-Russian consensus". See Jarausch and Lindenberger. "Contours of a critical history of contemporary Europe." Having a national history based on mostly communicative memories, makes the mnemohistory of the Baltic States by definition very diverse and dynamic. See for more on these dynamics Inge Melchior. *Guardians of Living History: the Persistence of the Past in Post-Soviet Estonia*. Doctoral dissertation, VU University Amsterdam, 2015.

52 Mälksoo. *The Memory Politics of Becoming European*, 655.

Contemporary Europe', held from 14–16 May 2012 in Lund, Sweden, for their comments on my paper and their own inspiring presentations. The same goes for the presenters at the conference *'Nation States between memories of World War II and contemporary European politics'*, held from 27–29 June 2012 in Nottingham, UK. For financial support of my fieldwork period, I am grateful to the Graduate School of Social Sciences VU University Amsterdam, and the Estonian Institute in Tallinn (Estophilus grant).

References

Assmann, Aleida. "Four Formats of Memory: From Individual to Collective Constructions of the Past." *Cultural History and Literary Imagination*. Eds. Christian Emden and David Midgley. Oxford: Peter Lang, 2002. 19–37.

Assmann, Jan. "From 'Moses the Egyptian: The Memory of Egypt in Western Monotheism' and 'Collective Memory and Cultural Identity'." *The Collective Memory Reader*. Eds. Jeffrey K Olick, Vered Vinitzky-Seroussi and Daniel Levy. Oxford: University Press, 2011. 209–215.

Bauman, Zygmunt. *Liquid modernity*. Cambridge: Polity, 2000.

Berg, Eiki. "Local resistance, national identity and global swings in Post-Soviet Estonia." *Europe-Asia studies* 54.1 (2002): 109–122.

Berkhoff, Karel C. *Motherland in Danger: Soviet Propaganda During World War II*. Harvard: Harvard University Press, 2012.

Booth, James W. "Kashmir Road: Some Reflections on Memory and Violence." *Millennium – Journal of International Studies* 38.2 (2009): 361–77.

Climo, Jacob J. "Memories of the American Jewish Aliyah: Connecting the Individual and Collective Experience." *Social Memory and History: Anthropological Perspectives*. Eds. Jacob J Climo and Maria G Cattell. Oxford: Altamira Press, 2002. 111–130.

Eriksen, Thomas Hylland. "Human security and Social Anthropology." *A World of Insecurity: Anthropological Perspectives on Human Security*. Eds.Thomas Hylland Eriksen, Ellen Bal and Oscar Salemink. London/New York: Pluto Press, 2010. 1–22.

Giddens, Anthony. *Modernity and self-identity*. Cambridge: Polity, 1991.

Giesen, Bernhard. *Triumph and trauma*. London: Paradigm Publishers, 2004.

Hirsch, Marianne. "The Generation of Postmemory." *Poetics Today* 29.1 (2008): 103–28.

Honneth, Axel. *The Struggle for Recognition: The Moral Grammar of Social Conflicts*. Cambridge: Polity Press, 1995.

Jarausch, Konrad and Thomas Lindenberger. "Contours of a critical history of contemporary Europe: a transnational agenda." *Conflicted memories: Europeanizing contemporary history*. Eds. Konrad Jarausch and Thomas Linderberger. New York/Oxford: Berghahn Books, 2007. 1–22.

Judt, Tony. "The past in another country: myth and memory in post-war Europe." *Memory and power in post-war Europe*. Ed. Jan-Werner Müller. Cambridge: University Press, 2002. 157–183.

Kangilaski, Jaak, Virve Kask, Kalev Kukk, Jaan Laas, Heino Noor, Aigi Rahi-Tamm, Rein Ratas, Anto Raukas, Enn Sarv, and Peep Varju. "The white book: losses inflicted on the Estonian nation by occupation regimes 1940–1991." Ed. Riigikogu Estonian State

Commission on Examination of the Policies of Repression, the Government of the Republic of Estonia and Ministery of Justice. Republic of Estonia: Estonian Encyclopaedia Publishers, 2005.

Kattago, Siobhan. "Agreeing to disagree on the legacies of recent history: memory, pluralism and Europe after 1989." *European Journal of Social Theory* 12 (2009): 375–395.

Kõresaar, Ene. *Memory and History in Estonian Post-Soviet Life Stories*. Tartu, Estonia: Tartu University, 2004. (PhD thesis)

Kõresaar, Ene, ed. *World War II and Its Aftermath in Estonian Post-Soviet Life Stories*. Amsterdam / New York: Rodopi, 2011.

Kovács, Éva. "Communism and after: The cynical and the ironical – remembering Communism in Hungary." *Regio: Minorities, politics, society* 1 (2003): 155–169.

Klumbyte, Neringa. "Memory, Identity, and Citizenship in Lithuania." *Journal of Baltic Studies* 41.3 (2010): 295–313.

Laar, Mart. "When will Russia say 'sorry'?." *The Wall Street Journal*. Tallinn, 2004.

Levy, Daniel, and Natan Sznaider. "Memory Unbound: The Holocaust and the Formation of Cosmopolitan Memory." *European Journal of Social Theory* 5.1 (2002): 87–106.

Maclure, Jocelyn. "The politics of recognition at an impasse? Identity politics and democratic citizenship." *Canadian journal of political science* 36.1 (2003): 3–21.

Mälksoo, Maria. "The Memory Politics of Becoming European: The East European Subalterns and the Collective Memory of Europe." *European Journal of International Relations* 15.4 (2009): 653–680.

Melchior, Inge. *Guardians of Living History: the Persistence of the Past in Post-Soviet Estonia*. Doctoral dissertation, VU University Amsterdam, 2015.

Melchior, Inge and Oane Visser. "Voicing Past and Present Uncertainties: The Relocation of a Soviet World War II Memorial and the Politics of Memory in Estonia." *Focaal – Journal of Global and Historical Anthropology* 59 (2011): 33–50.

Olick, Jeffrey K. "Collective Memory: The Two Cultures." *Sociological Theory* 17. 3 (1999): 333–348.

Onken, Eva-Clarita. "The Baltic States and Moscow's 9 May Commemoration: Analysing Memory Politics in Europe." *Europe-Asia Studies* 59.1 (2007): 23–46.

Pakier, Malgorzata and Bo Strath. Eds. *A European Memory? Contested Histories and Politics of Remembrance*. New York/Oxford: Berghahn Books, 2010.

Raun, Toivo U. *Estonia and the Estonians*. Stanford: Hoover Press, 2001.

Stevick, E. Doyle. "The Politics of the Holocaust in Estonia: Historical Memory and Social Divisions in Estonian Education." *Reimagining Civic Education: How Diverse Societies Form Democratic Citizens*. Eds. E. D. Stevick and B. A. U. Levinson. Lanham. Maryland: Rowman & Littlefield Publishers, 2007. 217–244.

Taylor, Charles. "The Politics of Recognition." *Multiculturalism: Examining the Politics of Recognition*. Ed. Amy Gutmann. Princeton: Princeton University Press, 1994. 25–73.

Thomas, W. I. "The definition of the situation." *Sociological Theory: A Book of Readings*. Eds. Lewis A. Coser and Bernard Rosenberg. New York: The MacMillan Company, 1970.

Weiner, Amir. "The Making of a Dominant Myth: The Second World War and the Construction of Political Identities within the Soviet Polity." *Russian Review* 55.4 (1996): 638–660.

Zerubavel, Eviatar. "Social Memories: Steps to a Sociology of the Past." *Qualitative Sociology* 19.3 (1996): 283–299.

Yuliya Yurchuk
Red Carnations on Victory Day and Military Marches on UPA Day? Remembered History of WWII in Ukraine

This chapter seeks to investigate the reception of visitors to the monument to Klym Savur, the commander of the Ukrainian Insurgent Army (UPA), a nationalist military units formed in 1942 in Western Ukraine. "Klym Savur" is an alias of Dmytro Kliachkivs'kyi, who was born in 1911 in the town of Zbarazh, Eastern Galicia (now Ternopil' Oblast'). In the 1930s he became involved in the nationalist underground of the Organisation of Ukrainian Nationalists (OUN), which was founded in 1929 with the aim of fighting against the Polish state in order to gain Ukrainian independence.[1] In the beginning of its activities, the OUN carried out sabotage against Polish landlords. This led to a wave of new repression against Ukrainians, called "pacification" by the Poles. In response, the OUN started terrorist attacks on representatives of Polish authority.[2] This led to arrests and the imprisonment of OUN leaders in the end of the 1930s. Kliachkivs'kyi was arrested, first by the Polish police in 1937 and later by the Soviets in 1940, who sentenced him to death. With the beginning of the German-Soviet war, Kliachkivs'kyi escaped from prison and in 1943 became a leader of the UPA units in Volhynia, the UPA-North (1943–45). During the time when Kliachkivs'kyi was a commander of UPA-North, mass killings of Poles took place in Volhynia. Grzegorz Motyka contends that Kliachkivs'kyi was one of those responsible and that he most probably took the decision concerning the "replacement" of Poles that led to ethnic cleansings. This belief is based on the fact that Klym Savur submitted an order in September 1943 which states that former Kolkhozes, real estate and industries of "Polish colonizers" would be distributed among landless and poor Ukrainian peasants. These orders found sympathizers among the Ukrainian peasants, who supported the UPA in killing their Polish neighbours.[3]

---

[1] On the history Organization of Ukrainian Nationalists see: Franziska Bruder. *"Den ukrainischen Staat erkämpfen oder sterben!": Die Organisation Ukrainischer Nationalisten (OUN) 1929–1948.* Berlin: Metropol, 2007.
[2] Taras Hunchak. *Ukraina: persha polovyna XX st. Narysy politychnoi istorii.* Kyiv, 1993.
[3] Grzegorz Motyka. *Od rzezi wołyńskiej do akcji Wisła.* Kraków: Wyd. Literackie, 2011, 127.

In the summer of 1944 Western Ukraine was defeated by the USSR. On 21 April 1945 a Soviet-Polish treaty of Friendship was signed. It was amended by a border agreement in August to include Eastern Galicia and Volhynia in the UkrSSR with some reservations regarding Poland. Towards the end of the war the UPA intensified their attacks on Poles on the Polish side of the border. This led to the repression and deportation from Poland of the Ukrainian civilian population, and caused about 780,000 Poles to leave for Poland in 1944–46.[4] In 1945 about 208,000 Ukrainians were deported from South-Eastern parts of Poland.[5] These deportations of Ukranians were planned to bring an end to the "Ukrainian question" on Polish territories once and forever. Deportations and forced resettlement of population culminated in 1947 as a result of an operation titled "Vistula" (operacja "Wisła"). In such a way, operation Vistula formally ended the Polish-Ukrainian armed conflict.[6]

Dmytro Kliachkivs'kyi was killed near the village Sus'k in Rivne oblast' in 12 February 1945. After his death Kliachkivs'kyi became a hero in the OUN mythology, cherished in the circles of OUN-B members in exile.[7] Posthumously he was awarded the title of Colonel of the UPA. In 1952 he was decorated with the Order of the Golden Cross, the highest decoration in the UPA. In post-war Ukraine, though, he was hardly known, as the history of the OUN and the UPA was mainly suppressed during Soviet times because it contradicted the monolithic heroic image of the Great Patriotic War and Great Victory which functioned as a fundamental myth in the formation of the identity of *homo Soveticus*.[8] On the remembered history of the Ukrainian-Polish conflict, Russian historian Osipian commented: "In the after-war epoch any mentioning of the Ukrainian-Polish armed conflict was stamped by a 'worker-peasant' taboo. All the crimes committed during the war were ascribed to Nazis."[9] With the beginning of perestroika

---

4 Motyka. *Od rzezi wołyńskiej do akcji Wisła*, 187–188. See also: Grzegorz Motyka and Dariusz Libionka. *Antypolska Akcja OUN-UPA 1943–1944. Fakty i interpretacje*. Warszawa: Wyd. IPN, 2002.
5 Motyka. *Od rzezi wołyńskiej do akcji Wisła*, 191.
6 Ihor Ilyushyn. *Ukraiins'ka Povstans'ka Armiia i Armiia Kraiova: protystoiannia u Zahidnii Ukraiini (1939–1945 rr)*. Kyiv: Kyiv-Mohyla Academy, 2009.
7 Per A. Rudling. "The OUN, the UPA and the Holocaust: A Study in the Manufacturing of Historical Myths." *The Carl Beck Papers in Russian & East European Studies* 2107 (2011).
8 On the role of the Great Patriotic War in the identity of the Soviet people see: Amir Weiner. *Making Sense of War: The Second World War and the Fate of the Bolshevik Revolution*. Princeton: Princeton University Press, 2001; Nina Tumarkin. *The Living and the Dead: The Rise And Fall Of The Cult Of World War II In Russia*. New York: Basic Books, 1994.
9 Aleksandr Osipian. "Etnichiskie chistrki i chistka pamiati: Ukrainsko-Polskoe pogranichie 1939–1947 v sovremennoi politike i istoriografii." *Ab Imperio* 2 (2004): 297–328, 308.

and the declaration of glasnost in the mid 1980s, the situation changed. A great deal of attention in public discussions was devoted to the "blank spots" of history. Topics came to light which had been taboo within the Soviet ideology. Among these topics were the OUN, the UPA, operation Vistula, and the Ukrainian-Polish armed conflict. However, whereas the topics of the OUN and UPA fight against the Germans and Soviets were foregrounded, the wrong deeds of these organisations found little attention in memory space.

In Poland, on the other hand, the Volhynian conflict became one of the central themes in discussions of 'blank spots of history', with the main focus on the tragic fate of the victims. The exhortations to remember the victims of the Ukrainian-Polish conflict were institutionalized in organizations founded by former victims or their relatives, e.g. the organization of the Armija Krajowa (AK) veterans or organizations of victims of forced deportations (including Ukrainian victims of Operation Vistula). In 2000 the two-volume book *Genocide of Polish population committed by Ukrainian nationalists in Volhynia in 1939–1945* written by W. Siemaszko and E. Siemaszko was published (5000 copies, 1434 pp.) Its publication was financed by the President's administration, Ministry of Culture and Historical Heritage and the Council for Preservation of Memory of Fight and Martyrdom of Poland. The book was recommended teaching at schools. The fact that one of the authors of the book, W. Siemaszko, is a veteran of the AK, significantly influenced the tone of the book. Although, the selection of exclusively Polish testimonies in the book and the lack of critical distance from the material undermine its scientific value (Iliushyn 2003), the detailed accounts of thousands of testimonies of the victims and witnesses cannot be ignored. The constant pressure of right-wing parties and victims' organizations on the Polish Parliament to recognize the conflict as an act of genocide has continued for decades.

In the Summer of 2013, the year of the 70th anniversary of the Volhynian conflict, Poland's parliament was about to adopt an amendment to describe the events in Volhynia as genocide. This caused a torrent of debates on both sides of the border. The Ukrainian right-wing party, Svoboda, asked Bronisław Komorowski, the Polish president, to cancel a visit on 14 July to Lutsk, the region's capital, for a 70th anniversary commemoration. In contrast, the ruling Party of the Region together with the Communists asked the Polish Parliament to pass the amendment, in this way demonstrating their position to Svoboda rather than their attitude regarding the problem of the anniversary as such. In the Polish Parliament the opinions also diverged. In the end, a compromise amendment was adopted which stated that the events in Volhynia in 1943–44 were "ethnic cleansing with features of genocide" (czystka etniczna nosząca znamiona ludobójstwa). The tense atmosphere around the anniversary in both countries demonstrates that in dealing with the past conflict, the two nations concentrated mainly on their *national* histories. In Ukrainian public discourse, the Volhynian conflict was presented as one of the steps towards national independence, whereas in Polish public discourse the killings of Poles were depicted as the "Volhynian *tragedy*": the Volhynian conflict in 1943 was presented as the quintessence of the long-lasting Ukrainian hatred of Poles that culminated in the massacre. The Polish terms for the ethnic conflict include the "Volhynian *massacre*", "genocide", or "ethnic cleansing". Hence, these "tragedy" and "massacre" narratives cannot be reconciled in a historical framework that can be shared by both nations.

In 2002, the year when the monument to Klym Savur was erected, the Ukrainian-Polish relations regarding the Volhynian conflict were no less tense than in 2013. The then Ukrainian President, Kuchma, held more pro-Polish views, whereas then opposition leader Viktor Yushchenko was more pro-UPA. Despite the tension in relations between Poland and Ukraine, as well as between the ruling party and the opposition within Ukraine, the monument to such a controversial leader as Klym Savur was finally built shortly before the 60th anniversary of the tragic events. The building of the monument was discussed for almost the entire decade of the 1990s. A growing anti-Kuchma campaign that started in 2000 contributed to the favourable conditions that made the monument possible in the region, which was strongly saturated with anti-Kuchma forces. Keeping all these conflicts and tensions in mind, one can ask why the monument was needed at all? Robert Musil famously contented: "There is nothing in this world as invisible as a monument. They are no doubt erected to be seen – indeed, to attract attention. But at the same time they are impregnated with something that repels attention, causing the glance to roll right off, like water droplets off an oilcloth, without even pausing for a moment".[10] Thus, even when finally built, is the monument seen? Does anyone pause for a moment and glance at it? And when they do so, what does this monument say to the viewer about the history it represents? In short, what is the reception of the monument among the public?

---

[10] Robert Musil. *Posthumos Papers of Living Author*. Transl. Peter Wortsmann. Hygiene: Eridanos Press, 1987, 61.

The Reception of Monuments

The study of the reception of monuments is grounded in the reception theory that originated in the literary studies of Hans-Robert Jauss in the late 1960s.[11] The present work strives to engage in the dialogue about the critique that studies on memory do not adequately reflect the role of audiences. As the student of memory Kansteiner contended: "Most studies on memory focus on the representation of specific events within particular chronological, geographical, and media settings without reflecting on the audiences of the representations in question."[12] Likewise, James Young proposed that the study of memory as represented in public monuments should focus on "the constant give and take between memorials and viewers, and finally the responses of viewers to their own world in light of a memorialized past – the consequences of memory."[13]

Studies of reception stress that meaning is produced both by the speaker and the reader (listener, viewer, visitor, etc.). Hence, meaning arises only through the interaction between these two poles. In his theory of encoding and decoding Stuart Hall drew our attention to the fact that there is a discrepancy between a message encoded and a message decoded.[14] The size of the discrepancy depends on the shared codes, previous knowledge and the values of the encoders and decoders. The reception of monuments includes reception both of the materiality of the monument located in the landscape and of the history which this monument represents. The latter is the main concern of the present paper.

This chapter presents the results of participant observation and interviews conducted near the monument to Klym Savur. A monument may remain unnoticed for many, but when people are asked to reflect on its meaning they start making sense not only of the monument but also of the history embodied in that monument.

---

11 On reception theory see: Robert C. Holub. *Reception Theory: A Critical Introduction*. London: Methuen, 1984; Hans Robert Jauss. *Toward an Aesthetic of Reception*. Transl. Timothy Bahti. Minneapolis: University of Minnesota, 1982.
12 Wulf Kansteiner. "Finding Meaning in Memory: A Methodological Critique of Collective Memory Studies." *History and Theory* 41, 2 (2002): 179–197, 179.
13 James E Young. *The Texture of Memory: Holocaust Memorials and Meaning*. New Haven, Conn.: Yale University Press, 1993, IX.
14 Stuart Hall. *Encoding and Decoding in the Television Discourse*. Birmingham: Centre for Contemporary Cultural Studies, 1973.

Klym Savur Remembered

The first commemorations of the OUN and UPA started already in the beginning of the 1990s. Although Klym Savur has not become as popular a figure for celebration as such leaders of the OUN as Stepan Bandera or Roman Shukhevych, he is definitely an important local hero who is celebrated regularly in the places related to his biography. Thus, on 16 February 1992, just in the third month of Ukrainian independence, the first commemoration of Klym Savur took place near the village of Sus'k, where he had been killed. The commemoration included a church mass and a series of speeches of local activists and concluded with the erection of a wooden cross commemorating the killed commander. This commemoration had been initiated by the regional committee of the right-wing party Rukh, UPA veterans, and the youth organization "Plast". The wooden cross was consecrated by the priests of the Ukrainian Autocephalous Orthodox Church. Units of the newly formed Ukrainian Army were also present and saluted the event. The meeting was opened by the head of the Rivne Committee of National Rukh of Ukraine, Volodymyr Omel'chuk, who positioned the death of Klym Savur in the space of victimhood, sacrifice, heroism, and greatness that has to be remembered with gratitude by present generations:

> Dear community!
> We came here today to the place where in winter 1945 fell in the unequal battle together with his two brethrens the devoted son of the nation, the unbreakable fighter for independence and freedom of Ukraine, the commander of UPA-North Dmytro Kliachkivs'kyi. We were led here by the feeling of deep sorrow for those endless sacrifices which Ukrainian nation put on the altar for its freedom in fight with its oppressors. We came here with the feeling of great respect to these knights, feeling of deep gratefulness for their sacrifice, for they did not kneel in front of oppressors and paid with their lives for the idea of Independence and Unity (Sobornist') of Ukraine.[15]

It should be stressed that the above rhetoric, which is close to that of liturgical speeches, is repeated in many celebrations of the OUN and UPA, thus complicating any expression of critical views since the person commemorated is presented not only as a hero but is also worshiped as a martyr or a saint. The mode of commemoration creates an atmosphere in which one is invited to take part in a ritual that presupposes unanimous support and excludes questioning or debating. The presence of Ukrainian Church clergy at all the unveilings of monuments to OUN and UPA members associates the commemorations with Christian rituals prac-

---

15 Volodymyr Omel'chuk cited in the newspaper *Volyn*, 24 February 1992, 2.

ticed in commemorations of dead relatives; thus they create a special, intimate atmosphere where nothing bad can be uttered about the dead.

Another monument to Klym Savur was unveiled in July 5, 1995 in a small town of Zbarazh, the town where Klym Savur was born. It took almost another decade before the monuments to the OUN and UPA figures began to appear in the larger towns of Western Ukraine.[16] The monument in Rivne became one of the first monuments to the OUN and UPA built in a larger city, the administration center of the oblast' (an administrative unit in Ukraine). The monument was consecrated in October 2002 on the 60th anniversary of the Day of the Creation of the UPA. The Day of the UPA has been broadly celebrated since the 1990s in many West Ukrainian towns when UPA veterans and their sympathizers gathered for marches. In the 2000s the celebrations expanded into other cities of Ukraine as well. The first mass celebrations of the Day of the UPA in Kyiv took place in 2005. Probably the victory of Viktor Yushchenko in the events known as the "Orange Revolution" legitimized such celebrations in the capital of the country, which was actually divided by its memory.

The monument in Rivne is placed in one of the central streets, Soborna Street, that faces the main building of the largest University in the city. The monument is located on the same street where the City Council and the city's largest church (Sviatopokrovsky Sobor) are situated. From this perspective, the site is strategically well-selected, as it is almost impossible to visit the city and not to see the monument. However, the place was selected not only because of its favorable location. This place is allegedly the location where the commander was buried, as during war-time the street was adjacent to the main prison of the city, where thousands of Jews and political prisoners were killed. In such a way, the place is not only connected to the death of one person, it is linked to the deaths of thousands of victims. It should be stressed that behind the monument to Klym Savur there is a monumental stone in memory of "five hundred Soviet citizens tortured by Hitler's killers". The memorial plaque on a building nearby that served as a prison during the war states "thousands of Ukrainian patriots were incarcerated and tortured here during the years of Nazist occupation". It should be mentioned that in 2001 a small chapel in memory of "Klym Savur and heroes of national-liberation struggles 1918–1950" was consecrated in Rivne (the architect V. Kovalchuk). By this, the memory of Klym Savur and

---

16 The tendency to build monuments to the OUN and UPA did not extend into other regions of Ukraine. In the capital city Kyiv e.g. there is no monument to the OUN or UPA. The memory of these organizations remains mainly linked to the areas where the organizations were active – Halychyna and Volhynia.

other "heroes of national-liberation struggles" were positioned in a sacred space which presupposes not only remembering but also worshiping.

The monument's appearance reminds one of the well-recognized visual forms of Soviet monuments and bas-reliefs dedicated to WWII, where the soldiers' courage and bravery are celebrated, as in well-known bas-reliefs near the Rodina (Motherland) statue in Kyiv. Although the monument to Klym Savur is dedicated to a single person, it not only embodies the heroism of one individual, it also symbolizes the collective effort of a great many other men of arms who were fighting for the same cause, which is embodied in the elements of the monument. As will be argued below, the well-recognized features of the monument made it easier for the onlookers to read it as a monument to a hero, a military man who sacrificed his life for the motherland.

Fig. 1: Monument to Klym Savur in Rivne, built in 2002. Sculptor V. Sholudko, architects T. Mel'nychuk and V. Koval'chuk. Photo: Yurchuk, 2011.

Fig. 2: Fragment of the Klym Savur monument in Rivne. The fragment symbolizes the collective effort of a great many other men of arms who were fighting for the same cause. Photo: Yurchuk

Fig. 3: Fragment of the "Dnieper Offensive" sculptural complex at the Motherland statue in Kyiv. Sculptor Vasyl' Borodai. Photo: http://kievbum.com/rodna-mat/.]

James Young claimed that "how and what we recognize in the company of a monument depends very much on who we are, why we care to remember, and how we see".[17] In my study, I was most interested in what people thought about the history the monument represents as they passed by it. What did their ways of seeing, thinking, and remembering tell me about these "recipients"? Reception theory applies the notion of "reader" when referring to the public consumption of a text (where text is understood in a broad semiological sense). Scholars who investigate people's responses to archeological sites tend to speak about "recipients" instead of "readers".[18] I will follow this tradition while speaking about the people whom I interviewed. I am fully aware that it was I who drew the attention of passers-by to the monument and that they otherwise might have passed by without even noticing it. It was I who triggered the reception process itself, and indeed made the passer-by into a recipient. Still, I contend that when their attention is drawn to it, the monument can evoke emotions, reflections, and thoughts on the history represented by the monument. As soon as the monument becomes visible, it begins to matter. As a result of seeing it, the recipients shared not only their thoughts about history but also their emotions, values, hopes, and disappointments. Furthermore, monuments not only "immortalize the dead" they also "mark... the values they [particular personalities] represented and the ideals of political regimes".[19] In the discussions about the UPA, the predominant themes are the self-sacrifice and victimhood of the whole Ukrainian nation.[20] National independence is presented as the highest value, one that can even justify the wrong deeds committed in the name of the nation. The adherence to the heroic narrative of the UPA is often equated with a "real Ukrainian-ness", as one of the main sponsors of the Klym Savur monument argued at the city council meeting where the building of the monument was dis-

---

17 James E. Young. "*The Texture of Memory:* Holocaust Memorials in History." *Cultural Memory Studies. An International and Interdisciplinary Handbook.* Eds. Astrid Erll, Ansgar Nünning, in collab. with Sara B. Young. Berlin/New York: De Gruyter, 2008, 357–366, 364.
18 Cornelius J. Holtorf. "'Object-orientated' and 'problem-orientated' approaches of archaeological research – reconsidered." *Hephaistos* 13 (1995): 7–18.
19 Cathrine Moriarty. "Review Article: The Material Culture of Great War Remembrance." *Journal of Contemporary History* 34, 4 (1999): 653–662, 657.
20 See: John-Paul Himka. "War Criminality: A Blank Spot in the Collective Memory of the Ukrainian Diaspora." *Spaces of Identity* 5, 1 (2005): 9–24; David R. Marples. *Heroes and Villains: Creating national History in Contemporary Ukraine.* Budapest: CEU Press, 2008; Johan Dietsch. *Making Sense of Suffering: Holocaust and Holodomor in Ukrainian Historical Culture.* Lund: Media Tryck Lund University, 2006.

cussed: "not honoring them (the UPA) is simply *not being Ukrainian*. Our history is as it is, and we have to be proud of it"[21] (author's emphasis).

In this paper, I deal with the 'response' of those to whom these monumental representations were addressed: the public, the "common people", who just pass by the monument. In total, fifty-two semi-structured interviews were conducted (with fourteen female and thirty-eight male respondents). The interviews were conducted on 15 and 16 October 2011 at the monument to Klym Savur with passers-by who were willing to spend a couple of minutes to share their thoughts on the monument and on the history embedded in it. The interviews took place on the two days immediately after the Day of the Foundation of the UPA, traditionally celebrated on 14 October, which is also holiday of the Orthodox Church – Pokrova (Intercession of the Theotokos) celebrated in honor of the Virgin Mary. This fact might have made the "memories" about the UPA more vivid, as it was more probable that people occasionally had heard about the holiday on the radio or TV, or had seen or even taken part in the celebration near the monument. Every year the memory service takes place there, with right-wing parties holding meetings with national banners and solemn speeches, wreaths being placed at the foot of the monument, and with Ukrainian clergy holding a liturgy-like service. From my observations, however, it became obvious that the memory service had not become a practice shared collectively by most of the city residents. Despite such thoroughly planned celebrations that had been repeated from year to year for two decades, most of the passers-by I met near the monument the day after celebration did not know whom the monument depicted (only four people knew who he was), although almost all of them said that they had seen the monument many times (only four visitors said that they had never noticed it before). Having analyzed the interviews, I distinguished several main themes that re-appeared from one interview to another and functioned as topoi in weaving the entangled texture of the narrative about the history of the OUN and the UPA.

Ukrainian Heroes, Real Patriots, and the Opposition

When recipients were asked to identify the person depicted by the monument only judging from the monument's appearance, most of them guessed that it

---

[21] Vasyl Chervoniy. Excerpt of Minutes No. 25 of the 2nd meeting of 25th session of Rivne City Council of 2nd call dated 2 November, 2001.

was a soldier (11), a military hero or a hero of war (9), a Ukrainian/national patriot (5), someone connected to Ukrainian independence (3), one of Bandera's men ('banderivets') (1), Stepan Bandera himself (2), or a UPA hero (7). Some thought that it represented a poet or a writer (12). Although these responses are rather diverse, all of them indicate that people predominantly connected the monument to the period of the struggle for the independence of Ukraine and in their ponderings they often added that if this monument was quite a new one it meant that it was built in memory of someone who had fought for independence – either a person connected to the UPA or the UNR (the Ukrainian People's Republic, the proclaimed independent state which existed from 1918 to 1920). Only two respondents thought it was a monument to a Red Army soldier. When informed that it was a monument to Klym Savur, most recipients said that they were hearing his name for the first time. Nevertheless, when asked to guess who the person could be, people again linked this name either to the UPA (most of the cases – 26) or the UNR (14). Thus, people tended to associate the monuments built in independent Ukraine with specific episodes of history represented as the periods of struggle for independence.

The interviews demonstrated that state independence, national liberation and the struggle against occupiers are the foci from which the history of the UPA is perceived by most people. Although, recipients had trouble giving any precise details on the UPA, they all agreed that the UPA fought for independence (42), was a liberation army (32), was composed of Ukrainian patriots (12), contained fighters against the Soviet and fascist occupiers (40), and stood up in opposition to the Soviet regime (4). Curiously, in three cases out of four where the UPA was described as the "opposition", the respondents expressed their expectations and hopes for the present and for a future where Ukrainians would benefit if they had the kind of "opposition" the UPA represented. Younger people tended to express sorrow when they were speaking about the UPA, the sorrow that there is no UPA-like opposition now:

> They were a kind of opposition, active opposition which we do not have now. They were fighting for independence against the Soviets and fascists.[22]

In such a way memory links reflections on the past with present needs and worries as well as with hopes and fears about the future. Speaking about the past, people are not oriented exclusively to the past. They position the past within the context of the present wherein their evaluations and attitudes are shaped by ex-

---

22 Respondent G. Interviews. Rivne 15.10.2011. Author's private archive.

pectations for the future. In the excerpt cited above, we can perceive a sense of nostalgia for a strong opposition against the ruling authorities of the present.

In the answers to the question of whether it is necessary to commemorate the UPA, in particular in the form of monuments, the visitors expressed their evaluation of the past which was highly valuable for understanding the recipients' attitude to the UPA. Having died in the war and in the struggle for independence was perceived as a sacrifice, an expression of "real patriotism", and as a good reason for remembrance and commemoration in the monuments:

> They were fighting for independence, we must commemorate them.[23]

> It was during the war. But I think that if there had been no war, there still would have been the UPA. We always wanted independence.... Patriotism and heroism have to be remembered and commemorated. They were fighting till the death, they knew they would be killed, but they were fighting. We must remember their sacrifice.[24]

The Role of Family Stories in Recipients' Responses

Although most of the respondents said that they had never celebrated any event related to the UPA, most of them replied that they celebrated Victory Day (43): either by going to parades or watching parades on TV (21), giving flowers to veterans (12), going to demonstrations or meetings (4), laying flowers at the monument (1) or simply having time with friends and family (3). People in their 50 – 60s said that on Victory Day they went to cemeteries and put flowers on the graves of relatives who had fought in the war (7).[25] Strikingly, people were eager to speak about their families and related the questions asked during the interviews to their family experiences. Almost all of the respondents in their 40 – 60s said that they had lost someone in the war, or mentioned a relative who had been in the war. They said that Victory Day was the day that they remembered these relatives. Some said that they celebrated Victory Day by going to church and praying for the souls of those who had been killed in the war or died afterwards. Only nine respondents said they did not celebrate the Day of Victory. Sometimes people stressed that the holiday meant the victory over

---

23 Respondent G. Interviews. Rivne 15.10.2011.
24 Respondent O. Interviews. Rivne 15.10.2011.
25 Only 2 people said they celebrated the Day of the Foundation of the UPA; others knew about such a day but said that they celebrated the religious holiday Pokrova on that day, not the day of the UPA.

fascism for them although they did not celebrate the day in any special way: "It is a holiday for me, because I know that it is a day of victory over fascism. But I do not do anything special on this day."[26]

Although none of the respondents who shared their family stories said that they had any relatives in the UPA, some of them seemed positive about the commemoration of the UPA soldiers while linking their family members' beliefs to those of the UPA:

> My grandfather was in the Red Army. My grandmother told me horrific stories about how the Soviets killed hundreds of the UPA soldiers in the village nearby. It was terrible. Now, it is good that there are such monuments, because these UPA people were also killed... for somebody it is very important to honor them. But it is important for all of us to know our history.[27]

Sometimes the evaluations of history became more complicated in instances where people referred to their family memories involving negative experiences with the UPA:

> My mother told me a lot about banderivets [Bandera's men]. They were for independence, but they killed a lot of Ukrainians. She said they were afraid of them. When Soviets killed some banderivets in their village the villagers were afraid to bury them. Even the relatives of the killed... Either they were afraid or thought it was a disgrace to have such relatives who killed their own folk.[28]

> They (UPA) were fighters for independence, but their methods were questionable. My grandparents had different stories about them. You know, they killed Ukrainians too.[29]

Such instances show that people have trouble dealing with difficult knowledge about the past which they learned from their families. They had to face contradictions and accommodate them within the generally glorious picture of the UPA which is promoted in the region. The fact that the UPA were killing "their own folk" arouses questions and doubts. In these instances people make their own decisions about how to relate their subversive "private" knowledge to established public representations: "Maybe there are people who need these commemorations, I can understand it. But I do not support their (UPA) methods. Their methods of fighting are unacceptable."[30] Elsewhere in the interview the respond-

---

26 Respondent O. Interviews. Rivne 15.10.2011.
27 Respondent K. Interviews. Rivne 15.10.2011.
28 Respondent Nn. Interviews. Rivne 16.10.2011.
29 Respondent Y. Interviews, Rivne 15.10.2011
30 Respondent J. Interviews. Rivne 15.10.2011.

ent explained: "They (UPA) were fighting for the independence of Ukraine but they were killing everyone like fascists."[31]

Another respondent expressed his views in the following way:

> Why not have such monuments? It is very difficult to say now who was right who was wrong. It is all our history. My grandpa was in the Red Army... I know it was a difficult time.[32]

Time and again, the independence of Ukraine functions as a lifeline in taking a decision on how to evaluate wrong deeds presented with an aura of sacrifice for the nation. Noteworthy, in the above mentioned responses, the bereaved are those who belong to their "own folk", whereas there is no explicit mention of the suffering of other nationalities. The UPA heroism is mainly questioned when it is related to attacks against other Ukrainians. Thus, the space of victimhood is predominantly occupied by Ukrainians in imagination of the recipients.

The Space of Victimhood

The theme of victimhood is another focal point through which the history of the OUN and UPA is narrated in the interviews. Indeed, about one fifth of the respondents placed the UPA struggle within the years of the Holodomor[33] (10). Such a link between the UPA and the Holodomor leads us to think that the history of the UPA is placed by the recipients within the space of the victimhood of the Ukrainian people as whole. Remarkably, this placement is also realized through commemorative practices, where the Holodomor and the monument to Klym Savur have become linked together on the anniversaries of the Holodomor. As a respondent, who happened to be a history teacher, replied:

> It (the monument to Klym Savur) was built in 2002. I often bring my school children here. I am a history teacher. On the Holodomor anniversary we come here to tidy up and clean up

---

31 Respondent J. Interviews. Rivne 15.10.2011.
32 Respondent S. Interviews. Rivne 15.10.2011.
33 The Holodomor is the man-made famine in 1932–1933 in the Ukrainian SSR. For the representations of the Holodomor in memory culture in contemporary Ukraine, see insightful studies: Georgiy Kasianov. *Danse macabre: Holod 1932–1933 rokiv u politytci, masovii svidomosti ta istoriografii (1980-pochatok 2000).* Kyiv: Nash Chas. 2010; Dietsch, *Making Sense of Suffering. On the rememberance of the Holodomor in the Ukrainian Diaspora*; Vic Satzewich. *The Ukrainian Diaspora.* New York: Routledge, 2002, 165–190.

near the monument. We also meet with veterans, both Red Army and UPA veterans. I come here to participate in meetings organized by the Ukrainian People's Party (UNP).[34]

Positioning the UPA in the same space of meaning as the Holodomor makes it easier to accommodate difficult knowledge about the wrong deeds of the UPA together with the glorious representations of their deeds in the monuments. What we can also conclude from the kind of responses cited above is that the acceptance of a new portrayal of the past does not always presuppose the denial of the old one. As the case cited just above demonstrates, the respondent's occupation and affiliation with the UNP engaged her in memory work and in the shaping of new remembrances, but it did not exclude adherence to other kinds of remembrances, such as meeting with Red Army veterans. These two seemingly opposite kinds of war remembrances mutually reinforce each other, with the fact of fighting and dying in the war making both the Red Army and UPA equally worthy of remembering and commemorating. Importantly, family history strengthens this connection:

> They (the UPA) were fighting for the independence of Ukraine, against both fascists and the Soviets. My father was killed in Warsaw on the 5th of May, 1945, and I understand that we have to remember both Red Army veterans and UPA veterans.[35]

Thus, death on the battlefield renders equal the UPA and the Red Army and thereby diminishes the ideological differences between these rivals. Indeed, as Reinhard Koselleck contended: "Whether dressed in hope or cloaked in grief, symbols of death last longer than any individual case. Although the individual case of death may fade, death is nonetheless still in store for every observer."[36] The only identity that matters is that of the dead fallen in the war. Put bluntly, even in the instances the recipients had no idea about who the UPA was, the mere fact that the monument depicted a fallen soldier, as easily identified from the visuality of the monument, made them think that he was worth remembering and commemorating. In such a way, "[t]he formal language specific to war memorials is obsolete without ceasing to speak. Evidently, this language out-

---

34 Respondent Kk. Interviews. Rivne 16.10.2011.
35 Respondent Kk. Interviews. Rivne 16.10.2011.
36 Reinhart Koselleck. "War Memorials: Identity Formation of the Survivors." *The Collective Memory Reader.* Eds. Jeffrey Olick, Vered Vinitzky-Seroussi, and Daniel Levy. Oxford: Oxford University Press, 2011, 365–370, 370.

lives its unique, politically and socially determined causes, so that the signs are no longer understood politically but remain comprehensible nonetheless."[37]

Conclusion

To sum up, through the analysis of the interviews I came to the conclusion that independence and liberation are the the main thematic foci in the narration about the UPA. Furthermore, the UPA is situated in the space of victimhood closely connected to such an unquestionable symbol of victimhood for many Ukrainians as the Holodomor. This imagined connection makes it problematic to have a critical and non-emotional distance to the UPA. It covers up "unpleasant knowledge" about atrocities committed by the UPA against other nationalities as well as against Ukrainians who did not support the UPA's cause. At the same time such an emotional charge enables history to function as a building block in the formation of national and regional communal identities.

Remarkably, in their reflections on history people refer to the glorious pasts of the Soviets and the UPA wherein both traditions of remembering do not exclude each other but rather reinforce each other. In such a way, victimhood and national sentiments reconcile the Soviet and the UPA heroic narratives. Indeed, the interviews showed that on the grassroots level discussion about the UPA goes beyond the binary polarization, Soviet vs. anti-Soviet, Ukrainian vs. anti-Ukrainian representations and remembering of the war. The long-ago formed picture of WWII have a decisive impact upon respondents in their understanding of the UPA. The mere fact of war and death in the battlefield makes the fallen soldier into a hero, while other more troublesome details of history are shifted out of the memory space. These disturbing details are not repressed, censored or silenced explicitly; they are rather overshadowed by the emphasis on independence, sacrifice, struggle, and liberation. Indeed, the heroic memory of WWII informs the memory of the insurgency. The well-known forms of remembering the great victory provide moulds where celebrations, monumental forms and rituals connected to insurgency are forged. The present peaceful co-existence of parallel memories does not, though, imply that there is no potential for conflict that can be ignited at certain points in time and in certain contexts. Exhortations to past historical injustices were not the last things used for mobilizing and perpetuating other injustices. History has enough evidence of people

---

[37] Ibid.

who, having lived together for decades, were seemingly instantaneously turned into bitter enemies who fought each other to the death.

References

Bruder, Franziska. "Den ukrainischen Staat erkämpfen oder sterben!" *Die Organisation Ukrainischer Nationalisten (OUN) 1929–1948*. Berlin: Metropol, 2007.

Dietsch, Johan. *Making Sense of Suffering: Holocaust and Holodomor in Ukrainian Historical Culture*. Lund: Media Tryck Lund University, 2006.

Hall, Stuart. *Encoding and Decoding in the Television Discourse*. Birmingham: Centre for Contemporary Cultural Studies, 1973.

Himka, John-Paul. "War Criminality: A Blank Spot in the Collective Memory of the Ukrainian Diaspora." *Spaces of Identity* 5.1 (2005): 9–24.

Holtorf, Cornelius J. "'Object-orientated' and 'problem-orientated' approaches of archaeological research—reconsidered." *Hephaistos* 13 (1995): 7–18.

Holub, Robert C. *Reception Theory: A Critical Introduction*. London: Methuen, 1984.

Hunchak, Taras. *Ukraina. persha polovyna XX st. Narysy politychnoi istorii*. Kyiv: Lybid Press, 1993.

Ilyushyn, Ihor. *Ukraiins'ka Povstans'ka Armiia i Armiia Kraiova: protystoiannia u Zahidnii Ukraiini (1939–1945 rr)*. Kyiv: Kyiv-Mohyla Academy, 2009.

Jauss, Hans Robert. *Toward an Aesthetic of Reception*. Transl. Timothy Bahti. Minneapolis: University of Minnesota, 1982.

Kansteiner, Wulf. "Finding Meaning in Memory: A Methodological Critique of Collective Memory Studies." *History and Theory* 41.2 (2002): 179–197.

Kasianov, Georgiy. *Danse macabre: Holod 1932–1933 rokiv u politytci, masovii svidomosti ta istoriografii (1980-pochatok 2000)*. Kyiv: Nash Chas, 2010.

Koselleck, Reinhart. "War Memorials: Identity Formation of the Survivors." *The Collective Memory Reader*. Eds. Jeffrey K. Olick, Vered Vinitzky-Seroussi and Daniel Levy. Oxford: Oxford University Press, 2011. 365–370.

Marples, David R. *Heroes and Villains: Creating national History in Contemporary Ukraine*. Budapest: CEU Press, 2008.

Moriarty, Cathrine. "Review Article: The Material Culture of Great War Remembrance." *Journal of Contemporary History* 34, 4 (1999): 653–662.

Motyka, Grzegorz and Dariusz Libionka. *Antypolska Akcja OUN-UPA 1943–1944. Fakty i interpretacje*. Warszawa: Wyd. IPN, 2002.

Motyka, Grzegorz. *Od rzezi wołyńskiej do akcji Wisła*. Kraków: Wyd. Literackie, 2011.

Musil, Robert. *Posthumous Papers of Living Author*. Trans. Peter Wortsmann. Hygiene: Eridanoss Press, 1987.

Osipian, Aleksandr. "Etnichiskie chistrki i chistka pamiati: Ukrainsko-Polskoe pogranichie 1939–1947 v sovremennoi politike i istoriografii." *Ab Imperio* 2 (2004): 297–328.

Rudling, Per A. "The OUN, the UPA and the Holocaust: A Study in the Manufacturing of Historical Myths." *The Carl Beck Papers in Russian & East European Studies* 2107 (2011).

Satzewich, Vic. *The Ukrainian Diaspora*. New York: Routledge, 2002.

Snyder, Timothy. *The Reconstruction of Nations: Poland, Ukraine, Lithuania, Belarus, 1569–1999*. New Haven and London: Yale University Press, 2003.

Tumarkin, Nina. *The Living and the Dead: the Rise and Fall of the Cult of World War II in Russia*. New York: Basic Books, 1994.
Wanner, Cathrine. *Burden of Dreams: History and Identity in Post-Soviet Ukraine*. PA: Penn State Press, 1998.
Weiner, Amir. *Making Sense of War: The Second World War and the Fate of the Bolshevik Revolution*. Princeton: Princeton University Press, 2001.
Young, James E. *The Texture of Memory: Holocaust Memorials and Meaning*. New Haven, Conn.: Yale University Press, 1993.
Young, James E. "*The Texture of Memory:* Holocaust Memorials in History." *Cultural Memory Studies. An International and Interdisciplinary Handbook*. Eds. Astrid Erll, Ansgar Nünning, in collab. with Sara B. Young. Berlin/New York: De Gruyter, 2008. 357–366.

Archive material

Excerpt of Minutes No. 25 of the 2nd meeting of 25th session of Rivne City Council of 2nd call dated 2 November, 2001 (Rivne City Council Archive).
Interviews with recipients. (Private archive of the author).
Volodymyr Omel'chuk cited in the newspaper *Volyn*, February 24 1992, 2.
Rivne Regional Newspaper *Volyn* (Rivne Oblast' Library Archive, Department of Regional Studies of Volhynia)

Part 4: **Memorial Media Spaces**

Mārtiņš Kaprāns
Framing the Ukrainian Insurgent Army and the Latvian Legion: Transnational History-Writing on Wikipedia

In the past decade, social networking sites (SNS) have become a crucial frame of remembrance and history writing in post-communist societies. These societies, as Rutten and Zvereva suggest, are a major player on the digital map today, forming "a new topography with special places of memory discussions, commemoration and fights."[1] To be sure, Web 2.0 has provided new opportunities for discussing history, particularly the history of the twentieth century, a period which prompts troublesome collective memories.

Not only has SNS reinforced the will to discuss a controversial history, but more importantly, it has established a transnational platform where full-fledged and reconciliatory narratives can be elaborated. Along with what Kasianov calls the nationalization of history in post-communist societies, one may, however, ask whether these virtual platforms facilitate the coming to terms with the past.[2] In order to answer this question, this chapter looks at Wikipedia, an exemplary case of transnational and collaborative knowledge creation. Specifically, the chapter addresses the representation of the Ukrainian Insurgent Army (UPA) and the Latvian Legion (LL), two historical topics which still generate tensions in Ukraine and Latvia. Both military entities were established in 1943. UPA was the military wing of the Ukrainian Nationalist Organization (OUN), and its ultimate goal was to liberate Ukraine from the Soviet as well as Nazi dictatorship. The LL, on the other hand, was established as an ostensibly voluntary unit of Waffen SS, but, arguably, some of the legionnaires indeed saw in the creation of the LL an opportunity to regain the freedom of Latvia.

The controversy emerges from different frames applied to the UPA and LL in popular discourse as well as in historiography. On the one hand, they are seen as the supporters or auxiliary forces of the German army during the Second World War and have thus been associated with the Nazi crimes. On the other hand,

---

1 Ellen Rutten and Vera Zvereva. "Introduction: old conflicts, new media: post-socialist digital memories. *Memory, Conflict and New Media: Web Wars in Post-Socialist States.* Eds. Ellen Rutten, Julie Fedor and Vera Zvereva. Abingdon, New York: Routledge, 2013, 1–18.
2 Georgiy Kasianov. "'Nationalized' History: Past Continuous, Present Perfect, Future..." *A Laboratory of Transnational History Ukraine and Recent Ukrainian Historiography.* Eds. Georgiy Kasianov and Philipp Ther. Budapest/New York: Central European University Press, 2009, 7.

both military groups are linked to anti-communist resistance and the fight against Soviet aggression.³ These diverging narratives about the UPA and LL are decisive elements of fractured memory regimes vis-à-vis the Second World War. Such memory regimes, as Kubik and Bernhard suggest, emerge when major memory actors turn into warriors who tend to draw a sharp line between their "true" vision of the past, and "wrong" versions of history.⁴ Yet, domestic actors are not the only ones on the frontline of this war. Equally important are warriors in Russia, which constantly exploits the commemoration of the UPA and LL as sufficient evidence for its claims of the rebirth of Nazism in Ukraine and Latvia. Moreover, in its *memory war* against Latvia and Ukraine, Russia has looked for allies among other European countries.⁵ In a nutshell, Russia criticizes any attempts to reinterpret the UPA and LL as acting within the context of two evils, i.e. the Soviet and Nazi totalitarian regimes, which were similarly criminal and aggressive towards Eastern Europe and the Baltic States.⁶

Although formally it would be more appropriate to compare the Wikipedia representations of the LL and the 14th Waffen SS Grenadier Division where many Ukrainians from Galicia were enrolled, the UPA has become a more meaningful *lieux de memoire* in the Ukrainian mnemonic landscape. Thus the UPA and LL are compared as two primary and salient figures of collective memory and persistent sources of "memory events" of the Second World War.⁷ Nevertheless, one should acknowledge the differences of the memory regimes of Ukraine and

---

3 Andrievs Ezergailis. Ed. *The Latvian Legion: Heroes, Nazis, or Victims?* Riga: Historical Institute of Latvia, 1997; Per A.Rudling. "Theory and Practice: Historical Representation of the War Time Activities of the OUN-UPA (the Organization of Ukrainian Nationalists – the Ukrainian Insurgent Army)." *East European Jewish Affairs* 36.2 (2006): 163–189.
4 Michael Bernhard and Jan Kubik. "The Politics and Culture of Memory Regimes: A Comparative Analysis." *Twenty years after Communism*. Eds. Michael Bernhard and Jan Kubik. New York: Oxford University Press, 2014, 261–296.
5 Eva-Clarita Onken. "The Baltic states and Moscow's 9 May commemoration: Analysing memory politics in Europe." *Europe-Asia Studies* 59.1 (2007): 23–46; Nils Muižnieks. Ed. *The Geopolitics of History in Latvian–Russian Relations*. Riga: Academic Press of the University of Latvia, 2011; Georgiy Kasianov. "'The Nationalization' of History in Ukraine." *The convolutions of historical politics*. Eds. Alexei Miller and Maria Limpan. Budapest/New York: Central European University Press, 2012, 141–174.
6 For the recent scholarly discussion on this paradigm see Michael Geyer and Sheila Fitzpatrick. Eds. *Beyond Totalitarianism. Stalinism and Nazism Compared*. New York: Cambridge University Press, 2009; Timothy Snyder. *Bloodlands: Europe between Hitler and Stalin*. New York: Basic Books, 2010.
7 Alexander Etkind. *Memory Events in the Transnational Space*. Paper presented in Memory at War Inaugural Workshop, King's College, Cambridge, June 2010. http://tinyurl.com/mvwaao (23 March 2015).

Latvia. The Latvian political elite has officially sought for the past 15 years to abstain from using the memory of LL to boost national pride or strengthen collective identity. In 2000, Latvia's parliament removed 16 March, the commemorative day of Latvian legionaries, from the official calendar. Regardless of the annual conflictual discourse that revolves around 16 March until today, the majority of Latvian politicians avoid attending the unofficial commemorative events of 16 March in Riga. Many of them, however, admit the tragedy of legionaries in the war and after that.

Ukrainian politicians, in contrast, have used the commemoration of UPA as political currency during the presidencies of Yuschenko and Yanukovych.[8] Unlike his predecessors, the current president, Petro Poroshenko, has refused to exploit the history of UPA for political purposes. On 16 May 2015, however, Poroshenko signed a controversial law that along with other organizations qualified the UPA as "fighters for Ukrainian independence". This law makes it a criminal offense to deny the legitimacy of "the struggle for the independence of Ukraine in the twentieth century" and public denial of the same is to be regarded as an insult to the memory of the fighters (see Draft law no. 2538–1). Thus, as critics have pointed out, questioning this claim, and implicitly questioning anything "fighters for independence" did, is being made a criminal offense.[9]

Differences between Latvia and Ukraine can also be observed on the societal level: the attitude towards the LL is clearly divided along the ethno-linguistic lines (Latvians vs. Russian speakers), while the social memory regarding the UPA is divided on a regional basis (East vs. West). In the 1990s and 2000s, one could observe a rather syncretic commemoration of the Second World War rivalries in Ukraine.[10] These contradictory attitudes were also evident in history teaching, where different narratives of the Second World War were taught in different parts of Ukraine, thus reinforcing the confrontation with respect to the UPA.[11] Conversely, syncretism and uncertainty are less characteristic of Latvia's

---

8 Nils Muižnieks and Vita Zelče. Eds. *Karojošā piemiņa. 16. marts un 9. maijs*. Rīga: Zinātne, 2011; Yuliya Yurchuk. *Reordering of Meaningful Worlds Memory of the Organization of Ukrainian Nationalists and the Ukrainian Insurgent Army in Post-Soviet Ukraine*. Doctoral Dissertation. Stockholm University, 2014.
9 Marples, David R. "Open Letter from Scholars and Experts on Ukraine Re. the So-Called 'Anti-Communist Law.'" *Krytyka* April (2015). http://krytyka.com/en/articles/open-letter-scholars-and-experts-ukraine-re-so-called-anti-communist-law (10 May 2015).
10 Andre Liebich and Oksana Myshlovska. "Bandera: memorialization and commemoration." *Nationalities Papers: The Journal of Nationalism and Ethnicity* 42.5 (2014): 750–770.
11 Lina Klymenkoa. "World War II in Ukrainian school history textbooks: mapping the discourse of the past." *Compare* 44.5 (2013): 756–777; Korostelinaa, Karina. "Constructing na-

mnemonic landscape, where the Russian-speaking minority systematically challenges the relatively strong consensus of Latvians on the Second World War and to some extent also on the LL; this consensus corresponds to the official historical interpretation.[12] Namely, unlike the triumphant narrative of Russian speakers, the Latvian narrative suggests that the war did not bring freedom to Latvia and legionnaires were largely victims of the war. Hence one may argue that Latvia's mnemonic culture has been more bipolar than the Ukrainian one in terms of WWII.

Taking into account communalities and actual dissimilarities, one might expect somewhat different representational practices regarding the UPA and LL on Wikipedia. Yet, Wikipedia resembles a Habermasian coffeehouse of the eighteenth century, where universal and rational guidelines are supposed to define discussions and lead to consensus.[13] That is, general principles rather than the nationally defined imperatives of political or social memory should prevail in the historical representations generated through Wikipedia. In practice, however, Wikipedia challenges the ideals of the Enlightenment by creating a digital heterotopia "which juxtapose[s] many otherwise incompatible spaces, online and offline, experts and amateurs, science and popular culture".[14] In such conditions, as this chapter suggests, a comparative analysis of Wikipedia is a useful tool to decipher the interaction between consensus building and nation-building contexts with respect to controversial history in general and to the UPA and LL in particular.

Wikipedians as a community of practice

The paradigmatic transformation of the media landscape in the 2000s and the emerging participatory culture has tremendously changed media consumption, shifting "from individualized and personalized media consumption towards con-

---

tion: national narratives of history teachers in Ukraine." *National Identities* 15.4 (2013): 401–416.
12 Mārtiņš Kaprāns and Olga Procevska. *Latvijas sociālās atmiņas monitorings*. Riga: Latvijas Universitāte, 2013. http://tinyurl.com/pjkok55 (24 March 2015).
13 Jürgen Habermas. *The Structural Transformation of the Public Sphere: An Inquiry into a category of Bourgeois Society*. Cambridge: Polity, 1989.
14 Jutta Haider and Olof Sundin. "Beyond the legacy of the Enlightenment?" *First Monday* 15.1 (2010). http://firstmonday.org/article/view/2744/2428 (24 March 2015).

sumption as a networked practice".¹⁵ Along with many other consequences caused by these changes, this transformation has certainly expanded the understanding of the mediality of memory. As Hoskins admits, "the increasingly digitalized networking of memory not only functions in a continuous present but is also a distinctive shaper of a new mediatized age of memory."¹⁶ Memory here and elsewhere is understood in its broadest sense as a culturally shaped representation of the past.

The idea of SNS is embedded in the maximalist understanding of media participation which highlights heterogeneity and multidirectional engagement in creating and consuming media content. It certainly intensifies the remediation of history and enables a greater participation in public discourse about the shared past. Likewise, SNS foster the development of a new (trans)national communicative space where knowledge and attitudes towards history can be exhibited, discussed, refined, and reinterpreted. One may even argue that SNS have increased the role of agency, thereby expanding the Halbwachsian conception of collective memory where an individual has a rather marginal role. Yet, SNS are far from perfect, and they reflect more general issues related to using the Internet. These problems are related to reflexivity, listening to others and working with difference, identity verification, processes of domination and exclusion, and the expansion of economic interests.¹⁷ Similar shortcomings arise in the online remediation of history: daily discourse about history is often sporadic, superficial, fragmented, polemic, obtrusive, and anonymous.

History is a widely demanded topic on Wikipedia. Spoerri, for example, found that articles in the combined category of politics and history received more visits than science or computer-related topics.¹⁸ Perhaps Wikipedia is also the most popular and visible place of transnational history writing. Critics, nevertheless, admit that the articles are "narrowed by a limited historical imagination that gives precedence to political and military history, especially the feats

---

15 Henry Jenkins. *Convergence Culture: Where Old and New Media Collide.* New York: University Press, 2006, 244.
16 Andrew Hoskins. "Digital network memory." *Mediation, Remediation, and the Dynamics of Cultural Memory.* Eds. Astrid Erll and Ann Rigney. Berlin: De Gruyter, 2009, 98.
17 Lincoln Dahlberg. "The Internet and democratic discourse: Exploring the prospects of online deliberative forums extending the public sphere." *Information, Communication and Society* 4.1 (2001): 615–633.
18 Anselm Spoerri. "What is popular on Wikipedia and why?" *First Monday* 12.4 (2007). http://tinyurl.com/ogkhrwe (24 March 2015).

of great men, over social, economic, or environmental history".[19] On the other hand, Wikipedia is not just a communication tool or knowledge repository, it is also a cultural system in its own right.[20] The Wikipedia guidelines accompanied by everyday participation practices and a common communication style define Wikipedians as a particular community of practice whose members have a joint enterprise, mutual engagement and shared repertoire.[21] However, as Wenger argues, not only unity, but also disagreements, challenges, and competition may be an essential component of such communities; therefore "a community of practice is neither a haven of togetherness nor an island insulated from political and social relations."[22] *Wikipedia* facilitates the competition of historical narratives and furthers collisions and conflicts, the flipside of participatory culture. Clearly, such a community of practice can entail different mnemonic agents who are located in the same consensual universe, sticking together through shared negotiation practices, but not necessarily through shared representations of the past. At the same time, Wikipedians coming from different cultural backgrounds, (inter)act along the culturally specific behavioral norms.[23] Hence it seems more appropriate to categorize Wikipedians as culturally bounded communities of practice who, regardless of a shared understanding of collaborative work, can significantly differ on the level of participation and interaction.

Talk pages and editing are the milestones of Wikipedia's culture. This culture embraces collaboration as well as the fight for meaning and authority. The Wikipedian's authority, as Bender et al. demonstrate, is usually established through *external claims* which are based on outside authority or sources of expertise, such as books, magazine articles, websites, written laws, etc.[24] Likewise, in

---

19 Brendan Luyt. "The Inclusivity of Wikipedia and the Drawing of Expert Boundaries: An Examination of Talk Pages and Reference Lists." *Journal of the American Society for Information Science and Technology* 63.9 (2012): 1876.
20 Christian Pentzold. "Fixing the floating gap: The online encyclopaedia Wikipedia as a global memory place." *Memory Studies* 2.2 (2009): 255–272; Michela Ferron and Paolo Massa. "Beyond the encyclopedia: Collective memories in Wikipedia." *Memory Studies* 7.1 (2014): 22–45.
21 *Wikipedia: List of guidelines*. http://en.wikipedia.org/wiki/Wikipedia:List_of_guidelines (24 March 2015).
22 Etienne Wenger. *Communities of practice: Learning, meaning, and identity*. Cambridge, UK: Cambridge University Press, 1998, 77.
23 Noriko Hara, Pnina Shachaf and Khe Foon Hew. "Cross-cultural analysis of the Wikipedia community." *Journal of the American Society for Information Science and Technology* 61.10 (2010): 2097–2108.
24 Emily M. Bender, et al. "Annotating Social Acts: Authority Claims and Alignment Moves in Wikipedia Talk Pages." *Proceedings of the Workshop on Language in Social Media*. Oregon: Association for Computational Linguistics, 2011, 48–57.

order to construct authority, Wikipedians often use *forum claims* or codified rules of behavior, e. g. that one should use reliable sources or avoid imposing personal opinion. It has been argued that unlike external claims which might lead to reconciliation, forum claims are more likely to cause negative alignment between Wikipedians.[25] Yet, both types of establishing authority may create exclusionary conditions that constrain engagement. For instance, the requirement to prove the reliability of sources or to apply the rules of behavior appropriately may discourage from creating the content of Wikipedia. Moreover, the number of actual editors also casts doubts on Wikipedia's heterogeneity: fewer than 10 per cent of the authors are responsible for more than 90 per cent of all contributions. As a result, Wikipedia is more and more often characterized as a hierarchical platform. König insists that in light of authority claims and gate-keeping, which are intrinsic to Wikipedia's participatory architecture, "exclusion cannot be avoided, which leaves Wikipedia in a dilemma".[26]

Linking these general observations to the actual research field, it is important to acknowledge the different roles that English and Russian Wikipedia play in Latvia and Ukraine. Russian Wikipedia is definitely an important site for Ukrainian editors as well as users. In 2014, more than half (55,5%) of all Wikipedia views from Ukraine were registered in Russian Wikipedia; English Wikipedia, on the other hand, received only 10% of views from Ukraine.[27] The editing practices also exemplify the central role of Wikipedia.ru: 43,8% of the Wikipedia edits from Ukraine were made in Russian Wikipedia, which falls just slightly behind Ukrainian edits in Ukrainian Wikipedia (48,7%).[28] Dounaevsky explains this interest in Russian Wikipedia by Ukrainian linguistic and cultural duality and ambiguity.[29] Conversely, in Latvia, English Wikipedia is the most popular site, which received 43,2% of views from Latvia in 2014, while Russian Wikipedia attracted a significantly smaller viewership (20,2%). Nevertheless, Latvian editors are more active in Russian than in English Wikipedia, contributing 37,8% and 12,8% of edits, respectively. These data suggest that Russian and English Wikipedia most likely have a different impact on the countries in question; howev-

---

25 Ibid, 55.
26 René König. "Between lay participation and elite knowledge representation." *Information, Communication & Society* 16.2 (2013): 171.
27 *Wikimedia Traffic Analysis Report*. http://tinyurl.com/ohzfgvt (24 March 2015).
28 *Wikimedia Traffic Analysis Report* http://tinyurl.com/ph667oy (24 March 2015).
29 Helene Dounaevsky. "Building Wiki-History: Between Consensus and Edit Warring." *Memory, Conflict and New Media: Web Wars in Post-Socialist States*. Eds. Ellen Rutten, Julie Fedor and Vera Zvereva. Abingdon, New York: Routledge, 2013. 132.

er, Russian Wikipedia is perhaps a more salient site of ideological struggle in both countries.

Methodology

In order to understand how the reconciliatory potential of Wikipedia is used, this chapter explores four Wikipedia articles on the Ukrainian Insurgent Army (UPA) and the Latvian Legion (LL).

To demonstrate how the articles on the UPA and LL were created, this chapter deals with both English and Russian Wikipedia. Both versions can be seen as transnational sites of history writing. Arguably, the English Wikipedia is a rather global platform which attracts diverse editors, whereas the Russian Wikipedia has a more regional character and largely appeals to the users of post-Soviet countries where the Russian language is still the lingua franca. Hence the empirical material includes different transnational realms, which might mean different practices of consensus building on controversial historical topics.

In this chapter, two different versions of each Wikipedia article (2010 and 2014) are explored, which helps to better understand the dynamics of consensus.[30] To conduct a comparative analysis, I have examined different datasets related to Wikipedia articles: edit histories, users' profiles, and talk pages. I have also used various external data collection tools to obtain quantitative information about editors and revision history. Likewise the qualitative research software *Nvivo 8* was used to extract additional data from Wikipedia articles and talk pages and to map relations between the most active editors. *Nvivo* facilitates the analysis of large amounts of text by providing various techniques for obtaining qualitative (e. g. open coding) as well as quantitative data (e. g. word frequency, tag clouds). The collected data are analyzed on two levels: narrative and agentic. On the narrative level I focus on the structure of Wikipedia articles and dominant themes that recur in talk pages. On the agentic level the most active Wikipedians are explored. In particular, I shall look at interaction patterns that emerge among the Wikipedia editors. For the sake of clarity, particular abbreviations are used to designate each Wikipedia article: EnUPA (English Wikipedia article on the UPA),

---

30 See *Ukrainian Insurgent Army*, retrieved from http://en.wikipedia.org/wiki/Ukrainian_Insurgent_Army; *Latvian Legion*, http://en.wikipedia.org/wiki/Latvian_Legion; *Украинская повстанческая армия*, http://tinyurl.com/o94md3b; *Латышский добровольческий легион СС*, http://tinyurl.com/jvuqxe2 (24 March 2015).

RuUPA (Russian Wikipedia article on the UPA), EnLL (English Wikipedia article on the LL), and RuLL (Russian Wikipedia article on the LL).[31]

Wikipedia Narratives

Although formally Wikipedia articles provide encyclopedic representations of history, these analytical texts retain narrative qualities, putting forward particular constellations of events, characters, and images. In Wikipedia, as Page puts it, "the burden of narration is distributed between different contributors, who in turn may include citations from materials authored by others and quotations attributed to various protagonists represented in the narrative in question."[32] In addition, articles' talk pages are often used by editors to coordinate narration, so as to make an article comprehensible to a layman.

The Wikipedia articles analyzed in this chapter show considerable structural variation which illuminates the diverse framing strategies that editors have agreed upon. EnUPA depicts the UPA's relations with numerous nations and countries, also pointing to the UPA's criminal or morally undermining activities (the ethnic cleansing of Poles in Volhynia and Galicia, ambiguous relations with Nazi Germany and Jews). To be sure, the first paragraphs of EnUPA link the UPA's activities to the Ukrainian Nationalist Organization's main goal: to re-establish a united, independent national state on Ukrainian ethnic territory. Thus, the violence of the UPA is primarily seen as a political tool. Notably, the national and political marker 'Ukrainian' has become more salient over time and is used more frequently in the 2014 version than in 2010. The editors of the English article have also agreed to use neutral titles for sections that deal with the most problematic issues (e.g. "Germany", "Poland", "UPA and Jews"). Yet, EnUPA emphasizes the uneasy memory work with respect to the UPA in today's Ukraine (reconciliation, commemorative places for victims and combatants, recognition of the UPA). The visual material of EnUPA has been expanded over the years, particularly stressing the military nature of the UPA and commemorative sites dedicated to the UPA.

Conversely, RuUPA is more prone to outlining the prehistory of the UPA, its nationalist origins and motivation for collaborating with the Nazis. The opening paragraphs of the article stress the militant character of the UPA and its antag-

---

[31] The first version of EnUPA was created in 2004, RuUPA in 2005, EnLL in 2006, RuLL in 2007.
[32] Ruth Page. "Counter narratives and controversial crimes: The Wikipedia article for the 'Murder of Meredith Kercher'." *Language and Literature* 23.1 (2014): 71.

onism toward Soviet partisans and the Polish underground army (i.e. those who fought against the Nazi invasion) during and after the Second World War. In such a way the Russian article highlights the UPA's violent activities, simultaneously downplaying the underlying political intentions behind that violence. However, the word frequency analysis suggests that the UPA's violence against Poles and Jews is more prominent in EnUPA than in RuUPA. This shows the varying salience of transnational contexts in both articles: while RuUPA accentuates the aggression towards the Soviets, EnUPA is more inclined to stress the UPA's violence toward ethic groups. In addition, the editors of RuUPA have decided to use more emotional and sensational section headings ("Collaboration with Wehrmacht, German police and SD", "The activities of the UPA against civilians", "Collaboration of the UPA with foreign secret services"). A separate section describes the liquidation of the UPA, emphasizing various tactics used by Soviet institutions to destroy the UPA. The Soviet measures taken against the UPA are framed as "the liberation of the Soviet lands", thus repeating the Soviet interpretative scheme of history. The vocabulary of RuUPA has largely remained the same over the years. The same persistence applies to the visual material, which again focuses on the UPA's violence.

To sum up, one may argue that the editors of EnUPA have reached a certain consensus by agreeing on a syncretic perspective. Namely, the UPA is characterized as a group of combatants who were ready to fight for their cause by any means during and after the Second World War. Although the crimes committed by the UPA are not downplayed, they are definitely not used as a dominant representational context. The editors of RuUPA, in contrast, have reached a narrower consensus. The Russian article only emphasizes the criminal character of the UPA, which thus legitimizes the liquidation of this military organization by the Soviets. In other words, the narrative of RuUPA overlooks alternative interpretations of the UPA's errant activities. It is noteworthy that the visual material also conveys these different representations. While the embedded pictures in EnUPA brings forward the symbolic dimension (commemorative sites, military symbols, stamps), RuUPA's visual material illustrates the victims of the UPA.

Similar patterns emerge within articles on the Latvian Legion. EnLL draws attention to conditions that led to the formation of the LL and explains the motivation of people who were involved in the LL. The English Wikipedia persistently defines Latvian legionnaires as conscripts who were by and large forcefully recruited by Hitler. Unlike the Russian article, the English article draws attention to a post-war incident in 1946 when the government of Sweden extradited soldiers from the LL who had fled to Sweden from the USSR. This story and the Swedish apology after Latvia regained independence stress the tragic destiny of the legionnaires. The narrative of EnLL has not changed significantly over the years, thus demonstrating a somewhat rigid consensus among editors.

The Russian Wikipedia, on the other hand, emphasizes the voluntary basis of LL, even though it simultaneously admits that the voluntary nature of their service was a rather formal pretext exploited by Nazis to mobilize Latvian conscripts. Notably, legionnaires in RuLL are also called Hitlerians (*Gitlerovci*), the ideological label inherited from the Soviet historical discourse and widely used in the Russian popular parlance nowadays. In a nutshell, these Wikipedia articles highlight a different understanding of the locus of control vis-à-vis the LL (as established by Nazis vs. established by Latvians and Nazis). The basis of this juxtaposition is much broader, i.e. it stems from a fundamentally different interpretation of the guilt for Nazi crimes. While EnLL admits that some members of LL were indeed involved in Nazi crimes, it states that these crimes happened before the LL was actually established in 1943. Moreover, the English Wikipedia article insists that "many Latvian historians maintain that the Latvian Legion itself was a front line combat unit and did not participate in any war crimes". In contrast, RuLL refers to several poorly sourced and rather unreliable cases related to Poland and Belarus, which allegedly prove the criminal nature of the LL; and a research-based conclusion that the absolute majority of the LL soldiers were not involved in Nazi crimes is presented as merely the opinion of Latvian historians. Nevertheless, all four articles point to the Nuremberg trials, which concluded that the UPA and the LL were not involved in committing Nazi crimes.

Sources are yet another important element in Wikipedia articles. They determine the quality of articles and hence are regularly discussed on talk pages. As Sundin argues, "There is a hierarchy of trustworthy genres in Wikipedia, which often mirrors hierarchies of sources as they are treated outside Wikipedia".[33] An obligation to use authoritative sources is a rule that is regularly applied by Wikipedia editors. Verification of sources is thus "one mechanism by which a dominant narrative can be established or a counter narrative excluded from a Wikipedia article".[34] However, when Wikipedians have conflicting opinions on the credibility of a particular source – which happens quite often – this leads to editing wars.

The editors of EnUPA and RuUPA have used various sources to create a reliable text about the UPA (Table 1). The bibliography of EnUPA entails 91 units. They are dominated by books and news media, while academic journals and var-

---

33 Olof Sundin. "Janitors of knowledge: constructing knowledge in the everyday life of Wikipedia editors." *Journal of Documentation* 67.5 (2011): 852.
34 Page. "Counter narratives and controversial crimes," 71.

ious Internet sources are used less frequently. Similar pattern can be observed in RuUPA, where the reliance on books and ignorance of ongoing scholarly discussions in academic journals is even stronger. Archival or video materials are rarely used in the analyzed articles and that shows a heavy dependence on secondary sources.

Table 1: The ratio of different sources[35]

	Books	News Media	Academic Journals	Internet	Other*
EnUPA	33%	29,7%	12,1%	12,1%	13,2%
RuUPA	47%	19%	9%	7%	16%
EnLL	56%	0	16%	16%	16%
RuLL	17,8%	31,1%	8,9%	20%	22,2%

* Government and NGO reports, PhD thesis, archives etc.

Table 2: The publication year of sources

	1940s	1950s	1960s	1970s	1980s	1990s	2000s	2010s	NI*	Total
EnUPA	1	5	3	0	4	12	24	21	21	91
RuUPA	3	2	2	1	1	12	41	11	17	90
EnLL	0	1	0	1	3	4	9	4	3	25
RuLL	1	2	0	0	3	6	21	4	8	45

* Impossible to identify the publication year

Regardless of structural similarities, the sources used in articles on the UPA reveal that dissimilar informative backgrounds have formed the editors' knowledge about the topic. If EnUPA is based on English and Ukrainian sources, the editors of RuUPA have preferred Russian and Ukrainian sources. There are only 10 (11%) bibliographical units which are used in both articles and they are published mostly in English. In other words, English rather than Ukrainian sources create a shared ground for both articles which, otherwise, have dissimilar origins. Yet, the topicality of UPA as regards Ukraine's memory politics in the past 15 years have obviously played a role in selecting sources, i.e. the bulk of sources have been published in the 2000s (Table 2).[36] Hence the recency of sources makes the political context more salient in Wikipedia articles and increases, particular-

---

35 The data represents the Wikipedia articles as they were on 15 September 2014.
36 The sources of EnUPA, however, represent a more dispersed timeframe than RuUPA.

ly in RuUPA, the likelihood that editors have remediated rather biased discourses about the UPA. It is also important to point out that many sources used have been published in the last five years. This evidently demonstrates that the work on writing the history of the UPA is ongoing, but also highlights the fragility of the consensus reached by Wikipedians in 2007–2009, when the most active editing and discussions occurred. The data show, though, that the updating of sources is more characteristic of EnUPA, which again suggests the limited informative background of RuUPA.

The number of information sources for EnLL and RuLL is significantly smaller than for both EnUPA and RuUPA. This shows, among other things, a correlation between the number and activity of editors and the number of sources used in a Wikipedia article. For example, EnLL has the lowest number of edits among all four articles (Table 3), and correspondingly it has the lowest number of sources. The narrative of EnLL is based on books, whereas RuLL's sources are dominated by news media, where sensationalism and biased assessment is more characteristic. Essentially, the English article on the LL can be seen as more reliable than the Russian article, whose accusatory perspective is principally grounded in the often superficial discourse of media and the Internet. One can again notice a considerable differentiation of sources: EnLL is dominated by English, while RuLL is based on Russian sources. Yet, both articles assign Latvian sources an auxiliary role. Furthermore, both articles have just two common sources thus having a completely different informative background. Similarly to articles on the UPA, the majority of sources are published in the period when the controversy around the LL evolved and when it became a regular topic in the bilateral relations of Latvia and Russia (from 1998 onwards).[37] In light of this controversy, a juxtaposition of the Latvian national, pro-Russian (often also pro-Soviet) and the Western European representations of the Second World War reveals an exacerbation of differences.

The selection of sources reveals that the predominance of English or Russian sources leads to a decreased interaction as well as to a stronger consensus which largely excludes counter narratives, as can be seen in the case of EnLL and RuLL. Conversely, competition of sources increases interaction and leaves room for counter narratives. This, however, can be used for different purposes, as can be seen in EnUPA and RuUPA. While the editors of EnUPA strive to integrate

---

37 Kārlis Kangeris. "Western pressure in the writing of Latvian history." *Inheriting the 1990s: The Baltic Countries. Studia Uralica Upsaliensia No. 37.* Ed. Baiba Metuzale-Kangare. Uppsala: Uppsala University Press, 2010, 191–198; Nils Muižnieks. "History, Memory and Latvian Foreign Policy." *The Geopolitics of History in Latvian–Russian Relations.* Ed. Nils Muižnieks. Riga: Academic Press of the University of Latvia, 2011, 21–30.

counter narratives in a common picture, the editors of RuUPA are ultimately inclined to establish the hegemony of a pro-UPA or anti-UPA narrative.

Agentic level

The editing history of Wikipedia articles reveals an already familiar participatory pattern: all four articles are created by a small group of editors and the top 10% of editors have made more than half of all edits (Table 3). The data suggest that RuLL has the lowest potential of pluralism, as the top five editors have made 63% of edits and have added 93.6% of the text.[38] RuUPA, in turn, has the most decentralized and scattered 'editing staff'; this diversity is also projected on the RuUPA's talk page, where some editors are even more tended to discuss than to edit the article (Table 5).

Table 3: Editing activity

Wikipedia article	Total revisions	Number of editors	Edits made by the top 10% of editors	% edits made by top five editors	% of text added by top five editors
EnUPA	2956	566	73.1%	39.9%	69,8%
RuUPA	3147	711	65%	26.6%	51,9%
EnLL	330	103	57.6%	41.2%	60,9%
RuLL	634	125	75.2%	63%	93,6%

Since many editors maintain a high level of anonymity, the assessment of individual Wikipedians is a more complicated task. Yet, the available information on user pages and talk pages provides sufficient data to describe the most active editors and their mutual relations. There are up to three leading editors in each article who usually also dominate on talk pages. The editors of EnUPA largely avoid using an accusatory rhetoric in their discussions (Table 4). The two editors most critical towards the UPA are Xx236 and Jo0doe. While Xx236 is related to Poland (Polish is indicated as his native language),[39] Jo0doe imposes somewhat pro-Russian interpretations, trying to frame the UPA as merely a Nazi collaborator. Moreover, Jo0doe has constantly vandalized articles and incited edit warring, both on EnUPA and RuUPA. It is also interesting to note that the most sizable

---

[38] The top five editors in both categories do not necessarily overlap.
[39] Ethnic cleansing of Poles in Galicia and Volynia is often mentioned as the most striking evidence of UPA's criminal activities.

contribution among anonymous editors comes from Poland, whereas the contribution of anonymous editors from the Russian Federation is insignificant.[40] This suggests that Polish editors of EnUPA have provided the most important input for the critical appraisal of UPA. Nevertheless, it is striking to see how editors who take nominally opposing sides try to reach a certain consensus, even if still disagreeing on crucial aspects of UPA. The editors who attempt to create a comprehensive article invite other Wikipedians to ignore Jo0doe's aggressive behavior and concentrate on the article.

> I think we are all better off if we simply integrate the info into an article if it is sourced and valid and correct the Jo0Doe's English. His own credibility matters little. It is his sources that matter. I find his sources valid even though his interpretation is one-sided. I deal with his edits to Holodomor in exactly same way. The sources he brings in are excellent. As for his attacks on credibility of other editors, those are best ignored. Articles' content is all that matters in the end of the day. – Irpen, 23 December 2007

> Believe me, this personal attitude ('you (OUN)', 'why do you lie' etc.) is not going to be healthy to either of you. Why don't you both stick to the article and try to avoid making the remarks directed at other editors ? – Lysy, 29 January 2008

This ongoing consensus building, as the communicative activity on talk pages suggests, is particularly characteristic of EnUPA. The content of the EnUPA's talk page emerges to a large extent from the polemic discourse between Faustian and Jo0doe, and other editors act as the supporters or opponents of these two leading editors (see Chart 1). As Faustian's position attracts more supporters, his balanced approach to the UPA prevails in the talk page as well as in the Wikipedia article.

Table 4: The top 10 editors of EnUPA

Editor's name	Description*	Edits	Entries on talk page	Attitude towards UPA**
Faustian	Pro-Ukrainian attitude	618	1024	B
Jo0doe	Blocked in EN and RU versions. Accused of vandalism and falsification of sources, pro-Russian/pro-Soviet	561	1029	C
Lvivske	Pro-Ukrainian attitude	186	34	B
Lysy	Ukrainian	110	25	B

---

40 *Wiki Trip*. http://sonetlab.fbk.eu/wikitrip/#|en|Ukrainian_Insurgent_Army (24 March 2015).

Table 4: The top 10 editors of EnUPA *(Continued)*

Editor's name	Description*	Edits	Entries on talk page	Attitude towards UPA**
Xx236	Polish is native language	81	46	C
Bobanni		61	46	B
Irpen	Russian	51	38	B
Volunteer Marek	Scholar from USA, member of Eastern European Mailing List	48	37	B
Iryna Harpy	Descendant of the Zaporozhian Cossacks, lives in Australia	40	52	B
Bandurist	Pro-Ukrainian attitude	40	10	S

* This information is obtained from user's profiles as well as from discussions on talk pages.
** B – balanced, C – critical, S – supportive

Conversely, the RuUPA's talk page displays interaction between various equally active editors. Yet, this ostensibly pluralistic pattern is, in fact, based on a highly conflictual discourse that evolves amongst the supporters of pro-Ukrainian and pro-Russian interpretations of UPA.

> I'm completely sure there was no particular 'Banderovites' violence'. That is to say, of course there was one most likely. [...] But I don't place the UPA on the same plaque where the SS and the like are placed. People [of UPA] were ultimately fighting for freedom. – Harding, 6 December 2006[41]

> One wants to hide the other side of the real history of one's fathers and relatives: how the families of the Red Army officers were betrayed to the SD and SS; how hundreds of thousands of Jews were 'released' to another world; how Poles were cleansed with the assistance of the Ukrainian SS. Well, of course, in one's own eyes, it's better to be the offspring of fighters and the victims of the regime than that of war criminals. – Jo0doe, 7 August 2008

Remarkably, two of the leading RuUPA editors (Jo0doe and Chobitok Vasilii [Чобиток Василий]) who indiscriminately condemn the UPA have been banned from Wikipedia because of their constant vandalism and violation of Wikipedia rules. To be sure, RuUPA demonstrates how a scattered and dispersed interaction of profoundly bias editors hampers consensus building as regards historical top-

---

[41] All quotes taken from Russian Wikipedia were originally published in Russian. The translation to English was done by me.

ics. That is to say, conflicting representations make consensus more fragile particularly in terms of the Russian article.

Table 5: The top 10 editors of RuUPA

Editor's name	Description	Edits	Entries on talk page	Attitude towards UPA
Martin89	From Ukraine	237	3	S
Jo0doe	Blocked in EN and RU Wikipedia. Accused of vandalism and falsification of sources, pro-Russian/pro-Soviet stances	216	152	C
Crow	Russian, pro-Ukrainian attitude, jurist, born in 1976, real name: Ivan. Has lived in Eastern Ukraine.	146	152	S
Wulfson	Born in Russia, real name: Sergey, currently lives in Russia, but has lived in Ukraine for long time, administrator of the article	142	188	B
Viggen	Pro-Ukrainian attitude, jurist	97	137	S
Nordrimidgard	Russian is native language	93	0	
Glossologist		86		
Чобиток Василий	Pro-Soviet, banned from Wikipedia, accused of vandalism	93	152	C
Ffederal		55	1	
Klip game	Supporter of communist ideas, offline name: Pavel Liahovsky (Ляховский Павел Юрьевич)	86	10	B

The relations between the editors of EnLL and RuLL significantly differ from those of editors of Wikipedia articles on the UPA. The most visible dissimilarity is a tremendously low participation in Wikipedia talk pages about the LL. If the talk pages regarding the UPA articles reveal attempts to create transnational historical narratives by including controversial interpretations of the UPA, the editing of articles on the LL is not accompanied by such discussions. In particular, this inactivity can be observed on the EnLL's talk page, where even the most active editors (Vecrumba and Zalktis) have made just a few entries. Perhaps, the missing discussions have resulted in a somewhat quick consensus, thus leaving it unchallenged over the years. The majority of the editors (including anonymous editors) of EnLL are either living in or are closely related to Latvia. Hence the transnational background of this Wikipedia article is somewhat limited. It should be noted, however, that EnLL and RuLL advocate completely divergent representations of the LL. While EnLL is intertwined with a balanced and slightly justificatory perspective, the Russian article is again dominated by a critical and accusatory tone. This contrast between interpretations is more conspicuous than the one observed between EnUPA and RuUPA.

Table 6: The top 10 editors of EnLL

User name	Description	Edits	Entries on talk page	Attitude towards LL
Vecrumba	Related to Latvia, lives in New York	40	7	B
Zalktis	Related to Latvia	34	5	B
Andris	Latvian	28	0	
Nug	Related to Estonia	18	2	B
Paul Siebert	PhD	16	3	B
Nedrutland		14	0	
Darouet	Student of evolutionary biology with interests in history, literature and philosophy	11	0	
Philaweb	An active member of WikiProject Latvia	9	1	
Xil	Constantly improves and develops WikiProject Latvia	6	3	B
GBE	Proud to be a European	6	0	

Table 7: The top 10 editors of RuLL

User name	Description	Edits	Entries on talk page	Attitude towards LL
Zac Allan	From Moscow, Zionist, supports pan-Slavic ideas	158	49	C
Abols	From Latvia	131	64	B
Knyf		66	15	C
Doomych	From Moscow, works in IT, also has a username Викискладе	22	5	B
Scriber	Russian	22	0	
Gaujmalnieks		19	0	
Silent1936	From Novosibirsk, currently has changed the username to Andrey FCSN	17	13	B
81.198.35.224	IP is registered in Latvia	13	0	
207.10.232.172	IP is registered in Fairport (NY), USA	10	1	
Gweorth		6	0	

Numerous editors have also co-edited other articles on the history of Eastern Europe in general and on Ukraine and Latvia in particular. For instance, the data provided by Editor Interaction Analyzer[42] show that Faustian and Lvivski, the editors of EnUPA, have participated in the talk pages of other English Wikipedia articles related to Ukraine (Organization of Ukrainian Nationalists, the Ukrainian right-wing party "Svoboda", etc) and Vecrumba and Nug have co-edited and discussed topics from Soviet history on English Wikipedia, particularly with respect to the Baltic states. This means that the most active editors are rather determined and knowledgeable Wikipedians, whose interactions have a longer history and whose arguments have been tempered in various contexts. Nonetheless, among the ten most active editors only Knyf, Silent1936 and Jo0doe have contributed to more than one of the Wikipedia articles analyzed in this chapter which means that the transnational communities of practice are isolated from each other.[43]

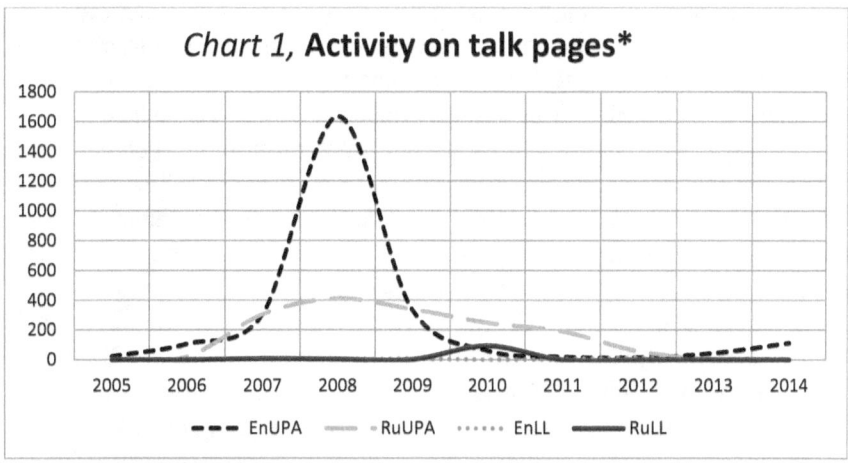

*Total number of entries per year

The data also show groups of Wikipedians who are tied together not just because of a shared interest in writing articles, but also because of national or regional origins. Taking into account this background, one may notice that EnUPA is largely written by a scattered transnational community (Table 4), whereas the

---

[42] Editor Interaction Analyzer, available at https://tools.wmflabs.org/sigma/editorinteract.py (23 March 2015).
[43] Knyf has edited both Russian articles, being more engaged in RuLL than in RuUPA. Knyf's attitude varies from somewhat indifferent towards the UPA to explicitly critical towards the LL. Silent1936, in contrast, demonstrates a balanced attitude towards both topics of Russian Wikipedia.

bulk of RuUPA is largely created by Russian and Ukrainian editors (Table 5). Hence, RuUPA emerges from regional rather than global discussions on history. The most active editors of EnLL and RuLL, are related to Latvia and Russia, respectively (see Table 6 and 7). On the one hand, this local perspective has obviously reduced the level of controversies on the LL, helping to cement a shared representation already dominating in each offline community. On the other hand, there have been limited transnational efforts to build the Wikipedia consensus on the LL.

Wikipedia has for long time been a battlefield for editors interested in Central and East European history. The Digwuren case is a good example to epitomize this ongoing struggle. In 2007, Wikipedia user Irpen submitted a case for the Arbitration Commission of English Wikipedia against user Digwuren. Irpen accused a group of active Wikipedians of vandalism and of blocking alternative views on the Baltic and East European history of the twentieth century. Many members of this group who took part in these editing wars were allegedly working behind the University of Tartu firewall and were members of the East European mailing list (EEML).[44] This well-coordinated group of Wikipedia editors, as it was argued, advocated anti-Russian, anti-communist and nationalist views and "attacked" those who disagreed with such a perspective. The Arbitration Commission decided to warn the involved editors that future attempts to use Wikipedia as a battleground by making generalized accusations that persons of a particular national or ethnic group are engaged in Holocaust denial or harbor Nazi sympathies may result in the imposition of summary bans (for more details on this controversy see Wikipedia: Arbitration). Several editors (e.g. Vecrumba, Nug (also Martintg), Irpen) of EnUPA and EnLL were also involved in the Digwuren case and EEML. Presuming that there are also other and not necessarily explicitly coordinated collaboration practices behind Wikipedia articles, one may argue that the clashes with respect to the UPA and LL to a considerable extent can be seen as the rivalry between well-established, but very small, groups of editors.

Conclusions

In this chapter, I have sought to show how Wikipedia as a transnational social networking site is involved in dealing with controversial episodes of the Second

---

[44] See Wikipedia: Arbitration/Requests/Case/Eastern European mailing list, retrieved from http://tinyurl.com/lynv4f (24 March 2015).

World War which are still sensitive issues in the collective memory of Latvia and Ukraine. The analysis of various datasets has revealed differences that help us understand and explain the potential of transnational history-writing in Wikipedia.

This research suggests that transnational conditions in English and Russian Wikipedia are used for diverse purposes. The leading editors of English Wikipedia have mainly addressed historical issues of the UPA and LL in a balanced and collaborative manner, producing a comprehensive narrative on controversial topics. Notwithstanding their attempts to follow the best practices of Wikipedia, the most active Russian Wikipedians, on the other hand, prefer a conflict oriented interaction. Apparently, Russian Wikipedia is more often seen as a battlefield where Russian, Ukrainian, and Latvian editors can impose their national historical narratives. This inevitably generates polemical rather than pluralistic and transnational history-writing. Therefore RuUPA and RuLL and behind the scene activities on talk pages reveal a more rigid juxtaposition of dominant and counter narratives.

The varying relations between competing narratives, in fact, show the conditionality of the argument that Wikipedians are prone to generate more neutral points of view as time goes by.[45] English Wikipedians are indeed more inclined to reach *global consensus* on the UPA and LL by bringing forward complexity rather than by reducing the essence of both military organizations to representatives of nationalism or perpetrators of Nazi crimes. These sites are also open to additional or new information and sources. Russian Wikipedians, however, tend to reinforce/criticize the *national consensus* of Ukraine or Russia and to a lesser extent that of Latvia. To be sure, the Russian language invokes power relations between Russia and other post-communist nations. This language formed the hegemonic representation of the Second World War in the Soviet era. And today the most assertive arguments that challenge the narratives of a "subaltern European past" are expressed in Russian.[46] In a nutshell, my research demonstrates that English Wikipedia advances a somewhat inclusionary narrative whereas Russian Wikipedia is seen as the site for exclusionary history-writing. This finding corroborates the argument that the English Wikipedia is more useful as a neutral

---

45 Ferron and Massa. "Beyond the encyclopedia: Collective memories in Wikipedia," 1327.
46 Maria Mälksoo. "The memory of becoming European: The East European subalterns and the collective memory of Europe." *European Journal of International Relations* 15.4 (2009): 653–680.

ground where local discussions can be revived and brought to the attention of the Anglophone Internet audience.[47]

Along with the exclusionary and inclusionary dimensions of Wikipedia, it is also important to take into account the differences in editing activity which are caused by the size of a particular nation. By referring to the cases of UPA and LL, it can be argued that one may expect a higher variety of sources, discussions and narrative complexity in those Wikipedia articles which deal with the controversial historical topics of larger nations.[48] In other words, the effect of the nation's size should be integrated in media literacy programs and should be emphasized when teaching critical thinking about Wikipedia as the source of historical knowledge.

Acknowledgement

The research was supported by the European Union through the European Social Fund (Mobilitas grant No GSHRG409MJD).

References

Bender, M. Emily, et al. "Annotating Social Acts: Authority Claims and Alignment Moves in Wikipedia Talk Pages." *Proceedings of the Workshop on Language in Social Media*. Oregon: Association for Computational Linguistics, 2011. 48–57.

Bernhard, Michael and Jan Kubik. "The Politics and Culture of Memory Regimes: A Comparative Analysis." *Twenty years after Communism*. Eds. Michael Bernhard and Jan Kubik. New York: Oxford University Press, 2014. 261–296.

Dahlberg, Lincoln. "The Internet and democratic discourse: Exploring the prospects of online deliberative forums extending the public sphere." *Information, Communication and Society* 4.1 (2001): 615–633.

Dounaevsky, Helene. "Building Wiki-History: Between Consensus and Edit Warring." *Memory, Conflict and New Media: Web Wars in Post-Socialist States*. Eds. Ellen Rutten, Julie Fedor and Vera Zvereva. Abingdon, New York: Routledge, 2013. 130–142.

Draft law no. 2538–1 "*Проект Закону про правовий статус та вшанування пам'яті борців за незалежність України у XX столітті*", http://w1.c1.rada.gov.ua/pls/zweb2/webproc4_1?pf3511=54689

Editor Interaction Analyzer, available at https://tools.wmflabs.org/sigma/editorinteract.py (23 March 2015).

---

[47] Rolf Fredheim, Gernot Howanitz and Mykola Makhortykh. "Scraping the Monumental: Stepan Bandera through the Lens of Quantitative Memory Studies." *Digital Icons: Studies in Russian, Eurasian and Central European New Media* 12 (2014): 29.

[48] The language barrier also matters. Latvians are certainly not able to discuss in Russian at the same level and amount as Ukrainians.

Ezergailis, Andrievs. Ed. *The Latvian Legion: Heroes, Nazis, or Victims?* Riga: Historical Institute of Latvia, 1997.

Etkind, Alexander. *Memory Events in the Transnational Space*. Paper presented in Memory at War Inaugural Workshop, King's College, Cambridge, June 2010. http://tinyurl.com/mvwaao (23 March 2015).

Ferron, Michela and Paolo Massa. "Beyond the encyclopedia: Collective memories in Wikipedia." *Memory Studies* 7.1 (2014): 22–45.

Fredheim, Rolf, Gernot Howanitz and Mykola Makhortykh. "Scraping the Monumental: Stepan Bandera through the Lens of Quantitative Memory Studies." *Digital Icons: Studies in Russian, Eurasian and Central European New Media* 12 (2014): 25–53.

Geyer, Michael and Sheila Fitzpatrick. Eds. *Beyond Totalitarianism Stalinism and Nazism Compared*. New York: Cambridge University Press, 2009.

Habermas, Jürgen. *The Structural Transformation of the Public Sphere: An Inquiry into a category of Bourgeois Society*. Cambridge: Polity, 1989.

Haider, Jutta and Olof Sundin. "Beyond the legacy of the Enlightenment?" *First Monday* 15.1 (2010). http://firstmonday.org/article/view/2744/2428 (24 March 2015).

Hara, Noriko, Pnina Shachaf and Khe Foon Hew. "Cross-cultural analysis of the Wikipedia community." *Journal of the American Society for Information Science and Technology* 61.10 (2010): 2097–2108.

Hoskins, Andrew. "Digital network memory." *Mediation, Remediation, and the Dynamics of Cultural Memory*. Eds. Astrid Erll and Ann Rigney. Berlin: De Gruyter, 2009. 91–106.

Jenkins, Henry *Convergence Culture: Where Old and New Media Collide*. New York: University Press, 2006.

Kangeris, Kārlis. "Western pressure in the writing of Latvian history." *Inheriting the 1990s: The Baltic Countries. Studia Uralica Upsaliensia No. 37*. Ed. Baiba Metuzale-Kangare. Uppsala: Uppsala University Press, 2010. 191–198

Kaprāns, Mārtiņš and Olga Procevska. *Latvijas sociālās atmiņas monitorings*. Riga: Latvijas Universitāte, 2013. http://tinyurl.com/pjkok55 (24 March 2015).

Kasianov, Georgiy. "'Nationalized' History: Past Continuous, Present Perfect, Future..." *A Laboratory of Transnational History Ukraine and Recent Ukrainian Historiography*. Eds. Georgiy Kasianov and Philipp Ther. Budapest, New York: Central European University Press, 2009. 7–24.

Kasianov, Georgiy. "'The Nationalization' of History in Ukraine." *The convolutions of historical politics*. Eds. Alexei Miller and Maria Limpan. Budapest, New York: Central European University Press, 2012. 141–174.

Klymenkoa, Lina. "World War II in Ukrainian school history textbooks: mapping the discourse of the past." *Compare* 44.5 (2013): 756–777.

König, René. "Between lay participation and elite knowledge representation." *Information, Communication & Society* 16.2 (2013): 160–177.

Korostelinaa, Karina. "Constructing nation: national narratives of history teachers in Ukraine." *National Identities* 15.4 (2013): 401–416.

Latvian Legion, http://en.wikipedia.org/wiki/Latvian_Legion (24 March 2015).

Liebich, Andre and Oksana Myshlovska. "Bandera: memorialization and commemoration." *Nationalities Papers: The Journal of Nationalism and Ethnicity* 42.5 (2014): 750–770.

Luyt, Brendan. "The Inclusivity of Wikipedia and the Drawing of Expert Boundaries: An Examination of Talk Pages and Reference Lists." *Journal of the American Society for Information Science and Technology* 63.9 (2012): 1868–1878.

Marples, David R. "Open Letter from Scholars and Experts on Ukraine Re. the So-Called "Anti-Communist Law." *Krytyka* April (2015). http://krytyka.com/en/articles/open-letter-schol ars-and-experts-ukraine-re-so-called-anti-communist-law

Mälksoo, Maria. "The memory of becoming European: The East European subalterns and the collective memory of Europe." *European Journal of International Relations* 15.4 (2009): 653–680.

Muižnieks, Nils. Ed. *The Geopolitics of History in Latvian–Russian Relations*. Riga: Academic Press of the University of Latvia, 2011.

Muižnieks, Nils. "History, Memory and Latvian Foreign Policy." *The Geopolitics of History in Latvian–Russian Relations*. Ed. Nils Muižnieks. Riga: Academic Press of the University of Latvia, 2011. 21–30.

Muižnieks, Nils and Vita Zelče. Ed. *Karojošā piemiņa. 16. marts un 9. maijs*. Rīga: Zinātne, 2011.

Onken, Eva-Clarita. "The Baltic states and Moscow's 9 May commemoration: Analysing memory politics in Europe." *Europe-Asia Studies* 59.1 (2007): 23–46.

Page, Ruth. "Counter narratives and controversial crimes: The Wikipedia article for the 'Murder of Meredith Kercher'." *Language and Literature* 23.1 (2014): 61–76.

Pentzold, Christian. "Fixing the floating gap: The online encyclopaedia Wikipedia as a global memory place." *Memory Studies* 2.2 (2009): 255–272.

Rudling, Per A. "Theory and Practice: Historical Representation of the War Time Activities of the OUN-UPA (the Organization of Ukrainian Nationalists – the Ukrainian Insurgent Army)." *East European Jewish Affairs* 36.2 (2006): 163–189.

Rutten, Ellen and Vera Zvereva. "Introduction: old conflicts, new media: post-socialist digital memories. *Memory, Conflict and New Media: Web Wars in Post-Socialist States*. Eds. Ellen Rutten, Julie Fedor and Vera Zvereva. Abingdon, New York: Routledge, 2013. 1–18.

Snyder, Timothy. *Bloodlands: Europe between Hitler and Stalin*. New York: Basic Books, 2010.

Spoerri, Anselm. "What is popular on Wikipedia and why?" *First Monday* 12.4 (2007). http://ti nyurl.com/ogkhrwe (24 March 2015).

Sundin, Olof. "Janitors of knowledge: constructing knowledge in the everyday life of Wikipedia editors." *Journal of Documentation* 67.5 (2011): 840–862.

Ukrainian Insurgent Army. http://en.wikipedia.org/wiki/Ukrainian_Insurgent_Army

Wenger, Etienne. *Communities of practice: Learning, meaning, and identity*. Cambridge, UK: Cambridge University Press, 1998.

Wikipedia: List of guidelines. http://en.wikipedia.org/wiki/Wikipedia:List_of_guidelines (24 March 2015).

Wikipedia:Arbitration/Requests/Case/Eastern European mailing list, retrieved from http://tinyurl.com/lynv4f (23 March 2015).

Wiki Trip. http://sonetlab.fbk.eu/wikitrip/#|en|Ukrainian_Insurgent_Army (24 March 2015).

Wikimedia Traffic Analysis Report. http://tinyurl.com/ohzfgvt (24 March 2015).

Wikimedia Traffic Analysis Report http://tinyurl.com/ph667oy (24 March 2015).

Yurchuk, Yuliya. *Reordering of Meaningful Worlds Memory of the Organization of Ukrainian Nationalists and the Ukrainian Insurgent Army in Post-Soviet Ukraine*. Doctoral Dissertation. Stockholm University, 2014.

Латышский добровольческий легион СС, http://tinyurl.com/jvuqxe2 (24 March 2015).

Украинская повстанческая армия, http://tinyurl.com/o94md3b (24 March 2015).

Volodymyr Kulyk
Negotiating Memory in Online Social Networks: Ukrainian and Ukrainian-Russian Discussions of Soviet Rule and Anti-Soviet Resistance

Although collective memory is widely associated first and foremost with state-controlled ceremonies, monuments and history textbooks, scholars have become fully aware of the fundamental role of the media in its production and maintenance. Moreover, while television is still considered the most important medium in terms of its impact on collective memory, memory studies increasingly turn to the so-called new media, which fundamentally change memory in general and collective memory in particular. The "accessibility, transferability and circulation of digital content"[1] extend the production of collective memory well beyond the state and its authorized agents and, no less importantly, free this production from its traditional containment within national borders. It is the combination of globalization and digital technologies that creates what Reading calls the "globital memory field" as, on the one hand, the circulation of mediated memories that "are less costly, globally connected, and reproducible across different media" and, on the other, as a "struggle by memory agents over the assemblage, mobilization, and securitization of memory capital."[2]

At the same time, in their fascination with the novel features of the digital production of memory, scholars often neglect more familiar but no less important aspects. Most theoretical and empirical studies focus on the new media's capacity to publicize and memorialize current and often private events. However, these media also contribute to the transmission and transformation of memories of events from the more distant past, which are widely recognized as part of collective memory (usually called history) but whose interpretations continue to be contested. As Jakubowicz argues, stories presented in various Internet repositories and forums "have become increasingly potent elements in wider socio-polit-

---

[1] Joanne Garde-Hansen, Andrew Hoskins and Anna Reading. "Introduction." *Save As ... Digital Memories*. Eds. Joanne Garde-Hansen, Andrew Hoskins and Anna Reading. Houndmills and New York: Palgrave Macmillan, 2009, 3.
[2] Anna Reading. "Memory and digital media: Six dynamics of the globital memory field." *On Media Memory: Collective Memory in the New Media Age*. Eds. Motti Neiger, Oren Meyers and Eyal Zandberg. Houndmills and New York: Palgrave Macmillan, 2001, 242.

ical struggles over legitimacy, authenticity and claims to truth."[3] Similarly, scholars seem to be more interested in the global flow of visual images and English-language texts than in the circulation of products in less widespread languages whose capacity to transcend national borders is limited to migrant communities and post-imperial entities. While transnational diaspora networks on the Web have received considerable attention,[4] little research has been carried out into the online communication between people who have found themselves in different states due to geopolitical changes but who continue to speak the same language and, in many cases, to consider themselves members of the same nation.[5] Last but not least, the dominance of the Western perspective results in a focus on the globalization-induced erosion of the national framework in established states, thus leading to the neglect of attempts to *create* such a framework in newly independent countries, which must compete both with old imperial perspectives and new global tendencies.

This chapter contributes to filling in these gaps by examining social network discussions of two historical phenomena crucial to the production of collective memory and national identity in independent Ukraine, namely Soviet rule and anti-Soviet resistance. Although the inherently transnational interaction in online networks precludes the containment of the discussions within the Ukrainian national borders, the participation is limited to people who believe that they have a stake in the collective memory of post-Soviet Ukrainians. Apart from Ukrainians themselves, this includes residents of other countries of the former USSR, first and foremost Russia, many of whom consider the countries' shared past to be a basis for a shared future. While the use of local languages, Ukrainian and Russian, significantly contributes to the exclusion of outsiders, it also reflects the participants' perception of their primary addressees (and, of course, their own linguistic skills). At the same time, the participation of non-Ukrainians ensures that the Soviet past is discussed not only from the Ukrainian national perspective but also from the post-Soviet transnational one. The contestation thus concerns not only specific content of the Ukrainian collective memory

---

3 Andrew Jakubowicz. "Remembering and recovering Shanghai: Seven Jewish families [re]-connect in cyberspace." *Save As … Digital Memories*. Eds. Joanne Garde-Hansen, Andrew Hoskins and Anna Reading. Houndmills and New York: Palgrave Macmillan, 2009, 98.
4 See e.g. Vinay Lal. "The politics of history on the Internet: Cyber-diasporic Hinduism and the North American Hindu diaspora." *Diaspora* 8.2 (1999): 137–172; Brenda Chan. "Imagining the homeland: The Internet and diasporic discourse of nationalism." *Journal of Communication Inquiry* 29.4 (2005): 336–368.
5 Among exceptions, see Shih-Diing Liu. "Undomesticated hostilities: The affective space of Internet chat rooms across the Taiwan Strait." *positions* 16.2 (2008): 435–455.

and national identity but also its salience vis-à-vis a competing supranational perspective positing a common past and future of all peoples of the former USSR.[6]

Historical memory in "old" and "new" media

As with many other media effects, the production of collective memory is medium-specific. It depends heavily on the composition of the audience of a particular type of media, the technology of production and distribution, and the state's policy with regard to the type in question. All of these are, of course, specific to a particular country with its political regime, the ethnolinguistic composition of its population, and the tradition of relations between the media, state and society. The analysis below focuses on the specific case of Ukraine[7] but similar features in the production of memory in certain media types are to be found in many other countries.

Newspapers, historically the first type of what came to be known as the mass media, combine relatively cheap production and relatively slow delivery. On the one hand, newspaper editors can usually afford to commission an original text aimed at giving their audience what they think it wants, rather than republishing what they hope their readers will find acceptable. On the other hand, in order to give the readers a new issue as soon as possible, it is preferable to publish or at least print newspapers regionally rather than nationwide, which also makes possible the supply of regionally adjusted texts, published either in separate outlets or in regional varieties of national ones. In multilingual countries, therefore, newspapers can also accommodate the linguistic preferences of their audiences, which means publishing primarily in the main language of a given locality or region. In Ukraine, the territories of two predominant languages are delineated both by region and type of settlement, with Ukrainian prevailing in the centre-west and the countryside, and Russian in the south-east and in large cities. The lead of Russian over Ukrainian on the newspaper market is due to the prev-

---

[6] On the content, salience and contestation of identity, see Rawi Abdelal et al. "Identity as a variable." *Perspectives on Politics* 4.4 (2007): 695–711; Volodymyr Kulyk. "The media, history and identity: Competing narratives of the past in the Ukrainian popular press." *National Identities* 13.3 (2011): 288.

[7] For more detail, see Volodymyr Kulyk. "War of memories in the Ukrainian media: Diversity of identities, political confrontation, and production technologies." *Memory, Conflict and New Media: Web Wars in Post-Socialist States.* Eds. Ellen Rutten, Julie Fedor and Vera Zvereva. London: Routledge, 2013, 63–81.

alence of urban readers, who are easier to reach for distributors and more attractive to advertisers. Moreover, while both languages are largely understood throughout the country, Ukrainian-speakers are more ready to consume media products in the familiar Russian than Russian-speakers are to accept Ukrainian, which most of them had no need to use in Soviet times. Nevertheless, the availability of outlets in both Ukrainian and Russian allow the overwhelming majority of westerners and easterners to read in their respective languages of preference.[8]

While the newspaper market as a whole is characterized by considerable ideological pluralism, each individual outlet often embodies a rather narrow range of ideological propositions. It is only elite (quality) newspapers that engage with different views of the issues under discussion, including those pertaining to history, and these are presented in overtly ideological genres such as opinion articles and letters to the editor. At the same time, elite newspapers also represent historical matters in less expressly ideological genres such as historical calendars, personal memoirs and news reports on anniversaries and commemorative dates. In tabloids, which are dominant on the newspaper market, such uncontested representations and seemingly non-ideological genres clearly prevail. Disguised as ideologically neutral descriptions of events or individual lives, tabloid texts embody one of the competing historical (meta)narratives[9], as their choice of topics and interpretative frames more or less consistently imbue Ukrainian history with particular content and salience vis-à-vis the histories of other nations and non-national collectivities. Since apparent neutrality is easier to achieve in texts implicitly embodying assumptions that the audience perceives as common sense rather than those challenging such assumptions, tabloids usually adhere to the dominant historical narrative, which in the case of Ukraine means the narrative continuing, albeit with some modifications, the Soviet interpretation of the past.[10]

On television, in contrast, the production is much more expensive and the delivery is virtually instantaneous, which makes it preferable for commercial broadcasters to buy domestic and foreign products that can be expected to at-

---

[8] Volodymyr Kulyk. "Language policy in the Ukrainian media: authorities, consumers and producers." *Europe-Asia Studies* 65.7 (2013): 1430–1431.
[9] A metanarrative is a "global or totalizing cultural narrative schema which orders and explains knowledge and experience". See John Stephen and Robyn McCallum. *Retelling Stories, Framing Culture: Traditional Stories and Metanarratives in Children's Literature*. New York: Garland 1998, 6. Usually such schemata are simply called narratives, e.g. narratives of Ukrainian history, and it is to this prevalent use of the term that I will adhere.
[10] Kulyk. "The media, history and identity," 294–301.

tract a broad audience. As in many countries across the globe, television is the most popular medium in Ukraine, meaning that television audiences are inclusive both socially and geographically, and thus also linguistically and ideologically. The most popular channels broadcast nationwide and, therefore, must provide content acceptable for people in all parts of the country, although they are particularly interested in urban residents, who are more attractive to advertisers. Linguistically, this means a combination of Ukrainian and Russian on each channel, a practice that has been used since Soviet times, first with the heavy dominance of Russian and then with an increasing share of Ukrainian as required by post-Soviet legislation. The greater readiness of the audience to watch in Russian and the higher economic effectiveness of such products, which can be consumed without translation in many post-Soviet countries, encourage most channels to fill the prime time with Russian-language films and series, while scheduling the Ukrainian-language products in less popular timeslots. Moreover, both Russian and Ukrainian producers tailor their films, serials, and game and reality shows primarily for Russian audiences, since Ukrainian viewers are fewer and supposedly less demanding. These products are usually shown on Ukrainian channels in Russian, while most Western products are translated into Ukrainian, a practice both reflecting and shaping viewer preferences. Most channels limit their own production to news, talk shows and occasional documentaries, while filling the lion's share of the air time with films and series purchased from Russian, Ukrainian or Western producers.[11]

While Western movies, documentaries and other products influence the Ukrainian viewers' memory and identity by turning their imagination and empathy to foreign places and people, Russian and Russian-oriented Ukrainian products can also affect the viewers' beliefs regarding their own country. They portray events in Russia or, less frequently, Ukraine or other parts of the former USSR, which are almost completely cleansed of any linguistic, ethnocultural and ideological features other than Russian and, at the same time, presented as common to the whole post-Soviet space (thus, in effect, equating this space with Russia). As far as historical memory is concerned, most movies and series deal with the Soviet or Russian imperial past, which is portrayed as a time of East Slavic commonality. These products thus covertly present the Ukrainian identity as compatible with or even subordinate to the Russian one.[12] In contrast, those domestically-tailored products that embody a clearly non-Russian Ukrainian identity

---

[11] Volodymyr Kulyk. *Dyskurs ukraïns'kykh medii: identychnosti, ideolohiï, vladni stosunky*. Kyiv: Krytyka, 2010, 218–230; Kulyk. "Language policy in the Ukrainian media," 1425–1426.
[12] Kulyk. *Dyskurs ukraïns'kykh medii*, 305–307.

usually do so much more conspicuously, which largely results from genre conventions, as in political talk shows where memory-related issues are discussed if they happen to have caused political controversies. Even in the less obviously ideological genre of news, stories on historical matters usually draw clear connections between past and present, which makes underlying ideological propositions more visible and increases the likelihood that the audiences perceive as partisan the embodied versions of memory and identity. Moreover, the cumulative share of these more visibly ideological products in the daily broadcasting of most Ukrainian channels is much smaller than that of the seemingly neutral products, and the average rating is considerably lower.[13]

The Internet combines very low production cost and very fast delivery of products which cannot be hindered by state borders or effectively controlled by the authorities. Moreover, the unprecedented ease of access to the production and transmission of verbal and audiovisual texts radically democratizes the mediated communication. The broadcast-era "mass-produced, mass-disseminated content mass-consumed by a large audience" is supplemented and increasingly replaced by "peer-to-peer, horizontal, personal communications"[14] between millions of people, often separated by thousands of miles, political borders and socioeconomic gaps, which results in a high level of ideological, cultural and linguistic pluralism. At the same time, the online communication perpetuates, and in some cases exacerbates, inequalities within and between countries. On the one hand, better-off and technologically savvy people are more likely to get access to the Web and use it more actively, which means that professionals, urbanites and the youth are often overrepresented among the producers of Internet content.[15] On the other hand, while the participation in online communication has extended to the most distant parts of the world, the production of truly popular and influential texts is still largely concentrated in the few countries with high technological capacity, vast financial resources and populations possessing good skills in transnational languages. Accordingly, it is the ideological perspectives favoured by the producers in these countries that prevail in global communication. Although the spread of the Internet increases the online use of dozens of languages, English remains the main means of transnational

---

13 Ibid, 218–225.
14 William Merrin. "Understanding me-dia: The second reformation." *Media Studies 2.0.* http://mediastudies2point0.blogspot.com. Personal blog. 6 March 2010 (20 December 2012).
15 For evidence from Ukraine, see "KMIS: Chyslo internet-korystuvachiv v Ukraïni zroslo do 40%." *Dzerkalo tyzhnia. Ukraïna*, 15 December 2011. http://news.dt.ua/TECHNOLOGIES/kmis_chislo_internet-korystuvachiv_v_ukrayini_zroslo_do_40–93827.html (25 December 2011).

communication, which affects the users' language proficiencies and, eventually, preferences even in purportedly "domestic" interaction. However, in the former colonial/imperial peripheries, their metropolitan languages successfully compete on the Web both with English, which remains much less known, and with local languages, which cannot boast adequate production in many genres, all the more so because many active users are not sufficiently proficient in or attached to these languages.[16]

In Ukraine, both internal and external disparities contribute to the predominance of the Russian language: that is, given the much larger scope of the Russian compared to the Ukrainian segment of the Web, Ukrainian users are often tempted to read and post in Russian, which thereby exacerbates the linguistic disparity within Ukraine's online community due to the overrepresentation of urbanites and well-to-do strata. Since Russian sites appear more prominently in the results of Internet searches, even those made in Ukrainian, Ukrainians tend to use Russian resources for various purposes, except for those having to do with exclusively domestic affairs. Moreover, ostensibly Ukrainian sites heavily republish texts from Russian ones, thus further blurring the line between the two segments. Even in the Ukrainian segment, most sites operate in Russian or in both languages (some use three, adding English, while many others offer it *instead* of Ukrainian). Purely Ukrainian-language resources are limited to few portals, blogs and specialized sites.[17] Accordingly, a 2012 survey revealed that respondents read Internet material exclusively or predominantly in Russian four times as often as they read exclusively or predominantly in Ukrainian, a much greater disparity than for newspapers and television.[18]

Discourse on historical memory is one important manifestation of the Ukrainian Internet's peculiar combination of diversified production and truncated post-imperial transnationality, or rather continued reproduction of imperial quasi-nationhood. In contrast to the "old" media, Ukrainian online outlets have been relatively free from state control and are thus able to pursue topics

---

[16] David Chrystal. *Language and the Internet*. Cambridge: Cambridge University Press, 2001; *The Multilingual Internet: Language, Culture, and Communication Online*. Eds. Brenda Danet and Susan C. Herring. New York: Oxford University Press, 2007, ch. 13–18.
[17] Lesia Chornopys'ka. "'Zruchna' mova ukraïns'kykh internet-ZMI." *Slovo Prosvity*, 8–14 September 2005. http://slovoprosvity.com.ua/modules.php?name=News&file=article&sid=2033 (15 July 2006); V. B. "Shcho take 'ukraïnomovnyi Internet'?" *Ukraïns'kyi Prostir*, 14 June 2011. http://ukr-net.info/2011/06/14/scho-take-ukrajinomovnyj-internet (15 August 2011).
[18] The nationwide representative survey (N=2029) was conducted in February 2012 by the Kyiv International Institute of Sociology. It was made possible by a grant awarded to me by the Shevchenko Society in America (from the Natalia Danylchenko Endowment Fund).

of their choice. Moreover, because of the low production cost, online media, in principle, can afford not to care much about advertisements and ratings which, in turn, makes it possible for many outlets to focus on political and cultural issues and employ analytical formats that are marginalized in more commercial media. These factors make the Internet a particularly suitable medium for expressing the preoccupation with memory and other aspects of identity, all the more so because interactive communication encourages discussion of various perspectives on the topic under consideration. Not only do many online news media pay close attention to matters of history and memory, but numerous archival or discussion-oriented websites also deal primarily with these matters. Perhaps the most prominent online media contributor to the production of Ukrainian historical memory is the website called *Istorychna Pravda* (a subsidiary of one of Ukraine's leading Internet publications, *Ukraïns'ka Pravda*), which features original and republished texts on various aspects of Ukrainian and other countries' history.[19] The editors consciously assume the role of public historians, which manifests itself in their presentation of the outlet as "a site of scholarly and journalistic discussions of the politics of history and memory" as well as a "source of news" on relevant topics and "storage of artefacts."[20] Most participants in memory-related discussions on this and many other Ukrainian websites seem to be residents of Ukraine or Ukrainian migrants abroad, but some posters declare or otherwise reveal their identity as foreigners, in most cases Russians. Although the use of Ukrainian in many original publications and responses thereto impedes the participation of people with inadequate knowledge of the language, many Russians understand enough Ukrainian to express their opinions and/or care too much about the topic under discussion to refrain from doing so.[21]

Soon after blogs and social networks became popular in Ukraine, they came to be used for, among other purposes, discussions on history and the politics of memory, which also mainly engage Ukrainians and Russians. Many blogs presented as outlets of organizations and localities limit their history pages to reference-based information, which is usually taken from encyclopaedias or other normative publications. Local history and tourist blogs, while seeking to give the audience interesting information on particular localities, buildings or per-

---

[19] *Istorychna Pravda*. http://www.istpravda.com.ua.
[20] Vakhtanh Kipiani and Pavlo Solod'ko. "Pro proekt." *Istorychna Pravda*, (2010), http://www.istpravda.com.ua/about (10 December 2010).
[21] In occasional discussions of the matter in various Internet outlets, many users with inadequate knowledge of Ukrainian report using Google Translate, similarly to what they do to read texts in other foreign languages.

sonalities, likewise tend to adhere to the dominant narrative of the past. Even a collective blog that focuses on little-known events and unusual interpretations and thus claims to present an "alternative history", while sometimes mentioning sympathetically the Ukrainian struggle for independence, otherwise implicitly denies its legitimacy by portraying the Russian imperial past as common to all East-Slavic peoples.[22] However, some blogs unequivocally undermine the established post-Soviet narrative, either in occasional comments reflecting on current events or, as in a collective blog, *Ukraïns'ka istoriia*, by purposefully disseminating "correct" interpretations of various episodes of the past, first and foremost those that the Soviet regime allegedly silenced or falsified.[23]

Much more popular than topical websites or blogs, however, are social networks, the interaction in which is one of the most important uses of the Internet in Ukraine (reported by 46% of all users in 2011), second only to emailing (51%) and surpassing even information searching (38%), let alone communication in forums, chats and blogs (14%). In contrast to most parts of the world, in the post-Soviet space Russian-based networks intended as a local response to Facebook (FB) quite successfully compete with the global giant. The largest of these networks, *VKontakte* (VK), is the most popular network and one of the most popular Web resources in Russia, Ukraine and other post-Soviet countries, particularly among young people.[24] As of late 2011, this network encompassed 67% of Ukraine's Internet users, compared to 43% for Facebook and 6% for the most popular of the blog platforms, Livejournal. While VK is particularly popular with the youth (95% of Internet users between 16 and 25 years reported having registered), the use of FB is rather evenly distributed among all age groups.[25]

The two most popular social networks, *VKontakte* and Facebook, contribute to the production of collective memory in several main ways. To begin with, the participants' personal pages may contain texts, pictures or links to other Web resources. Some quasi-personal pages are established in the name of prominent historical personalities or organizations. In addition, there are topical pages featuring particular historical events or commemorative initiatives. But perhaps the

---

22 *Al'ternativnaia Istoriia*. http://alternathistory.org.ua.
23 *Ukraïns'ka istoriia*. http://history-ua.livejournal.com.
24 Facebook. http://www.facebook.com; VKontakte. http://vk.com.
25 "Issledovanie: samymi populiarnymi sredi ukraintsev sotssetiami iavliaiutsia Vkontakte i Odnoklassniki." *Korrespondent*, 22 November 2011. http://korrespondent.net/business/mmedia_and_adv/1285832-issledovanie-samymi-populyarnymi-sredi-ukraincev-socsetyami-yavlyayutsya-vkontakte-i-odnoklassniki (25 November 2011); "VKontakte", "Odnoklassniki" ta Facebook lidyruiut' sered sotsial'nykh merezh v Ukraïni, (2011). http://www.gfk.ua/public_relations/press/press_articles/009018/index.ua.html (20 December 2012).

most important of the memory-related practices are participation in topical groups or communities which facilitate a rather equal exchange of information and opinions (even though the group administrators often have the power to "ban" those participants seen as violating the rules). A group can be started by any user with an opinion, a question, a link or another means of suggesting a topic for discussion, thereby provoking responses in the form of answers to the question, comments on the opinion, or links to publications more or less loosely related to the suggested topic. In VK, the interaction can also be continued by suggesting a new "topic" within the same group, which often results in dozens or even hundreds of separate exchanges with little interaction among them. Some administrators limit the membership in their groups to prevent abuse by ideologically hostile or simply irresponsible people, but most groups remain open to all users of the network and, therefore, to all views on the issues under discussion. Given the predominantly Russian-speaking profile of the Ukrainian users and the predominant practice of conducting transnational interaction in a commonly understood language, most discussions take place in Russian, particularly in VK. However, many original or later posters use Ukrainian, either presupposing primarily domestic, communicative partners or refusing to accommodate foreign ones, particularly those with opposing views. Among the millions of groups on VK, thousands focus on issues of history and historical memory in Ukraine, with group memberships ranging from dozens of thousands to the initiator alone and the number of posts in specific discussions ranging from thousands to a single entry. Particularly popular are the groups focusing on controversial episodes of history and contemporary commemorative initiatives, the latter contributing to the discussion and contestation of the former.[26]

Discourse on twentieth-century Ukrainian history on Facebook and *VKontakte*

Of all the differences between the historical memories of different groups in the Ukrainian population, the most dissimilar and divisive are the perceptions regarding twentieth-century developments. Although the evaluations of the Russian-dominated entities of the more distant past also vary considerably across regional, ethnolinguistic and ideological groups, it is the interaction between

---

[26] Cf. Vera Zvereva. "Historical events and the social network 'V Kontakte'." *East European Memory Studies* 7 (2011). http://www.memoryatwar.org/enewsletter-nov-2011.pdf (25 March 2012).

public representations and personal or family memories that makes the attitudes toward the Soviet rule particularly hard to change and, therefore, to reconcile. In fact, rather than seeing such reconciliation as imperative for national unity, Ukraine's political elites have often exploited the differences for their own electoral purposes. This was particularly the case after the Orange Revolution, when the confrontation between two main political groupings manifested itself, among other things, in a stronger emphasis on their respective versions of the national past presented as important elements of the identities of their core constituencies.[27] As many media outlets not only provided a discursive arena for confrontation but also supported the position of their political patrons, public discourse was characterized by the competition of the two contrasting views of the Ukrainian past, which also implied very different choices for the present. The competition of memory discourses within Ukraine was also exacerbated by representations of history emanating from Russian politicians and media who believed they had a stake in the debate about the identity of the neighbouring population, and did not lack channels to make their opinion heard, all the more so because of the above-mentioned heavy presence of Russian media products in Ukraine.[28]

These two versions, or (meta)narratives, of Ukrainian history differ first and foremost in their interpretations of certain periods of interaction between Ukraine and Russia. One of these narratives I call *East Slavic* or *Soviet*, the former name referring to an emphasis on East Slavic commonality and the latter to the embodiment in the Soviet official discourse, from which this narrative was adopted by its post-Soviet adherents. This narrative continues the Soviet view of a common history uniting the East Slavic peoples and treats the Russian Empire and the USSR as voluntary unions of Russians and Ukrainians. In contrast, the *nationalist* or *anti-Soviet* narrative sees Ukraine's incorporation in Russian-dominated entities as imperial subjugation established and sustained largely by force. The two narratives contest in particular the interpretation of two symbolically important phenomena of the twentieth century. While the nationalist narrative considers the Great Famine of 1932–1933 (Holodomor) genocide against

---

[27] Andrei Portnov. *Uprazhneniia s istoriei po-ukrainski.* Moscow: OGI, Polit.ru, Memorial, 2010, 79–101; Tatiana Zhurzhenko. "'Capital of despair': Holodomor Memory and Political Conflicts in Kharkiv after the Orange Revolution." *East European Politics and Societies* 25.3 (2011): 610–633; Volodymyr Kulyk. "Natsionalistychne proty radians'koho: istorychna pam'iat' u nezalezhnii Ukraïni." *historians.in.ua*, 20 September 2012. http://historians.in.ua/index.php/istoriya-i-pamyat-vazhki-pitannya/379-volodymyr-kulyk-natsionalistychne-proty-radianskoho-istorychna-pamiat-u-nezalezhnii-ukraini (20 December 2012).
[28] Kulyk. *Dyskurs ukraïns'kykh medii*, 296–312.

Ukrainians, its competitor views it as a tragedy of all Soviet peoples and a crime of the Stalinist regime rather than of Russian imperialism.[29] Even more contrasting are the views of the Ukrainian Insurgent Army (Ukraïns'ka Povstans'ka Armiia, UPA), the nationalist military organization of the 1940s and the early 1950s, which appears as a force struggling for national independence in the anti-Soviet narrative and as a collaborator with the Nazi occupiers in the East Slavic one.[30] It is the East Slavic version of the Soviet past in general and of these two controversial phenomena in particular that have been clearly favoured in Russia since Vladimir Putin came to power in 2000, which has been reflected in Russian political and media discourse constantly spilling over into Ukraine.[31]

While the views of Russian elites are explicitly or implicitly presented in all kinds of media, ordinary Russians can reach their Ukrainian counterparts primarily through social networks, which are also the main site of ideological discussions within each country. Given the huge differences of views, both within Ukraine and across the Ukrainian-Russian border, it is little wonder that the discussion of memory-related matters often becomes tense or outright hostile, particularly with regard to symbolically charged phenomena such as the Holodomor and the UPA. Discussion is often intentionally provoked by the use of opinion-eliciting genres such as surveys and quizzes, by an offensive style or an overly radical position. Moreover, many participants enter the interaction not only for the sake of seriously discussing the topic at hand but also, or even primarily, for expressing their ethnocultural identity or simply having fun. Such diverse uses and abuses are facilitated by the generally liberal politics of "befriending" other network users (eager to have many online friends, people often send friendship requests to – and accept them from – complete strangers who have little in common with themselves) and by easy access to topical groups (most such groups are open, and administrators rarely ban anyone for misbehaviour). The confrontation and hostility seem to be more characteristic of VK, where ideological discussions tend to involve larger numbers of people who, moreover, often remain anonymous and are thus less constrained by the perceived norms of interpersonal interaction. This manifests itself, in particular, in the

---

29 Mykola Riabchuk. "Holodomor: The Politics of Memory and Political Infighting in Contemporary Ukraine." *Harriman Review* 16.2 (2008): 3–9; Portnov. *Uprazhneniia s istoriei po-ukrainski*, 84–90.
30 Mykola Riabchuk. "Kul'tura pamiati i politika zabveniia." *Otechestvennye zapiski* 34.1 (2007): 42–55; Wilfried Jilge. "Nationalukrainischer Befreiungskampf: Die Umwertung des Zweiten Weltkriegs in der Ukraine." *Osteuropa* 58.6 (2008): 167–186.
31 See e.g. Boris Dubin. "Pamiat', voina, pamiat' o voine. Konstruirovanie proshlogo v sotsial'-noi pamiati poslednikh desiatiletii." *Otechestvennye zapiski* 4 (2008): 6–21.

widespread phenomenon of "trolling" i.e. intentionally frustrating the interaction in groups or on personal pages perceived as hostile. While a nuisance to those participants primarily interested in substantive discussion, trolling is often tolerated as contributing to more lively interaction and fun. In addition to trolling-opposing groups, VK users frequently complain to the network administration about those groups' allegedly inappropriate functioning (including the fomenting of ethnic hatred), which sometimes leads to their being blocked, particularly if complaints become numerous.

One way to assess the level of contestation of memory and identity in a group or on a page is by comparing the frequencies of two prevalent responses to its (memory-related) posts over a considerable period of time (long enough to level post-to-post variation). In contrast to *likes*, which signal the reception of and general agreement with a statement made in the post, *comments* can be both supportive and critical. Moreover, even support is often expressed in comments with either a qualification or elaboration, thereby more or less modifying the original proposition. Therefore, the comments to likes ratio can be seen as a rough estimate of the degree of contestation in particular online arenas or with regard to particular kinds of statements (by topic, genre, author, etc.). Table 1 presents the ratios for assorted groups and pages in the two networks (FB and VK) that feature posts having to do with twentieth-century Ukrainian history and collective memory. In addition to three groups, all related to the Ukrainian Insurgent Army, and a quasi-personal page established in the name of the UPA and its core political grouping, the Organization of Ukrainian Nationalists (OUN), the table includes a personal page by a prominent Ukrainian journalist Vakhtang Kipiani who has, among his other roles, been the editor of the *Istorychna Pravda* website (in the last case, I only analyze those posts having to do with history or memory). To give the reader some idea of what these groups and pages are like, I also indicate the number of members for the groups and the number of friends or subscribers for the pages (as of 1 May 2012), the number of posts in the month of April 2012 (for which the likes and comments were counted), and the share of posts having to do exclusively or partially with Ukraine. Notwithstanding the great variation within each network, it is clear that contestation is much stronger in VK groups, where participants comment on posts they have read at least as frequently as they express their liking thereof. In contrast, the two collective entities on FB, while differing greatly in the scope of participation and posting, have equally low levels of commenting, which demonstrates the primarily ritualistic nature of most people's association with them as members or subscribers. At the same time, Kipiani's public prominence and posting inventiveness ensure significant readership of and rather active response to his posts, although more often with likes than comments.

Table 1. Contestation of memory in assorted memory-related groups and pages on Facebook and *VKontakte* in April 2012[32]

Group/ page, network	Participation as of 1.05.2012	Number of posts in April 2012	Percentage of posts regarding Ukraine	Number of likes per post	Number of comments per post	Comments to likes ratio
OUN-UPA (FB)	4,996	6	100.0	3.3	0.2	0.09
Novyny pro OUN-UPA (FB)	303	56	66.1	1.0	0.2	0.20
Vakhtang Kipiani page (FB)	4,620	67	46.3	59.5	19.1	0.32
OUN-UPA (VK)	1,961	149	59.7	3.1	3.2	1.03
Protiv OUN-UPA (VK)	21,636	280	45.7	4.1	6.7	1.63

Turning to qualitative analysis of particular discursive practices, I would like to begin with a characteristic example of a confrontation which does not leave any chance for a compromise between staunch supporters of the opposing narratives. Such confrontations often result in one party quitting the discussion, usually with a newcomer to the group leaving the terrain that turned out to be dominated by the "enemy." The example comes from a group that defines itself as being "Against the OUN-UPA and other Nazi collaborators" and, accordingly, is dominated by supporters of the East Slavic narrative. In early April 2012, a routine reference to a Ukrainian nationalist publication intended to evoke the group participants' indignation was met, among expected responses, by a voice of strong condemnation of the prevalent view, thus provoking a heated exchange

---

32 Included are the following: Facebook page under the name of OUN-UPA. http://www.facebook.com/profile.php?id=100001085783391&fref=ts; Facebook group "Novyny pro OUN-UPA" [News on OUN-UPA], http://www.facebook.com/groups/209568449142720/?fref=ts; Facebook page by Vakhtang Kipiani. http://www.facebook.com/vakhtang.kipiani?fref=ts; *VKontakte* group "OUN-UPA, Stepan Bandera ta Novitni Natsionalisty" [OUN-UPA, Stepan Bandera and Modern Nationalists], http://vk.com/novitninatsionalisty; *VKontakte* group "Protiv OUN-UPA i prochikh posobnivov fashizma" [Against OUN-UPA and other Fascist collaborators], http://vk.com/club1001828. Posts were counted in early May 2012 and some of them have since been removed, particularly on FB. The names and addresses of the pages and groups are listed as at the time of my last accessing them for this writing (20 December 2012).

between supporters of that view and the dissident. The latter soon left the group in protest, accompanied by another participant who only took the floor to announce his departure. While most of the defenders of the East Slavic narrative did little more than strongly condemn the dissenter and thereby assert their own identity and legitimacy, one discussant referred to unspecified documents that would supposedly back his view of the UPA combatants as Nazi collaborators, a reference obviously intended to lend more authority to his claim to truth. Most of the participants used the language primarily associated with the narrative they stood for, namely Russian, but one of them resorted to Ukrainian, perhaps in order to make his words more persuasive to his Ukrainian-speaking opponent. At the same time, one of those protesting against the dominant position started his departure announcement in Russian but then switched to Ukrainian, which he must have viewed as more appropriate for such a statement. Whatever the language, most posters make explicit or implicit claims to true Ukrainian identity (in this case, none reported coming from another country) and, by the same token, deny the legitimacy of such claims by their opponents. One discussant countered the perception of the UPA combatants (also called Banderites, after the name of a OUN leader, Stepan Bandera) as Ukrainian heroes by referring not just to their allegedly criminal deeds but more specifically to their crimes against fellow Ukrainians. The following is a shortened version of the exchange (in Russian and Ukrainian, Ukrainian-language parts italicized):

OP: ... School children in Lviv painted Easter eggs in the Nazi colours [this is the title of a publication followed by a link thereto]
PKh: Schoolchildren are not to blame. They have been taught to do so by Nazi remnants.
YaA: Yeah. But in about ten years they will grow up and become the most active part of society.
PKh: Will they live that long? It is dangerous to be a Nazi.
SB: *If one does not like Ukraine and the UPA, then there are two options: either this person is mad or an enemy. These people contradict themselves, live in Ukraine, communicate in Russian, ridicule its [Ukraine's] language and history. Think who you are. Who has imposed [on you] this way of thinking and living?*
PKh: Why are you, a bunch of freaks, sticking your UPA to our Ukraine? For us Ukrainians they were and remain Nazi. Just like you are Nazi for us, a bunch of defective heroizators of the criminal Banderite gang. And besides, it is funny when a bunch of freaks is calling the country to think)))) ...
DZ: If a person views as heroes those people who carried out their antihuman ideas, this person is a moral freak.
OI: *If you do not like Soviet Ukraine and the Soviet troops which liberated almost entire Europe, then you can separate from Ukraine and make your heroes anybody including Hitler!!!!!!*
SB: *The Soviet regime, by safely concealing everything, made it impossible for those who lived not in the west to learn the true history. I was deceived too when I was studying,*

> *and although I am from central Ukraine I did not lack brains to learn history first-hand from a UPA soldier.*

PKh: Don't mind the Soviet [regime]... German, American, Polish documents and even confessions of the UPA bastards themselves, did the Soviet regime made them impossible too? One who is not up in the clouds but studies everything thoroughly, knows history!... in contrast to your bunch of brainless idiots. A soldier? Since when has a Nazi slut become a soldier???? Did they have any fights or win any great battles? A terrorist cannot be a soldier. This is stupid. There are many mummers too. You better read documents rather than listening to gossiping grannies.

AK: I am leaving the group, *good bye!*

PKh: Well, *good bye*... It is even strange you did not bark 'Glory to Ukraine!'[33] It means you are still having doubts... My advice to you is to read documents and to think for yourself without listening to anybody. There is no one else in this [Ukrainian] state to help you with this. Think for yourself. ...

PKh: The lost generation of the five Orange years manifests itself. I pity them.

SB: *I pity that part of people who are affected by the 'Russian ideology'. A Ukrainian is one who loves Ukraine and its language, one who respects its history. And one who vilifies the history of people who fought for independent Ukraine is an enemy and a traitor, in other words, a khokhol* [derogatory word for a Ukrainian]. *Good bye.* ...

DZ: for the likes of [SB] the words 'independent Ukraine' has already become an exhortation; one can do whatever one wishes, kill, rob, rape and once you are doing all these vile things with the words 'Glory to Ukraine' you have an absolution!! Do they have any squeamishness to prevent them from receiving and being proud of how these 'heroes' fought for independent Ukraine?? I do not want anything that was obtained in such a criminal way. By the way, it would be worth knowing that those fighters for Ukraine killed with equal ease similar fighters for Ukraine who just happened to be in rival organizations and that was sufficient [crime to be killed].[34]

Sometimes, however, adherents of the same narrative may disagree with a memory proposition made in a certain post. Right after the above-quoted exchange with Ukrainian nationalists, the anti-OUN-UPA group was thrown into a debate about the final episodes of World War II as represented in a recent Russian-German coproduced movie called *4 Days in May*. The movie makers' portrayal of an

---

[33] This traditional greeting of the OUN-UPA is a ritual expression used by their followers to declare their identity and, in conflicting situations, to antagonize ideological opponents, which is why it is often employed for trolling. Since the Euromaidan protests of 2013–2014, this greeting was embraced by large masses of supporters of Ukraine's independence and redefined as pertaining to all heroes fighting for it in the past and present. See Volodymyr Kulyk. "Ukrainian nationalism since the outbreak of Euromaidan." *Ab Imperio* 3 (2014): 101.

[34] *VKontakte* group "Protiv OUN-UPA i prochikh posobnivov fashizma." Posts dated 6 and 7 April 2012 (20 December 2012). Here and in the following quoted exchange, names are abbreviated.

attempted rape of a German girl by a Soviet officer in May 1945, even though presented as an isolated event rather than a widespread case (which such rapes arguably were in those days) was perceived by defenders of the iconic view of the Red Army as a distortion of historical truth, a slander. But not all group members shared this view: one participant called for accepting this black spot on the generally bright image of the army and, by extension, the state it fought for. In this case, the defenders of the established Soviet narrative aimed their indignation not at Ukrainian nationalists but at Russian "liberasts", a label made by combining the words "liberal" and "pederast" and thereby presenting liberalism as inseparable from or even identical to (the support for) homosexuality, in other words, as a perversion. For staunch supporters of the established East Slavic narrative, any critic thereof, either Ukrainian or Russian, was a "stinker." In contrast, moderate supporters of East Slavic commonality were not only ready to recognize some Soviet sins but also believed that it was such recognition that set them apart from their Ukrainian nationalist opponents, whom they viewed as flatly rejecting any critique of the anti-Soviet position. In the passage quoted below, the adherence to the same narrative and the same identity is reflected in the use of the same language, Russian, except for the word "Ukrainophobes", which is rendered in the original language to mark it as a term of the Ukrainian nationalist discourse:

AG: Once again, lousy liberasts vilify our grandparents... [included is a link to the movie's trailer]
PKh: There are a lot of stinkers in Russia, too.
SS: Why stinkers? There were no rapists and bandits in the Red Army or what?
PKh: No there weren't. Rapists and bandits were tried by a [military] tribunal and after that they were no longer Red Army soldiers.
PKh: They [the movie's makers] just took out an old tale of raped German women and begin to harp on it. What else can one say about them? Stinkers, nothing else.
SS: It is not a tale but a fact. You are making saints out of the Red Army. There were among them rapists, marauders and robbers. One must look at both sides. Otherwise, you are no different than the Ukrainian nationalists. They too, if one has a different view than theirs, start howling stinkers, *Ukrainophobes*. ...[35]

Surveys occasionally initiated in VK groups are interesting not only as triggers of discussion that highlights nuances of opinions but also as an indication of the degree of disagreement about a given issue among group members. While most respondents give answers in tune with the prevalent mood in the group, the share of opposing answers can be seen as a rough estimate of the strength

---

35 Ibid. Posts dated 9 April 2012 (20 December 2012).

of (any) dissent, at least when the general number of responses is fairly large. Another, somewhat discordant estimate is the ratio of comments to votes, similar to the comments to likes ratio discussed above. In particularly controversial cases, more participants express their opinions, not only by choosing one of the suggested answers but also by elaborating on their choice in comments, which often trigger responses from others. Some surveys also encourage comments by inviting the respondents to specify some options or add their own.

For example, the same anti-OUN-UPA group quoted above featured the following question in April 2012: "Still, what do you believe the UPA did for Ukraine (Little Rus')?" The author implicitly guided the respondents toward the East Slavic view by using two names for Ukraine, with the second one derived from the imperial Russian tradition, which was thereby presented as perfectly legitimate. At the same time, the list of options included not only two negative evaluations but also four various positive answers and one that allowed the respondents to suggest their own version of the UPA's "merits." Although the unequivocal denial of any merit ("They did nothing good, they were losers, traitors and enemies") turned out to be the most popular, with 30% out of nearly 10,000 responses, this combined with the other critical view ("When they failed [to achieve their goals], they hid, robbed and killed in order to survive", 13%) did not get the support of a majority of those who chose to respond. Considerable portions thereof opted for positive evaluations such as "They liberated [their] land from the enemies" (14%), "They have other merits (to be specified in comments)" (11%) and "They created a new state" (7%). Rather surprisingly, the disagreement did not in this case lead to a long debate, as demonstrated by a rather low number of comments on the matter (70). With just one exception, the dissident respondents refused to elaborate on their opinions, so the supporters of the prevalent negative view were left to debate among themselves, not so much on the UPA as on the Soviet regime against which the nationalist movement had fought.[36] In contrast, a survey on the attitude toward the former USSR in a group of OUN-UPA supporters and "modern nationalists" provoked a long stream of comments (290) traded over a period of eight months, despite a much lower number of respondents (119) and a prevalent support for the negative attitude (63%). Only 9% declared the outright positive attitude, 12% defined their position as combining "the positive and the negative" and further 16% opted for the view of the bygone state as "just the past." While some comments were limited to unequivocal condemnations, others reflected on both negative and positive aspects

---

[36] Ibid. Post dated 14 April 2012 and responses dated 14 to 27 April 2012 (20 December 2012).

of the Soviet rule, with nuances of the positions being discussed no less actively than radical differences.³⁷ These examples suggest that while the ratio of comments to votes indicates the degree of any disagreement among the group members, the distribution of responses shows how radically their views differ, that is, whether the disagreement primarily takes place between or within distinct narratives.

However, the production of collective memory in social networks is by no means limited to overt debates among adherents of the opposing historical narratives or even between different versions of the same narrative. Many posts in history-related groups, let alone on personal pages of network users, contribute to this production by history-related statements that remain almost or completely unopposed. This pertains in particular to commemorative statements such as those reminding one's readers (other group members or friends/subscribers having access to one's personal page) about an anniversary of a certain event or a certain person's birth or death. Although in the case of most controversial figures critical comments may question the legitimacy of (any) commemoration thereof, in many other cases commemorative acts are met with few if any comments, a reaction which can be seen as a sign of tacit support or indifference, with a large number of likes increasing the likelihood of the former interpretation. For example, the group of OUN-UPA supporters responded lukewarmly to a number of posts by one participant commemorating prominent figures of the Ukrainian nationalist narrative. Even a post about the anniversary of the assassination of Yevhen Konovalets, the founding leader of the OUN, was met with only four likes and not a single comment.³⁸ Although he was killed by a Soviet agent (which the post did not mention), Konovalets was not nearly as prominent or controversial a figure as Bandera, who led the organization at a later stage and became a symbol of its fight against the Soviet regime. This makes the former figure less known, less interesting and less strongly felt about than the latter, which helps explain the otherwise surprising silence following this affirmation of the Ukrainian nationalist narrative. Much more enthusiastic was the anti-OUN-UPA group's response to a commemorative post about an anniversary of the 1944 Soviet "liberation" of Odesa from the German troops, featuring a picture of the main war memorial in the city highlighted with the candle-formed words "Motherland remembers" and a red flag of the former USSR which indicated

---

37 *VKontakte* group "OUN-UPA, Stepan Bandera ta Novitni Natsionalisty." Topic "Shcho dlia vas oznachae SSSR?" Posts dated 16 May 2011 to 30 January 2012 (20 December 2012).
38 Ibid. Post dated 22 May 2012 (20 December 2012).

what motherland they referred to.[39] There were no comments but as many as 71 likes and 13 shares (reproduction of the post on readers' own pages, another possible response to posts in both networks), which shows that the act of commemoration was supported by the bulk of the group and thus can be considered quite successful. Although such commemorations primarily engage people who already lean to the historical narrative featuring the event or person in question, the unopposed reaffirmation of the high value of this episode reproduces not only the narrative itself but also an identity it ascribes to contemporaries through their posited relation with the past.

It is such unopposed reaffirmation that prevails on Facebook, where groups and personal pages are more likely than in *VK* to be sites of the respectful exchange of opinions and emotions between like-minded people. Even on much-visited pages such as that of Vakhtang Kipiani, there appear few voices radically disagreeing with posts pertaining to history and memory. When Kipiani harshly criticized in August 2012 the Ukrainian communist leader Petro Symonenko's suggestion to hold a referendum on the state symbols since those currently in use were allegedly discredited due to having been employed by Ukrainian nationalists collaborating with the Nazis, the poster's attitude was shared by an overwhelming majority of those who expressed their opinions in comments. Out of 94 comments, only one voiced a clearly dissenting opinion on the matter. Even more indicative of the prevalent support were 588 likes and 87 shares.[40] The only cases of heated debate on Kipiani's history-related posts in 2012 were those triggered by his approving reference to a text on *Istorychna Pravda* that raised the issue of ethnic Ukrainians' involvement in anti-Jewish pogroms in western Ukraine under the Nazi occupation and by his opinion on the inappropriateness of using a traditional Ukrainian word for Jews, *zhydy*, which many Jews view as derogatory and anti-Semitic, all the more so because of its use by the Nazi occupiers and their Ukrainian collaborators. These challenges to the Ukrainian nationalist narrative were vehemently opposed by many of Kipiani's nationalist-minded friends, although some supported his call for the reappraisal of certain factually or ethically problematic tenets of the narrative. The relative frequency of different responses confirms that the level of disagreement was much higher than with regard to the state symbols: for the post on the Ukrainian participation in the pogroms, there were as many as 237 debating comments, many more than tacitly supportive likes (70) or shares (40).[41] In other

---

39 *VKontakte* group "Protiv OUN-UPA i prochikh posobnivov fashizma." Post dated 9 April 2012 (20 December 2012).
40 Facebook page by Vakhtang Kipiani. Post dated 9 August 2012 (20 December 2012).
41 Ibid. Posts dated 21 December and 27 November 2012 (22 December 2012).

cases, most of his friends seemed to be in agreement on the issues of history and memory.

That people supporting Ukraine's Western orientation and distinctly non-Russian national identity seem to prevail in most FB discussions is partly because their ideology and identity have influenced their choice of social network in the first place. Rather than debating the past and its implications for the present with fellow post-Soviets, many Facebook users (myself included) tend to discuss memory-related and various other issues within the global/Western context, with people in Ukraine and across the globe who are linked by personal acquaintance, professional or leisure interest and/or ideological affinity and often rely on English for transnational communication.[42] Although nationalist agendas sometimes clash with the Western-dominated cosmopolitan perspective, the interaction between more or less liberal nationalists from various countries is generally less contentious than that between adherents of the opposing versions of Ukrainian identity. However, the prevalence of the nationalist/Western version on Facebook can only be ascertained among those users who engage in the production of a clearly Ukrainian identity, albeit in interaction with other civic, cultural and social ones. At the same time, many Ukrainians having an FB account (often in addition to one in VK) may contribute to the reproduction of the East Slavic transnational commonality and thus remain largely invisible to research focused on the discussions of distinctly Ukrainian history and memory.

Conclusion

In the words of Erll and Rigney: "Fighting about memory is one way of keeping it alive and [...] the history of cultural memory is marked as much by crises and controversies running along social fault lines as it is by consensus and canon-building."[43] The above analysis has shown that in contemporary Ukraine, the

---

[42] A good example of such a cosmopolitan memory-oriented community on Facebook is the Memory at War forum (http://www.facebook.com/groups/memoryatwar), a group founded by the eponymous research project at the University of Cambridge which focuses on the politics of memory in Russia, Poland and Ukraine. As of early 2015, the group comprised about 1700 scholars, journalists and other interested people from a number of Western and post-communist countries, including several dozen Ukrainians. The main language of interaction is English, although many posts refer to texts in various languages of the post-communist region and beyond.
[43] Astrid Erll and Ann Rigney. "Introduction: Cultural memory and its dynamics." *Mediation, Remediation, and the Dynamics of Cultural Memory.* Eds. Astrid Erll and Ann Rigney. Berlin: De Gruyter, 2009, 2.

memory of Soviet rule and anti-Soviet resistance is very much alive and anything but consensual. The controversy along the regional and ethnolinguistic lines within Ukraine is exacerbated by a Ukrainian-Russian trans-border gap in the perceptions of the formerly common state. While both intra- and international differences are sustained to some extent by purposeful efforts of the political and cultural elites, it is primarily through the social networks that ordinary Ukrainians and Russians perform and assert their memories and identities to peers in other parts of their own country and across the border. Easily transcending the newly drawn border, but largely contained within the established linguistic realm, the interaction in the social networks and other new media contributes to the preservation of the post-imperial framework of collective memory and the frustration of the effort to replace it with the national one. At least this was true before the Russian military intervention in Ukraine in 2014 instigated unequivocal loyalty to Ukraine and alienation from Russia, which resulted in severing of many trans-border lines of discursive interaction and a more pronounced orientation toward dealing with "ones' own people."[44] While many people opposed this preservation of post-Soviet ties, their opposition was articulated in the very transnational space they sought to compartmentalize. Much of the memory discourse on the Internet was a fierce confrontation between the two irreconcilable narratives, a "memory war" impeding the development of a coherent view of the past that would facilitate national unity in the present. Although confrontation between opposing views is to be found in the social network interaction across the globe, in a deeply divided post-imperial society such as Ukraine, it challenges the very foundation of national identity, which has not yet been secured by political and cultural institutions. At the same time, many network participants engage in more constructive debate over particular aspects of collective memory within the confines of a shared narrative. Last but not least, many people participate in various inconspicuous practices of the reproduction of a certain version of memory and identity, often without being aware of the process to which they contribute.

References

Abdelal, Rawi, Yoshiko M. Herrera, Alastair Ian Johnston and Rose McDermott. "Identity as a variable." *Perspectives on Politics* 4.4 (2007): 695–711.

Chan, Brenda. "Imagining the homeland: The Internet and diasporic discourse of nationalism." *Journal of Communication Inquiry* 29.4 (2005): 336–368.

---

[44] Kulyk. "Ukrainian nationalism since the outbreak of Euromaidan," 106–113.

Chornopys'ka, Lesia. "'Zruchna' mova ukraïns'kykh internet-ZMI." *Slovo Prosvity*, 8–14 September 2005. http://slovoprosvity.com.ua/modules.php?name=News&file=article&sid=2033 (15 July 2006).

Chrystal, David. *Language and the Internet*. Cambridge: Cambridge University Press, 2001.

Danet, Brenda and Susan C. Herring. Eds. *The Multilingual Internet: Language, Culture, and Communication Online*. New York: Oxford University Press, 2007.

Dubin, Boris. "Pamiat', voina, pamiat' o voine. Konstruirovanie proshlogo v sotsial'noi pamiati poslednikh desiatiletii." *Otechestvennye zapiski* 4 (2008): 6–21.

Erll, Astrid and Ann Rigney. "Introduction: Cultural memory and its dynamics." *Mediation, Remediation, and the Dynamics of Cultural Memory*. Eds. Astrid Erll and Ann Rigney. Berlin: De Gruyter, 2009. 1–11.

Garde-Hansen, Joanne, Andrew Hoskins and Anna Reading. "Introduction." *Save As ... Digital Memories*. Eds. Joanne Garde-Hansen, Andrew Hoskins and Anna Reading. Houndmills and New York: Palgrave Macmillan, 2009. 1–21.

"Issledovanie: samymi populiarnymi sredi ukraintsev sotssetiami iavliaiutsia Vkontakte i Odnoklassniki." *Korrespondent*, 22 November 2011. http://korrespondent.net/business/mmedia_and_adv/1285832-issledovanie-samymi-po-pulyarnymi-sredi-ukraincev-socsetyami-yavlyayutsya-vkontakte-i-odnoklassniki (25 November 2011).

Jakubowicz, Andrew. "Remembering and recovering Shanghai: Seven Jewish families [re]-connect in cyberspace." *Save As ... Digital Memories*. Eds. Joanne Garde-Hansen, Andrew Hoskins and Anna Reading. Houndmills and New York: Palgrave Macmillan, 2009. 96–114.

Jilge, Wilfried. "Nationalukrainischer Befreiungskampf: Die Umwertung des Zweiten Weltkriegs in der Ukraine." *Osteuropa* 58.6 (2008): 167–186.

Kipiani, Vakhtang and Pavlo Solod'ko. "Pro proekt." *Istorychna Pravda* (2010). http://www.istpravda.com.ua/about (10 December 2010).

"KMIS: Chyslo internet-korystuvachiv v Ukraïni zroslo do 40%." *Dzerkalo tyzhnia. Ukraïna*, 15 December 2011. http://news.dt.ua/TECHNOLOGIES/kmis_chislo_internet-koristuvachiv_v_ukrayini_zroslo_-do_40-93827.html (25 December 2011).

Kulyk, Volodymyr. *Dyskurs ukraïns'kykh medii: identychnosti, ideolohiï, vladni stosunky*. Kyiv: Krytyka, 2010.

Kulyk, Volodymyr. "The media, history and identity: Competing narratives of the past in the Ukrainian popular press." *National Identities* 13.3 (2011): 287–303.

Kulyk, Volodymyr. "Natsionalistychne proty radians'koho: istorychna pam'iat' u nezalezhnii Ukraïni." *historians.in.ua*, 20 September 2012. http://historians.in.ua/index.php/istoriya-i-pamyat-vazhki-pitannya/379-volodymyr-kuly-k-natsionalistychne-proty-radianskoho-istorychna-pamiat-u-nezalezhnii-ukraini (20 December 2012).

Kulyk, Volodymyr. "War of memories in the Ukrainian media: Diversity of identities, political confrontation, and production technologies. *Memory, Conflict and New Media: Web Wars in Post-Socialist States*. Eds. Ellen Rutten, Julie Fedor and Vera Zvereva. London: Routledge, 2013. 63–81.

Kulyk, Volodymyr. "Language policy in the Ukrainian media: authorities, producers and consumers." *Europe-Asia Studies* 65.7 (2013): 1417–1443.

Kulyk, Volodymyr. "Ukrainian nationalism since the outbreak of Euromaidan." *Ab Imperio* 3 (2014): 94–122.
Lal, Vinay. "The politics of history on the Internet: Cyber-diasporic Hinduism and the North American Hindu diaspora." *Diaspora* 8.2 (1999): 137–172.
Liu, Shih-Diing. "Undomesticated hostilities: The affective space of Internet chat rooms across the Taiwan Strait." *positions* 16.2 (2008): 435–455.
Merrin, William. "Understanding me-dia: The second reformation." *Media Studies 2.0.* http://mediastudies2point0.blogspot.com. Personal blog, 6 March 2010 (20 December 2012).
Portnov, Andrei. *Uprazhneniia s istoriei po-ukrainski.* Moscow: OGI, Polit.ru, Memorial, 2010.
Reading, Anna. "Memory and digital media: Six dynamics of the globital memory field." *On Media Memory: Collective Memory in the New Media Age.* Eds. Motti Neiger, Oren Meyers and Eyal Zandberg. Houndmills and New York: Palgrave Macmillan, 2001. 241–252.
Riabchuk, Mykola. "Kul'tura pamiati i politika zabveniia." *Otechestvennye zapiski* 34.1 (2007): 42–55.
Riabchuk, Mykola. "Holodomor: The Politics of Memory and Political Infighting in Contemporary Ukraine." *Harriman Review* 16.2 (2008): 3–9.
Stephen, John and Robyn McCallum. *Retelling Stories, Framing Culture: Traditional Stories and Metanarratives in Children's Literature.* New York: Garland, 1998.
V. B. "Shcho take 'ukraïnomovnyi Internet'?" Ukraïns'kyi Prostir, 14 June 2011. http://ukr-net.info/2011/06/14/scho-take-ukrajinomovnyj-internet (15 August 2011).
"VKontakte", "Odnoklassniki" ta Facebook lidyruiut' sered sotsial'nykh merezh v Ukraïni (2011). http://www.gfk.ua/public_relations/press/press_articles/009018/index.ua.html (20 December 2012).
Zhurzhenko, Tatiana. "'Capital of despair': Holodomor Memory and Political Conflicts in Kharkiv after the Orange Revolution." *East European Politics and Societies* 25.3 (2011): 597–639.
Zvereva, Vera. "Historical events and the social network 'V Kontakte.'" *East European Memory Studies* 7 (2011). http://www.memoryatwar.org/enewsletter-nov-2011.pdf (25 March 2012).

Tea Sindbæk Andersen
Football and Memories of Croatian Fascism on Facebook

On 19 November 2013, when Croatia's national football team defeated Iceland and thus secured Croatia's participation in the World Championship 2014 in Brazil, Croatian defender Josip Šimunić celebrated by leading a chant associated with the fascist Ustasha regime that governed Croatia and Bosnia during the Second World War. As a result, Šimunić was fined by Zagreb's county court for inciting racist hatred, and the International Football Association, FIFA, banned him from participating in 10 international matches including the World Championship. By late November 2013, a Facebook page set up in defence of Šimunić had received 150,000 likes and many lengthy comments. Moreover, the page promoted an online petition, which soon gathered more than 30,000 signatures, aimed to convince FIFA that Šimunić had been misunderstood. Both the Facebook page and the petition and its comments were evidence of a deep engagement in negotiating the meaning of Šimunić's chant, and in questioning its connection to fascism. Attempts were made to rethink Croatia's fascist past and to reframe history to emphasize Croatia's victimization through the crimes of others.

This chapter investigates the types of memory transmission and negotiation taking place on the Facebook page supporting Šimunić and on the petition webpage. The Šimunić affair is an example of a pop-cultural event actualizing memory through a highly charged symbol, the chant, and of social media distributing it quickly and widely, engaging an unusually large and varied group of memory actors, who were then able to contribute, comment and retransmit the posts on the Facebook page and beyond. Yet, as the chapter seeks to explore, perhaps these engagements are rather short-lived and superficial. Indeed, social media allows for fast and unbounded sharing of memory mediation, and they invite interactivity and reactions in the forms of likes, comments and signatures. But this type of participation also raises questions: What happens to the content and the memory narrative in these highly fluid and interactive types of memory mediation? And what can we learn from these digital forms of interacting and such minimal participatory acts as clicking the 'like' button?

Šimunić and the 'Za dom spremni' chant

In a highly unusual act to celebrate the victory of the Croatian national football team over Iceland and the much-wanted ticket to the World Championship 2014 in Brazil, Croatian defender Josip Šimunić grabbed a microphone and conducted the remaining spectators in a chant. Four times Šimunić yelled 'In battle' (u boj) to which the audience answered 'For your people' (za narod svoj), and afterwards the player shouted four times, 'For the home(land)' (Za dom), to which the audience replied 'Ready' (Spremni).[1] While both phrases are obviously nationalistic appeals, 'Za dom spremni' is especially problematic because of its close association with the fascist Ustasha regime that governed Croatia and Bosnia during the Second World War. The Ustasha and their leader, Ante Pavelić, are known for their extreme violence, their assistance to Nazi extermination policies and their death camps and genocidal campaigns against Serbs, Jews, Roma and regime opponents in general, policies which caused the deaths of several hundred thousand civilians in Croatia and Bosnia.[2] 'Za dom spremni' was the official greeting of the Ustasha regime and its armed forces.

Šimunić's celebration was quickly and widely condemned. Croatia's Minister of Education and Sports, Željko Jovanović, wrote on his own Facebook page "Oh my Šimunić, you need a history lesson. If you wish, I will personally help you to find a good professor and to understand what kind of yell 'Za dom spremni' is". Jovanović then officially notified the heads of the Croatian Football Association and the Croatian Olympic Committee, calling on them to react.[3] International media also reacted to Šimunić's celebration, referring to it as involving a "pro-Nazi chant".[4] To Šimunić himself, however, the Ustasha connotations of his celebration were unproblematic. After the match, he allegedly defended his act, stating that "I have always wanted to do that. Who is going to punish me? I

---

[1] See for example this video clip and article: Graeme Yorke. "Croatia's Josip Simunic slapped with 10 game ban and will miss the World cup because of Nazi chanting." *Mail Online* 16 December 2013. http://www.dailymail.co.uk/sport/worldcup2014/article-2524741/Croatias-Josip-Simunic-slapped-10-game-ban-miss-World-Cup-Nazi-chanting.html (10 August 2014).
[2] See eg. Jozo Tomasevich. *War and Revolution in Yugoslavia, 1941–1945. Occupation and collaboration.* Stanford: Stanford University Press, 2001.
[3] Ivica Kristović. "Jovanović: E moj Šimuniću, tebi treba lekcija iz povijesti." *Večernji list* 20 November 2013. http://www.vecernji.hr/hrvatska/jovanovic-e-moj-simunicu-tebi-treba-lekcija-iz-povijesti-903984 (8 August 2014).
[4] Anon. "Croatia's Josip Simunic defends 'pro-Nazi' World Cup celebration chant." *The Guardian* 20 November 2013. http://www.theguardian.com/football/2013/nov/20/croatia-josip-simunic-defends-apparent-pro-nazi-chant (8 August 2014).

have done nothing wrong. I support Croatia, my home, and if that bothers anyone that is his problem".[5] As a result of the chant, Šimunić was taken to trial and fined by the Croatian state a few days after the Iceland match. In mid-December 2013 the International Football Association, FIFA, insisted that 'Za dom spremni' is a wartime salute of the fascist Ustashe movement and thus against the association's disciplinary codex. FIFA therefore banned Šimunić from participating in 10 international matches, which included the matches at the World Championship, thus practically ending the Croatian defender's international career.[6] Šimunić protested, but his appeal was turned down in May 2014 by the Court of Arbitration of Sports in Lausanne, which upheld the original judgement.

Šimunić, however, insisted on a different meaning of his celebration chant. Commenting on the final verdict in Lausanne, Šimunić stated that "to me, home ("dom") is a symbol of love and fatherland, of community", and that "the greeting "Za dom" I experience as patriotic and I said it exclusively for that reason ... I am a man who loves his fatherland and I think you judge me unfairly".[7] In an exclusive interview with the journal *Hrvatski tjednik*, Šimunić again expressed his love for his homeland and insisted that he would not have behaved differently had he known of the consequences. About the chant, he said: "Someone has written that no one in the whole world has a greeting so valuable, beautiful and inspiring to dignity, no one has an informatively richer, patriotically and familywise more attractive greeting than the one we Croats have: Za dom- spremni! It isn't clear to me why some think that we should renounce this one. Unfortunately, some people deliberately misinterpret this old Croatian patriotic greeting."[8] Thus, to Šimunić, the Ustasha connotations of 'Za dom spremni' were apparently irrelevant in comparison with what he saw as the chant's patriotic meaning. There are several aspects of this disagreement between Šimunić and his critiques from the football organizations and on the part of official Croatia. On the surface the question seems to be whether 'Za dom spremni' is in fact an Ustasha symbol. But below this, and, somehow more disturbingly, lie the questions of whether

---

5 Kristović. "Jovanović: E moj Šimuniću."
6 Bojan Arežina. "DORH Šimuniću izrelao maksimalno novčanu kaznu." *Večernji list* 21 November 2013. http://www.vecernji.hr/crna-kronika/drzavno-odvjetnistvo-simunicu-izreklo-maksimalnu-novcanu-kaznu-904274 (8 August 2014); Hrvoje Delač. "Šimuniću 10 utakmica suspenzije zbog ustaškog pozdrava!" *Večernji list* 16 December 2013. http://www.vecernji.hr/nogomet/simunicu-velika-kazna-dobio-deset-utakmica-suspenzije-909525 (6 August 2014).
7 Hina. "Šimonić: Pozdrav s'Za dom spremni' je patriotski; Sud u Lausannei: 'Ne, to je ratni poklič ustaša", *Jutarnji list*, 12 May 2014. http://www.jutarnji.hr/simunic-pozdrav-za-dom-do zivljavam-kao-patriotski-cas-ne-to-je-bez-sumnje-ustaski-uzvik-/1190847/ (6 August 2014).
8 Vjekoslav Magaš. "Eksklusivni intervju." *Hrvatski tjednik* 5 June 2014, 22.

the chant's Ustasha connection is at all problematic, and whether Croatia's Ustasha history should in fact be condemned. These issues, as well as the role and character of Šimunić as a person and football player, were also at stake in the debates in electronic and other media following Šimunić's chant and the resulting penalty.

Šimunić's own attitude to the chant 'Za dom spremni' and its history and connotations are strongly influenced by his personal background. Josip Šimunić was born in Australia in 1978 to Croatian parents who had emigrated from Hercegovina. Šimunić played as a central defender for the Melbourne Knights before moving to German football in 2001 and in 2011 on to Dinamo Zagreb, where he was captain in 2013. Until the Iceland match, Šimunić had also been an experienced key player on the Croatian national team with a record of 103 matches.[9] According to sports sociologist John Hughson, Šimunić and his actions should be understood within the context of his experience from Australian football in the 1990s, where extremist fans of Croatian immigrant clubs such as Sidney Croatia were highly nationalistic and subscribed to a certain version of Croatianness, with a view on Croatian history based mainly on oral traditions, which the fans often took over from fathers or uncles.[10] In this version of Croatian history, an idea of a "Croatian struggle" featured prominently. The extremist fans saw Ante Pavelić, the leader of the Ustasha, as a historical hero and "freedom fighter", and they paid lip service to fascism, paraded Nazi and Ustasha symbols or chanted about violence and atrocities. Hughson sees these practices as acts of defiance by a marginalized Croatian community, which used football terraces as stages for unhindered expression of ethnic identity.[11] Thus, the Croatian-Australian football sub-culture, where Josip Šimunić had learned the rules of the game, was influenced by a passionate, long-distance nationalism, which was inevitably accentuated by the war in Croatia and the fight for an independent state in the 1990s.

---

9 See the description on the webpages of Dinamo Zagreb, http://gnkdinamo.hr/hr/1-momcad/igraci/obrana/josip-simunic1/ (5 April 2014) and FIFA's webpage, "Josip Šimunić." http://www.uefa.com/worldcup/season=2014/teams/player=49993/profile/ (5 April 2014).
10 In 1993 the club was renamed Sydney United, during the Australian Soccer Federation's campaign in the early 1990s to de-ethnicize Australian football culture. See John Hughson. "Football, folk dancing and fascism: diversity and difference in Multicultural Australia." *Journal of Sociology* 33 (1997): 167–186; and also the webpage of the club, "About Sidney United 58 fc." http://www.sydneyunited58fc.com/history/sydney-united-58-fc/ (5 April 2014).
11 Hughson, "Football, folk dancing and fascism", see also Centre for South East European Studies, Graz, Interview with John Hughson (University of Central Lancashire). "Josip Šimunić and his Australian context". http://www.youtube.com/watch?v=NFvavWNUzDs (6 August 2014).

Yet, Šimunić spent most of his adult years in European football and was by 2013 an experienced player in both the European and the Croatian football arenas. He must have had some ideas about what the effects would be of leading this particular chant at Zagreb's main stadium after a significant victory. Indeed, as several commentators have pointed out, the really problematic matter is not that Šimunić as an individual expressed an ignorant and worrisome personal take on Croatia's darkest history, but rather that a large part of the crowd responded enthusiastically to his chant, apparently sharing his point of view.[12] As suggested by Dario Brentin, the message sent at the stadium in Zagreb seems to say something much more sinister about views on Croatia's darkest past and about right-wing historical revisionism and flirting with fascist history in Croatian sports culture and in Croatian society more generally.[13]

Josip Šimunić is certainly not the first to have an ambiguous relationship to Ustasha memory in Croatia. In the 1990s, the Croatian state's history politics questioned the Yugoslav communist version of Croatian history, which had thoroughly condemned the Ustasha regime. Though the Ustasha was never officially rehabilitated, the Croatian government in the 1990s followed a somewhat ambiguous line, never properly condemning the Ustasha as such, while allowing the renaming of streets in honor of high-ranking members of the Ustasha. President Franjo Tudjman, himself a historian and the author of several revisionist publications aimed at lowering the estimation of the number of the victims of the Ustasha, promoted reconciliation between the left and the right (that is the Communists and their opponents, including the Ustasha) in Croatian politics.[14] Moreover, the government accepted the Croatian political far right's open flirting with Ustasha symbols and values.[15] But after the change of regime in Croatia in early 2000, followed by a wave of liberalization of Croatia's political system,

---

[12] See e.g. Florian Bieber. "Ready for the Homeland? Simunic and a bit of normal fascism." *Balkan Insight*, 21 November 2013. http://www.balkaninsight.com/en/blog/ready-for-the-homeland-simunic-and-a-bit-of-normal-fascism (10 October 2014).

[13] See also Dario Brentin. "Fascist Groundhog day? The issue with 'Za dom spremni' in Croatian football." *Balkan Insight*, 11 April 2015. http://balkanist.net/fascist-groundhog-day-issue-za-dom-spremni-croatian-football/ (10 May 2015).

[14] Tea Sindbæk. *Usable History? Representations of Yugoslavia's difficult past, 1945–2002*. Aarhus: Aarhus University Press, 2012, 190–199.

[15] Vjeran Pavlakovic. "Flirting with Fascism: The Ustaša legacy and Croatian politics in the 1990s." *The Shared History. The Second World War and National Question in Yugoslavia*. Novi Sad: Centar za Istoriju, demokratiju i pomirenje, 2008, 115–143.

steps were taken to curb the use of Ustasha symbols, both in the public sphere and among youth groups, for example at rock concerts.[16]

Yet, football fan groups have remained difficult to control, given their notoriously defiant attitude and consciously provocative use of symbols. And as the enthusiastic response to Šimunić's chant on 19 November 2013 in Zagreb showed, a significant group of the football audience had a sufficiently positive or playful attitude to this symbolism to be willing to sing along. However, as the chant and the case against Šimunić became widely known through both Croatian and international media coverage, a much larger audience reacted on the Internet through social media. In this electronic public forum, Šimunić gathered ample support and various other reactions, which in the end constituted a complex and open negotiation of the historical symbol of 'Za dom spremni' and its connected memory narratives.

Šimunić on facebook

Šimunić's chanting brought to worldwide attention the question of a specific historical symbol, 'Za dom spremni', and the related memory of the Ustasha. This occurred initially on one of the biggest stages of international popular culture, the football World Cup, and subsequently also in political discourse, as Croatian ministers and other public figures reacted to the incident. Šimunić thus very efficiently actualized a rather problematic part of Croatia's collective memory. To which extent, then, did the use of Facebook and the online petition pages influence the presence and negotiation of this memory?

Šimunić's chant and the public condemnation of it certainly caused a great many reactions on the Internet. Several Facebook pages were set up to gather support for Šimunić. The most popular one, 'Support for Josip Šimunić' (Potpora Josipu Šimuniću), was created on 20 November 2013 and received within the same day 50,000 expressions of support in the form of a click on the button 'like'. Three days later, on the 23 of November, the page had received 150,000 'likes' and many lengthy comments. Moreover, the page promoted an online petition, which by late November 2013 was signed by more than 30,000, with the aim to convince FIFA that Šimunić had been misunderstood.[17] Both the Facebook

---

[16] On Croatian politics, see for example Sabrina P. Ramet, "Politics in Croatia since 1990." *Croatia since independence. War, politics, society, foreign relations.* Ed. Sabrina P. Ramet, Konrad Clewing and Reneo Lukić. Munich: R. Oldenbrug Verlag, 2008, 31–57.
[17] See the petition webpage on: http://www.change.org/p/fifa-support-for-josip-%C5%A1imuni%C4%87 (14 August 2014).

page and the petition and its comments revealed a deep commitment to negotiating the meaning of Šimunić's chant, questioning its connection to fascism and to tying the chant to pure patriotism. After the final verdict against Šimunić in Lausanne, the Facebook page 'Support for Josip Šimunić' remained active, but gradually transformed into a fan page for Šimunić. By August 2014 the explosive growth in support and reactions had definitely stopped; the page had by then received 160,776 likes, that is, an increase of a little more than 10.000 since 23 November 2013. Even though the page remained active and still discussed football, fandom and the meaning of nationalist chants, the amount of attention it received was on a different and much less significant scale.

Through the Facebook page and the petition, as well as other media sites, such as electronic newspapers and Youtube, Šimunić's actualization of the Ustasha memory thus had a significant electronic afterlife. This afterlife of widespread electronic reactions is indeed a new possibility opened up by Internet and social media.

The difference in the situation caused by social media may be illustrated by comparing the digital reactions in the Šimunić case with a somewhat similar incident that took place 9 years earlier. In November 2004 Milan Gurović, a basketball player for the Partizan club in Belgrade and a star of the Serbian national team, was banned from playing a game in Croatia, because he refused to cover a tattoo on his left shoulder showing the face of the Serbian Chetnik leader Draža Mihailović. The Croatian Ministry of the Interior denied Gurović's entry into the country, since the tattoo was seen as violating a Croatian law prohibiting the display of symbols that may inspire hatred or violence on the basis of racial, religious or ethnic affiliation. During the Second World War, Chetnik militias collaborated with the Axis occupiers of Yugoslavia and committed war crimes and large scale massacres of Muslims, Croats and other groups of civilians in Croatia, Bosnia and Serbia. Moreover, Serbian paramilitary groups adopted Chetnik symbols and language during the Yugoslav wars in the early 1990s. In Croatia, Bosnia-Herzegovina and other formerly Yugoslav states, Draža Mihailović is therefore regarded as a war criminal, and Chetnik symbolism is highly offensive. To Gurović, however, Mihailović was the opposite of a Fascist and a war criminal. The incident featured prominently in Serbian media. For days, Gurović's portrait covered the front and back pages of Serbian tabloids, while journalists and editorials expressed offense and disbelief at the Croatian stance. Moreover, Serbian ministers felt compelled to comment on what they saw as unnecessary problem-making and an undemocratic decision directed against "individual iconography".[18] Thus, as in the Šimunić case, a sports hero actualized a controversial and potentially highly offensive historical symbol, creating a significant media reaction and a debate that reached a wide public and the highest political level. Yet, little was said after November 2004, and no Facebook movement or online petition was created in support of Gurović. Clearly, digital and social media have opened new possibilities for transmitting and recycling news, as well as for enabling significantly different forms of participation in debates or media events.

A main aspect of various types of social media on the Internet is the enabling of various forms of audience participation. The level of participation may vary significantly. According to media sociologist Simon Lindgren, Internet users may treat an Internet service such as YouTube as an expanded version of television, or they may engage in small communities sharing a certain enthusiasm, contributing viewpoints and knowledge. A study from 2008 showed that while some users are mainly consumers and others primarily produce, the largest group consists of users who are both consumers and producers, thus constituting an active participatory audience.[19] Internet and social media also function as sources of information and as news channels where major events are broadcast. Reactions on social media are quick, but unlike the coverage of sensational events in traditional media, online discussion fora may remain active for years, discussing the events in question and relating them to other events.[20] Online fora can thus create an active electronic archive of events and debates, thus ensuring an electronic afterlife to media events. Moreover, by commenting and sharing, Internet users create forms of community. Internet services such as YouTube, while facilitating large technical networks, also serve as spaces for developing networks of enthusiasts or various types of electronic communities and interest groups. The Facebook page in support of Šimunić created an electronic interest group, which, through the ongoing debate about the 'Za dom spremni' chant, also became a forum for memory negotiation, or, perhaps, a very loosely connected memory community.

---

[18] Tea Sindbæk. "The Fall and Rise of a National Hero: Interpretations of Draža Mikailović and the Chetniks in Yugoslavia and Serbia since 1945." *Journal of Contemporary European Studies* 17.1 (2009): 47–59.
[19] Simon Lindgren. "Collective problemsolving and informal learning in networked publics. Reading vlogging networks on YouTube as knowledge communities." *Interactive Media Use and Youth: Learning, Knowledge Exchange and Behavior.* Ed. E. Dunkels, G. Frånberg & C. Hällgren. Hershey: IGI Global, 2011, 50–64.
[20] Simon Lindgren. "Youtube gunmen? Mapping participatory media discourse on school shooting videos". *Media, Culture and Society* 33.1 (2010): 1–14.

Facebook, which hosts the support page for Josip Šimunić, was specifically designed as a social networking site enabling self-representation and global connection with friends and colleagues. Moreover, as the Šimunić page exemplifies, it also connects and helps to create interest groups. The discussions on the Facebook page link to other Internet services, but also to older types of media. It is thus part of a much wider media landscape that is heavily drawn upon and linked to. As Lindgren points out, social media enable 'many to many' communication.[21] In the case of a Facebook page, this may take the form of the owner of the page making entries, which then receive likes, comments, or even chains of comments. An essential feature of Internet communication is that users can decide to be anonymous, or, if they want, identify themselves, or, indeed, invent a completely new identity for the purpose of online activities. Another characteristic of online interaction is the lack of control and reprisal, which may explain the widespread and unconstrained use of abusive and racist language in some fields and fora.

The characteristics of Internet communication influence the ways in which history and memory may be represented and debated online. Memory debates can be fast, unbounded, anonymous and unregulated.[22] According to Ellen Rutten and Vera Zvereva this has significant implications: while the Internet offers many new possibilities of memory communication and negotiation, it also causes a semantic shift in the basic concept of memory. Users, they argue, are not primarily preoccupied with recollections but rather with basic concepts such as group solidarity, emotions and belonging.[23] Indeed, memory has always been about identity creations in the present, but in the case of memory debates on the Internet this becomes even more apparent – and more dominant. This was certainly the case with the Šimunić discussions on Facebook.

---

21 Simon Lindgren. "The Sociology of Media and Information technologies". *Introduction to Sociology: Scandinavian Sensibilities*. Ed. G.C. Aakvaag, M. Hviid Jacobsen & T. Johansson. London: Pearson, 2010, 140–159.
22 Andrew Hoskins. "7/7 and connective memory: international trajectories of remembering in post-scarcity culture". *Memory Studies* 4.3 (2011): 269–280.
23 Ellen Rutten & Vera Zvereva. "Introduction. Old conflicts, new media: post-socialist digital memories." *Memory, Conflict and New Media. Web Wars in Post-socialist States*. Ed. Ellen Rutten, Julie Fedor & Vera Zvereva. London: Routledge, 2013, 1, 5.

Facebook memory narratives

The character of material and texts – or the content – on digital social media is different from that in printed media, and so is the relationship of the media users towards the content. According to media scholar José van Dijck, "user-generated content is considered unfinished, recyclable input".[24] This makes authorship unclear, and it also makes texts and narratives less linear, more fragmented and sometimes even collagelike in their compilation of different bits of content. Inevitably, this influenced the types of debates and memory narratives created and distributed on Facebook in connection to Šimunić and 'Za dom spremni'.

The Facebook page 'Support for Josip Šimunić' was established on 20 November 2013, the day after Croatia's victory over Iceland and Šimunić's infamous chant.[25] The very first entry was a link to a YouTube clip on which former President of the Croatian football association Vlatko Marković states on TV that the greeting 'Za dom spremni' is "completely normal" and not necessarily connected to the Ustasha movement. The clip was several years old. Marković, who was known for controversial statements against gay rights, had retired from his post in 2012 and had died in September 2013.[26] The entry received 1,038 likes and 64 comments. The vast majority of the comments were supportive of Marković's statement and of Šimunić. Most users expressed this through a simple 'bravo' or 'Za dom spremni'. Yet, the entry also received a number of more lengthy comments. A handful of comments reacted to the official critic of Šimunić from the Minister of Education and Sports, by suggesting in abusive and sexualized language what to do with Minister Jovanović, and also with Serbs in general.

A few comments were explicitly political, suggesting that the minister must go or that Šimunić must have the right to free speech. A couple of comments were explicitly supportive of the Ustasha and Ante Pavelić, and some even celebrated Ustasha atrocities. A handful of comments specifically related to public understandings of history, suggesting that journalists and politicians have no understanding of history, if they considered Šimunić's chant offensive; and one asked why the Ustasha are always treated as the bad guys, while the Serbian

---

24 José van Dijck. *The culture of connectivity: A critical history of social media.* New York: Oxford University Press, 2013, 35–36.
25 https://www.facebook.com/josip.simunic.officialfanpage?fref=ts (14 August 2014).
26 See e. g. the UEFA webpage, "Croatia mourns Vlatko Marković." 23 September 2013. http://www.uefa.com/memberassociations/association=cro/news/newsid=2000125.html (6 April 2014) and Anon. "Croatia football chief Vlatko Markovic hit by gay group's backlash." *Guardian*, 14 November 2010. http://www.theguardian.com/football/2010/nov/14/gay-backlash-croatia-football-chief (6 April 2014).

Chetniks are not. Finally two comments were critical of Šimunić and the original entry, pointing out that the Ustasha were indeed evil. In general, the chain of comments expressed extremely fragmented and rather diverse points of views that did not really relate to one another. The vast majority of participation took the form of a click on Facebook's 'like' button.

The second entry, also made on 20 November, was simply a picture of Šimunić during his chant. It received 342 'likes' and 9 comments of the same type as to the first entry. Apparently the Facebook page was now well established and started to attract attention. The third entry, a statement from the authors of the page explaining its purpose, received 9,228 likes and 1,028 comments. This entry certainly represents a contribution to the debate about the meaning of 'Za dom spremni' and the memory of Croatia's Ustasha past. The authors (the text makes it clear that there is more than one) state that the page was set up to back Šimunić because of his chanting and the attacks from media and politicians: "On this page we do not wish to politicize nor to glorify anyone... We only wish to show the real truth of the greeting 'Za dom spremni'", the authors claim, suggesting a somehow naïve and one-sided view on the question of historical symbols. The authors rather lengthily argue that expressions almost similar to 'Za dom spremni' were used on Croatian battlefields and in literature in the sixteenth, eighteenth and nineteenth centuries. Moreover, the authors claim, the Ustasha salute was slightly different, and it was only in the communist period that the link between the Ustasha movement and 'Za dom spremni' was created, thus making the salute synonymous with a Croatian version of 'Heil Hitler'. The entry thus seeks to discredit the official and mainstream historians' view by describing it as based on communist – and Serbian dominated – propaganda. Finally, according to the authors of this entry, 'Za dom spremni' was widely used by Croatian forces during the war in 1991–1995, and the expression is now a popular salute among Croatian football fans. Clearly, the main strategy of the authors' statement is to distance 'Za dom spremni' from Croatia's Ustasha past and tie it to other parts of Croatian history, thus turning it into an 'innocent' and purely patriotic greeting. At the same time, the entry suggests that this is the current popular meaning of the chant in Croatia. How did Facebook users react to these strategies?

With more than 9,000 likes and more than 1,000 comments, this second entry certainly called forth quite a reaction. Indeed, the chain of comments to this particular entry constitutes a text of more than 200,000 words. Yet, the character of the comments seems quite as fragmented as in the case of the first entry. They span from the occasional call to "hang the Serbs" to plain praise of Šimunić or simply stating 'Za dom spremni', sometimes even abbreviated as "ZDS"; and they span from critique of Minister Jovanović to critique of the page itself. Nevertheless, the vast response also allows for some examination of which types of comments were most likely to create reactions, at least in the form of 'likes'. By far the most popular reaction to the second entry was a plain picture of Šimunić with the statement "Za Dom", which was 'liked' by 1,327 people. Another popular response stated: "It is shameful that the Minister of Education seeks a history teacher for our Šimunić, but when at Marakana the Croatian flag was burned, he accidentally didn't notice", thus suggesting that the minister is busy hunting down his own player, while ignoring assaults on Croatian national symbols in the famous Belgrade stadium. This comment created its own sub-chain of 9 comments, primarily suggesting in various ways that the Minister of Education rather than Šimunić needed a history teacher. Most of these entries received a handful of 'likes', while no one 'liked' a comment abusing the minister in highly sexualized, homophobic and anti-Serbian terms. Thus, the comments in this sub-chain manifestly questioned the minister's right to intervene, but even more fundamentally, they questioned the official interpretation of the salute 'Za dom spremni' and thus implicitly the official position on Ustasha history.

Fig. 1: The Facebook page "In Support of Josip Šimunić" on 28 November 2013, proudly boasting of its more than 150,000 supporters

Many comments framed the debate within an idea of a Serbian-Croatian conflict. In this context, it also served to delegitimize Jovanović, emphasizing his alleged Serbianness. The question of Jovanović's proposed pro-Serbian or anti-Croatian leaning was also linked to the government's politics regarding the rights of the Serb minority in Slavonia and around Vukovar to write place signs in their own language and alphabet, which was severely criticized and condemned. While the dominant tone in the many comments was one of supporting what was presented as Šimunić's patriotism, the discussions about Šimunić and the nature of his chant also morphed to include general debates on the nature of patriotism, Croatian history, relations to Serbs, the unpatriotic line of the government and the economic crisis in the country. And next to it all were the recurring pro-Ustasha statements, but also the almost as regularly repeated comment criticizing the ignorance and cruelty of other comments.

At this point, the communication spread quickly. Indeed, the vast majority of comments to the authors' statement were left on 20, 21 or 22 November. Moreover, the life span of the commenting activity was apparently quite limited; the most recent comment in the above-mentioned chain was left on 28 of November 2013. Interaction between commenters was usually rather limited. While the first 50 comments did cause some reaction, at least in the form of 'likes', the remaining 978 hardly ever received more than one or two likes, which seems to suggest that they were rarely attracting particular attention and probably rarely read. Rather than an ongoing debate, this appears to be a long series of personal statements, somewhat like tagging one's name on an important wall, leaving a stone on top of a pile marking a mountain track, or perhaps just identifying oneself as belonging to a group. Indeed, basic expressions of in-group solidarity and group belonging seem to be the main point of most of these comments.

Nevertheless, the negotiating of Croatian and Ustasha history on the Facebook page was constant and took many forms. One very frequent practice was to contest the official interpretation and invest 'Za dom spremni' with different meanings. A quote from Šimunić himself in an entry on 20 November stated that: "Those who are bothered by the shout 'Za dom spremni', let them learn some history. Any FARE [the international organization Football Against Racism in Europe], whichever accusation, penalty, I have nothing to be ashamed of." This entry proudly contested the views of the Croatian Minister of Education and Sport and the international football world, suggesting that they were the ones who got history wrong. The same defiance was expressed by the authors of the Facebook page. An entry on 20 November called out: "Thank you everyone for the support for our Šimunić! JOSIP HANG ON! WE ARE WITH YOU! Za dom : SPREMNI ♥". The eerie positioning of this particular expression next to the symbol of a heart boldly challenged the usual association of the greeting with Ustasha fanaticism and cruelty. Moreover, in a number of entries, starting on 23 November, the authors of the Facebook page systematically referred to "the old-

Croatian cry 'Za dom spremni'", thus again seeking to connect the Ustasha greeting to different associations.

Fig. 2: A post from 20 November 2013 proudly announces that the Facebook page has succeeded in attracting attention from the media and calls to support for Šimunić. By situating a heart next to the Ustasha greeting, the post apparently seeks to associate that greeting with love rather than violence and cruelty.

Moreover, the authors of the page as well as numerous comments repeatedly argued that Croatian history was characterized by Croats being victims of others, mainly communists and Serbs, and often the posts and comments did not distinguish between these two parties. The accounts of communist and Yugoslav/Serbian crimes were often connected to descriptions of anti-Croatian chants by Serbian football fans and abuse of Croatian symbols in Serbian football stadiums. Rather than justifying the Ustasha or Šimunić, this rhetoric seems to suggest that others were much worse and used more offensive symbols, so why should Jovanović and the Croatian government criticize and persecute Šimunić. Inevitably this led to relativization of Šimunić's chant, but also of the crimes and violence of the Ustasha movement as such. The authors of the Facebook page supporting

Šimunić were involved in a difficult balancing act when they tried to justify Šimunić's use of the chant as pure patriotism while simultaneously rethinking Croatian history from a victim perspective, tying the Ustasha symbol of 'Za dom spremni' to a distant past, and comparing it to 'worse' crimes committed by Serbs, Communists and Chetniks. Often they came close to justifying Ustasha crimes by foregrounding the crimes of others.

While the relativization of historical crimes and the attempts to distance 'Za dom spremni' from the Ustasha movement were quite popular, especially if they criticized Minister Jovanović (one such post received 11,652 'likes' and 507 comments), the absolutely most popular posts seem to be the ones that simply supported Šimunić himself. One entry on 22 November quoted a press release from the Croatian Football Association which stated that Šimunić was shocked that anyone would connect him with "the darkest period in Croatian history". The entry then suggested that one 'like' equaled one 'support' for Šimunić, thereby gaining 17,674 likes.

Rather than coherent texts, the content on the Facebook page in support of Šimunić constituted chaotic compilations of material. While some posts and entries transmitted memory narratives and symbols, others added new aspects, sometimes completely changing the direction of the communication, and very many simply signaled support or, much less frequently, disapproval. Among the interesting trends on the Facebook page is the use of other media. The authors of the page as well as the commenters often inserted clips or links in the entries, in order to underline, substantiate or illustrate a point, or just to impress and entertain. Sometimes this was done without any explanation, leaving the reader to establish a meaningful link between posts on the Facebook page and the clips and sequences from other media. Especially clips, links and pictures that include the personal appearance of Josip Šimunić were usually very popular and seemed to need no context. The Facebook page thus interacted with other sources and served as a nucleus in the debate. This practice certainly expanded the scope of what went on, but it also contributed to the fluid and fragmented character of the communication and commenting on the page.

Another feature characterizing this Facebook debate is the systematic and very frequent recycling of pieces of text. The long entry by the authors explaining the aims of the page was regularly copied and reused in other posts, both by the authors and by commenters. Sometimes bits were cut out and others inserted, but long sequences of the text, if not all of it, are literally word-for-word identical to the original entry, sometimes with a new short introduction or a brief invitation to "read the truth". On the one hand, this seems to suggest a presumption that this 'truth' will be more convincing by being frequently repeated. On the other, it may also reflect the assumption that the original entry will be very quickly gone from the eye of the public, and that it therefore needs to be refreshed and kept present. Also, it reveals an interesting view on text and authorship: apparently the moment this entry was posted, it also became public and shared property, free for anyone to adopt and repost in their own name with no specification of ownership or original source. It seems an underlying premise that if one shares the views expressed by another, one also has ownership of the text. And substantiation of any kind of the claims and arguments made in the text is seemingly quite unnecessary. Yet, users and contributors may add different types of substantiation, for example a link to a news service or a clip with a person publicly making similar claims. Parts of the audience thus contribute to a collective creation of a kind of community knowledge with its own community-internal rules of validation.

Yet, the participation and contribution from Facebook users also caused problems. The somehow anarchic character of the Internet and Facebook meant that it was very difficult to control comments and statements, and the positions expressed by the authors behind the Facebook page inevitably appealed to members of Croatia's extremist right-wing groupings, and apparently also attracted highly offensive comments. The regular use of curses and abusive, obscene language seemed to challenge the aims of the Facebook page. The fact that from the very beginning this was indeed a problem for the authors behind the page is clear from an entry posted on 20 November, in which the authors stated: "We ask you to restrain unsuitable comments, curses, because we do not wish that the page be reduced to curses and insults! We ask you not to glorify any regime, because that is not suitable and we do not wish that!" There was clearly a fear that the cause may be tainted or hindered by both obscene language and pro-Ustasha statements. Furthermore, it is clear from other entries that there was a risk that the page might be closed or banned. Thus, while the medium of Facebook allowed the authors of the page to reach a large audience very quickly and invite them to participate in and support their project, users and commenters challenged and confused the aims and strategy of this project. Indeed, the participatory audience on Facebook constituted a real danger to the existence of the project's platform.

While the messages on the Facebook page 'Support for Josip Šimunić' certainly spread quickly, it is hard to say how far they reached. Though commenters frequently pointed out that they lived outside Croatia or had a somehow non-Croatian background, entries and comments on the page were held predominantly in Croatian with rare comments or questions in German, English or other languages. Yet, the page has certainly reached migrant communities outside Croatia. In Munich a group of Croatian football supporters staged a small demonstration and sent photos of it to the 'Support for Josip Šimunić' page, where they were posted on 25 November and received nearly 8,000 'likes'. In a way, the Facebook page thus served to create a memory community across international borders.

As stated above, starting on 23 November, the Facebook page also promoted a petition in support of Šimunić and addressed it to FIFA president, Sepp Blatter. This petition was initiated in the UK and formulated bilingually in English and Croatian, and it did get support from all over the world and in both languages. The petition text largely repeated the arguments from the Facebook page, but it also gave some further explanations for supporting the protest against Šimunić's punishment, one being that young Croats were sick of being connected to a Fascist past and having to stand trial for the crimes of the Ustasha, and another that they wanted freedom to express patriotism.[27] Some of the signatories left comments explaining why they supported the petition. Many simply stated that Šimunić was a patriot, not a Fascist, and that patriotism is not a crime. Others gave historical explanations similar to those on the Facebook page, and one posted the complete text of one of the versions of the original entry explaining the aims of the Facebook page. Yet, in spite of the more than 30,000 signatories, the petition had no influence on FIFA's final decision, which was to confirm that Šimunić was banned from 10 international matches. But it did unite a dedicated international Internet community and thus contributed to a transnational memory debate.

The statements and explanations made by signatories of the petition were more homogenous and in line with the original intent of the petition text than was the case on the Facebook page. Obviously, participation was quite regulated in connection to the petition, as only signatories were able to comment. Moreover, it may be argued that a signature and a comment stating the reasons for signing are more serious and committed ways of expressing one's support than a 'like' on Facebook. The petition may be regarded as having created a loose and transcultural virtual memory community of people with fairly similar views on a particular element of Croatia's past. While the petition's electronic community reached a membership of 34,000, the Facebook page, with its much less controllable participatory audience, reached 160,000 followers. The petition page is somehow a finished activity, whereas the Facebook page stays active. Though the page gradually turned into a more ordinary kind of fan club platform for supporters of Josip Šimunić, it remained nationalist and very right wing, with connections to ultra-nationalist popular culture and veterans'

---

[27] See the petition webpage on: http://www.change.org/p/fifa-support-for-josip-%C5%A1imuni%C4%87 (14 August 2014).

organizations. Moreover, the page continued to make entries and create chains of comments debating the meaning of Croatian historical symbols, fascism and patriotism, albeit on a much smaller scale, and with much less intervention. Thus, there is still a digital afterlife of the debate caused by Josip Šimunić's fascist chant, but it is hardly vibrant.

Conclusion

The Facebook page 'Support for Josip Šimunić' contributed to a very rapid dissemination of a particular set of views on the Šimunić case. It reached a large group of people, who somehow expressed their support through a click on 'like'. Parts of this group also engaged more actively through commenting, posting clips and links, and recycling the main statements of the page's authors, thus sharing and confirming a certain view of the past. We may regard this group, and also the somewhat similar group of petition signatories, as a very large and very loose virtual memory community. Yet, the chaotic and anarchic character of the commenting practices suggests that this is a very fragmented and loose community at best. Indeed, most commenters do not really relate to comments from other group members.

Many commenters use the Šimunić debates to condemn Croatia's political elite or to make a provocation. Yet, the vast majority of users of this page only click on 'like', which is certainly a minimal kind of participation. The speed, unboundedness and participation, though minimal and enigmatic, open completely new possibilities of memory transmission on the Internet and on Facebook. Yet, it is hard to say whether, in a case like that of Josip Šimunić, Facebook communication has a much larger reach and impact than other types of memory mediation, such as printed media. The support page for Josip Šimunić had an audience of 160,000 at the most. A tabloid newspaper such as *Večernji list* has a print run of around 60,000, presumably reaching 285,000 readers, and it has 881,000 readers online. It seems fair to assume that most Croats learned of the Šimunić case through these channels, though this tells us nothing of their views.

The Facebook page may be as much an example of the general fragmentation within Croatian society with regard to the memory of Croatia's fascist past. Both the Facebook page and the petition certainly constitute a contestation of the official and politically accepted view on the issue. Especially the Facebook page's posts and comments promote a series of somehow loosely defined memory narratives, which presents Croatia's history as a long struggle for national freedom and independence, with its people often victimized and suffering from the crimes of others. In these narratives, the Ustasha history is certainly not prominent, but certainly also less evil than so many other historical dark figures. Indeed, in these narratives, the Ustasha do not seem to be taken sufficiently seriously to be allowed to taint Croatian patriotism in any way. Thus, their role with regard to the salute 'Za dom spremni' is presented as too insignificant to have any consequence. The Facebook page, and to a lesser extent the petition also, thus promoted massive banalization, trivialization and downplaying of Croatia's darkest past. Indeed, the discourse on these pages suggests a lack of confrontation with Croatia's difficult Ustasha history, and in this it may reflect a more general problem of coming to terms with this past in Croatian society. Though the political establishment clearly condemns this part of Croatia's history, the legacies from the ambiguous memory politics in the 1990s have left parts of Croatian society in a memorial grey zone with an unclear relationship to the Ustasha past.

References

"About Sidney United 58 fc." http://www.sydneyunited58fc.com/history/sydney-united-58-fc/ (5 April 2014).
Anon. "Croatia football chief Vlatko Markovic hit by gay group's backlash". *Guardian*, 14 November 2010. http://www.theguardian.com/football/2010/nov/14/gay-backlash-croatia-football-chief (6 April 2014).
Anon. "Croatia's Josip Simunic defends 'pro-Nazi' World Cup celebration chant", *The Guardian*, 20 November 2013. http://www.theguardian.com/football/2013/nov/20/croatia-josip-simunic-defends-apparent-pro-nazi-chant (8 August 2014).
Arežina, Bojan. "DORH Šimuniću izrelao maksimalno novčanu kaznu". *Večernji list*, 21 November 2013. http://www.vecernji.hr/crna-kronika/drzavno-odvjetnistvo-simunicu-izreklo-maksimalnu-novcanu-kaznu-904274 (8 August 2014)
Bieber, Florian. "Ready for the Homeland? Simunic and a bit of normal fascism" *Balkan Insight*, 21 November 2013.
http://www.balkaninsight.com/en/blog/ready-for-the-homeland-simunic-and-a-bit-of-normal-fascism (10 October 2014).
Brentin, Dario. "Fascist Groundhog day? The issue with 'Za dom spremni' in Croatian football." *Balkan Insight* 11 April 2015. http://balkanist.net/fascist-groundhog-day-issue-za-dom-spremni-croatian-football/ (10 May 2015).
"Croatia mourns Vlatko Marković. " *UEFA webpage* 23 September 2013. http://www.uefa.com/memberassociations/association=cro/news/newsid=2000125.html (6 April 2014)
Delač, Hrvoje. "Šimuniću 10 utakmica suspenzije zbog ustaškog pozdrava!", *Večernji list*, 16 December 2013. http://www.vecernji.hr/nogomet/simunicu-velika-kazna-dobio-deset-utakmica-suspenzije-909525 (6 August 2014).
Dijck, José van. *The culture of connectivity: A critical history of social media.* New York: Oxford University Press, 2013.
"Dinamo Zagreb Prva Momčad." http://gnkdinamo.hr/hr/1-momcad/igraci/obrana/josip-simunic1/ (5 April 2014)

Graeme Yorke. "Croatia's Josip Simunic slapped with 10 game ban and will miss the World cup because of Nazi chanting". *Mail Online* 16 December 2013. http://www.dailymail.co.uk/sport/worldcup2014/article-2524741/Croatias-Josip-Simunic-slapped-10-game-ban-miss-World-Cup-Nazi-chanting.html (10 August 2014).

Hina. "Šimonić: Pozdrav s'Za dom spremni' je patriotski; Sud u Lausannei: 'Ne, to je ratni poklič ustaša", *Jutarnji list* 12 May 2014. http://www.jutarnji.hr/simunic-pozdrav-za-dom-dozivljavam-kao-patriotski-cas-ne-to-je-bez-sumnje-ustaski-uzvik-/1190847/ (6 August 2014).

Hughson, John. "Football, folk dancing and fascism: diversity and difference in Multicultural Australia". *Journal of Sociology* 33 (1997): 167–186

"Josip Šimunić." http://www.uefa.com/worldcup/season=2014/teams/player=49993/profile/ (5 April 2014).

"Josip Šimunić and his Australian context (Interview with John Hughson)." http://www.youtube.com/watch?v=NFvavWNUzDs (6 August 2014).

Hoskins, Andrew."7/7 and connective memory: international trajectories of remembering in post-scarcity culture". *Memory Studies* 4.3 (2011): 269–280.

Kristović, Ivica. "Jovanović: E moj Šimuniću, tebi treba lekcija iz povijesti" *Večernji list*, 20 November 2013. http://www.vecernji.hr/hrvatska/jovanovic-e-moj-simunicu-tebi-treba-lekcija-iz-povijesti-903984 (8 August 2014).

Lindgren, Simon. "Youtube gunmen? Mapping participatory media discourse on school shooting videos". *Media, Culture and Society* 33.1 (2010): 1–14.

Lindgren, Simon. "Collective problemsolving and informal learning in networked publics. Reading vlogging networks on YouTube as knowledge communities." *Interactive Media Use and Youth: Learning, Knowledge Exchange and Behavior*. Eds. E. Dunkels, G. Frånberg & C. Hällgren. Hershey: IGI Global, 2011. 50–64.

Lindgren, Simon. "The Sociology of Media and Information technologies." *Introduction to Sociology: Scandinavian Sensibilities*. Eds. G.C. Aakvaag, M. Hviid Jacobsen & T. Johansson. London: Pearson, 2012. 140–159.

Magaš, Vjekoslav. "Eksklusivni intervju." *Hrvatski tjednik* 5 June 2014, 22.

Pavlakovic, Vjeran. "Flirting with Fascism: The Ustaša legacy and Croatian politics in the 1990s." *The Shared History. The Second World War and National Question in Yugoslavia*. Novi Sad: Centar za Istoriju, demokratiju i pomirenje, 2008. 115–143.

"Potpora Josipu Šimuniću." https://www.facebook.com/josip.simunic.officialfanpage?fref=ts (14 August 2014)

Ramet, Sabrina P. "Politics in Croatia since 1990." *Croatia since independence. War, politics, society, foreign relations*. Eds. Sabrina P. Ramet, Konrad Clewing and Reneo Lukić. Munich: R. Oldenbrug Verlag, 2008. 31–57.

Rutten, Ellen & Vera Zvereva. "Introduction. Old conflicts, new media: post-socialist digital memories." *Memory, Conflict and New Media. Web Wars in Post-socialist States*. Eds. Ellen Rutten, Julie Fedor & Vera Zvereva. London: Routledge, 2013: 1–18.

Sindbæk, Tea. "The Fall and Rise of a National Hero: Interpretations of Draža Mikailović and the Chetniks in Yugoslavia and Serbia since 1945". *Journal of Contemporary European Studies* 17.1 (2009): 47–59.

Sindbæk, Tea. *Usable History? Representations of Yugoslavia's difficult past, 1945–2002*. Aarhus: Aarhus University Press, 2012.

"Support for Josip Šimunić." http://www.change.org/p/fifa-support-for-josip-%C5%A1imuni%C4%87 (14 August 2014).

Tomasevich, Jozo. *War and Revolution in Yugoslavia, 1941–1945. Occupation and collaboration*. Stanford: Stanford University Press, 2001.

Elvin Gjevori
Collective Memory and Institutional Reform in Albania

After the fall of communism across Eastern Europe, repressed memories resurfaced vengefully and became potent tools of political struggle. In the Balkans and some former Soviet republics such memories were even used to fuel protracted wars and ethnic cleansing. Consequently, many social science debates have been interested in analysing memory conflicts and the way that they have been used by national elites to elicit mobilisation or acquire popular legitimacy.[1] Although this analytical focus has been enlightening, collective memory viewed from this perspective has almost exclusively been characterized as a destructive instrument of political struggle. I argue that collective memory can also be an appropriate analytical framework to understand the profound and positive changes that have occurred in post-communist countries. Specifically, collective memory can be instrumental in explaining the differing paths of institutional reforms across and within emerging democracies.

In this regard Albania presents an interesting case through which to test collective memory as an explanatory mechanism behind institutional reform, specifically institutionalisation defined as the situation whereby "[a]uthority and power are depersonalized, and resource mobilization and principles of resource allocation are routinized."[2] After the fall of communism, in addition to the economy, Albania had to reform the armed forces and judiciary since they were the main power centres through which the communist regime had built one of the most repressive dictatorships in Eastern Europe. Both reforms started in 1991 and initially suffered from the same symptoms of politicisation, nepotism and corruption. After the pyramid scheme crisis of 1997, which resulted in the almost total collapse of the state, both the armed forces and the judiciary had to begin

---

[1] Ed Cairns and Mícheál D. Roe. Eds. *The Role of Memory in Ethnic Conflict*. Basinstoke: Palgrave Macmillan, 2003; Craig Larkin. *Memory Conflict in Lebanon: Remembering and Forgetting the Past*. London: Routledge, 2012; Conny Mithander, Maria Holmgren Troy and John Sundholm. Eds. *Collective Traumas: Memory of War and Conflict in 20th Century Europe*. Brussels, Belgium: Peter Lang, 2007; Victor Roudometof. *Collective Memory, National Identity and Ethnic Conflict*. Westport: Preager Publishers, 2002; Meir Litvak. Ed.*Palestinian Collective Memory and National Identity*. New York: Palgrave Macmillan, 2004; Katharina Hall and Kathryn Jones. Eds. *Constructions of Conflict*. Oxford: Peter Lang, 2011.
[2] Johan Olsen. "Change and Continuity: An Institutional Approach to Institutions of Democratic Government." *European Political Science Review* 1.1 (2009): 5.

anew and were again politicised. Although their history under communism was similar since they were politicised and their early transition reforms were also similar, from the early 2000s on there has been progress towards institutionalisation in the military while that of the judiciary lags behind. The success of military reform culminated with NATO accession in 2009, while the failure of judicial reform became one of the main impediments to advancing Albania's EU integration. This raises the question as to why Albania was more successful in institutionalising its military than the judiciary.

Collective memory and preference formation

Explaining why Albania was successful in institutionalising its military more substantially than the judiciary can be approached from different angles, the most prominent of which would be a rationalist, interest-based approach. Indeed elite interests are crucial to explain institutional reforms. However, in emerging democracies experiencing prolonged and volatile transitions, interests are highly mutable, making it difficult for elites to identify and use them as guides to their political behaviour. In Albania, the mutability of interests is even more accentuated because it experienced major uncertainty not only in 1991, when communism fell, but also in 1997, when the above-mentioned pyramid schemes collapsed and resulted in popular revolt, and again in 1999 during the Kosovo war, when half a million refugees entered its territory. Therefore, undertaking an analysis of institutional reform in Albania by identifying elite interests in a particular moment and then connecting them to decisions would be neither enlightening nor correct. In emerging democracies like Albania, one has to analyze the events that happen before interests crystallised because such events affect interest formation, which in turn affects political behaviour. So I do not deny the role of interests in explaining variation of political behaviour; I instead explain how interests are shaped. This perspective is particularly important for studying transitioning democracies as it enables researchers to understand differing institutional developments across and within countries.

Therefore, I argue that in transitioning countries with unstructured institutions, a process of social construction occurs, prior to institutional consolidation, during which actors create an understanding of the problem and the way to address it. Under conditions of uncertainty, where the old has been repudiated, the future is unclear and the high hopes of the first days of freedom have been dampened by the unavoidable crises of transition, actors have to reassess their goals, reshape their interests and only then can they act. So to understand institutionalisation reform, one has to understand how problems are perceived, how history is made sense of, how preferences are shaped and then analyze their effects on institutions. For this reason, I rely on a constructivist account of interest formation with collective memory as an explanatory mechanism to account for institutionalisation in Albania. The evolution of collective memory defined as "social representations concerning the past which each group produces, institutionalizes, guards and transmits through the interaction of its members"[3] provides a variety of frameworks through which diverse actors develop an understanding of the past and confront the challenges of the future, especially in periods of uncertainty. It is through such frameworks that actors form preferences and against which they evaluate choices. The analysis of elite collective memory therefore is key to understanding pre-institutionalisation preference formation.

Based on the theoretical understanding laid out above, this chapter's main argument is that the differing degrees of military and judicial institutionalisation in Albania from the beginning of its democratic transition in 1992 to its NATO accession in 2009 can be explained by the development of elite collective memory. I argue that the combination of the memory of the communist regime and the memory of the main crises during the transition created the frameworks through which political elites ranked priorities enabling substantial institutionalisation in the military only.

Methodology – tracing collective memory

Tracing the development of collective memory is generally difficult, in Albania even more so since data on public opinion are either missing or unreliable. The most effective and practical method by which one can measure such development is through the analysis of newspaper coverage of military and judicial reform. Newspaper coverage is an appropriate medium through which to analyze collective memory because written language is one of the main mechanisms through which memory is conveyed, becomes available to the linguistic entity, and shapes interest formation.[4] Studying the language used by politically affiliated newspapers in particular enables researchers to gain an understanding of the political elite's perspective, their memory of the previous regime, their understanding of the crises they faced, and the future they envision. Newspaper cover-

---

[3] Paolo Jedlowski. "Memory and Sociology. Themes and Issues." *Time and Society* 10.1 (2001): 33.
[4] Peter Berger and Tomas Luckmann. *The Social Construction of Reality: A Treatise in the Sociology of Knowledge*. New York: Random House, 1967, 63.

age is not only representative of the elite's view, but it also reaches and affects public opinion on a wide scale. Therefore, by analysing newspaper coverage of military and judicial reform I can trace elite interest formation over time. To do so, I focus on the level of politicisation based on the assumption that institutionalisation and politicisation are inversely related. I rely on content and discourse analysis of newspaper articles to investigate how the politicisation of military and judicial reform has developed over the years and to identify the causal mechanisms explaining any observed change.

I have chosen two newspapers: *Rilindja Demokratike (Democratic Rebirth)*, the official organ of the centre-right Democratic Party and *Zëri i Popullit* (Voice of the People) the official organ of the centre-left Socialist Party. These newspapers provide the official position of the two political parties which have governed Albania since the fall of communism. Both newspapers are thoroughly political during the period under analysis and their articles represent the official positions of their respective parties. Because of tight party control, any change in their coverage cannot come out of the changing nature of the newspapers, but out of the political parties controlling their editorial line. I examined all the editions of these newspapers from 1992 to 2009 and collected all substantive, policy-oriented articles regarding military and judicial reform. Articles containing 'simple' reporting of a story, without analysing and assigning merit/blame were not collected. At the end of data collection I built a dataset of 1535 articles covering military and judicial reform from 1992 to 2009.

The collected articles were classified by newspaper, by topic (military/judiciary) and by type of coverage (non-politicised/politicised). The third categorisation requires some explanation. An article is deemed to provide non-politicised coverage if it has one of the following attributes: 1. States that the military/judiciary is an independent institution. 2. States that the military/judiciary is undergoing positive reform increasing professionalism and de-politicisation. 3. Defends military/judicial reform and calls on the 'other side' to refrain from politicisation. An article is deemed to provide politicised coverage if it has one of the following: 1. States that the military/judiciary is a politically controlled institution lacking independence and serving the sitting government's interests. 2. Accuses the government of politicising the military/judiciary through political appointments.

Lastly, from 1992 to 2009 there were three changes of power: in 1992 the Democratic Party (DP) won the elections and became the first non-communist party to lead Albania since 1944. In 1997 the Socialist Party (SP) came to power after pyramid schemes collapsed followed by anarchy, and in 2005 the DP returned to power. This variation enables me to analyze whether newspaper coverage of military and judicial reform is connected to the political fortunes of the DP and SP. It should be noted that military policy has been remarkably steady as both sides have constantly downsized the military, relied on the same strategic partners and provided similar budgetary support. Therefore, if I notice any change in the newspaper coverage of military reform, it is unlikely that it reflects policy change.

Findings

Both newspapers dedicate considerable attention to military and judicial reform, an indication that they see them as problematic. The more significant finding is that coverage of judicial reform is politicised throughout the period under scrutiny. The level of politicisation oscillates in accordance with the Democratic Party and the Socialist Party being in power and opposition. Each time the DP is in power, its newspaper Democratic Rebirth (DR) covers the government's judicial reforms as positive while the Voice of the People (VP) sees them as attempts to politicise the judiciary. Each time the SP is in power the VP defends the government's judicial reforms while DR accuses it of politicisation. Regarding military reform, during the 1990s, its coverage follows the politicised trajectory of judicial reform. However, from 2002 on, it becomes increasingly less politicised and no longer oscillates when DP and SP are in and out of power. The graphs below (Figures 1 and 2) illustrate the fluctuation of politicisation of newspaper coverage of judicial and military reform in relation to the ideological orientation of the government.

As the graphs show, judicial reform coverage is consistently politicised while military reform coverage is politicised in the 1990s only and becomes increasingly less so in the 2000s. So it is natural to ask, why did the coverage of military reform change in the second decade of the transition? Since both institutions had been similarly politicised during communism and the first decade of transition, why did the political elites change their approach in the second decade of the transition, only for the military? What is this change indicatory of? To answer these questions, the following sections will analyze DR's and VP's newspaper articles to identify the justificatory mechanisms which allowed their coverage of judicial reform to be politicised throughout the period under analysis and the justificatory mechanisms which enabled the de-politicisation of military reform coverage in the second decade of transition.

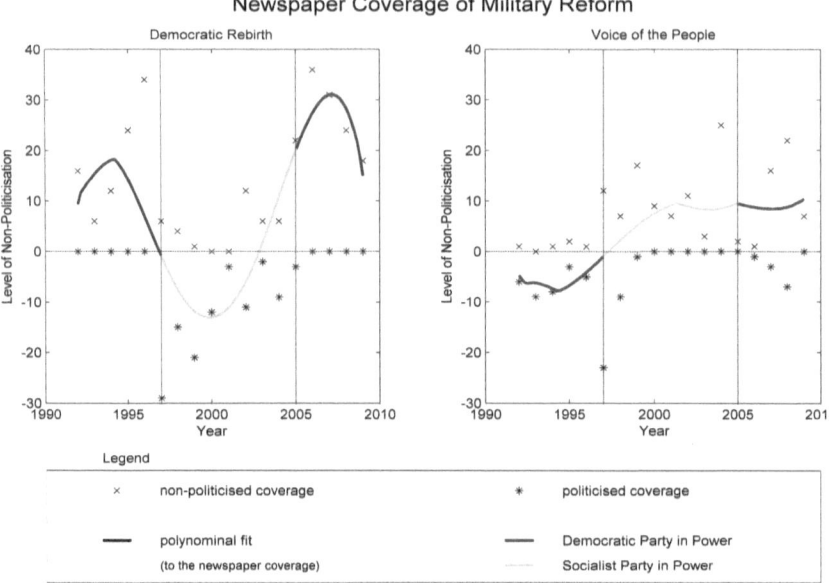

Fig. 1

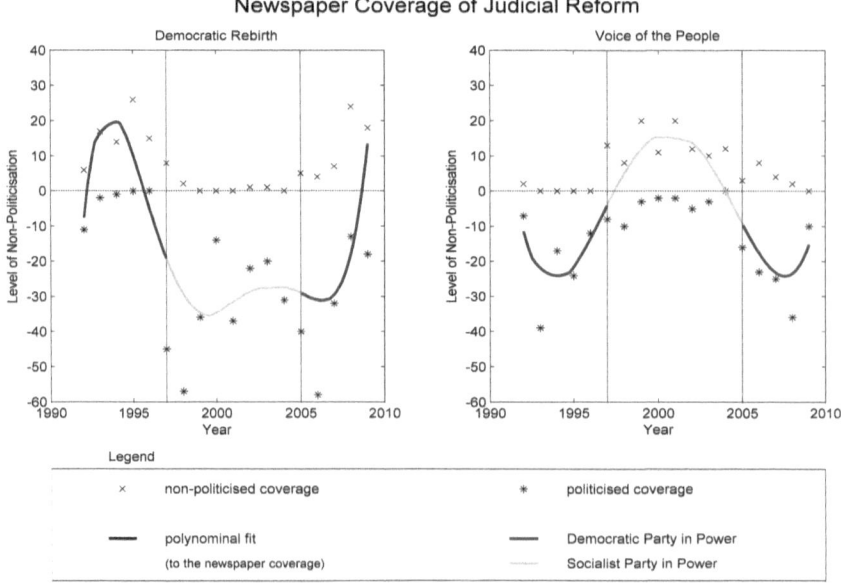

Fig. 2

Coverage of Judicial Reform

Except for 1992, the Democrats' first year in power, Democratic Rebirth (DR) provided a non-politicised coverage of judicial reform so much so that in 1995 and 1996 it had no politicised articles. The coverage was primarily concerned with a comparison of the democratic judiciary with that under communism. An article on 16 February 1996 is a good illustration of this approach, as it stated:

> [W]e inherited from the communist regime a judiciary which was uniquely dependent on politics. Only in Albania the ministry of justice and the defence lawyer were abolished in 1967. After the establishment of democracy these institutions were introduced again [...] Since the fall of communism, judicial independence has been accepted as the main priority for the construction of the new state.[1]

The message is clear, Albania has come out of one of its darkest periods, and in the years of the DP government the healthy foundations of a new judiciary have been built. This, however, was DR's message late in the Democratic Party's term; before defending the judiciary and judicial reforms, DR applied strong pressure on the judiciary to follow the government's political goals. Early in DP's term DR pressured the judiciary to put on trial the former communist leadership and accused the SP of sabotaging the trials since when they had been in power "the trial was delayed because the SP found it difficult to punish its spiritual inspirers [...] Only after the victory of [DP] democracy in March 22 1992 the trial restarted."[2] Thus, the first elements of the connection between the ideological orientation of the government and judicial effectiveness are surfacing as DR argued in this article that only when the Democratic Party is in power the judiciary is effective and apolitical. Attention to the expected trials of the communist leadership continued and so did DR's 'advice' to the judiciary by stating:

> [T]he people directly responsible for communist crimes will scream: 'What good comes out of these trials? What do we gain from punishments? This is not justice, it is revenge [...]' They lie, they are afraid of being punished and this is why they scream. They know there can be no reconciliation, no rule of law, no social justice without analysing the past and punishing those responsible for this great tragedy.[3]

---

[1] For practicality, the name of the newspapers and titles are translated in the footnotes while the original name and title are placed alongside the translation in the bibliography.
Democratic Rebirth. "The Albanian judiciary aims to reach contemporary standards." 15 February 1996, 4.
[2] *Democratic Rebirth.* "Nears the time for the trial of the communist cast." 11 July 1992, 1.
[3] *Democratic Rebirth.* "No revenge just justice." 20 October 1992a, 3.

Here, DR called for the use of the judiciary to try the former communist leadership as a way to analyze the past and punish those responsible for it. Not only was DR in favour of using the judiciary, but it argued that it could be done only under the DP government because the SP was the successor of the communist regime. This perspective was destined to politicise the discussion of judicial reform, as the opposition – accused of being camouflaged communists – would see it as an attempt to control the judiciary and use it against the opposition.

While in 1992 and early 1993 DR pressured the judiciary to investigate the communist leadership as an indirect way to de-legitimise the SP accused of harbouring them, by the end of 1993 the calls to investigate the SP itself became more direct. DR called upon the judiciary "to fulfil its duty" in investigating the corruption of the Socialists, whom it saw as a continuation of Enver Hoxha's[4] Labour Party.[5] DR argued that Socialists claimed the accusations were political because they knew they were guilty. The paper incited the judiciary to action by saying, "[T]he judiciary MUST HAVE NO MERCY for ordinary thieves like [SP Chairman] Fatos Nano."[6] DR not only accused the SP leader of being corrupt and the SP of being the inheritor of communism, but it accused the opposition of being against judicial reform because they wanted to control it as they had when they were communists. "Such behaviour can be expected only by those who have never accepted the rule of law, who, when in power, controlled the judiciary according to their arbitrary wills, who eliminated the right to legal counsel so that people were left exposed to the cruelties of the dictatorship."[7] These articles connected DR's overall argument: the communist leadership politicised the judiciary, was criminal and corrupt, for which it had to be investigated. Secondly, and more importantly, the SP was the inheritor of the communist mentality of political control over the judiciary, which positioned it against judicial reform.

Just as it used the memory of the communist regime to de-legitimise the opposition, DR also referenced the abuses of the communists as part of its rhetoric in defending the government's judicial reform. In doing so, DR continued to de-legitimise any Socialist criticism by arguing that they were unreformed communists in favour of a politicised judiciary. For example, in late 1993, DR defended the government's decision to graduate new lawyers in six-month courses to re-

---

4 At the head of the Labour Party, Enver Hoxha was the leader of Albania's one-party state during 1944–1985.
5 *Democratic Rebirth*. "Now it is the judiciary's time to fulfil its duty." 8 May 1993, 2.
6 *Democratic Rebirth*. "The Judiciary must have no mercy on ordinary thieves like Fatos Nano." 15 May 1993a, 1.
7 *Democratic Rebirth*. "Only a band of thieves can come to the defence of a thief." 18 February 1994, 3.

place those judges and investigators considered as co-operators of the communist regime in an article stating "the Albanian judiciary was the field where communism was the most dominant; otherwise Albanians would not have experienced that kind of dictatorship for fifty years."[8] Those who had been delivering 'justice' in the name of the people, claimed the article, were products of the communist caste and in their education they learned only the Labour Party's directives, making them nothing other than Party commissars. For that reason, DR claimed, most judges and prosecutors had to be replaced by lawyers educated during democracy. It is clear that DR presents judicial reform as a process in which the old judges need to be replaced with new ones and this new judiciary then needs to 'fulfil its duty' and condemn the communist caste and its camouflaged inheritors.

The balancing between defending the government's judicial reform and attacking the Socialist opposition continued in an editorial in which the SP was accused of being "ready to sacrifice – for the sake of political capital and power – law, justice and democracy."[9] In fact it could not be otherwise; if the reform is presented as a way to punish communists hidden in the SP and corrupt Socialists, the latter cannot be anything but enemies of judicial independence. DR reinforced its accusations and stated that the SP attacked the judiciary because, they controlled it when they were communists and they yearn to control it again. That is why the new judiciary should make sure that "criminals like [SP Chairman] Fatos Nano are tried for genocide [...] the communist leadership must answer for the blood of innocent victims, the people killed in the streets, those burned alive, the mothers left alone, the destruction done to this country."[10]

From late 1992 on DR was persistent in its message: the SP is the continuation of the Labour Party and the communist regime, and thereby guilty of its crimes and of the politicisation of the judiciary. Secondly, the SP, as evidenced by the trial of its chairman, was also characterised as guilty of corruption and abuse of power. That is why the SP was against judicial reform, and that it why, in DR's eyes, its complaints were illegitimate since corrupt unreformed communists were not to be trusted. The contours of this coverage hold steady until 1997, when the DP goes into opposition.

---

8 *Democratic Rebirth*. "Military reform will not be stopped by the communist screams of the VP." 19 November 1993b, 4.
9 *Democratic Rebirth*. "Even Fatos Nano will submit to the law and the judiciary." 14 February 1994a, 1.
10 *Democratic Rebirth*. "Criminals like [SP Chairman] Fatos Nano should be tried for genocide also." 1 June 1995, 1.

For the same period VP's coverage was the exact opposite. After the Socialist Party (SP) lost the 1992 elections, the VP was initially hesitant to put forth a full-throated criticism of judicial reform. These reservations, however, soon started waning as at the end of 1992 it analyzed the appointment of the new Prosecutor General (PG) arguing that:

> [F]or precious services rendered to the DP, by breaking the law in favour of the power-holders, Mr Dragoshi was rewarded with the position of the PG [...] while the former PG Maksim Haxhia, who refused to break the law and harm the independence of the judiciary, was fired unceremoniously.[11]

This was the first accusation against the government for politicising the judiciary and was followed by many more. For example, VP published a long article where it analyzed DP's judicial reform and noted that in Albania instead of the rule of law, one found a situation where "the pressure of authorities on the judiciary to follow 'central directives' is clear evidence of the flagrant attempts to build a political and police state which aims to side-track the rule of law."[12] So by the end of 1992, the VP had set the contours of its approach towards DP's judicial reform by arguing that it was a politically motivated attempt to control the judiciary. This kind of coverage was on display in early 1993 when the VP accused the DP of pressuring the judiciary with the aim of using it politically:

> [T]his was what the Labour Party tried to do and this is what the DP is doing under the banner of 'fighting judicial corruption and communists in the judiciary.' The latest decisions of the High Council of Justice[13] to cleanse the judiciary reached a new peak of politicisation, which will continue in the future.[14]

While DR accused the SP of being unreformed communists, the VP replied by arguing that the DP-led government was beset by a communist mentality of maintaining political control over the judiciary.

Besides accusing the government of aiming to control the judiciary, the VP was also specific in its criticisms by analysing sensitive legislative initiatives. For example, VP criticised the law on defence lawyers, which it saw as a continuation of "the psychological violence on the organs of the judiciary to not dare follow their juridical consciences in cases involving the party in power [...] this

---

11 *Voice of the People*. "Party knows best." 2 December 1992, 3.
12 *Voice of the People*. "What kind of state are we building in Albania: a political or a legal state?" 17 December 1992a, 1–2.
13 Constitutionally independent body governing judicial appointments and promotions.
14 *Voice of the People*. "The judiciary under the DP's attack." 6 January 1993, 1, 3.

law is deeply political."[15] In addition, as part of its campaign to denounce the government's control of the judiciary, the VP joined the debate on the condensed courses graduating judges and prosecutors. The VP stated that "the preparation of the 'Party's faithful' in the three-month courses is a sign of the dangers to individual rights."[16] Interestingly, VP, the newspaper founded by Enver Hoxha, increasingly compared the government's decisions to the actions taken by communists when they gained power. From VP's perspective, DP's reform was as politicised and thirsty to control the judiciary as the communists were when they came to power.

Attacks on the judiciary reached unprecedented levels when a proceeding for corruption was initiated against SP Chairman Fatos Nano. The trial provided VP the most opportune moment to demonstrate that indeed the DP had been working to politicise the judiciary in order to use it against the opposition. The VP argued that: "the judiciary is under the control of the rightist-fascist state"[17] and one month later writes "the judiciary is scared. The Constitutional Court is afraid to defend the law, is afraid to demonstrate its independence, is afraid to show democratic emancipation, and is afraid to escape the claws of political control."[18] After accusing the DP of politicising the judiciary and using the Nano trial as evidence of its submission, VP argued that the judiciary was merely an extension of the government.[19] After Mr Nano was declared guilty and given a long prison sentence, VP concluded "the judiciary is under the total control of politics."[20] VP's coverage of judicial reform conveyed the message that the judiciary was politicised and presented DP's judicial reforms as attempts to 'capture' the judiciary and use it as an instrument against the opposition. On numerous occasions the VP accused the government of following in the footsteps of the communist regime by building a politicised judiciary. This editorial line continued until 1997 when the SP gained power.

In 1997, after growing protests over the failure of pyramid schemes, the declaration of a state of emergency, and the looting of military depots, the DP-led

---

15 *Voice of the People*. "The judiciary under accusation." 10 January 1993a, 5.
16 *Voice of the People*. "The preparation of the Party's faithful in 3-month courses shows the danger to human rights in Albania." 10 April 1993b, 1.
17 *Voice of the People*. "The judiciary under the feet of the rightist fascist state." 27 July 1993c, 1.
18 *Voice of the People*. "A scared judiciary." 11 August 1993d, 1.
19 *Voice of the People*. "The independence of the judiciary in Albania: a reality or a piece of paper?" 13 October 1993e, 2.
20 *Voice of the People*. "The judiciary under the claws of the political state." 8 April 1994, 1.

government resigned and new elections were held and won overwhelmingly by the SP. This change of power was reflected in the direction of newspaper coverage. As soon as President Berisha[21] and the DP were out of power, DR began accusing the government of politicising the judiciary. Remarkably, however, the content of the accusations did not change. If during 1992–97 DR de-legitimised SP accusations against judicial reform on the basis that the SP was not to be trusted as the heir of the communist regime, after 1997, it used the same accusation to label SP's judicial reform as politicised. For example, on the day of the swearing in of the new president and the official removal of Berisha, DR wrote "today begins the aggression of the ex-communists on the constitution and independent institutions."[22] DR maintains the same line of attack against the SP whether in opposition or in government: unreformed communists are not to be trusted.

This approach was on clear display a few days later when DR wrote:

> [Justice Minister] Kondi presented yesterday the Socialists' platform of aggression against judicial independence. The barbarity of the SP and its henchmen against the young judges who implemented judicial reform transforming Albania from the country where people were killed to a country where freedom was protected and guaranteed, was to be expected.[23]

As far as DR was concerned, the return of the SP to power was equivalent to the return of the communist methods of judicial politicisation. In addition, DR, as it had done when the DP was in power, continued to attack the SP for connections with political crime. For example, DR argued that "[President] Meidani, [Minister of Justice] Kondi and the SP are expected to vote in favour of the reintroduction of communist criminals and murderers in courts and the Prosecutor's Office to transform the judiciary into an obedient tool for the elimination of political opponents."[24] The article referred to the government's initiative to return to work a number of judges and prosecutors removed by the DP government. However, from DR's perspective this was equivalent to the return of the former communist judicial cast.

Accusations against the government for politicising the judiciary continued with high intensity even after the troubled year of 1997. For example, in an interview with the former DP-appointed and SP-fired Chief Justice of the Constitution-

---

21 Albania's first post-communist President who was forced to resign in 1997 and lead the Democratic Party in opposition.
22 *Democratic Rebirth*. "The President is stripped of all power." 29 July 1997, 1.
23 *Democratic Rebirth*. "The judiciary under the guillotine." 31 July 1997a, 1.
24 *Democratic Rebirth*. "The judiciary under the leadership of crime." 28 August 1997b, 2.

al Court, DR quoted him saying that "the year 1999 will be a continuation of the destruction of the judiciary; its further corruption and political revenge against those few left who do not obey the government."[25] This quote encapsulates the continuous attacks regarding politicisation and corruption, which were crucial to DR's de-legitimatisation of the government's judicial reform. DR continued to maintain the same hard line accusing the Socialist government of politicising the judiciary. In 2000 DR provided an overview of SP's judicial reform since their accession to power:

> [A]fter removing all the chairmen of district courts, the chairmen of appellate courts, and after inventing political tests as a way to remove judges who did not follow their political orders, [President] Meidani and [Justice Minister] Kondi now have come out openly with their plan to install SP militants in the organs of the judiciary.[26]

Clearly, after the DP lost power in 1997 DR's coverage of judicial reform changed significantly by attacking it as politicised. Substantially however, DR's case against SP's judicial reform relied on the same justificatory mechanisms it used when it was in power. When the DP was in power DR argued that Socialists were not to be trusted because they wanted to turn the clock back to the communist practices of politicised judiciary; after going into opposition DR argued that the SP was in fact turning the clock back to the politicised communist judiciary. DR's coverage followed the same editorial line throughout its opposition until it returned to power in 2005.

The opposite is true of the Voice of the People's (VP) coverage of judicial reform after the Socialists won the elections in 1997. From VP's perspective everything needed to begin anew. Therefore, the paper wrote that the government must prioritise the creation of a new and independent judiciary.[27] As SP's efforts to reform the judiciary began, in an article entitled "[T]he court mafia collapses" the paper informed its readers that the new High Council of Justice (HCJ) has begun judicial reform. Claiming a new beginning for the judiciary, the VP wrote that "during the five years of the DP government, judges did not wear the black toga of the judge, but the blue [colour of the DP] apron of the DP. Courts made political decisions, not judicial ones."[28]

Similarly to DR, the VP shows remarkable stability in the content of its coverage as it continues to attack the DP for the politicisation of the judiciary and

---

25 *Democratic Rebirth*. "The anti-law and thefts are blooming." 9 January 1999, 7.
26 *Democratic Rebirth*. "Political cleansing in the judiciary continues." 12 January 2000, 4.
27 *Voice of the People*. "Let us build an independent judiciary." 6 September 1997, 2.
28 *Voice of the People*. "The court mafia collapses." 25 September 1997a, 4.

attempts to connect DP's reforms to Albania's former communist regime. Such an approach is best encapsulated by an article which analyzed the development of the judiciary as follows: "the [Labour] Party politicised the judiciary and intervened directly in its affairs. Important trials were conducted under Hoxha's leadership, which is a clear indication of the absence of an independent judiciary." After identifying the first problem as coming from communism, the VP identified the second one: "[President] Berisha took control of the communist judicial machinery and simply repainted it blue [...] Berisha at the head of the DP state created an intellectual and professional desert in the judiciary in order to harass his political opponents for absurd alleged crimes."[29] It is clear that VP attempted to draw a straight line between the judicial reform during communism and DP's judicial reform during 1992–97. In drawing this straight line, it aimed to discredit DP's past reform, justify the need for SP's reform, and pre-emptively to de-legitimate any DP accusations.

With time, as the Socialist-led reform is implemented, the VP no longer mentions judicial politicisation. In fact, the VP decreases its coverage of judicial reform and in 2004, SP's last full year in power, it writes only twelve articles. As far as the VP was concerned, SP's judicial reform had been successful. Just as DR's coverage became politicised once the DP was out of power, VP's coverage became non-politicised once the SP gained power. However, although the newspapers change the direction of their coverage, the content remains almost intact. DR continues to accuse the SP of being the institutional heir of the Labour Party, while the VP continues to accuse the DP of being the ideational heir of the Labour Party. Both sides use the memory of communism and tie it to their opponent to de-legitimise their policies, belittle their objections, and justify their own reforms.

In 2005, the DP returned to power after eight years of opposition, and just as in 1992 and 1997 both newspapers change the direction but not the substance of their coverage. During 1992–97 Socialists were accused of being unreformed communists falsely attacking DP's judicial reform of politicisation. During 1997–2005 Socialists were accused of applying their communist heritage to politicise the judiciary and use it against the opposition, and after 2005 they were again accused by DR of pretending to defend the judiciary to maintain their political control over it.[30] There is remarkable continuity in DR's coverage of judicial reform as it continuously accused the SP of politicising the judiciary because

---

[29] *Voice of the People*. "The judiciary should not serve politics." 23 October 1999, 9.
[30] *Democratic Rebirth*. "The war against crime and corruption confuses the SP." 26 February 2006, 1; *Democratic Rebirth*, "Criminal bands in the SP leadership." 22 April 2007, 1.

of its communist heritage. The VP on the other hand, just as it did when it was first in opposition, after 2005 accused Berisha of being a communist-inspired politician who wanted to regain political control over the judiciary. Once the SP moved into opposition, VP's coverage of judicial reform was re-politicised and the newspaper accused the government of usurping the judiciary.[31] As importantly, VP relied on the same ideational mechanisms it used during SP's 1992–97 opposition, equating Berisha's reform with the communist practices of judicial politicisation.

Preliminary Conclusion

During this seventeen-year span it is clear that DR and VP covered judicial reform in a politicised way. Each time the DP and SP were in power, their newspapers portrayed the judiciary as undergoing positive reform. Inversely, each time the DP and SP were in opposition their newspapers accused the government of politicising the judiciary and using it against the opposition. Secondly, and as importantly, there is one element that both newspapers share and that connects their articles on an ideational level; the memory of communism. There was little analysis of what happened to the judiciary during communism, but both newspapers agreed that it was politicised to enable the regime to maintain power. Consequently, the memory of communism became a label for a politicised judiciary. This is why DR, in their first term continually accused the SP of being beset by the communist mentality of judicial politicisation while the ex-communist VP accused the DP of applying communist methods to implement its own politicisation. The accusations of communist tendencies or mentality were used to de-legitimise the other side's judicial reform or accusations of judicial politicisation.

These accusations of communist mentality/heritage precluded the 'other side' from being viewed as a legitimate partner in judicial reform. If the other side was communist, then it was by definition against an independent judiciary, and had an ingrained interest in fighting against judicial institutionalisation. Therefore, both DR and VP viewed judicial reform as the complete validation of one side and the political denunciation of the other undemocratic side. That is why the reform of one side was based on the rollback of the reforms applied by the other. As is clear through this analysis, from 1992 to 2009 this was the framework through which judicial reform was portrayed. This coverage made

---

[31] *Voice of the People.* "The majority does anything to invade the HCJ." 4 October 2006a, 4; *Voice of the People.* "The judiciary under the control of the DP." 24 October 2007, 1.

the achievement of a bipartisan agreement impossible because if the other side was made up of unreformed communists longing to turn back to the communist practices of a politicised judiciary, agreement was not possible. If the other side is presented, as both newspapers did, as antithetical to the democratic values of independent institutions and good governance, then it must be fought and not accommodated.

Coverage of Military Reform

After the Democratic Party (DP) came to power in 1992, Democratic Rebirth (DR) defended military reform and argued that the Socialist Party (SP) was against it because of its communist mentality and heritage. As a result, DR reminded readers of the communist practices of military politicisation as a way to de-legitimise Socialist criticism:

> The Labour Party of yesterday and the SP of today are responsible for the haemorrhaging in the military. The inhuman, anti-Albanian and anti-democratic actions – the politicisation of the military – started when the most vehement anti-Albanian and craziest adventurer Enver Hoxha usurped military leadership [...] It became even more evident after 1960 when, mercilessly, Hoxha eliminated military officials whom he deemed, through his demonic mind, part of enemy groups.[32]

From the beginning, military reform was covered in a highly politicised tone, even more so than with judicial reform, as DR did not just blame the communist regime for politicising the military, but also equated it with the SP in opposition. This approach set the stage for the politicisation of military reform, which continued with its harsh language as the SP was accused of being "a committed opponent of military reform [since] its military doctrine is identical to Enver Hoxha's people's military."[33] So, DR claimed that military reform was not just a repudiation of the communist politicisation of the military, but also a repudiation of the SP as an unreformed communist-inspired party. Just as it did with judicial reform, DR claimed that DP was undoing communist politicisation of the military and the SP stood in the way because of its communist heritage and ideology.

---

[32] *Democratic Rebirth.* "The SP is responsible for the haemorrhaging in the military." 6 October 1992b, 1, 3.
[33] *Democratic Rebirth.* "SP: A committed opponent of military reform." 7 August 1992c, 2.

So, for military reform also, the communist past was an important lens through which reform was evaluated. Although communism could be recalled in many ways, for DR such coverage had one main angle: communism as a state which used politically-inspired violence to maintain power. Time and again, when using communism as a justificatory mechanism in its articles on military reform, DR described the communist regime as criminal and murderous and stated that "the entire domestic and international activity of Hoxha's regime was criminal and anti-national." DR argued that after the communists came to power, "they began a campaign of persecutions, arrests, imprisonments, tortures, killings with no trial, violence against families, entire villages and intellectuals [...] aiming to eliminate that part of the population which would not accept the communist dictatorship."[34] Of the many elements that could have been chosen to describe the communist period, DR focused on the violent nature of Hoxha's regime. So when DR argued that the government was undoing communist military politicisation and that the SP was a communist-inspired party, it had a specific kind of communism in mind. DR claimed that DP's military reform would ensure that the violence inherent to the communist regime never returned, while the SP was longing to bring it back. This approach aimed to undercut SP accusations and de-legitimise it as a partner in military reform. DR's coverage maintains the same editorial line until the end of DP's governance by presenting military reform as a great achievement and accusing the SP of being a communist-inspired party aiming to politicise the military.

The VP on the other hand saw the government's military reform as fully politicised. From accusations of treason, fascism, and communism no punches were spared in the heated exchanges:

> Mussolini's fascists and Nazi Germans, those who are still alive at least, their supporters in Albania, the Greek monarchical-fascists, the Serbian chauvinists, and all the enemies of the Albanian people, finally can rejoice at the condition in which the Albanian military finds itself [...] The DP has purged 15,000 officers who left the country as refugees while hundreds of others are locked in prison cells because they have been stained with political accusations.[35]

While DR accused the SP of being unreformed communists, VP replied that DP's military reform was not only politicised, but was also harming the country's na-

---

34 *Democratic Rebirth.* "The SP responsible for the haemorrhaging in the military." 20 October 1992d, 1, 3.
35 *Voice of the People.* "Who is responsible for the haemorrhaging in the Albanian military?" 2 October 1992b, 1.

tional defence. VP criticised military reform as unpatriotic, overly politicised and consequently weakening the country:

> [T]housands of officers are witnesses of the fact that this reform is based upon political criteria. It is sad, but true, that military appointments are approved by DP's offices. It is unfortunate that the present military leadership is entirely politicised. This is not only illegal, but also very dangerous for the fate of the military and the nation's defence.[36]

According to the VP, DP's government was acting just like the communist regime did by politicising the military and using it for its own purposes. This is why in an article entitled "[t]he reform in the armed forces is not led by the law but by DP's politics" VP strongly criticised the reform for lacking vision, competence and for being politicised.[37] Evidently, the early exchanges on military reform were highly politicised and aimed to discredit DP's reform as unpatriotic, undemocratic, and a continuation of communist politicisation. Such coverage, first by DR and then by the VP, precluded the other side from being viewed as a partner in military reform.

Accusations of a politicised military reform continued in 1994 also. In early June VP accused the Ministry of Defence (MoD) of using soldiers as 'travelling voters' so that the DP would win a special election. The VP analyzed this issue and argued that DP's politicisation of military reform was endangering Albania's democratic future. The article further accused the leadership of the MoD of using the military for overtly political reasons as an "instrument of DP's interests."[38] This issue was again analyzed and the MoD was accused of "being committed to follow the road of the anti-law [and] use the Albanian military, similarly to third world countries, to keep power at any cost."[39] During SP's opposition, the VP maintained the same editorial line accusing the government of undertaking a politicised reform and using the military to achieve its political aims. It is clear that during DP's first term, coverage of military reform was remarkably similar to that of judicial reform. DR argued that Democrats were reforming the military and that the SP was a communist-inspired party against military institutionalisation. The VP, on the other hand, argued that DP's reforms simply replaced communist politicisation.

---

36 *Voice of the People*. "Military reform is defended through facts and laws, not demagoguery." 10 February 1993 f, 3.
37 *Voice of the People*. "Military reform is led by the DP not the rule of law." 20 August 1993 g, 4.
38 *Voice of the People*. "The military should serve the nation, not DP's political games." 11 June 1994a, 1.
39 *Voice of the People*. "You are committed to break the law." 24 June 1994b, 1, 2.

In 1997, after the collapse of the pyramid schemes, the declaration of the state of emergency, the attempted use of the military to subdue popular revolts and the latter's refusal to follow orders, the military disbanded, its depots were looted and public order collapsed. As a result, in June 1997 new elections were held and won by the SP. After the DP lost the elections, DR's coverage of military reform changed direction and became accusatory against the SP for undertaking a 'communist rebellion' to take power, undo reforms and re-politicise the military:

> [O]nly the leaders of the Labour Party and their heirs in the SP are the authors of this destruction [...] Communism, which destroyed every national value, destroyed the military also. When the military started breathing again, the same people who applied crime and destruction, through their communist elements, hit a new, killed again and re-destroyed the military.[40]

Although the direction of DR's coverage changed, its content remained intact as it continued to accuse the SP of being a communist-inspired party aiming to re-politicise the military. This approach became clearer when DR accused the government of preparing a deep political cleansing in the military and intending to replace existing officers with political appointees and bandits who overthrew the democratic government. DR stated that this was "the most severe hit against the military since 1967 [...] underneath the declarations of the Minister are the hideous intentions to bring back all the incriminated people who served the dictatorship."[41] Similarly, on 24 August DR wrote an article in which it stated that "the return of the old communist officers is equivalent to the politicisation of the armed forces."[42] Clearly, after the SP gained power DR's coverage of military reform changed direction by accusing the government of politicising the military along the lines of the previous communist regime and appointing party militants at the expense of professionals.

The articles of 1997, however, were not just a reflection of the immediate heat produced by the events of 1997. For example in 1999, an article written by two former military officers during the time Mr Berisha was President stated:

> [T]he left executed the 1997 armed rebellion to its bitter end, concluding with the barbaric destruction of the armed forces to gain power by force [...] After the SP came to power

---

40 *Democratic Rebirth.* "Who destroyed the military?" 1 November 1997c, 7.
41 *Democratic Rebirth.* "The defence minister: Prison for all Democrats." 5 August 1997d, 4.
42 *Democratic Rebirth.* "The recall of former officers re-politicises the military." 24 August 1997e, 4.

through violence, it has used Byzantine methods to damage the military as its 'mother party' had done for fifty years."[43]

This quote encapsulates DR's overall argument after 1997. It continued to rely on accusations of communism to de-legitimate the SP and used the 1997 crisis, which it labelled as a 'communist rebellion,' as an example of a communist-inspired armed revolt to take power by force and re-politicise the military. This approach continued as DR published in two full pages the official DP analysis of the national security strategy and reform of the armed forces. DR's article began by stating that "the 1997 armed revolt lead by the extreme left, which wanted power at any cost, besides spectacular economic damage [...] destroyed the military."[44] Even worse, according to DR, after the left came to power, it implemented a political reform similar to that of the communist regime in which young officials were replaced by the old communist nomenclature. So DR not only accused the SP of politicising the military, and not only continued to use communism as a de-legitimating tool, but it also presented an image of the 1997 crisis as a military failure, and depicted 1997 as the year in which the military was attacked by unreformed communists who wanted power at any cost and once in power re-politicised the military.

On the other hand, after the SP won the 1997 elections, the VP refrained from attacking the MoD except for those military officers who were connectable to the DP and President Berisha. VP's main focus was on the analysis of the 1997 crisis as a justificatory mechanism for the government's upcoming reform. The VP argued that after the 1997 crisis the approach to military reform must change and that it was worrying that "the DP wants to maintain the same structures in place and consequently to continue with the failed politicisation of the military."[45] So while it aimed to present a conciliatory tone, VP continued to accuse the DP of being against the de-politicisation of the military. Similarly, in another article the VP argued that in 1997 the military "was destroyed by Sali Berisha; it was destroyed by the high leadership of the Democratic Party."[46] The paper continued to present the argument that the politicisation of the military destroyed its foundations by arguing that "DP's criteria for military reform were a hidden facade to humiliate the military [...] DP militants were awarded with military ranks [...] military preparation was replaced by political party preparation [...] the objec-

---

43 *Democratic Rebirth*. "For a professional and disciplined military." 19 September 1999a, 12, 13.
44 *Democratic Rebirth*. "DP's national security strategy." 29 September 1999b, 12, 13.
45 *Voice of the People*. "Popular revolt and the dissolution of the military." 9 April 1997b, 4.
46 *Voice of the People*. "Who destroyed the Albanian military?" 23 April 1997c, 8.

tives of the military were replaced with the objectives of the DP."⁴⁷ To show the repercussions of the politicisation of the military and the effects of the 1997 crisis, VP presented an overview of the 1997 destruction: "1311 murders, 75 killed children, 1450 people injured, 52 police officers killed [...] 1200 out of 1500 military depots destroyed, 562,000 weapons looted, 1,56 billion bullets stolen, 3,5 million grenades, 24 million artillery bullets and explosives, 1 million mines, and 3600 tons of explosive devices unaccounted."⁴⁸

Interestingly, both DR and VP agreed that in 1997 the military was destroyed and portrayed the events of 1997 as a military/security failure. Although they blamed one another, they identified politicisation as the cause for the destruction of the military. Despite the agreement that the politicisation of the military was wrong and that such politicisation produced the 1997 crisis, they still did not seem able to find a way to break the vicious cycle of politicised coverage. It seemed that military reform had entered a stable binary mode of mutual accusations and de-legitimisation, similar to the situation regarding judicial reform, which could have become a self-reproducing vicious cycle.

In 2002 however, the politicised coverage of military reform was broken, as this was the first year in which DR had more non-politicised than politicised articles on military reform while in opposition. The reversal in 2002 was evident through two elements. First, the criticism of military reform became less military-centred, coverage of military reform became more NATO-integration oriented, and accusations of military politicisation decreased drastically.⁴⁹ Besides breaking the cycle of politicised coverage while in opposition, after the DP came to power in 2005, DR did not support policy reversal, did not point the finger at the previous government for everything wrong with the military, and presented DP's reforms as a continuation of Socialist reforms.⁵⁰ Importantly, after the SP moved into opposition in 2005, VP either paid little attention to military reform or when it covered the topic, was supportive and almost never accused the government of wanting to politicise it.⁵¹

---

47 *Voice of the People*. "Why was the military destroyed?" 9 May 1997d, 6.
48 *Voice of the People*. "The tragedy through numbers." 23 September 1997e, 4.
49 *Democratic Rebirth*. "Albanians support America and NATO." 11 September 2002, 5; *Democratic Rebirth*. "The military celebrates its 90ᵗʰ anniversary." 5 December 2002a, 2.
50 *Democratic Rebirth*. "The furthering of cooperation with NATO, USA and the EU." 11 September 2005, 11;
Democratic Rebirth. "For the transformation of Albanian defence." 11 September 2005a, 13.
51 *Voice of the People*. "Rumsfeld in Tirana: appreciation for our soldiers." 6 July 2006, 5; *Voice of the People*. "SP Resolution: Let us fulfil the obligations for NATO membership." 9 January 2008, 1, 3; *Voice of the People*. " Majko: The invitation to join NATO will be the final goodbye to the Albanian transition." 9 February 2008a, 13.

So how can one account for what seems an unexpected but stable change of military reform coverage by DR and VP? What changed between 2000 – when the VP was still comparing DP's reforms to communist politicisation while DR was accusing the government of bringing back communist officers – and 2002 which can account for the shift in newspaper coverage? Let me start with what stayed the same. The political climate was similarly polarised, the players were the same and distrust was still high. Albania's democratisation standards remained similarly low, as both the local elections of 2000 and general elections of 2001 were contested by the opposition as manipulated. The international situation also had not changed substantially as Albania's partners were not any closer to accepting it as a possible NATO member. For example, in 2002 Albania was refused to even be considered for potential NATO membership. While domestically and internationally Albania's conditions were stable and at first sight did not point to any factors that could break the vicious cycle of military politicisation, the 1999 Kosovo war changed the dynamics of military reform coverage dramatically, although not immediately. When NATO decided to bombard Yugoslavia because of its treatment of the Kosovo Albanians, NATO was seen as righting an historical injustice. Secondly, and importantly, the 1999 Kosovo war re-opened the debate on the 1997 destruction of the military under a new perspective, allowing the meaning of the 1997 crisis to be remoulded. I argue this is the slow developing mechanism which allowed the 'sudden' shift in 2002 and beyond. The following overview will demonstrate how this process progressed.

During the Kosovo war DR presented an image of NATO as the defender of freedom and the Albanian people. DR wrote that NATO "has firmly positioned itself as the protector of the peaceful people of Kosovo. NATO has shown that it is willing to shorten Balkan dictatorships to defend democratic values."[52] DR also reported that Mr Berisha called upon the Albanian people to unite around NATO to win the fight and praised NATO for being close to the Albanian people in such a difficult moment.[53] Similarly, DR published a declaration of Mr Berisha in which he stated that "the arrival of NATO troops in Albania is a historic development in our already positive relationship [...] we can say that Albania is a de facto NATO member and the Albanian people a faithful and dignified NATO ally."[54] Lastly, after the Kosovo war ended DR wrote, "NATO begins the liberation of Kosovo [...] Albanians welcome NATO with jubilation."[55] In these articles, and

---

52 *Democratic Rebirth*. "NATO takes over Albania's airports." 13 June 1998, 3.
53 *Democratic Rebirth*. "The Albanian nation a faithful NATO ally." 23 April 1999c, 3.
54 *Democratic Rebirth*. "Albanians, unite to deserve the victory." 23 April 1999d, 3.
55 *Democratic Rebirth*. "NATO begins the liberation of Kosovo." 13 June 1999e, 1.

others, NATO is presented as the liberator of Albanians, as the defender of democratic values, and as an effective organisation since it managed to do what Albanians had never been able to: drive the Serbs out of Kosovo.

Besides cementing NATO's positive reputation, the Kosovo war brought back to the surface the discussion of the destruction of the military in 1997. As the Yugoslav army was shelling border regions, the Albanian military was incapable of reacting. In 1999 DR covered extensively the shelling of border villages and towns by the Yugoslav artillery as a proxy to illustrate the ineffectiveness of the Albanian military. For example, DR wrote "the Serbian army burns Albanian villages while our armed forces 'kept their cool' and did not respond to the provocation"[56] because they could not. A few days later DR again wrote that the northern border was at the mercy of local farmers since the military could defend it.[57] These kinds of articles showed the incapacity of the Albanian military, after 1997, to defend the border. To establish the connection between the military's incapacity to defend the border and its 1997 destruction, DR commented that "the destruction of the military during the 1997 communist rebellion has significantly lowered its capacity to defend the nation."[58]

As the heat of the Kosovo war was dissipating, DR continued the analysis of the military's ineffectiveness and published an article by two former officers stating that "after the Kosovo war NATO members are analysing their militaries' performance in the conflict. We should also do the same – but with one difference – our analysis should begin from the destruction of the military in 1997."[59] Lastly, at the end of 1999, DR wrote a long analytical article and argued that the destruction of the military in 1997 produced its inability to defend the country. According to DR this failure:

> [b]ecame clear to the public, especially to those living in the north-eastern areas, because the military was not able to defend the country against Serbian attacks. The state was not capable to defend the sovereignty and integrity of the nation; it was not able to defend the life of its citizens.[60]

---

56 *Democratic Rebirth.* "The Serbian military burns Albanian villages." 14 April 1999f, 1.
57 *Democratic Rebirth.* "Serbs invade the villages of Tropoja." 20 April 1999 g, 4.
58 *Democratic Rebirth.* "Reith: The Albanian military is far from NATO's standards." 28 August 1999p, 2.
59 *Democratic Rebirth.* "For a professional and disciplined military." 19 September 1999a, 12, 13.
60 *Democratic Rebirth.* "DP's national security strategy." 29 September 1999b, 12, 13.

The argument is clear; when the military was needed to defend the country's territorial integrity, it was incapable of doing so because it had been destroyed in 1997. The contrast between the Albanian military and NATO armies could not be starker. NATO defended Albanians while their own military could not because they had been destroyed it in 1997.

The VP covered the Kosovo war extensively as an existential threat to and military aggression against Albania. In early 1999 the VP reported on the PM's visit to the border region with Yugoslavia, where he was quoted as saying, "we have to be ready to defend what we hold dearest: our sovereignty."[61] One month later the VP wrote that "in the northern region tanks and cannons are ready for any eventuality."[62] While at the end of March the VP stated "the entire military has been installed in the north."[63] As the border scuffles intensified, the VP wrote "our tanks fire back against 120 Serbs."[64] Lastly, in an article titled "Serbs want war with Albania"[65] the paper reported that military incidents had increased exponentially and that the military was doing its best to defend the country. Clearly, VP presented the Kosovo crisis as a serious military threat in which the armed forces were called upon to perform their duties and did so in an admirable way. Nevertheless, the VP, on numerous occasions argued that in cases where the Albanian military would not suffice, then NATO would be called upon.[66]

The reassurance that in cases where the Albanian military were not able to defend the country NATO would step in is an indication that the VP was aware of the military's limitations. Nevertheless, any admission of the military's incapacity to perform its role was blamed on the 1997 events. For example, the VP quoted the Minister of Defence as saying that "the military is encountering difficulties in fulfilling its mission because of a lack of resources and the effects of the 1997 destruction."[67] In a sense the VP was saying that the government was bequeathed a very poor situation by the predecessors and was trying its best in a difficult environment. Similarly, in 1999 the VP quoted the MoD as saying that "the armed forces are ready to defend the country ... after its almost total destruction in

---

61 *Voice of the People*. "Albanians are ready to defend their sovereignty." 30 January 1999a, 3.
62 *Voice of the People*. "Në veri topa e tanke janë gati." 27 February 1999b, 1.
63 *Voice of the People*. "The entire military is in the north." 24 March 1999c, 3.
64 *Voice of the People*. "Tanks fire back against 120 Serbs." 12 May 1999d, 1.
65 *Voice of the People*. "Serbs want war with Albania." 8 June 1999e, 2.
66 *Voice of the People*. "The USA will defend us." 4 February 1999f, 1; *Voice of the People*. "NATO: Bombardments until the Serbs pull back." 12 May 1999 g, 1; *Voice of the People*. "Cohen: Albania an important NATO ally." 13 July 1999p, 3.
67 *Voice of the People*. "The Albanian military ready to defend the nation." 9 June 1998, 2.

19997, amid countless difficulties, the military has been rebuilt."⁶⁸ Again, the message was the same: the military was destroyed and it has been rebuilt, but still it faced difficulties. So, while the VP presented the situation at the northern border as a military aggression against Albania for which the military was needed, it also argued that the destruction of the military in 1997 inhibited it from fulfilling its mission.

This kind of coverage – the connection of the 1997 crisis to the military's inability to defend the border in 1999 – affected DR's approach, making it more supportive of military reform under the NATO-integration perspective. For example DR wrote that "government and opposition consider NATO's presence in the region as a factor in favour of peace and stability, which should be finalised with Albania's NATO integration."⁶⁹ While in 2004 DR wrote, "after the horrible events of 1997 and the 1999 Kosovo war in which the military had to fight a 'real' war, Albania began its most difficult battle, the battle to join NATO."⁷⁰ After the Kosovo war DR's coverage became non-politicised, as it relied on the re-framed memory of the 1997 crisis to support military reform to join NATO, which had helped Albania during its hour of need and provided a template of an effective and apolitical military organisation. The NATO-integration perspective based on the lessons of the crisis during the transition became dominant in VP's coverage also as in 2004, while the SP was in government, it wrote:

> Ten years ago [DP's first term] we were a source of weapons for dictatorships around the world, seven years ago [1997 crisis] the military disintegrated, for three years after that we consumed the security of our neighbours and were not able to defend ourselves [Kosovo war]. Now our military ensures there is peace around the world [Albanian peace-keepers in NATO missions in Iraq and Afghanistan].⁷¹

Even after the SP went into opposition the VP maintained the same NATO-integration perspective as it wrote that the SP "encourages all military personnel to engage without reservation in fulfilling all obligations for NATO accession."⁷² Clearly, after the Kosovo war both sides looked at military reform from the NATO-integration-perspective, which enabled them to depoliticise its coverage

---

68 *Voice of the People*. "The military is ready to defend the nation." 16 January 1999q, 4.
69 *Democratic Rebirth*. "Government and opposition with a common position on NATO integration." 5 July 2002b, 4.
70 *Democratic Rebirth*. "NATO General speak about Albania." 10 August 2004, 15.
71 *Voice of the People*. "29 November, everything has been rebuilt, even the military." 30 November 2004, 4.
72 *Voice of the People*. "The DP applies political pressure on the organs of the judiciary." 7 December 2008, 3.

and find bipartisan agreement to join the organisation which saved Albanians in their hour of need and provided them a template to emulate.

Preliminary Conclusion

Newspaper coverage of military reform in the 1990s was strikingly similar to judicial reform coverage. Both DR and VP accused the SP and DP respectively of politicising military reform and of continuing the communist practices of politicisation. Based on the military reform coverage of the 1990s, its similarity to the judicial reform coverage, and to the coverage of the 1997 crisis which was viewed by both sides as vindication of their worst fears about the other side, there was no reason to expect the change identified in the 2002.

The coverage of the Kosovo war enabled the re-framing of the 1997 military destruction. After 1997 both SP and DP agreed that politicisation destroyed the military, but they were too distrustful of each other to undertake a bipartisan military reform; they blamed each other for what happened and saw one another as antithetical to democracy. The agreement that the military was not capable of defending the country in 1999 because it had been destroyed in 1997 – an event for which they continued to accuse each other – enabled them to get over the deep mutual distrust. The 1997 crisis seen through the prism of the Kosovo war showed that military politicisation did not have just domestic adverse effects, but also harmed national interests which transcended political divisions. The connection of the 1997 crisis with the 1999 Kosovo war, and the conclusion that the 1997 crisis had led to the inability to defend the country in 1999 produced the shift identified in 2002. The delay from the end of the Kosovo war in 1999 to DR's shift to a non-politicised coverage in 2002 is attributed to two factors. First, elites require time to analyze events, reach conclusions and then make them public. Second, and as important, political elites need to find the right timing to come out in favour of such major policy change. The years 2000 and 2001 were hotly contested electoral years and thereby not appropriate for DR to publically change its views on military reform.

Conclusion

Based on the above analysis, I conclude that the Kosovo war coverage enabled the change identified in the second decade of transition, but only regarding military reform. The way the 1999 Kosovo war was covered by both newspapers has some striking similarities. First, NATO is presented as an institution on the side of Albanians and an efficient defender of the values of Western democracy. Second, the military's incapacity to defend the border during the Kosovo war enabled a re-framing of the 1997 crisis. The Kosovo war demonstrated that the politicisation and then destruction of the military had major negative repercussions for Albania and Albanians in the Balkans. The one time both sides agreed that the military was needed to defend the country, they could not use it because they had destroyed it. The combination of these two elements – NATO as the defender of Albanians and the Albanian military's incapacity to defend its own people after the 1997 destruction – enabled the two sides to see the 1997 crisis through a new prism. The Kosovo war showed that the way the Albanian military had been politicised affected not just domestic politics, but also the country's ability to defend itself and the Albanian populations outside the official borders.

In addition to the re-framing of the 1997 crisis, NATO's intervention in Kosovo provided Albanian elites with a model they could strive towards and which enjoyed an overwhelming backing by Albanians, who viewed it as their defender. The Kosovo war coverage created a permission structure which allowed both sides to depoliticise the debate on military reform. They could still blame each other for the 1997 crisis, as they still do, but they could not deny the reality that when the military was needed most they could not use it because it had been destroyed. That realisation, and NATO's popularity, created the opening to slowly change the coverage and from 2002 on to view military reform from the 'NATO integration' perspective as an objective uniting Socialists and Democrats.

From this analysis it is clear that the main reason for the temporal shift between the first and second decades of transition in the coverage of military reform has to do with the development of the collective memory of the events of 1997 and its re-framing after the 1999 Kosovo war. This conjunction is the most likely explanatory mechanism which enabled elites to see the 'apocalypse of 1997' and their defencelessness during the Kosovo war as the result of military politicisation begun in 1944. The fear of another 1997, when the military was disbanded, combined with the fear of another 1999, where the military could not defend the country because it had been destroyed two years earlier, enabled the shift in military reform coverage in the early 2000s. The fear of another 1997 and another 1999 created the condition for a broad agreement to institutionalise the armed forces to reach NATO standards and membership since NATO showed how a professional military could serve Albania well.

Acknowledgement

This publication was supported by a Swedish Institute Research Grant.

References

Berger, Peter and Tomas Luckmann. The Social Construction of Reality: A Treatise in the Sociology of Knowledge. New York: Random House, 1967.

Cairns, Ed and Michéal D. Roe. Eds. The Role of Memory in Ethnic Conflict. Basinstoke: Palgrave Macmillan, 2003.

Mithander, Conny, Maria Holmgren Troy and John Sundholm. Eds. Collective Traumas: Memory of War and Conflict in 20th Century Europe. Brussels: Peter Lang, 2007.

Hall, Katharina and Kathryn Jones. Eds. Constructions of Conflict. Oxford: Peter Lang, 2011.

Jedlowski, Paolo. "Memory and Sociology. Themes and Issues." Time and Society 10.1 (2001): 29–44.

Larkin, Craig. Memory Conflict in Lebanon: Remembering and Forgetting the Past. London: Routledge, 2012.

Litvak, Meir Ed. Palestinian Collective Memory and National Identity. New York: Palgrave Macmillan, 2004.

Roudometof, Victor. Collective Memory, National Identity and Ethnic Conflict. Westport: Preager Publishers, 2002.

Olsen, Johan. "Change and Continuity: An Institutional Approach to Institutions of Democratic Government." *European Political Science Review* 1.1 (2009): 3–32.

Rilindja Demokratike. "Afron koha për gjyqin a bllokmenëve" (Democratic Rebirth, "Nears the time for the trial of the communist cast"), 11 July 1992: 1.

Rilindja Demokratike. "Aspak hakmarrje, vetem drejtesi" (No revenge just justice). 20 October 1992a: 3.

Rilindja Demokratike. "PP(S) – shkaktare dhe pergjegjese per hemoragjine ne ushtri" (The SP is responsible for the haemorrhaging in the military). 6 October 1992b: 1 and 3.

Rilindja Demokratike. "PS: Kundërshtare e vendosur e reformës në drejtësi" (SP: A committed opponent of military reform). 7 August 1992c: 2.

Rilindja Demokratike. "PP(S) shkaktare dhe përgjegjëse për hemoragjinë në ushtri" (The SP responsible for the haemorrhaging in the military). 20 October 1992d: 1 and 3.

Rilindja Demokratike. "Tani e kanë rradhën organet e drejtësisë të kryejnë detyrën" (Now it is the judiciary's time to fulfil its duty"). 8 May 1993: 2.

Rilindja Demokratike. "Drejtësia nuk duhet të ketë mëshirë për uzurpatorë të korruptuar dhe hajdutë ordinerë si Fatos Nano" (The Judiciary must have no mercy on ordinary thieves like Fatos Nano). 15 May 1993a: 1.

Rilindja Demokratike. "Reformën e drejtësisë nuk mund ta pengojnë ulërimat komuniste të ZPsë" (Military reform will not be stopped by the communist screams of the VP). 19 November 1993b: 4.

Rilindja Demokratike. "Vetëm një bandë hajdutësh mund të dale në mbrojtje të hajdutit" (Only a band of thieves can come to the defence of a thief). 18 February 1994: 3.

Rilindja Demokratike. "Ligjit dhe Drejtësisë do t'i nënshtrohet dhe Fatos Nano" (Democratic Rebirth, "Even Fatos Nano will submit to the law and the judiciary"). 14 February 1994a: 1.

Rilindja Demokratike. "Kriminele si Fatos Nano i pret gjykimi edhe per genocid" (Criminals like [SP Chairman] Fatos Nano should be tried for genocide also). 1 June 1995: 1.

Rilindja Demokratike. "Sistemi Shqiptar i drejtesise synon te arrije standartet bashkekohore" (The Albanian judiciary aims to reach contemporary standards). 15 February 1996: 4.

Rilindja Demokratike. "Presidenti dorëzon Mejdanin" (The President is stripped of all power). 29 July 1997: 1.

Rilindja Demokratike. "Drejtësia në gijotinë", (The judiciary under the guillotine). 31 July 1997a: 1.

Rilindja Demokratike. "Drejtësia vihet nën sundimin e krimit" (The judiciary under the leadership of crime). 28 August 1997b: 2.

Rilindja Demokratike. "Kush e shkaterroi ushtrine?" (Who destroyed the military?). 1 November 1997c: 7.

Rilindja Demokratike. "Brokaj: burg për gjithë demokratët" (The Defence Minister: Prison for all Democrats). 5 August 1997d: 4.

Rilindja Demokratike. "Rithirrja e ish-oficerëve politizim i ushtrisë" (The recall of former officers re-politicises the military). 24 August 1997e: 4.

Rilindja Demokratike. "NATO merr aeroportet e Shqipërisë" (NATO takes over Albania's airports). 13 June 1998: 3.

Rilindja Demokratike. "Antiligji dhe vjedhjet jane ne lulezim" (The anti-law and thefts are blooming). 9 January 1999: 7.

Rilindja Demokratike. "Për një ushtri profesioniste dhe të disiplinuar" (For a professional and disciplined military). 19 September 1999a: 12 and 13.

Rilindja Demokratike. "PD për mbrojtjen dhe sigurinë e vendit" (DP's national security strategy). 29 September 1999b: 12 and 13.

Rilindja Demokratike. "Kombi Shqiptar, aleat besnik i NATO" (The Albanian nation a faithful NATO ally). 23 April 1999c: 3.

Rilindja Demokratike. "Shqiptarë, të bashkojemi për të merituar fitoren" (Albanians, unite to deserve the victory). 23 April 1999d: 3.

Rilindja Demokratike. "NATO fillon clirimin e Kosovës" (NATO begins the liberation of Kosovo). 13 June 1999e: 1.

Rilindja Demokratike. "Ushtria Serbe djeg fshatrat e Tropojës" (The Serbian military burns Albanian villages). 14 April 1999f: 1.

Rilindja Demokratike. "Serbët pushtojnë fshatrat ne Tropojë" (Serbs invade the villages of Tropoja). 20 April 1999 g: 4.

Rilindja Demokratike. "Reith: Ushtria Shqiptare larg standardeve të NATOs" (Reith: The Albanian military is far from NATO's standards). 28 August 1999p: 2.

Rilindja Demokratike. "Spastrimet politike ne gjyqësor vazhdojnë" (Political cleansing in the judiciary continues). 12 January 2000: 4.

Rilindja Demokratike. "Shqiptarët me Amerikën dhe NATOn" (Democratic Rebirth, "Albanians support America and NATO"), 11 September 2002: 5.

Rilindja Demokratike. "Ushtria feston 90-vjetorin" (The military celebrates its 90th anniversary). 5 December 2002a: 2.

Rilindja Demokratike. "Pozitë-opozitë, qëndrim unik për NATO-n" (Government and opposition with a common position on NATO integration). 5 July 2002b: 4.

Rilindja Demokratike. "Gjeneralë të NATOs flasin për Shqipërinë" (NATO General speak about Albania). 10 August 2004: 15.

Rilindja Demokratike. "Zgjerimi i bashkepunimit me NATO-n, SHBA-te dhe BE-ne" (The furthering of cooperation with NATO, USA and the EU). 11 September 2005: 11.

Rilindja Demokratike. "Per transformimin e mbrojtjes Shqiptare" (For the transformation of Albanian defence). 11 September 2005a: 13.

Rilindja Demokratike. "Goditja e krimit dhe korruptionit dalldis PSnë" (The war against crime and corruption confuses the SP). 26 February 2006: 1.

Rilindja Demokratike. "Bandat e Krimit ne kupolën e PS" (Criminal bands in the SP leadership). 22 April 2007: 1.

Zëri i Popullit. "PD presion politik ndaj organeve të drejtësisë" (Voice of the People, "The DP applies political pressure on the organs of the judiciary"). 7 December 2008: 3.

Zëri i Popullit. "Atë punë e di partia." (Party knows best). 2 December 1992: 3.

Zëri i Popullit. "Cfarë shteti po ndërtohet në Shqipëri; shtet juridik apo shtet politik?" (What kind of state are we building in Albania: a political or a legal state?). 17 December 1992a: 1 and 2.

Zëri i Popullit. "Kush pergjigjet per hemoragjine ne ushtrine Shqiptare?" (Who is responsible for the haemorrhaging in the Albanian military?). 2 October 1992b: 1 and 3.

Zëri i Popullit. "Intelektualët e drejtësisë nën shenjestrën e PD" (The judiciary under the DP's attack). 6 January 1993: 1 and 3.

Zëri i Popullit. "Pushteti gjyqësor në bankën e të akuzuarve" (The judiciary under accusation). 10 January 1993a: 5.

Zëri i Popullit. "Përgatitja e 'Benikëve të Partisë' në kurse 3-mujore tregon se sa në rrezik janë të drejtat e njeriut në Shqipëri" (The preparation of the Party's faithful in 3-month courses shows the danger to human rights in Albania). 10 April 1993b: 1.

Zëri i Popullit. "Drejtësia nën këmbët e shtetit Ballisto-Fashist" (The judiciary under the feet of the rightist fascist state). 27 July 1993c: 1.

Zëri i Popullit. "Drejtësia a trembur" (A scared judiciary). 11 August 1993d: 1.

Zëri i Popullit. "Pvarësia e pushtetit gjyqësor në Shqipëri një fakt apo një nen në letër?" (The independence of the judiciary in Albania: a reality or just a piece of paper?). 13 October 1993e: 2.

Zëri i Popullit. "Reforma në ushtri mbrohen me fakte dhe ligje, jo me servilizëm dhe demagogji" ("Military reform is defended through facts and laws, not demagoguery"). 10 February 1993f: 3.

Zëri i Popullit. "Reforma në ushtri udhëhiqet nga PD dhe jo nga ligjet" (Military reform is led by the DP not the rule of law). 20 August 1993 g: 4.

Zëri i Popullit. "Drejtësia nën kthetrat a shtetit politik" (The judiciary under the claws of the political state). 8 April 1994: 1.

Zëri i Popullit. "Ushtria i shërben kombit, jo lojrave politike të PD" (The military should serve the nation, not DP's political games). 11 June 1994a: 1.

Zëri i Popullit. "Ju jeni i vendosur të enci në rrugën e anti-ligjit" (You are committed to break the law). 24 June 1994b: 1 and 2.

Zëri i Popullit. "Të bëjmë një drejtësi të pavarur" (Let us build an independent judiciary). 6 September 1997: 2.

Zëri i Popullit. "Bie mafia e gjykatave" (The court mafia collapses). 25 September 1997a: 4.
Zëri i Popullit. "Revolta popullore dhe shpërbërja e ushtrisë" (Popular revolt and the dissolution of the military). 9 April 1997b: 4.
Zëri i Popullit. "Kush e shkatërroi ushtrinë Shqiptare?" (Who destroyed the Albanian military?). 23 April 1997c: 8.
Zëri i Popullit. "Pse u shkatërrua ushtria?" (Why was the military destroyed?). 9 May 1997d: 6.
Zëri i Popullit. "Tragjedia përmes numrave" (The tragedy through numbers). 23 September 1997e: 4.
Zëri i Popullit. "Ushtria Shqiptare e gatshme të mbrojë vendin" (The Albanian military ready to defend the nation). 9 June 1998: 2.
Zëri i Popullit. "Drejtësi jo për t'i shërbyer politikës" (The judiciary should not serve politics). 23 October 1999: 9.
Zëri i Popullit. "Shqiptarët të gatshëm të ruajnë sovranitetin" (Albanians are ready to defend their sovereignty). 30 January 1999a: 3.
Zëri i Popullit. "Në veri topa e tanke janë gati" (In the north tanks and cannons are ready). 27 February 1999b: 1.
Zëri i Popullit. "Në veri është gjithë ushtria" (The entire military is in the north). 24 March 1999c: 3.
Zëri i Popullit. "Tanket qëllojnë mbi 120 Serbë" (Tanks fire back against 120 Serbs),12 May 1999d: 1.
Zëri i Popullit. "Serbët duan luftë me Shqipërinë" (Serbs want war with Albania). 8 June 1999e: 2.
Zëri i Popullit. "SHBA do të na mbrojnë" (The USA will defend us). 4 February 1999f: 1.
Zëri i Popullit. "NATO: Bombardime derisa Serbët të tërhiqen" (NATO: Bombardments until the Serbs pull back). 12 May 1999 g: 1.
Zëri i Popullit. "Cohen: Shqipëria aleati ynë i rëndësishëm" (Cohen: Albania an important NATO ally), 13 July 1999p: 3.
Zëri i Popullit. "Ushtria është e gatshme për të mbrojtur vendin" (The military is ready to defend the nation). 16 January 1999q: 4.
Zëri i Popullit. "Dokumenti i sigurimit kombëtar – shprehje e përgjegjësisë politike e kombëtare" (The document of national security strategy – an expression of political and national responsibility). 15 February 2000: 5.
Zëri i Popullit. "29 Nëntor, rimëkëmbet gjithcka, edhe ushtria" (29 November, everything has been rebuilt, even the military). 30 November 2004: 4.
Zëri i Popullit. "Rumsfeld ne Tiranë: vlerësim për ushtarët" (Rumsfeld in Tirana: appreciation for our soldiers). 6 July 2006: 5.
Zëri i Popullit. "Mazhoranca bën gjithcka për pushtimin e KLDsë" (The majority does anything to invade the HCJ). 4 October 2006a: 4.
Zëri i Popullit. "Sistemi i Drejtësisë në duart e PD" (The judiciary under the control of the DP). 24 October 2007: 1.
Zëri i Popullit. "PSSH Rezolutë: Të përmbushim detyrimet për anëtarësimin në NATO" (SP Resolution: Let us fulfil the obligations for NATO membership). 9 January 2008: 1 and 3.
Zëri i Popullit. "Majko: Ftesa për në NATO do të jetë një lamtumirë për tranzicionin Shqiptar" (Majko: The invitation to join NATO will be the final goodbye to the Albanian transition). 9 February 2008a: 13.

Igor Pietraszewski and Barbara Törnquist-Plewa
Clashes between National and Post-national European Views on Commemorating the Past: The Case of the Centennial Hall in Wrocław

In June 2007, the mayor of the city of Wrocław received a certificate from the UNESCO director-general. This document confirmed that the *Jahrhunderthalle*, designed by Max Berg and built in 1911–1913, had been added to the World Heritage List. The building, for 62 years (specifically since 1945) known to generations of Poles as *Hala Ludowa* ("People's Hall") was registered at the UNESCO office in Paris under its original historical Prussian name from 1913, which translates as "Centennial Hall". This was just one of many events and commemorations that have taken place in Wrocław in recent years. The name change is an important symbolic act symptomatic of the process of change in the city's historical memory narrative, and more broadly of the political and cultural transformations taking place in Poland. The processes that led to the new name can be traced to the changes in the politics of memory[1] at the macro (EU politics of memory), meso (politics of history of Poland and Germany) and micro (local politics of history) levels. In this article we concentrate in particular on the process on the micro scale, by analyzing the actions of mnemonic actors participating in the construction of the space of local historical memory in Wrocław. We aim to examine the local debate sparked by the name change. We consider this debate significant since in our view it represents a good example of the squabbles and conflicts witnessed in today's Europe between the proponents of a traditional, national approach to history and the advocates of a common European one (and the one supported by the EU and Council of Europe). This post-national idea of the past emphasizes the artifice of ideologically constructed national divides in the entangled national histories of Europe, encouraging instead the removal of the stereotypical and often ahistorical categorizations into "ours" and "yours" or friends and enemies. This vision of a European past strives to lib-

---

[1] We understand "politics of memory" as the top-down implementation by elites of ways for society to see the past, mostly for political-ideological objectives. For an insightful discussion on the definition of the politics of memory see Lech M Nijakowski. *Polska polityka pamięci*. Warszawa: Wyd. Profesjonalne i akademickie, 2008, 41–47.

erate the European memory narratives from any excessively emotional, national particularisms.²

Fig. 1: The Centennial Hall in Wrocław

Wrocław's history makes it a particularly good place to observe the disputes between these two ideologically deep-rooted ways of viewing the past affecting the way in which the formation of Europe's future is seen. It is a borderland city that during its long history has belonged to several countries: the Polish Crown, the Czech Crown, the Habsburg Empire, Prussia, Germany, and since 1945 to Poland. Moreover, after the Second World War the city experienced a complete exchange of population that was unprecedented in such a large settlement. Due to the changed borders and a decision by the Allies, the German population³ was

---

2 This project of a post-national, European community is articulated both at an intellectual level (see for example writings by Jürgen Habermas or Gerard Delanty,) and in political declarations of European institutions (e.g. the Lisbon Treaty) as well as expressed in practice (e.g. the European Culture Capital initiative, European Heritage Label, European Heritage Trails).
3 Officially and according to the orders of the authorities, no single German was to remain. In practice, though, a small group of Germans did stay, slowly diminishing as a result of Polonization or emigration to Germany. Since this was a long-lasting process, specific numbers are hard

forced to leave and was replaced by Poles. This complex history constitutes a challenge for the city's inhabitants. While making decisions about its development, they also have to take positions and express their attitude to the German past of the city in particular and their approach (national or post-national) to the past in general.

The analysis of the debate which follows is based mainly on media sources such as the press and comments on Internet forums. The latter communication channel would appear to be one of few widely available methods for people to articulate their views in the public space since it airs the views of people outside of the select group of the opinion-forming elites. When analyzing the situation regarding the change to the hall's name, we concentrate on the relationship between the "official memory"[4] and the reactions it triggers that are visible in Internet forums. We supplemented the Internet sources by holding several interviews with representatives of Wrocław's local authorities.[5]

In the analysis that follows, we treat the participants of the debate on the Centennial Hall as mnemonic actors participating in the construction of the space of local historical memory in Wrocław. We want to show the course of this process, as well as attempt to give a typology of the positions of the actors participating in it. To do this, we make use of theoretical concepts formulated by Michael Bernhard and Jan Kubik,[6] who stress that, through their actions in the cultural memory field,[7] mnemonic actors construct "memory regimes" – understood as organized ways of remembering a specific issue at a given moment.[8] Bernhard and Kubik offer a typology of memory regimes (fractured, pillarized, unified) based on the combination of different types of actors (whom they cate-

---

to come by – see Grzegorz Strauchold's article "Polityka narodowościowa na Ziemiach Zachodnich i Północnych w pierwszych latach po II wojnie światowej." *Pamięć i Przyszłość* 3.9 (2010).
4 We define "official memory" as the ways of remembering the past propagated by actors (political and other) in the public space. Cf. Michael Bernhard and Jan Kubik. Eds. *Twenty Years after Communism: The Politics of Memory and Commemoration*, New York: Oxford University Press, 2014, 2.
5 The interviews were held in 2013. When quoting them we retain the respondents' anonymity.
6 Bernhard and Kubik. *Twenty Years after Communism: The Politics of Memory and Commemoration*.
7 Cultural memory can be defined as representations of the past encapsulated in material objects (including written words). Cultural memory is a kind of institution. "It is exteriorized, objectified and stored away in symbolic forms that, unlike the sound of words or the sight of gestures, are stable and situation-transcendent"; see Jan Assmann. "Communicative and Cultural Memory." *Cultural Memory Studies: An International and Interdisciplinary Handbook*. Eds. Astrid Erll and Ansgar Nünning. Berlin/New York: De Gruyter 2008, 110.
8 Bernhard and Kubik. *Twenty Years after Communism: The Politics of Memory and Commemoration*, 15.

gorize as warriors, pluralists, abnegators) involved in the construction of these regimes. The whole set of memory regimes in a given society in a given period can be called "the field of memory" or "mnemonic field." In our analysis we see the change of the name of the famous building in 2007 in Wrocław as a construction of a memory regime aiming to contribute to the changes of the memory field in Poland in general and in Wrocław in particular. We try to identify the types of mnemonic actors involved in this process and the type of memory regime, and to describe the changes to the memory field.

The origins of the debate

During the communist era in Poland Wrocław was cast as an original Polish, Piast city which, although seized as a result of an unfortunate twist of fate for a long time by the Germans, Poland's eternal enemies, had been returned to the "mother ship" in 1945. This narrative lacked any positive evaluation of the German past input in Wrocław's development. The material traces of the German culture were neglected and sometimes simply destroyed. However, since the fall of communism in 1989 there has been a radical change in the local memory field.[9] In 1989, with the change to the political system and implementation of democracy, the generation that had created and struggled in the anti-communist opposition movement known as Solidarity came to power in Wrocław. This was manifested in the approach to history and the new memory narrative concerning the history of the city. As Bernhard and Kubik point out:

> A radical regime change, such as that experienced in Eastern Europe in 1989, is not only about the reconfiguration of economic interests, redistribution of political power, and reordering of social relations. It is also about the *reformulation of collective identities* and the *introduction or reinvigoration of the principles of legitimizing power* [emphasis ours]. These two tasks cannot be realized without a reexamination of the group's past, their historical memory.[10]

The elites ruling Wrocław from 1989, who came from liberal circles, officially adopted and approved the new vision of Wrocław's past, thus rejecting the narrative dominant in the communist era. The new narrative of the past is in tune with European models of narrating the past with focus on cultural encounters,

---

9 See Gregor Thum. *Uprooted: How Breslau became Wroclaw.* Princeton: Princeton University Press, 2011.
10 Bernhard and Kubik. *Twenty Years after Communism: The Politics of Memory and Commemoration*, 10–11.

mutual recognition and discourses of multiculturalism.[11] Thus the creators and proponents of the new narrative pay attention to the German cultural traces in Wrocław. At the same time they attempt to balance the sometimes bothersome weight of the German heritage in Wrocław by stressing the city's "multicultural" past, understood as memory of the fact that Wrocław's development was determined by many cultures. Wrocław's multiculturalism seems debatable, however, since although the city was for a long time dominated by German culture, today it is almost totally ethnically Polish. However, the creation of historical memory is rarely a simple attempt to formulate a "truthful" reconstruction of the past; it is usually about selective remembering and forgetting in order to create a specific vision of it for a number of reasons: political, ideological, existential and commercial.

The constructed myth of "multicultural" Wrocław is a conscious action of the authorities.[12] It has become part of the city's strategy,[13] and was used in its successful candidature for the title of European City of Culture 2016. According to the idea of a multicultural past, Wrocław should draw from its history to become an important European center, a modern "meeting place" in which both present and past inhabitants as well as people of various cultures and nations feel equally at home. At the same time, this means recognition of the co-existence of various memories in Wrocław, in particular the German and the Polish memory and their burden of conflicts. In the light of this idea, the authorities' decision to revert to the old German name of the hall designed by Max Berg seems reasonable.

The idea of registering the People's Hall on the UNESCO list was explained by a leading Lower Silesia official:

> Where did the Centennial Hall idea come from? Wrocław really wanted to have something put on the UNESCO list. The UNESCO list is already full of all kinds of things, and it's hard to find a reason to nominate something. Most of Wrocław's beautiful old buildings are reconstructions because they were rebuilt [...]. Added to which, the UNESCO list already has so many buildings like that that no more will get into that category. As it turned out, there was a gap for the early 20th century, the architecture from that time, something like that.

---

[11] For analysis of this discourse see for example Thomas Risse. *A Community of Europeans? Transnational Identities and Public Spheres*. Ithaca. NY: Cornell University Press, 2010; or Cris Shore."Inventing Homo Europaeus. The Cultural Politics of European Integration." *Ethnologia Europaea. Journal of European Ethnology* 29.2 (1999): 53–66.

[12] Stanisław Kłopot "Kreowanie mitu wielokulturowego Wrocławia." *Pamięć jako kategoria rzeczywistości społecznej*. Eds. J. Styka and M. Dziekanowska. Lublin: Wyd UMCS, 2012.

[13] "Strategy Wrocław 2000 Plus" from 1998, "Wrocław 2000 Plus. Studies on the city strategy", *Biuro Rozwoju Wrocławia* Bulletin 6.24 (1998): 48–52.

> Generally UNESCO had inscribed older ones. Perhaps someone noticed it might work. [...] So what could be nominated from Wrocław? [...] Oh, the People's Hall! But the People's Hall was built as the Centennial Hall. So if you lodged an application with a historical outline, then you'd probably have to refer to the historical name. [14]

One high-ranking official from the City Council described the way in which the name change was made as follows:

> When we decided to apply for the UNESCO list for the People's Hall, the specialists, the UNESCO administration in Paris, said that to make the addition of this entry successful we shouldn't use two names, because we were using the name the People's Hall and the historical name, the Centennial Hall. And to be honest they didn't order us, just said 'standardize' the nomenclature in the application that you're submitting. As a result, the group of historians writing the application made what was in my opinion the correct decision, to use the historical name, because it had from the beginning been called the Centennial Hall. [15]

As the above statements show, the people who put together and submitted the application for the hall to be added to the UNESCO list were convinced about the need to invoke the historical, Prussian name. This was a decision that fitted the strategy adopted in the 1990s to redefine the historical narrative about Wrocław, one with ideological, political and economic motivations. The policy-makers therefore did not expect any resistance.

The information that a change had been made to the name of the hall reached the public through diverse information in the media. There were questions as to what event the Prussian name commemorated. In nationwide and local newspapers and the Internet, differing historical interpretations concerning the name of the Centennial Hall began to appear. A fierce debate was unleashed.

What is commemorated by the name "Centennial Hall"?

The official version of the building's erection, as described on the hall's official website, is given in very neutral terms: "the Centennial Hall was designed by Max Berg, an architect and constructor. This facility is the most famous work of Wrocław Modernism. Its structure was erected between 1911 and 1913, and

---

14 Interview conducted by the authors in November 2012.
15 Interview conducted by the authors in November 2012.

its interiors held the Centennial Exhibition to commemorate the 100th anniversary of Napoleon's defeat at Leipzig."[16]

Writing in the right-wing national daily *Rzeczpospolita*, the well-known columnist Piotr Semka complained about the lack of historical context in this description. His article "Raising Prussian ghosts"[17] quoted information from German Wikipedia. According to this version, the official opening of the hall took place on 10 March 1913, the day on which, in an effort to increase the anti-French mood before the impending conflict with Napoleon's army, King Frederick William III of Prussia had founded the new order of the Iron Cross. According to Semka, this order:

> [...] was a fetish of Prussian glory at the time of Breslau's celebrations. This style was adopted by the Nazis [...] The proponents of a return to the old name are outraged at the identification of the hall with an order that has a strongly negative connotation in Poland, repeating that one can speak solely about the connection with the anniversary of Prussia's wars of liberation against Napoleon. But the thing is that there is no contradiction between the two – the cult of the Iron Cross was and is inextricably connected in German national mythology with the 1813 war and Breslau. Therefore, the circumstances in which the hall came into being are not quite so innocent for a Polish observer. [...] Regardless of the chauvinistic character of the centenary celebrations, though, another question arises. Why should we in Polish Wrocław revive a date that for Poland meant Napoleon's betrayal enacted by Prussia? A date that foreshadowed the defeat of the Duchy of Warsaw,[18] the annihilation of Prince Józef Poniatowski's army?[19] The date of the renewed alliance of Russia and Prussia, the two most aggressive partitioning powers? [...] The opponents of the name change pointed to the clandestine way in which it was reinstated and asked a simple question: "why should we even in a seemingly unimportant name celebrate the triumph of Prussian glory?"

A similar note was struck by history professor Jerzy Robert Nowak, a commentator and columnist for *Trwam* Television, Radio *Maryja*, the newspaper *Nasz Dziennik* and other Catholic right-wing media:

---

16 http://www.halastulecia.pl/en/historia?m=1 (16 January 2014).
17 http://archiwum.rp.pl/artykul/689783-Wywolywanie-pruskich-duchow.html (30 October 2013).
18 The Duchy of Warsaw was a Polish state established by Napoleon I in 1807 from the Polish lands ceded by Prussia. Following Napoleon's defeat, the duchy was occupied by Prussian and Russian troops until 1815, when it was formally partitioned between the two countries at the Congress of Vienna.
19 Prince Józef Poniatowski was a Polish military hero who led the Polish troops allied with Napoleon. His death at the Battle of Leipzig in 1813 became a legend, depicted in Polish national iconography.

The defeat of the Polish armies alongside the French at the Battle of Leipzig meant both further thwarting of hopes for independence and being plunged into the ever stronger bondage of the partitions, including that of Hohenzollern Prussia. To revert to the old name commemorating the centenary of the Prussian triumph at the Battle of Leipzig therefore means today in Polish Wrocław a kind of national masochism – reconciling ourselves with a name commemorating Poland's once again falling into long and hopeless slavery. This was the reason for the very turbulent disputes that arose over the name change, which unfortunately ended in triumph for the proponents of the Prussian name, mostly owing to the position of Wrocław's present stewards.[20]

Such interpretations of the name met with opposition from the liberal-oriented media. An especially active participant in the mounting debate was the *Gazeta Wyborcza* journalist Beata Maciejewska. As historian specializing in the history of Wrocław, she has written several dozen articles on this subject. Her response to the two statements cited above was as follows:

Whose centenary is it? This was evident in the last debate provoked by Prof. Jerzy Robert Nowak, the Radio Maryja ideologist, who claimed that Wrocław is being re-Germanized and has entered into battle with the Prussian invader and its Fifth Column. One of the most important items in the account of damages he lodged on the city's behalf was the change of the name of the People's Hall to the Centennial Hall. The opponents of this change stressed that it is a symbol of Prussian militarism, confirmation of the Prussian triumph in the Battle of the Nations at Leipzig. Its supporters spoke of respect for Wrocław's foreign history, and said that it is not worth using another name, as the building can be seen by its historic name on the UNESCO World Heritage List. I have been following this debate online: almost none of its participants used the most important argument – that the people of Breslau had no intention of honoring the hundredth anniversary of the Battle of Leipzig. Of course, the imperial court wanted this. But the liberal Breslau city council, in which almost half of the councilors were social democrats, decided to remember the proclamation of King Frederick William III, "To my people" (*An mein Volk*), in which the ruler called for a joint war for liberation "from foreign rulers". The councilors understood the royal appeal as giving some of the power to the nation, the victory of its democratic aspirations, incidentally more limited after the events of the 1848 revolutions. In such a situation it makes sense that Emperor William II did not give money for the building of the Hall, and that the city had to take out a loan, which was a huge burden for its budget. The emperor also failed to become a patron of the Centennial Exhibition (only the Four-Domes Pavilion was devoted to his historical honor, not the Hall) and he was not present at its opening. Note that the occasion was celebrated with a show of Gerhart Hauptmann's drama *Festspiel im deutschen Reimen*, about the Battle of Leipzig. The play had pacifist overtones, and portrayed Napoleon as the destroyer of the *ancien régime* and creator of common Europe. A scandal erupted, the European press was severe in its criticism, and the play had to be cancelled. And this should be

---

20 http://www.jerzyrobertnowak.com/artykuly/Nasz_Dziennik/2009/2009.02.18.php (21 November 2013).

remembered before we start to hold fervent orations about the "glorification of Prussian militarism". [...] The *Rzeczpospolita* columnist Piotr Semka has written that [the Iron Cross] is a symbol of Prussian militarism and a fetish of Prussian glory later adopted by the Nazis. Proof: the Nazis put the Iron Cross with a Prussian eagle in Wrocław's coat of arms from 1938. Indeed they did, but with the eagle of the Silesian Piasts. And the Iron Cross itself was something that many Polish officers fighting in the German army during the First World War had. [...] It is also worth remembering that today a stylised Iron Cross is a symbol of the German armed forces, with whom the Polish army is allied. History likes to complicate everything, so before passing censure it is better to learn it.[21]

The polemic over the name in the national and local press also soon-captured the attention of Wrocław's inhabitants. Rather than being the sole preserve of the elites (politicians, academic, journalists etc.), debate also flared on Internet forums. Wrocław residents displayed varying attitudes to the name change and the politics of historical memory pursued by the city's authorities. Some asked whether the building and street names given by the former partitioners and enemies of Poland should be reinstated, or monuments erected to eminent former German inhabitants of the city. Earlier initiatives of the authorities to put up monuments and plaques to remember famous German personalities such Friedrich Schiller or Dietrich Bonhoeffer had not aroused much opposition,[22] yet commemorating the Prussian victory brought a wave of indignation expressed especially online in the form of comments on articles addressing the hall's name change. Posts on forums revealed differences in positions regarding the complicated Polish-German history, and difficulties in bridging the line dividing the distinct memories of the victors and defeated. Furthermore, they demonstrated the problem of some Internet-users in assimilating Poland's post-war communist history.[23]

---

21 Beata Maciejewska. "Zakończmy wojnę wrocławsko-pruską." *Gazeta Wyborcza [Wroclaw, n. 74]* 28 March 2009.
22 See Thum. *Uprooted: How Breslau became Wroclaw.*
23 Discussed was the extent to which the name "People's" was tied to the legacy of communism. "Zdecydowanie Hala Ludowa. Lud to pojęcie niekomunistyczne", awas_awas, http://m.wroclaw.gazeta.pl/wroclaw/51,106542,14914957.html?i=6 (21 November 2013).

The debate on the Centennial Hall on Internet forums

Internet forums have become a unique communication channel open to all, in which anyone can articulate their views in the public space. Their anonymity means that people can speak freely. The hundreds of posts on the hall included not only those at odds with political correctness (and thus with the officially implemented politics of memory), but also those who expressed support for the name change or attempted to reconcile the two sides of the argument.

Using the above-mentioned typology suggested by Bernhard and Kubik, and based on the posts on the hall's name change, several categories of mnemonic actors can be distinguished.

The most obvious category is that of "mnemonic warriors." Their characteristic trait is that they claim to represent the sole legitimate truth. They also tend to espouse a single, unidirectional, mythologized vision of time. They see the present as permeated by the 'spirit' of the past. Thus, in their view, "the problems of the present (and the future) cannot be effectively addressed unless the whole polity is set on the proper foundation constructed according to the 'true' vision of history. The alternative visions of the past – by definition 'distorted' – need to be delegitimized or destroyed."[24] Mnemonic warriors in Wrocław include both proponents and adversaries of the name "Centennial Hall". Its opponents delegitimize supporters by accusing them of conscious or unconscious (resulting from stupidity) betrayal of national interests. The supporters of the new name delegitimize its opponents by presenting them as national chauvinists. Those against the name change often invoke national myths of the past ("Wrocław was always Polish", "Germany is our eternal enemy"). Those in favor promote a post-national vision and Europe, and also have a tendency to mythologize both the past and the future (applying the myth of a multicultural Wrocław).

Let us take a look at the dynamic of the debates raging on forums among mnemonic warriors. On the Website of the Wrocław club of the right-wing *Gazeta Polska* newspaper, the following proclamation appeared:

> As residents of Wrocław *we express our deep concern, which has recently only heightened, at the process of Germanisation of our city* [emphasis ours]. Aware as we are that the time of Wrocław's greatest development came at a time when it found itself in German hands, this

---

24 Bernhard and Kubik. *Twenty Years after Communism: The Politics of Memory and Commemoration*, 18.

does not stop us from invoking its Polishness. We believe that, as Poles living for over half a century in Wrocław, *we have every right to shape our national identity* [emphasis ours], cultivate Polish tradition and honor. Polish heroes. The restoration of German building and street names, which takes place *under the aegis of being part of the European trend* [emphasis ours], is possible thanks to the exploitation of Wrocław's citizens' ignorance and is happening without a broad debate on the topic. A clear example is the already universally used name "Centennial Hall", which is a faithful translation of the German name "Jahrhunderthalle". One should recall that the name given to the building after it was erected in 1913 alludes to the hundredth anniversary of the Battle of Leipzig (1813). We have no doubt that *for Poles to celebrate the anniversary of the tragic "Battle of the Nations" is at the very least regrettable* [emphasis ours], since it brought the victory of the partitioners of Poland over Napoleon's army together with its ally, the Army of the Duchy of Warsaw. This was a defeat which put an end to the possibility to create a free Poland. It was also here that one of the greatest Polish national heroes, the Commander in Chief of the Polish Armies of the Duchy of Warsaw Prince Józef Poniatowski, fell. The remarkable cult which arose after his death gave the Polish Nation heart for over 100 years as it awaited its victory. The French historian Bainville described him as a "symbol of Poland faithful though in vain", while late in his life, Napoleon – acknowledged as the greatest leader in world history – admitted that Poniatowski was "the true king of Poland".

Given the divergence between the actual name, associated with the People's Republic of Poland, the Wrocław People's Hall Company Sp. z o.o.[25], and the name in public circulation for several years, "Centennial Hall", we propose an entirely new name, which also makes reference to the building's history. Our compromise suggestion is "Prince Józef Poniatowski Hall".[26]

The idea to give the hall the name of Prince Józef Poniatowski, a Polish national hero who died at the Battle of Leipzig fighting at Napoleon's side, did not go down well with the supporters of the Centennial Hall name. One person to react fiercely was the aforementioned Beata Maciejewska, one of the main "mnemonic warriors", and as a *Gazeta Wyborcza* journalist someone with a tremendous influence on the formation of the historical narrative in Wrocław. She used her articles and columns[27] to criticize and ridicule this idea and met with an emotional reaction from some readers through comments on Gazeta Wyborcza. The followings are representative comments from eight readers participating in the discussion; we report their posts maintaining the same readers' nick-

---

25 "Sp. z o.o." means limited liability corporation.
26 "Wrocław: Chcą zmienić nazwę Hali Ludowej." *Gazeta Polska* http://wroclaw.naszemiasto.pl/artykul/1208639,wroclaw-chca-zmienic-nazwe-hali-ludowej,id,t.html (29 November 2013).
27 "Hala Stulecia czy imienia Poniatowskiego [FELIETON]." *Gazeta Wyborcza* http://wroclaw.gazeta.pl/wroclaw/1,35771,11201458,Hala_Stulecia_czy_imienia_Poniatowskiego__FELIETON_.html (29 November 2013).

names, as they appear on the Webpage: "wrocławianin", "45rtg", "WK", "1410_tenrok", "Flying_jureczek", "jerzyt21", "karakalla" and "Jacek".

> the standard of journalism at gw [Gazeta Wyborcza] has hit rock bottom... and as for changing the name of the hall to Józef Poniatowski, I'm absolutely in favour, as you can't have much between the ears if you celebrate the victory of the Prussians over Napoleon [...] why stick to that? Since we have centennial hall why not name it after hakata[28] or good old uncle Adolf?[29]

Another post:

> What, Maciejewska, does it hurt that only your paper uses the name you made up for the People's Hall? That the people of Wrocław say "People's Hall", just as they always have? Come on then Maciejewska, get used to the fact that you can't get everything done through your paper's "social actions" that have the finesse and standard of honesty of the "spontaneous workers" actions' in Gomułka's time.[30]

And one more comment:

> Wait a moment. After convincing the lemmings that the People's Hall "must" be the Centennial Hall (as if the name in Polish is of any significance for foreigners), the time will come for an exhibition of the eminent figures who have appeared there. And then, to respect history (after all, 'our' city was faithful to the Nazi Party and Hitler like few others in the Third Reich), we will have to hang up a portrait of Hitler.
>
> Ms Maciejewska, it's time to write a justification – what are you waiting for? In the meantime – as an exercise – please show what the difference is between renaming the Imperial Bridge the Grunwaldzki Bridge[31] and renaming the Centennial Hall the Prince Józef Poniatowski Hall.[32]

---

28 *Hakata* – colloquial name for the German nationalist organisation Deutscher Ostmarkenverein, which sought the Germanisation of the Polish lands in the Prussian partition.
29 Posted by "wrocławianin" [Timestamp: 22.02.12, 11:02] http://forum.gazeta.pl/forum/w,72,133591012,133592060,Re_Hala_Stulecia_czy_imienia_Poniatowskiego_FEL.html (29 November 2013).
30 Posted by "45rtg". Gomułka was the leader of Communist Poland from 1956 to 1970. http://wroclaw.gazeta.pl/wroclaw/1,35771,14914957,Co_ma_wspolnego_Hala_Stulecia_z_Poniatowskim_i_inne.html?v=1&obxx=14914957#opinions (29 November 2013).
31 This refers to a historic Wrocław bridge, known in pre-war German Breslau as Imperial Bridge and renamed by the Poles after 1945 as Grunwaldzki Bridge.
32 Posted by "WK" [Timestamp: 22.02.12, 11:17] http://forum.gazeta.pl/forum/w,72,133591012,133592601,Przyjdzie_czas_i_na_portret_Hitlera_w_Hali.html (20 November 2013).

The comments under the articles on the hall's name included both individual posts and entire discussions. It is worth quoting an extract that is symptomatic of the dispute over the name. Particularly notable is the amount of historical knowledge and emotional involvement of the participants using the login names "WK" and "1410_tenrok". They present differing positions towards historical interpretation. "WK"'s stance seems to be characteristic of a traditional, national understanding of history, whereas "1410_tenrok" presents a new, European model of post-national memory that relativizes the traditional, national view of history. This user writes, for example:

> Two hundred years post factum, nobody comprehends those events. Unfortunately Napoleon was a kind of Hitler of the early nineteenth century! He did little for the Polish cause, if anything! [...] It's worth remembering that this was by no means a Polish battle, but just a battle of nations who wanted to defeat a troublemaker and usurper [...].[33]

"WK" countered this comment as follows:

> Absolutely agree, the battle was not Polish and THAT'S WHY WE HAVE NO REASON TO COMMEMORATE IT!
> [...] By what right should we in Poland refer to the brand of a hall from the worst period of Prussian militarism, whose immediate successor was after all Hitlerism? If it was the "Bierut", "Stalin", "Polish Workers' Party", 'People's Republic Workers' Hall (or something like that), that would be a disgrace, but what's wrong with the name "People's"?[34]

The reaction of "1410_tenrok" was fierce, underlining its arguments, taking the role of teacher and accusing opponents of chauvinism:

> [...] The Centennial Hall is a hall that was built for various reasons [...]. In 1811 it was in Breslau that the Prussian Revolution broke out. It was here that Frederick William's famous proclamation was made, aimed at the nation. It was from here, from the church in Sobótka-Górka, that the revolutionary units went off to fight for the freedom of Prussia, which several years later at the Congress of Vienna was acknowledged as more of a Slavic than a Germanic country, as it was Slavs (not just Poles) who were in the majority. There was no thought at the time of militarism, but rather of such prosaic matters such as secularisation and freeing the peasants from serfdom. Interesting, eh???
> This was the fundamental reason for which this great monument was raised. *The whole moronic discussion, especially on the part of nutty chauvinists, ought to remember* [em-

---

[33] Posted by "1410_tenrok" [Timestamp: 22.02.12, 11:59] http://forum.gazeta.pl/forum/w,72,133591012,133594165,i_kto_tu_jest_lemingiem_WK_.html **Fehler! Textmarke nicht definiert.**(20 November 2013).
[34] Posted by "WK" [Timestamp: 22.02.12, 12:36] http://forum.gazeta.pl/forum/w,72,133591012,133595505,Re_i_kto_tu_jest_lemingiem_WK_.html (20 November 2013).

phasis ours] that in oh so Catholic Rome the Pantheon still exists, the place in which all the main deities of the people conquered by the Romans were put. And nobody ever thought of changing its name to, for instance, the papal church or something similar. In recognition of its sacredness even, great Italians were buried there. Lay off history. This is not a game for little kids. History is too complicated.[35]

"WK" remained unconvinced, answering:

"That 'famous' proclamation called for a battle with Napoleon, did it not? Moreover, it proved a success – the coalition formed defeated Napoleon at Leipzig. The struggle for the freedom of Prussia was not a struggle for the freedom of Poland. Indeed, Poles made up a sizable proportion of the population of Prussia (after all, there weren't many Sorbs, or perhaps we're now starting to distinguish the Masurians – I'm no expert on the trends of spreading 'local patriotism'), and later on, that fact was one of the main arguments for forced Germanisation.

In London there's a Waterloo station and in Paris, Austerlitz – not the other way round. The years pass and somehow nothing changes. No nation celebrates foreign victories or foreign nationalism.[36]

WK's comments are supported by another user, who writes:

It's one thing to restore German street names like "Garden Street", and quite another to return to a name commemorating the victory of Germans in a war with the French, or anyone else. It's not our victory, and not in our interest to celebrate it. History should be treated seriously.[37]

We should stress that those taking part in the debate were not just "mnemonic warriors", but also representatives of another type of mnemonic actors: "mnemonic pluralists." Such people respect the rights of others to distinct, equivalent interpretations and visions of the past. They are open to searching for a common truth and ready to construct a common memory regime, which Bernhard and Kubik call a "pillarised mnemonic regime" in which competing visions of the past coexist.[38] This type of actor is represented by the two following posts:

---

[35] Posted by "1410_tenrok" [Timestamp: 22.02.12, 13:17] http://forum.gazeta.pl/forum/w,72,133591012,133596870,i_znowu_dosc_nieprawda_niestety_.html (20 November 2013).
[36] Posted by "WK" [Timestamp: 22.02.12, 13:51] http://forum.gazeta.pl/forum/w,72,133591012,,Hala_Stulecia_czy_imienia_Poniatowskiego_FELIE_.html?v=2, (20 November 2013).
[37] Posted by "Flying_jureczek" [Timestamp: 28.07.08, 11:34] http://forum.gazeta.pl/forum/w,72,63944931"Kto_sie_boi_Hali_Stulecia (20 November 2013).
[38] Bernhard and Kubik. *Twenty Years after Communism: The Politics of Memory and Commemoration*, 12.

> Geez, what's up with all of you? Two names have been adopted anyway. It's not the only instance of something like this, e.g. La Manche/English Channel, Persian Gulf/Arab Gulf, and Mount Everest has over a dozen names. I know what the Centennial Hall is and the People's Hall, too. And I live "a stone's throw" from the HALL. I'd protest if someone wanted to call it "Caterpillar Hall".[39]

And:

> But there is already an excellent, uncontroversial idea for the name: Max Berg Hall. With all the problematic burdens of connotations removed, associated with both the People's Hall and the Centennial Hall, honoring an outstanding architect for the city, and at the same time stressing that the history of Wrocław didn't begin in 1945.[40]

However, "mnemonic pluralists" are very much in the minority on Internet forums. The least visible users, meanwhile, are of course the so-called "mnemonic abnegators", who by definition are not interested in history and do not involve themselves in it. They "tend to be uninterested in thinking in terms of mythical time, treat the past as a reservoir of useful tests of practical solutions, focus on the present, and strive to avoid participating in cultural (including mnemonic) wars".[41] From time to time, however, their voices are heard on forums. For example:

> Don't you have bigger problems? Everyone's got used to the People's Hall. Who's it bothering?[42]

As well as:

> They should get working. There are more important things to do in the city than thinking about changes to the name of the Centennial (People's) Hall. Leave one of the most precious buildings in the city in peace...[43]

---

[39] Posted by "jerzyt21." http://wroclaw.gazeta.pl/wroclaw/1,35771,14914957,Co_ma_wspolnego_Hala_Stulecia_z_Poniatowskim_i_inne.html#LokWrocTxt, (26 November 2013).
[40] Posted by "karakalla." http://wroclaw.gazeta.pl/wroclaw/1,35771,14914957,Co_ma_wspolnego_Hala_Stulecia_z_Poniatowskim_i_inne.html#LokWrocTxt (26 November 2013).
[41] Bernhard and Kubik. *Twenty Years after Communism: The Politics of Memory and Commemoration*, 19.
[42] Posted by "Jacek" [Timestamp: 2012–02–01 07:50:41] on the article "Wrocław: Chcą zmienić nazwę Hali Ludowej"
http://wroclaw.naszemiasto.pl/artykul/1208639,wroclaw-chca-zmienic-nazwe-hali-ludowej,id,t.html (26 November 2013).
[43] Posted by "Wrocławianin" [Timestamp: 2012–04–14 09:59:13] on the article "HalaLudowa, StuleciaczyPepi?" http://wroclaw.naszemiasto.pl/artykul/1362563,hala-ludowa-stuleciaczy-pepi,2,id,t,nk.html#skomentuj (26 November 2013).

Although the quantitative research on knowledge and interest in Wrocław's history[44] has shown that a large percentage of the city's residents are memory abnegators, the debate on the hall revealed that this situation may change. As the number of articles on the hall grew, more and more people started to show an interest in issues concerning Wrocław's historical memory and to participate in the debate on Internet forums. This is a good illustration of the dynamic accompanying the processes of collective memory construction. A certain mnemonic equilibrium exists until some political entrepreneur (in the case described here – the opinion-makers representing the nationalist right) finds an effective discursive strategy to champion a vision of the past that challenges the hitherto dominant view. What happens then is that with the entrance of a mnemonic warrior a memory regime constructed as pillarised (based on peaceful coexistence) or unified (based on consensus) becomes "fractured."[45] This means that the memory regime becomes a field of political struggle. This conflict will last until the warriors transform into pluralists and/or abnegators who do not see any advantage in engaging in memory conflicts. A mnemonic equilibrium can then be reinstated, only to be shaken again as soon as a new memory warrior is able to ignite a memory conflict.

The reactions of the local decision-makers

The heatedness of the debate on the name change came as a surprise to the Wrocław authorities. As the name that was "new" to Poles, i.e. Centennial Hall, had already been added to the UNESCO World Heritage List, it could not be changed without their losing face, and they therefore compromised, allowing both names to be used. As one journalist dealing with the city's history put it:

> ...those in power were put up against the wall, they had some German toy pistol pointed at them and started to have their patriotism picked apart. They started to think slightly conservatively, sat astride the barricade, getting hit on the backside and neither right nor left.

---

[44] See results of the research conducted by Paweł Czajkowski and Barbara Pabjan. "Formy Pamięci Historycznej Miasta. Architektoniczne Dziedzictwo Kulturowe Miasta w Świadomości Młodzieży." *Pamięć jako Kategoria Rzeczywistości Społecznej*. Eds. Józef Styka and Małgorzata Dziekanowska. Lublin: Wyd.UMCS, 2012.

[45] Kubik and Bernhard. *Twenty Years after Communism: The Politics of Memory and Commemoration*, 16. The authors discern three kinds of memory regimes: "(1) a fractured regime when at least one actor is a warrior, (2) a pillarized regime when there is no warrior in the mix and at least one actor is a pluralist, and (3) a unified regime when no actor is a warrior or a pluralist; that is, all are abnegators."

> They don't want to make any courageous decisions. Look at the wretched Centennial Hall. It was registered at UNESCO as the Centennial Hall. That's the trade mark, there's even a plaque in the wall etc. All over the city we have tourist signs pointing to the "Centennial Hall". If we go out somewhere, it's the Centennial Hall, but the company is called "People's Hall".[46]

The politicians' behavior can be understood by reading Bernhard and Kubik, who point out that mnemonic actors often try to treat history instrumentally, but are not totally free in their construction of historical memories. There are limits to malleability in the presentation of the past imposed by the visions of history that the target audience cultivates and considers valid.[47] If the mnemonic actor crosses the line between credible and non-credible visions of the past, his legitimacy and power is weakened.[48] We can assume that it was the controversies revealed by the name change (and then discussed broadly on Internet forums) that made the authorities worry about their legitimacy, thus leading to the delay in the official process of the hall's renaming. Along with the criticism, ideas surfaced in the public space of giving it an entirely new name, such as that of its creator, "Berg Hall", or of the Polish pope – "John Paul II Hall". The idea was not accepted by the authorities. A high-ranking official representing the local government gave the following reasons:

> But even if you'd called it the Berg Hall, you'd still have to write in the application, "Berg Hall, once known as Centennial Hall", and that was what the administrators wanted, to avoid that context. And then [...] a discussion began over whether it should be called Centennial Hall or People's Hall. I took the position in this discussion that I personally like Centennial Hall, and don't like People's Hall. I don't like People's Hall because it derives from communism, and I have more against the name People's Hall than against the name Centennial Hall, but I said that we wouldn't change the name of the "Hala Ludowa" [People's Hall] business, it'd still be called "Hala Ludowa, sp. z o.o. [ltd]" and people could say what they wanted. And it is interesting that the language usage is clearly flowing towards Centennial Hall. And I must insist here that the great majority say Centennial Hall, not People's Hall. There were certain controversies over it, but with the hindsight of a few years I'd say actually pretty negligible controversies. If we meet in five years we

---

46 Interview conducted by the authors in November 2012.
47 Such visions evolve and sometimes even become radically modified in a complex process involving a play of mutual adjustment between what the mnemonic entrepreneur proposes and what a given audience is prepared to accept, see Kubik and Bernhard. *Twenty Years after Communism: The Politics of Memory and Commemoration*, 11–12.
48 Ibid.

won't even remember that there were any significant disagreements over what it should be called.[49]

This analysis is hard to fault. The generation is slowly diminishing that remembers the German crimes of the Second World War and has been most strongly emotionally involved in the debates over the name change. Communicative memory becomes cultural memory.[50] Debates over history and memory become ever less personal ideological disputes, which will doubtless before long cease to have the same significance as they still do today. The space is opened for reinterpretation of history and commemorations free from the burden of individual historical memory. In this kind of situation, politicians fighting for votes do not have to make controversial decisions and become involved in disputes. If for any reason a situation is arrived at that triggers social tensions, the rational strategy of action is to calm emotions and set the matter aside to "sort itself out" later. The field of political memory is a unique place:

> ...it is here where political success depends heavily on skillful interweaving of "realpolitik" manoeuvres (often behind the scenes) with an effective formulation and communication of cultural interpretations, including public presentation of mnemonic positions. Effective positions are those that are consonant with the cultural terrain of target groups, those that resonate with their images of the past.[51]

In this case, the unambiguous views of Internet posts demonstrated a clear aversion on the part of some residents to the hall's name change. At the same time, the authorities' behind-the-scenes activities "did not meet" the "images of the past" and expectations held by a proportion of potential voters. The most sensible political strategy was to call to a halt the official process of the name change and trust that the new name – whose proposal and dissemination exploited all possible means (such as signs pointing to the hall, information in guide books, maps and tourist guides, support in some media) – would with time become consolidated in the public consciousness of its own accord.

---

49 Interview with a high official, politician, born 1959, conducted by the authors in October 2012

50 According to Jan Assmann communicative memory means daily memory, representations of the past expressed just orally, thus not leaving material traits. See Assmann. "Communicative and Cultural Memory," 110.

51 Kubik and Bernhard. *Twenty Years after Communism: The Politics of Memory and Commemoration*, 16.

Conclusions

If we take into account the conceptual framework proposed by Bernhard and Kubik[52] and adopted in this case study, it is clear that what we are dealing with in Wrocław is a political form of a fractured memory regime, dominated by mnemonic warriors. The decisions taken in the field of memory and the creation of new memory regimes require important calculations that, as pointed by Bernhard and Kubik, are of two kinds:

> One – positional – is based strictly on the grounds of the (political) cost/benefit analysis [e.g. "Do I improve my electoral chances by inviting 'them' to form a coalition?"]. The second consideration – semiotic – is about cultural consequences of such a decision (e.g., "What kinds of meanings can be attached to my decision of forming this coalition?"). In this second calculation a set of possible interpretations of one's actions is considered. The most successful politicians calculate political efficacy and cultural significance simultaneously".[53]

During the decision process on the hall's name change, several factors were doubtless taken into account. Among these were not only the material benefits resulting from the possibility of securing European funding for its renovation, but also the change in the historical narrative of Wrocław and the idea of Wrocław's multicultural history that came from the EU memory field. Having been a feature of the city development strategies for well over a decade, Wrocław's new memory narratives are seeping into the residents' consciousness, but the process is not as fast as the city's authorities would like it to be. In their political calculation (political efficacy and cultural significance), Wrocław's authorities in fact failed to appreciate correctly two fundamental factors in the field of memory politics: the *cultural* and *instrumental-political*.[54] In the former case, they reckoned without the persistence of traditional, national, Polish approaches to the past. They presumed that the inhabitants either shared the new view on the city's past propagated since the 1990s, or that the majority of them were "mnemonic abnegators." This was why they did not see the need to consult with the city's residents on the change of the hall's name. The local authorities were actually unprepared for the scale and intensity of negative reactions expressed by two (partially overlapping) groups: conservative and nationally oriented mnemonic

---

52 Kubik and Bernhard. *Twenty Years after Communism: The Politics of Memory and Commemoration.*
53 Ibid, 15–16.
54 Ibid, 19.

warriors marginalized in the local, public discourse, as well as the older residents of the city who had become used to the name "People's Hall" over the decades. The latter associated the name "People's" with their happy (isn't it always?) youth, and not with a remnant of dreary communism. As for the champions of a conservative, national vision of history, it is no easy task to convince the opinion leaders in these communities and social circles of the EU's post-national historical narrative. At the meso (state) level, these people are often ideologically associated with the conservative, national-Christian Law and Justice party (PiS).

Regarding structural factors, it seems that the local authorities overestimated their capacity to influence and control public opinion. The unbroken hold of liberal parties in the city government since 1989 has restricted the access of right-wing nationalists to local opinion-forming circles and official media. What the local authorities did not expect was that this hegemonic position could be challenged by the new social media, but this was precisely what happened.

Internet forums became the most important and accessible platform for articulating rightist-nationalist views, seen by Wrocław's authorities as "politically incorrect". Today this is the city's main communication channel through which the struggle between supporters of the traditional, national historical narrative and those who strive to reinterpret it in the European and post-national spirit is fought. It is probable that the Wrocław controversy may have its counterparts in other cities in contemporary Europe, as the European integration process is the backdrop for a constant tension between the national and the European. A visible dispute is going on between champions of the renationalization of the memory of individual national communities and the common European memory.

The case of the Centennial Hall described here shows the great importance of continual public dialogue in the process of the construction of a European, post-national memory. This does not mean aiming for the political construction of a "unified memory regime", as Wrocław's city authorities have tried to do, but rather the creation of a "pillarised regime" based on respectful co-existence of different memories and an understanding for different experiences and perspectives. Only on this basis can a difficult compromise be built. A good note to close on is the historian Robert Traba's diagnosis:

> Europe today wants and is seeking elements of a common memory. Yet constructing a cultural memory requires that the dialogue be made civic, shifted from the political level to that of heated public debate, in which the heightening of differences will generate a new value – the living memory of twenty-first century Europe.[55]

---

55 Robert Traba. "Wprowadzenie." *Pamięć: Wyzwanie dla nowoczesnej Europy = Erinnerung :*

References

Assmann, Jan. "Communicative and Cultural Memory." *Cultural Memory Studies: An International and Interdisciplinary Handbook.* Eds. Astrid Erll and Ansgar Nünning. Berlin/New York: De Gruyter 2008: 109–118.

Bernhard, Michael. Jan Kubik. Eds. *Twenty Years after Communism: The Politics of Memory and Commemoration*, New York: Oxford University Press, 2014.

Kłopot, Stanisław. "Kreowanie mitu wielokulturowego Wrocławia." *Pamięć jako kategoria rzeczywistości społecznej.* Eds. J. Styka and M. Dziekanowska. Lublin: Wyd UMCS, 2012.

Maciejewska, Beata. "Zakończmy wojnę wrocławsko-pruską." *Gazeta Wyborcza [Wroclaw, n. 74]* 28 March 2009: 129–139.

Nijakowski, Lech M. *Polska polityka pamięci.* Warszawa: Wyd. Profesjonalne i akademickie, 2008.

Czajkowski, Paweł. Barbara Pabjan. "Formy Pamięci Historycznej Miasta. Architektoniczne Dziedzictwo Kulturowe Miasta w Świadomości Młodzieży." *Pamięć jako Kategoria Rzeczywistości Społecznej.* Eds. Józef Styka and Małgorzata Dziekanowska. Lublin: Wyd.UMCS, 2012: 141–155.

Risse, Thomas. *A Community of Europeans? Transnational Identities and Public Spheres.* Ithaca, NY: Cornell University Press, 2010.

Shore, Cris. "Inventing Homo Europaeus. The Cultural Politics of European Integration." *Ethnologia Europaea. Journal of European Ethnology* 29.2 (1999): 53–66.

Strauchold, Grzegorz. "Polityka narodowościowa na Ziemiach Zachodnich i Północnych w pierwszych latach po II wojnie światowej", *Pamięć i Przyszłość* 3.9 (2010): 8–18.

Thum, Gregor. *Uprooted: How Breslau became Wroclaw.* Princeton: Princeton University Press, 2011.

"Wrocław 2000 Plus. Studies on the city strategy", *Biuro Rozwoju Wrocławia* Bulletin 6.24 (1998): 48–52.

Traba, Robert. "Wprowadzenie." *Pamięć: Wyzwanie dla nowoczesnej Europy = Erinnerung : eine Herausforderung für das moderne Europa.* Ed. Robert Traba. Olsztyn: Stowarzyszenie Wspólnota Kulturowa "Borussia", (2008): 19–20.

---

eine Herausforderung für das moderne Europa. Ed. Robert Traba. Olsztyn: Stowarzyszenie Wspólnota Kulturowa "Borussia", 2008, 19.

Notes on contributors

Tea Sindbæk Andersen is assistant professor of Balkan Studies at the Department of Cross-Cultural and Regional Studies, University of Copenhagen, and vice-chair of the COST-action network "In Search for Transcultural Memory in Europe. Her research focuses on the contemporary history of South-Eastern Europe, especially issues related to uses of history, cultural memory, identity politics and popular culture in the former Yugoslav area. She is the author of *Usable History? Representations of Yugoslavia's Difficult Past from 1945 to 2002* (Aarhus University Press, 2012) and a number of scholarly articles on cultural memory and uses of history, popular culture, school books, historiography and political discourse.

Barbara Törnquist-Plewa is professor of Eastern and Central European Studies, Head of the Centre for European Studies at Lund University in Sweden and chair of the COST-action network "In Search for Transcultural Memory in Europe". In her research she focuses on nationalism, identity and collective memories in Eastern and Central Europe. She is the editor and author of many books and articles in English, Swedish and Polish, all dealing with modern history and culture of Eastern and Central Europe. Among the latest is the collection *Which Memory, Whose Future? Remembering Ethnic Cleansings and Lost Cultural Diversity in Central, Eastern and South-eastern European Cities*, published by Berghahn, 2016.

Cecilie Felicia Stockholm Banke is a senior researcher at the Danish Institute for International Studies where she works with Danish and European foreign policy, specializing in the politics of memory in international relations. From 2009– 2013 she was in charge of Holocaust and genocide studies at DIIS, and since 2014 she is Head of the Danish Delegation to the International Holocaust Remembrance Alliance. Her recent publications include *Playing Second Fiddle. Contending Visions of Europe's Development* with Bo Petersson & Hans Åke Persson (2015)and "Between Accommodation and Awareness. Jewish resistance in Scandinavia under Nazism" in Patrick Henry (Ed.) *Jewish Resistance Against the Nazis* (2014).

Tuomas Forsberg is professor of International Politics at the University of Tampere and deputy director of the Centre of Excellence on Choices of Russian Modernisation at the Aleksanteri Institute of the University of Helsinki. Previously he worked at the University of Helsinki, at the George C. Marshall European Center for Security Studies, Garmisch-Partenkirchen, Germany and at the Finnish Institute of International Affairs. He gained his PhD at the University of Wales, Aberystwyth in 1998. His research has dealt primarily with European security issues, focusing on the EU, Germany, Russia and Northern Europe. His publications include *Divided West: European Security and the Transatlantic Relationship* (co-authored with Graeme Herd, Blackwell 2006) and articles in journals such as *International Affairs, Journal of Peace Research, International Studies Review, Security Dialogue* and *Journal of Common Market Studies*.

Davide Denti is a PhD candidate at the School of International Studies, University of Trento, Italy. His research focuses on EU state building and member state building, with a case study on Bosnia and Herzegovina. He has published in edited books and in peer reviewed journals (*Croatian International Relations Review, Contemporary Southeastern Europe, Südosteuropa*). He holds an MA in International Relations from the University of Milan and an MA in European Studies from the College of Europe, Bruges, where he also served as teaching assistant.

Sophie Oliver completed an interdisciplinary PhD at the University of London in 2010. Her doctoral research examined the possibility of an ethics of secondary witnessing based on theories of embodiment, in particular in relation to cultural memory. During an Alexander von Humboldt Foundation research fellowship at the University of Konstanz and the Max Planck Institute Berlin, she has further developed her thinking in a project about the aesthetics of secondary witnessing in relation to Holocaust memorials in Berlin. She has published numerous articles in peer-reviewed journals, and is a contributor to various edited books on a range of themes including human rights, cultural theory and media representations of trauma.

Birga U. Meyer studied History and Cultural Studies at the University of Bremen before receiving her PhD at the University of British Columbia in Vancouver. For her PhD thesis, *Difficult Displays: Holocaust Representations in History Museums in Hungary, Austria and Italy,* she analyzed and compared the ways museums in these three countries represent the Holocaust today. Specialized in the contemporary history of Europe, she works on National Socialism, the Holocaust and its aftermath with a keen interest in how museums conceptualize the past in visual, textual and spatial representations. Focusing on research that combines public history and academic enquiry, Birga U. Meyer currently works at the *Project Museum Friedland*, a museum about the history of the German transit and refugee camp in Friedland, which was established in 1945.

Notes on contributors

Andrej Kotljarchuk is associate professor in history and senior researcher at Södertörn University. His research focuses on minorities and the role of expert communities, mass violence and the politics of memory. His recent publications include *In the Forge of Stalin. Swedish colonists of Ukraine in the totalitarian experiments of the twenties century*, published by Stockholm and Södertorn Universities, 2014; the book chapter "The Nordic Threat: Soviet Ethnic Cleansing on the Kola Peninsula" (Södertörn, 2014); and the articles "Nazi Genocide of Roma in Belarus and Ukraine: the significance of census data and census takers", in *Etudes Tsiganes* (2015) and "World War II Memory Politics: Jewish, Polish and Roma Minorities of Belarus", in *Journal of Belarusian Studies* (2013).

Anna Wylegała is a sociologist and an assistant professor at the Institute of Philosophy and Sociology, Polish Academy of Sciences. She was a fellow of the Imre Kertesz Kolleg Jena (2013) and United States Holocaust Memorial Museum (2014). Her field of interests includes biographical and collective memory and identity, as well as post-war social change in Central and Eastern Europe. She has recently published *Przesiedlenia a pamięć. Studium (nie)pamięci społecznej na przykładzie ukraińskiej Galicji i polskich "ziem odzyskanych"* (*Resettlements and Memory. A Study of Social Memory in the case of Ukrainian Galicia and Polish 'Recovered Lands'*) Toruń, 2014.

Inge Melchior recently defended her PhD thesis entitled *Guardians of living history: the persistence of the past in post-Soviet Estonia* at the VU University Amsterdam. As a sociologist and anthropologist, she focuses on the social practice of collectively remembering of the Second World War and the Soviet period among Estonians, both on the personal/familial and a political level. Her research is primarily based on ethnographic fieldwork, combined with statistic analyses of representative survey data. She has published "Voicing past and present uncertainties: The relocation of a Soviet World War II memorial and the politics of memory in Estonia" *Focaal: European Journal for Anthropology*, 2011, and several other contributions to journals and edited books.

Yuliya Yurchuk, obtained her PhD in history from Stockholm University. Her thesis *Reordering of Meaningful Worlds: Memory of the Organization of Ukrainian Nationalists and the Ukrainian Insurgent Army in Post-Soviet Ukraine* was defended in 2015. She is currently working at Center for Baltic and East European Studies, Södertörn University, Sweden. Her main field of interests includes memory politics in East European countries, history of the Second World War, and nation-building in Ukraine.

Mārtiņš Kaprāns is a researcher at the Institute of Philosophy and Sociology, University of Latvia. He received his PhD in communication science from University of Latvia in 2012. From 2013 to 2015, Kaprāns was research fellow at the Institute of Government and Politics, University of Tartu. His current research interests are focused on long-distance nationalism, transnational remembering, and representation of the past in social networking sites. Kaprāns has recently published articles in *Journal of Media and Communication*, *Journal of Baltic Studies* and *Memory Studies*.

Volodymyr Kulyk is a head research fellow at the Institute of Political and Ethnic Studies, National Academy of Sciences of Ukraine. His main research topics are the politics of language, politics of memory, nationalism and media discourse, on which he has published three books and dozens of articles and book chapters in English, Ukrainian, Russian, German, French and Polish. His latest book is Dyskurs ukraïns'kykh medii: identychnosti, ideolohiï, vladni stosunky (The Ukrainian Media Discourse: Identities, Ideologies and Power Relations) Kyiv: Krytyka, 2010.

Elvin Gjevori holds a PhD from Dublin City University, Ireland in International Relations and Politics. Currently, he is a Swedish Institute Post-Doctoral Researcher at Malmo University, Sweden. Previously he worked as a lecturer of politics at the Department of Applied Social Sciences at the European University of Tirana, Albania. Dr Gjevori's research focuses on institutional reform in post-communist countries and collective memory with a particular focus on the Western Balkans. He has published articles which have appeared in the Journal of Southeast European and Black Sea Studies and East European Politics.

Igor Pietraszewski, is an assistant professor at the Institute of Sociology at the University of Wrocław (Poland). His main research interest is the sociology of culture, music and memory. He has published articles in Polish, English and Slovak and is the author of *Jazz in Poland. Improvised Freedom* Peter Lang, 2014.

Index of names

Ahtisaari, Martti 53 f.
Antonescu, Ion 153
Appelbaum, Ralph 103
Arnold-de Simine, Silke 96, 99 f., 104, 106 f.
Ashdown, Paddy 78
Assmann, Aleida 4, 26, 31, 38, 96, 119, 208

Bandera, Stepan 5, 232, 238, 240, 251, 270, 286 f., 291
Berg, M. 219, 321, 351, 355 f., 365, 367
Berisha, Sali 330, 332 f., 337 f., 340
Berkhoff, Karel 153, 159, 211
Bernhard, M. 204, 212, 250, 353 f., 360, 364–369
Bonhoeffer, D. 359

Čavić, Dragan 79
Chametzky, Peter 106

Dačić, Ivica 85, 87
Drakulić, Slavenka 83 f.
Đukanović, Milo 77 f.

Ehrenburg, Ilya 157
Eisenman, Peter 29, 109–111
Erdogan, Recep Tayyip 21

Freudenheim, Tom 105

Gross, Andrew 5, 32, 113
Grossman, Vasily 157, 160
Gurović, Milan 303 f.

Halonen, Tarja 53–55
Harjes, Kirsten 109 f.
Hein, George E. 99
Heyl, Matthias 96 f., 101
Hirsch, Marianne 37, 112, 208
Hoffman, Martin 113 f.
Hooper-Greenhill, Eilean 99–101
Hoxha, Enver 326, 329, 332, 334 f.

Ignashchenko, Anatoly 163
Izetbegović, Bakir 84, 86

Josipović, Ivo 77, 83 f.
Judt, Tony 7, 27, 204

Kadishman, Menashe 115
Kaldor, Mary 65, 78
Kaplan, E. Ann 114
Karadžić, Radovan 65 f.
Kasztner, Reszö 133
Kipiani, Vakhtang 280, 285 f., 292
Kochubievsky, Mikhailo 154
Koivisto, Mauno 51 f.
Konovalets, Yevhen 291
Konstatinoskii, Ilya 153
Koštunica, Vojislav 81
Kozimirenko, Mikha 149, 163
Kritzman, Lawrence 151 f.
Kubik, J. 250, 353 f., 360, 364–369
Kuznetsov, Anatoly 159, 161

LaCapra, Dominick 113
Levada, Pirohova 158, 167
Libeskind, Daniel 96, 104–106, 108 f.
Linenthal, Edward 103
Lipponen, Paavo 54
Lisle, Debbie 99 f.

Maciejewska, B. 358 f., 361 f.
Marović, Svetozar 78
Meier, Lili / Lili Jákob 139
Mesić, Stipe 78
Milošević, Slobodan 66, 85
Mladić, Ratko 65 f.
Molotov, Vyacheslav 51, 153, 159, 210

Nano, Fatos 326 f., 329
Nikolić, Tomislav 66, 77, 83–87
Nora, Pierre 11, 151 f.
Nowak, J.R. 357 f.

Poniatowski, J. 357, 361 f., 365
Putin, Vladimir 53, 55, 57 f., 284

Radstone, Susannah 117
Rauterberg, Hanno 110

Schiller, F. 359
Šimunić, Josip 297–314
Šešelj, Vojislav 84
Sontag, Susan 114
Stead, Naomi 105–108

Tadić, Boris 77, 80f., 84–86
Thaçi, Hashim 85
Traba, R. 370f.

Trifunović, Darko 78
Turkey, Republic of 8, 21, 23f., 30, 33f.
Tyaglyy, Mikhailo 149, 155, 169

Witcomb, Andrea 99–101

Yeltsin, Boris 52f., 57, 59
Young, James 11, 22, 104f., 109, 139, 218, 231, 236, 238

Subject index

Act of Settlement of all Nomadic Gypsies 158
Affect 4, 10, 12, 22, 33, 37–40, 43, 47, 72, 97, 101, 103, 112–115, 117f., 140, 277, 279, 320, 322
Agency 132f., 135, 138, 141, 145f., 164, 183f., 187, 253
Albania 7, 15, 75, 319–322, 325–330, 332, 334–336, 338–343, 345
Ambiguity 66f., 74, 77f., 80, 88, 214f., 255
Anthropology 203f, 218f.
Apology 5, 13, 33, 38, 44–46, 59, 66–74, 76–87, 258
24 April 23, 32
Armenia 21–24, 30, 32–34
Armenian genocide 8, 12, 21f., 24f., 30, 32f.
Armenian massacres 22f.
Armenian tragedy 23f., 32
Audience 13, 15, 42, 68, 70, 73, 83, 96f., 231, 270, 275–278, 280, 298, 302, 304, 312–314, 367
Auschwitz-Album/Lili Meier Album 124, 136f., 139, 144
Auschwitz-Birkenau 129, 134, 136f., 139–141, 159

Babi Yar 149f., 153–155, 157–166, 168f.
Battle of Leipzig 357f., 361
Belarus 151, 155, 157, 170, 197, 200, 259
Bergen-Belsen 114
Bessarabia 156
Blog 59, 107, 111f., 116, 278–281, 301
Bosnia and Herzegovina 47, 65f., 78f., 87
Bosniaks 82, 86
Bosnian Serbs 79
Breslau 354, 357–359, 362f.
Bronze Soldier 1, 219f.
Bukovina 156

Chernihiv 150
Clash of memories 204
Collective memory 4f., 25f., 30f., 37–39, 152, 154, 162, 169, 177, 179, 204, 208f., 212, 231, 236, 242, 250, 253, 269, 273–275, 281, 285, 291, 294, 302, 319–321, 345, 366
Communicative memory 223, 368
Communism 1f., 6–8, 32, 124, 206, 211, 213, 223, 250, 319f., 322f., 325–327, 332f., 335, 337f., 353f., 359f., 364–370
Communities of practice 254, 267
Consensus building 252, 256, 263–264
Contestation of memory 285f.
Contested WWII memories 206
Cosmopolitanization of memory 25, 30
Cost-benefit analysis 73
Council of Europe 159, 166, 351
1997 crisis 338–340, 343–345
Croatia 6, 14, 77f., 80, 83–86, 152, 222, 297–303, 306–315
Cultural Memory 4f., 7, 9, 11, 31f., 96–98, 100–102, 112, 115, 118, 236, 253, 293, 353, 368, 370
Czech Republic 156

Dachau 114
4 days in May (movie) 288
Dayton Peace Agreements 65, 76
Democratic Party (of Albania) 322f., 325, 330, 334, 338
Democratisation 57, 75, 340
De-personification 157, 162f., 167
Difficult memory 191
Digital memory 15, 249f., 273f., 297f.
Disputed memory 3
Double experience 1f., 8
Dubrovnik 77f.

Eastern Europe 1–9, 12, 14, 38, 75, 130, 155, 213, 250, 266, 319, 354
East Slavic (Soviet) narrative 277, 283f., 286f., 289f., 293
Emotion 1–5, 10–13, 23, 41, 43, 45, 72, 95–97, 101–103, 108f., 112–114, 116, 118, 178, 186, 191, 193, 195, 205, 209, 218f., 223, 236, 292, 305, 368
Empathic distress 113f., 116, 118

Empathic unsettlement 113, 115, 117
Empathy 45–47, 69, 74, 96f., 103, 112–115, 118, 124, 135, 141, 277
Estonia 1, 8, 13, 203–224, 266
Estonian veterans 211–212
Ethnographic fieldwork 206–209, 219–220, 224
EU 1, 7f., 33, 47, 50, 54, 58, 75–77, 82f., 87, 166f., 170, 204–206, 212, 221, 320, 339, 351, 369f.
EU accession 66, 76f., 86, 212, 217, 219
EU membership 75, 80f., 88
European belonging 222
European City of Culture 355
Europeanisation 67, 74, 219
European memory 1, 8f., 15, 27, 123, 177, 203, 205, 209, 213f., 218, 223, 282, 352, 370
European memory politics 7, 13
European Parliament (EP) 24, 81
European Union 7, 56, 58, 80–83, 86, 151, 204, 213, 270
Exhibition design 102, 125f.
Extraordinary Commission for Investigation of War Crimes (ChGK) 149f., 157f., 160, 169

Facebook 14f., 281f., 286, 292f., 297f., 302–315
Fascism 14, 154, 211, 220, 240, 297, 300f., 303, 314, 335
Feelings of insecurity 205, 214
Finland 13, 37f., 47–59
First World War 22f., 30, 33f., 359
Football 14, 163, 297–303, 306f., 309–312
Football world cup 302
Forgiveness 37f., 40–47, 59, 68f., 71, 73
Framing 124, 249, 257, 276, 344f.
Frederick William III (Friedrich Wilhelm III) 357f.

GDR Museum 98
Genocide 1, 6, 8, 12, 21–25, 28–31, 33f., 41, 65–67, 78f., 81f., 84f., 87, 102, 135, 149–151, 154–159, 161–163, 165–170, 211, 229f., 283, 327

Genocide in Bosnia (Bosnian genocide) 25, 81
German Emigration Museum 98
Global memory 8, 21, 25f., 33, 254
Greater Serbia 84
Great Patriotic War 55, 154, 228
Great Soviet Encyclopaedia 155

Hala Ludowa 351, 359, 367
Helsinki 47f., 50–53, 56f., 82
Historical memory 27, 57, 109, 118, 170, 208, 212, 214, 275, 277, 279f., 282, 351, 353–355, 359, 366, 368
Historical narrative (narrative of history, narrative of the past) 9, 43, 71, 105, 252, 254, 265, 269, 275f., 281, 291f., 354, 356, 361, 369f.
Holocaust 5–9, 11, 13, 21–25, 27–29, 31–33, 95, 97, 100–103, 105–107, 109–113, 115–118, 123–137, 140–145, 149–151, 153–162, 164, 166–170, 178, 203f., 211–213, 228, 231, 236, 268
Holocaust memory 8f., 25–27, 30, 123, 166, 211
Holocauszt Emlékközpont/Holocaust Memorial Center 123f., 128, 138
Holodomor 236, 241–243, 263, 283f.
Hybrid narrative 145

Iconic Images 114, 136
Independent State of Croatia (Fascist Ustasha regime) 297f., 298, 301
Institutionalisation 319–322, 333, 336
International Court of Justice (ICJ) 65, 82
International Criminal Tribunal for the former Yugoslavia (ICTY) 65f., 78
International Declaration on Human Rights of 1948 29
Internet 10, 14, 253, 260f., 270, 273f., 278–281, 294, 302–305, 312–314, 353, 356, 359f., 365–368, 370
Irit Dekel 109f.
Istorychna Pravda (website) 280, 285, 292
Izvestia 153f., 160f.

Jahrhunderthalle 351, 361
Jewish Council 133

Subject index — 381

Jewish Museum Berlin 97, 105f., 108f., 118
Jews, Jewish 1, 13, 23, 28f., 32, 96f., 103–106, 108–110, 112, 115, 118, 123–127, 129–134, 136f., 139–145, 149f., 153–155, 157–163, 167, 177f., 186, 203f., 206, 208, 210–214, 218, 233, 250, 257f., 264, 274, 292, 298
Judiciary 319f., 322f., 325–334, 343

Karelia 48f., 51–54
Karelian Isthmus 48, 54
1999 Kosovo war 340, 343–345
Koziatyn 158
Krasnaya Zvezda 153, 157
Kurenivka 162f.
Kyiv 58, 149f., 154–163, 166f., 169, 227f., 233–235, 241, 277, 279
Kysylyn 169

Literaturnaya gazeta 161
Livejournal 281
Local memory 8, 13, 354
London 3, 5, 7f., 14, 22, 33, 40f., 47, 50, 52, 71, 101, 104, 126, 132, 134f., 138, 153, 167, 196, 204f., 231, 275, 305, 319, 364

Material security 73
Media (mass media) 1f., 4, 9f., 12, 14f., 51, 54–56, 58f., 72, 118, 150, 152f., 159f., 162, 165, 167, 182, 207, 209, 231, 236, 247, 249, 252–255, 259–261, 270, 273, 275–280, 283f., 294, 297f., 300, 302–307, 310f., 314, 353, 356–358, 368, 370
Media product 276, 283
Mediation 3f., 9–11, 72, 253, 293, 297, 314
Meds Yeghern 32
Memorialization 150, 155, 167, 169f., 251
Memorial to the Murdered Jews of Europe 97, 103, 109f., 118
Memory activists 206f., 213f., 217
Memory at War 3, 250, 293
Memory communities (memory community) 8, 11, 13f., 304, 313–314
Memory conflicts 37–39, 41, 43, 48, 53–55, 58f., 319, 366
Memory negotiations 8, 14

Memory politics 8, 19, 152–155, 166, 170, 204f., 207, 209, 223, 250, 260, 315, 369
Memory regimes 7, 250, 353f., 366, 369
Memory representations 6, 9f.
Memory transmission 9f., 12–14, 297, 314
Memory war 14, 250, 294
Military 1f., 52, 55, 57f., 65, 125, 142, 153, 196, 198, 210, 227, 234, 238, 249f., 253, 257f., 269, 284, 289, 294, 320–323, 327, 329, 334–345, 357
Mnemonic communities 205, 209, 213
Mnemonic war 360f., 365
Molotov-Ribbentrop treaty 49, 51
Montenegro 65, 78, 84
Monuments 4, 9, 11–13, 52, 71, 96, 150–153, 155, 157–159, 161, 163f., 167, 169, 231–234, 236, 238–242, 273, 359
Moscow 48, 51, 53f., 59, 152f., 155, 157, 160, 204, 250, 266, 283
museum exhibitions 4, 135
Mykolaiv 169

Napoleon 357f., 361–364
National Historical Memorial Preserve Babyn Yar 164
National Identity 32, 38, 56, 58, 109f., 152, 219, 222, 274f., 293f., 319, 361
Nationalist (anti-Soviet) narrative 6, 14, 24, 81, 84f., 87, 124, 159, 163, 189, 227, 229, 249, 257, 268, 283f., 286, 288–293, 303, 313, 362, 366, 370
National Socialism 1f., 27f., 32
NATO 47, 212, 320f., 339–345
Nazis 2, 8f., 27–29, 32, 100, 140f., 153–155, 158–160, 162f., 206, 211, 216f., 223, 228, 250, 257, 259, 292, 357, 359
New Museology 99f., 104, 108
Newspaper 9, 14f., 21, 153f., 160f., 232, 275f., 279, 303, 314, 321–323, 325, 329f., 332–334, 340, 344, 356f., 360
New wars 65
Non-apology apology 80
Novorzhev 154
Nuremberg trial 27, 29, 259

Odesa 291
Odessa 158, 167, 169

Online community 279
Online petition 297, 302, 304
Ontological security 73
Operation Oluja 85
Ordinary people 166
Organization of Ukrainian Nationalists (OUN) 227, 250f., 267, 285
Ostarbeiters 163
Ostroushki 158, 167f.
Othering 142
Ottoman Empire 22f., 34
Ovcara 84

patriotism 239, 303, 309, 311, 313–315, 364, 366
Paulin Dvor 84
Pavlivka 166
Perpetrators 2, 41, 44, 46, 57, 67, 74, 79, 82, 124, 126, 131f., 134f., 140, 143–145, 156, 159, 203, 212, 269
Photography 112, 114, 134
Poland 5, 13, 32, 48, 156, 166, 177–184, 186, 188, 191f., 194, 196–198, 200, 210, 228–230, 257, 259, 262f., 293, 351f., 354, 357–359, 361–364
Political memory 368
Poltava 150, 167
Popular culture 181, 252, 302, 313
Post-communist countries 204, 222f., 269, 293, 319
Post-communist society 249
Postmemory 112, 208
Pravda 160f., 164, 280
Prussia 351f., 356–359, 362–364
Public apology/-ies 65–70, 73–80, 87f.
Pushkino 154

Racism 21, 128, 142–144, 166, 309
Rational choice 66
Ratne 169
Reactive memory 76
Reconciliation 6, 8, 13, 31, 37f., 40–43, 45f., 50, 54, 56f., 60, 66–70, 72, 76–79, 83f., 86–88, 166, 255, 257, 283, 301, 325
Regional cooperation 76

Representation of the past 39, 51, 253f., 353, 368
Republika Srpska (RS) 65f., 77–79
Resistance Fighters 141
Restorative justice 42f., 46, 66f., 69, 77, 87
Roma 13, 123f., 126–129, 131, 140–144, 149–151, 153–170, 232, 298
Romania 6, 124, 141, 153, 156–158, 167
Russia 1–3, 10, 13, 23f., 37f., 47f., 50–59, 151, 153, 155–158, 161–163, 169f., 180, 183, 204, 206, 210–213, 215–220, 223, 228, 250–252, 255–270, 273–277, 279, 281–284, 287–290, 293f., 357
Russian language 256, 269, 279
Rwanda genocide 25

Secondary witness 96
Second World War (see also Worl War II/ WWII) 14, 297, 298
Serbia 6, 13, 65f., 77f., 80–87, 303f., 306–310, 335, 341
Serbian Parliament 80–83
Serbian Progressive Party (SNS) 84
Serbian Radical Party (SRS) 84
Sijekovac 84
Site of memory 12, 153, 162
sites of memory 11–14, 93, 151f.
Socialist Party (of Albania) 322f., 328, 334
Sonderkommando 133f., 137
Sound 110, 127, 140
Sources 38, 132, 145, 150, 160, 162, 250, 254f., 259–261, 263, 265, 269f., 304, 311, 353
Soviet Union 48–51, 53, 55, 57–59, 155–157, 160f., 163, 178, 196, 203–205, 210f., 222
Spain 26f.
Spanish civil war 26
Srebrenica 12f., 65–67, 77–88
Stabilisation and Association Agreement (SAA) 81
Struggle for recognition 203, 222
Sumy 150, 167f.
Survey data 56, 209f., 216, 279, 289f.

Subject index — **383**

Television 79, 84f., 231, 273, 276f., 279, 304, 357
Terms 24, 27, 30f., 38, 41, 43f., 48, 71–73, 78, 83, 86, 113, 117, 130, 199, 207f., 215–217, 230, 249, 252, 265, 273, 308, 315, 356, 365
Text Panels 126
The Baltic states 2, 48, 55f., 204f., 221, 223, 250, 267
The Latvian Legion 249f., 256, 258f.
The Second World War 23f., 28f., 32, 37, 49, 65, 81, 100, 150, 155, 177, 211, 228, 249–252, 258, 261, 269, 297f., 301, 303, 352, 368
The Ukrainian Insurgent Army 2, 166, 227, 249–251, 256, 284f.
9 May commemoration 205
Topical group 282, 284
Torchyn 158
Tragedy 30, 32, 51, 79, 82, 125f., 130, 149f., 154f., 157, 159, 161–163, 165f., 169, 194, 230, 251, 284, 325, 339
Transcarpathia 156
Transcultural memory 313
Transgenerational polity 73
Transition 15, 47, 320f., 323, 339, 343–345
Transitional justice 5, 37, 41, 80
Transnational history 249, 253, 269
Transnistria 153, 158, 167
trauma 4, 31, 39, 41, 43, 56f., 96f., 100–102, 113f., 118, 123f., 126, 166, 193, 204, 212, 319
Troubling past 2, 11f., 15
Truth Claims/Authenticity 70, 72, 97, 101f., 112, 135, 274

Uefa 300
Ukraine 3, 6, 13f., 58, 149–151, 155–161, 163–170, 177f., 180–184, 191f., 197, 200, 227f., 230, 232f., 236, 238, 241f., 249–252, 255, 257, 260, 265–267, 269, 274–288, 290, 292–294
Ukrainian identity 277, 287, 293
Ukrainian Insurgent Army (Ukraïns'ka Povstans'ka Armiia, UPA) 2, 166, 187, 227–230, 232f., 236–243, 249–252, 256–265, 267–270, 284–288, 290–292
Ukrainian language 272. 279, 287
UNESCO 351, 355f., 358, 366f.
UN genocide convention 29
United States Holocaust Memorial and Museum 102
USSR 155, 161, 183f., 196, 228, 258, 274f., 277, 283, 290f.
Ustaša 297–303, 306–315

Vichy regime 28
Video Interviews 126, 132
Vilshanka 158, 167f.
Vinnitsa 150, 167
VKontakte 281f., 286, 288, 291f.
Volhynia 2, 150, 166, 195, 199f., 227–230, 233, 257
Vukovar 84, 309
Vyborg 48, 53, 154

Web 2.0 249
Website 65, 79, 98, 102, 106, 165, 207, 254, 280f., 285, 356, 360
Web War 14, 249, 255, 275, 305
Western Balkans 65, 67, 75–78
Wikipedia discussion pages (Wikipedia talk pages) 254, 256f., 262f., 267, 269
Wikipedia editors 256, 259, 268
Winter War 47–55, 57–59
Witness 52, 95, 97, 113, 118, 141, 150, 156, 160, 169, 229, 336
World War II 2, 12–14, 38, 40, 45, 49–52, 54–58, 80, 177, 203, 211, 218f., 224, 228, 251, 288
WWII 5f., 58, 149f., 152f., 156, 163, 166, 169f., 203–223, 227, 234, 243, 252

Yerevan 23

Za dom spremni 298–302, 304, 306–311, 315
Zionist Youth 133